E. Greatbatch, sc.

WASHINGTON IRVING, ESQRE

From the Original Painting by Newton.
Engraved by permission of John Murray, Esq.

ASTORIA

ADVENTURE IN THE PACIFIC NORTHWEST

BY WASHINGTON IRVING

Introduction by Kaori O'Connor

KPI
LONDON AND NEW YORK

First published in 1839

This edition published in 1987 by KPI Limited
11 New Fetter Lane, London EC4P 4EE

Distributed by
Routledge & Kegan Paul, Associated Book Publishers (UK) Ltd.
11 New Fetter Lane, London EC4P 4EE

Methuen Inc., Routledge & Kegan Paul
29 West 35th Street
New York, NY 10001, USA

J M Dent Pty Limited
112 Lewis Road, Knoxfield 3180, Victoria, Australia

Printed in Great Britain by
T. J. Press (Padstow) Ltd., Padstow, Cornwall

© This edition KPI Limited 1987

ISBN 0 7103 0255 X

INTRODUCTION

This is the story of one man's dream. The man was John Jacob Astor, America's first millionaire and multimillionaire, and his dream was to establish a trading empire on the northwest coast of America that would reach through the Pacific all the way to China. Written by Washington Irving and based largely on Astor's private papers, *Astoria* follows Astor's colourful band of Scottish adventurers, French creoles, Canadian *voyageurs*, Ameican trappers, Indians and Sandwich (Hawaiian) islanders as they struggle to reach the Pacific coast by land and sea, there to establish Astor's western outpost of Astoria and to strive against his bitter rivals, the men of the Northwest Company. *Astoria* is a compelling saga of daring, intrigue, heroism and betrayal, a true history of a great enterprise that, but for the outbreak of the War of 1812, would have changed the course of history.

Near the end of his life, when he had become the richest man in America, John Jacob Astor was fond of saying '*The only hard step in building up my fortune was the first thousand dollars. After that it was easy.*'[1] Born in Waldorf, Germany on July 17, 1763, Astor arrived in New York as a penniless immigrant at the age of 21, and within five years had gained a solid footing in the two fields – fur trading and merchandizing – that became the foundation of his vast wealth. Astor was a genius at buying and selling, with a particular gift for seeing 'how one form of commerce could be linked with another to the advantage of both.'[2] Thus, from the beginning of his career he carried on his operations as a general merchant and as a fur trader in tandem, exporting furs to Europe then reinvesting part of the profits in European general merchandize which he imported to America, selling part of the return cargo as a merchant and using the remainder as trade goods with which to barter for more furs.

During Astor's early years in America, Canadian domination of the North American fur trade amounted to a near-monopoly. American fur traders were bedevilled by restrictive trade agreements which prohibited direct commerce between Canada and America, and were further hampered by a continuing series of disputes over borders, frontier commerce and trans-Atlantic shipping that jeopardised peace between America and Britain for decades after the War of Independence and played havoc with American attempts to build up a flourishing foreign trade. When Jay's Treaty of 1794 eased the restrictions on Canada – America trade, Astor expanded his European import-export network and spread his American fur trading activities towards the Great Lakes. Despite the disadvantages under which he was operating, he was by the turn of the century reckoned to be worth $250,000.

In 1800, Astor entered the China trade, taking an interest in a ship that sailed for Canton loaded with furs and ginseng, and returned with a cargo of tea, silks, spices and chinaware. Canton was the most profitable fur market in the world, where prime pelts fetched good prices that could be reinvested in a return cargo of oriental goods that would fetch high prices in Europe and America. Canada had no direct access to the Canton market as the Canadians were restricted to England and America as markets for their pelts. Readily seeing the potential in a form of commerce that enabled him to undercut his Canadian rivals, to increase the range of goods in his merchandizing network and to make a double profit from a single voyage, Astor decided to make the China trade one of his main interests. By 1803 he was sending all his best furs to Canton, supplementing the smaller cargoes of furs he sent to Europe with Chinese teas and silks that fetched a higher price there than pelts. Astor's China trade continued to turn him a handsome profit until 1807, when a dispute between England and America over free trade led to an embargo on American foreign shipping. The irksome embargo lasted until 1809, and it was during this fallow period in his trans-Atlantic and China operations that Astor began to formulate the plans that led to the great Astoria adventure.

In 1803, America had acquired the vast Louisiana Territory, a region that included the Mississippi and Missouri rivers and the rich fur lands that lay to the west, but the Canadian companies had continued to exploit the region so intensively that three-fourths of the furs taken west of the Missippi went into Canadian hands. The American government was keen for the trans-Mississippi fur trade to pass into American control, and Astor had long been considering plans that would allow him to break the power of the Canadian outfits and to monopolize the American fur trade himself. At first he had been attracted to a scheme based on the Atlantic-orientated Canadian model, with New York to serve as headquarters for an American operation that would draw furs from the Mississippi area and the far west, transport them back to New York by way of the Mississippi and an overland route, and ship them from that port to Europe and China. Political considerations and his experience in the China trade led Astor to revise his original plan. The embargo demonstrated that it was unwise to rely on shipping through New York, and he knew that the pelts that fetched the highest prices in Canton were the seal and sea-otter skins that the Russians were taking along the Pacific Northwest coast. Astor's solution was to retain the overall scheme, but to shift the focus of operations from the Atlantic to the Pacific, with the idea of drawing furs taken in the interior *westwards* to a headquarters on the Pacific coast which would also collect seal and sea-otter skins, and despatch combined shipments to China. By February, 1808, Astor was writing to the American President, Thomas Jefferson, about his plans to establish a settlement on the Pacific coast 'which should assist in ousting British influence from the trans-Mississippi area,'[3] a plan Jefferson welcomed with enthusiasm. In April 1808 he obtained a charter for the American Fur Company, which would be the parent organization for his projected settlement, and when the embargo ended he moved quickly to set his plans in operation.

Washington Irving's comprehensive account of the founding of Astor's Pacific outpost and the events that led to Astoria's falling into the hands of the Northwest Company of Montreal requires no supplementing, but for a fuller picture of what Astoria might have been it is necessary to take up the story where Irving's narrative ends. The failure of Astoria would have destroyed most men, but Astor – whose motto when he suffered reverses was '*Make the best of things*'[4] – was able on this occasion, as he did many times in his long career, to turn an apparent defeat into victory. The ships that he had intended for Astoria were diverted to other enterprises in the Pacific, trading between the Russian settlements of the northwest, the Spanish settlements of the California coast and the Hawaiian islands with the supplies originally destined for the Columbia outpost. In Hawaii, Astor's brig *Forester* took the fancy of King Kamehameha I who purchased her in 1816 for a large quantity of sandalwood which another Astor ship, the *Enterprise* took to Canton along with a quantity of seal skins she had obtained on the northwest coast, selling the combined cargo for such a large profit that Astor resolved to make the Pacific trade and particularly the Hawaiian sandalwood trade, a major part of his China trade.

When the war that lost him Astoria ended in 1815, Astor plunged back into foreign trade with a vengeance, and now had two fleets of vessels operating out of New York, one playing the European trade routes, the other trading with China. Having realized that he could participate in the Northwest Coast fur trade without maintaining a settlement there, Astor now added a third, Pacific, fleet to his operations, and set up a Pacific trading network that in time embraced China, Hawaii and the coasts of North and South America. Astor's Pacific ships would sail for Hawaii from New York loaded with general merchandize, part of which would be sold to the chiefs for sandalwood, to be collected in future. The ship would then go on to the Russian settlements to exchange general merchandize for seal and otter skins, would drop down to the Columbia to trade for furs with the Indians, and would dispose of the last of her cargo on the California coast in exchange for silver and pearlshell, then return to Hawaii to pick up the promised cargo of sandalwood. The wood, furs, skins, shells and silver would be taken to Canton and a return cargo of China goods obtained for sale in Hawaii for more sandalwood, to the Russians for more skins and the remainder, not suitable for the Indian fur trade, would be taken south to Ecuador and Chile to be exchanged for copper and specie. The ship would return to Hawaii, pick up the second sandalwood cargo and sail for Canton, pick up another cargo of China goods and then sail for New York, where part of the goods would be sold on the American market and the rest taken on to Europe and the Mediterranean by Astor's Atlantic fleet. The Atlantic ships would return loaded with quicksilver, lead and specie which Astor's China ships would take to Canton supplemented with a cargo of fox and beaver skins from the American interior which fetched a lower price than the skins from the Northwest coast, but were still highly profitable. Astor was not the only Pacific trader, but the sophistication and intricacy of his Pacific operations were unrivalled, and his world-wide trading network unique. As the author of the definitive study of Astor's business activities observed,

> So the process went on, involving the interior and the west and the east coasts of North America, the west coast of South America, the Hawaiian islands, Canton, England, the Mediterranean, both Northern and Southern Europe – indeed all parts of the commercial world. Is it surprising, in view of the number of times that goods were turned over between the departure and return to New York, and the unsophisticated character of at least two of the races from whom Astor obtained the most important types of the commodities utilized in this commerce – from the Indians furs and from the Hawaiians sandalwood – that Astor became a multimillionaire of commerce at a time when simple millionaires were a rarity?[5]

Astor remained in Pacific trade until 1825 when, aged 62 and in uncertain health, he decided to concentrate on interests closer to home. China and the Pacific had by no means occupied all of Astor's attentions in the post-Astoria years, and although the Pacific Fur Company had been dissolved in 1814, the American Fur Company had continued to expand its operations under his direction. Astor now embarked on a vigorous campaign to place his company in a position of unchallenged supremacy in America by eliminating all rivals through ruthless competition or the takeover of rival firms. By 1833 he was the dominant figure in the American fur trade, held a commanding position in the London fur market despite the competition from the Hudson's Bay Company, and was in virtual control of the fur market at Canton. In 1834 Astor, now 70 and in bad health, retired from the American Fur Company, withdrew from all foreign and domestic trade and began to concentrate on real estate. From 1800 onwards, he had followed a policy of applying some two-thirds of the profits from his commercial ventures to investment in land on Manhattan Island, and it was largely the profits from his China and Pacific trades that enabled him to invest some $1,111,000 in Manhattan between 1800 and 1834. On his retirement from trade, Astor entered the field of property speculation, offering cash loans for Manhattan land-based securities, either free- or lease-hold, and plowing the revenue from earlier purchases back into the acquisition of new properties. His property holdings were so extensive that he was known as 'the landlord of New York', and at his death on March 29, 1848 his estate was worth between $20,000,000 and $30,000,000, a sum largely determined by the increase in value of his Manhattan properties.

However profitable, Astor's land speculations failed to absorb his interest as his fur and trading operations had done, and the only venture that remained close to his heart was Astoria which, as he confided to a friend in 1814, was 'that favorite plan by which I should have done all I wished, or ought to have desired.'[6] Astor never changed his mind about Astoria and, in 1834, took steps to ensure that his favourite plan would not be forgotten. Washington Irving, author of 'Knickerbocker's' History of New York, Bracebridge Hall and The Sketch Book of Geoffrey Crayon, including Rip Van Winkle and The Legend of Sleepy Hollow, had recently returned to America after a long residence in Europe. Irving was America's most popular writer, and the first American to gain recognition in European literary circles, and was regarded on both sides of the Atlantic with something near to adulation. Astor and Irving had met in Paris in 1821, and a friendship had since grown up between them. Astor now proposed that Irving should undertake a history of Astoria, confessing that he himself felt 'the want of occupation and amusement' and thought he might 'find something of both in the progress of the work'.[7] Astor put all his Astoria documents at Irving's disposal, a huge collection that included everything from the letters of the ill-fated Captain Thorn to the complete accounts of the Pacific Fur Company, and eventually an agreement was reached whereby Irving's nephew Pierre would undertake the preliminary work of sifting through the vast archive, with Irving to undertake the actual writing of the book. Astor paid Pierre $3,000 for his efforts, but Irving refused to accept compensation from Astor for his work, preferring to receive revenues from his publisher when the book should finally appear. 'He was too proverbially rich a man,' Irving wrote of Astor some years later, 'for me to permit the shadow of a pecuniary favor to rest on our intercourse.'[8]

Astor had stipulated that both Irvings should reside with him at Hells Gate, his country estate on the Hudson River, while the work was in progress. In June 1835, Irving moved out to Hells Gate, joining a bachelor establishment that consisted of the widowed Astor and his young grandson, Astor's confidential secretary the poet Fitz-Greene Halleck, and his own nephew Pierre. Astor revelled in the Irvings' activities, 'hovering in the next room, emanating anecdote, ready to send if necessary, for every survivor of the expedition,'[9] and doing everything possible, as Irving wrote to a friend, 'to render our residence with him agreeable, and to detain us with him.'[10] Irving set to work, filling notebooks with queries for Pierre to research, studying Astor's documents and published memoires by expedition veterans Bradbury, Brackenridge, Long, Cox and Franchere, and delving through the accounts of Lewis and Clark and other explorers for details that would show the Astoria project in a larger context. The manuscript was finished by the spring of 1836, and was published in October of that year to acclaim by critics and public alike.

Irving's *Astoria* was a literary *tour de force* that captured the restless, adventurous spirit of that pioneering and commercial age, captivated audiences for whom the West and the frontier were subjects of the deepest fascination, and celebrated the individualism that was then such a dominant note in the American character. Although drawn from the Astoria records supplemented by other sources, it was no mere reconstruction or compilation. As the reviewer of the London *Spectator* put it, *Astoria* was

the most finished narrative of such a series of adventures that ever was written, whether with regard to plan or execution.

The arrangement has all the art of a fiction, yet without any apparent sacrifice of truth or exactness. The composition we are inclined to rate as the *chef d'oeuvre* of Washington Irving. It has all the minute fulness and enough of the polished and elaborate elegance of other works, with more of closeness, pith and substance. . . . He has extracted the spirit from the Astorian archives and thrown off their dregs and dry matter.[11]

Irving's *Astoria* is a full-bodied, red-blooded book in its own right, a unique mixture of evocative description, skillful characterization, gripping narrative and artful anecdote. In his hands, the real-life figures of the feckless Pierre Dorion and his resourceful Indian wife, the dictatorial Captain Thorn, the canny one-eyed chieftain Comcomley and the scheming M'Dougal spring to life with a vivid intensity usually found only in the finest works of fiction, and the narrative, while never departing from the known facts of the expedition, is infused with such a thrilling spirit of adventure that it surpasses most works of pure romance in excitement. Irving's account of the fate of the *Tonquin* and Hunt's final descent towards the Columbia, his sensitive and sympathetic portraits of Indian life, and his deft sketches of wilderness trappers, swaggering Northwesters and *voyageurs* canoeing down the river to Astoria are among the finest passages in American literature. Yet for all its literary flourishes Astoria is ultimately a historical work of remarkable accuracy, and although it presents the issues very much from Astor's point of view, it is a faithful description of the frontier experience, and of early exploration and settlement on the Northwest coast. Nor is its interest limited to the history of the American coast, for *Astoria* demonstrates Hawaii's strategic and commercial importance at that early date, contains rare descriptions of life in the Hawaiian islands before the arrival of the missionaries, and sheds light on the activities of those native sailors like the Hawaiian known to the Astoria men as John Coxe,[12] who formed a significant part of Pacific sailing crews throughout the nineteenth century, and often settled permanently on the Northwest coast.

Astoria became the most popular book of its day, and was quickly translated into French, German and Russian. 'Old Mr Astor,' Irving noted, 'seems greatly gratified.'[13] But Astor's satisfaction with Irving's epic raises the questions of why a man who devoted his life to making money was anxious to immortalize a venture that brought him a huge financial loss, and why a man who had met with success in many fields should wish to be remembered for an enterprise that was a failure. The answer is to be found in a letter written to Astor by Thomas Jefferson on May 24, 1812 and quoted in part in *Astoria*:

> I considered, as a great public acquisition, the commencement of a settlement on that point of the western coast of America, and looked forward with gratification to the time when its descendants should have spread themselves through the whole length of that coast, covering it with free and independent Americans unconnected with us but by the ties of blood and interest, enjoying like us the rights of self-government.

It is unlikely that Astor ever envisioned himself as the political head of an independent republic, for his vast wealth gave him more real power than the limited authority enjoyed by American public figures of the time, and his interests and instincts were commercial rather than political. However, in view of his trading activities in the Pacific and China, it is clear that Astor's ultimate plans for Astoria went far beyond the establishment of a simple fur-trading settlement. If the Astoria project had not been brought to an end by the outbreak of the War of 1812, there is little doubt that, with his financial skills and resources, Astor would have linked the countries of the Pacific Basin into one of the greatest commercial empires in the world. This great plan, implicit in the whole Astoria enterprise, explains Astor's wish to perpetuate the memory of his lost Columbia outpost, trusting that his dream of a Pacific empire, little appreciated in his own time, would later be seen in a different light.

Astor's was, indeed, a golden vision – but it was not without its darker side. As head of the American Fur Company, he

> wrecked the government trading houses, which had for their purpose the furnishing of goods to Indians at fair prices, in order that his organization might secure their furs at low rates... paid low wages to his *voyageurs* and sold them necessary supplies at exorbitant rates, and... charged goods

to his subordinate traders at such high prices that they were forced to mortgage their lands to the Company.[14]

Astor shipped opium to China, sold liquor to Indians well knowing the destructive effect it would have, ran arms and ammunition to South American revolutionaries, cared nothing for the misery that his sandalwood trade with the chiefs inflicted on the common people of Hawaii and, closer to home, was apparently unconcerned about the 61 lives lost on the Astoria expeditions[15] that were so dear to his heart. Astor's Pacific empire would have brought him great profits, at a tremendous cost to others. And a commercial enterprise on the scale envisioned by Astor would inevitably have had profound political implications for the whole of the Pacific Basin. But these considerations cannot detract from the scope of Astor's vision, nor the brilliance of Irving's account of a great and heroic Pacific adventure.

Kaori O'Connor

NOTES

[1] Porter, Kenneth Wiggins *John Jacob Astor, Business Man* (2 vols), Harvard Studies in Business History, Russell & Russell, New York, 1966: p.1122.

[2] Ibid., p.940.

[3] Ibid., p.144.

[4] Ibid., p.1073.

[5] Ibid., p.665.

[6] Ibid., pp.342-3.

[7] Ibid., p.1053.

[8] Ibid., p.1054.

[9] Williams, Stanley T., *The Life of Washington Irving* (2 vols), Oxford University Press, New York, 1935 (ii), p.83.

[10] Porter, op.cit., p.1054.

[11] Williams, op.cit., (ii), pp.86-7.

[12] King Kamehameha I encouraged Hawaiians to serve on foreign ships in order to learn western ways, a practice that began in 1787. See Kittelson, David, 'John Coxe: Hawaii's First Soldier of Fortune', *Hawaiian Historical Review*, Honolulu, vol.I, no. 10 (January 1965).

[13] Porter, op.cit., p.1054.

[14] Ibid., p.1046.

[15] Ross, Alexander, *Adventures of the First Settlers on the Oregon or Columbia River*, Smith Elder & Co., London, 1849, p.283. Ross, a veteran of the

expedition, gives the breakdown as follows; 8 lost on the Columbia bar, 5 on the land expedition, 27 on the *Tonquin*, 8 on the *Lark*, 3 at Astoria, 9 in the Snake country and 1 during the final departure.

ASTORIA.

CHAPTER I.

Objects of American enterprise—Gold hunting and Fur trading—their effect on colonization—Early French Canadian settlers—Ottawa and Huron hunters—an Indian trading camp—Coureurs des Bois, or rangers of the woods—Their roaming life—Their revels and excesses—Licensed traders—Missionaries—Trading posts—Primitive French Canadian merchant—His establishment and dependants—British Canadian fur merchant—Origin of the North-West Company—Its constitution—Its internal trade—A candidate for the company—privations in the wilderness—North-west clerks—North-west partners—A North-west nabob—Feudal notions in the forest—The Lords of the Lakes—Fort William—Its parliamentary hall and banqueting-room—Wassailing in the wilderness.

Two leading objects of commercial gain have given birth to wide and daring enterprise in the early history of the Americans: the precious metals of the south, and the rich peltries of the north. While the fiery and magnificent Spaniard, inflamed with the mania for gold, has extended his discoveries and conquests over those brilliant countries scorched by the ardent sun of the tropics, the adroit and buoyant Frenchman, and the cool and calculating Briton have pursued the less splendid, but no less lucrative, traffic in furs amidst the hyperborean regions of the Canadas, until they have advanced even within the Arctic circle.

These two pursuits have thus in a manner been the pioneers and precursors of civilization. Without pausing on the borders, they have penetrated at once, in defiance of difficulties and dangers, to the heart of savage countries: laying open the hidden secrets of the wilderness; leading the way to remote regions of beauty and fertility that might have remained unexplored for ages, and beckoning after them the slow and pausing steps of agriculture and civilization.

It was the fur trade, in fact, which gave early sustenance and vitality to the great Canadian provinces. Being des-

titute of the precious metals, at that time the leading
objects of American enterprise, they were long neglected
by the parent country.   The French adventurers, however
who had settled on the banks of the St. Lawrence, soon
found that in the rich peltries of the interior, they had
sources of wealth that might almost rival the mines of
Mexico and Peru.   The Indians, as yet unacquainted
with the artificial value given to some descriptions of furs
in civilized life, brought quantities of the most precious
kinds and bartered them away for European trinkets and
cheap commodities.   Immense profits were thus made by
the early traders, and the traffic was pursued with avidity.

As the valuable furs soon became scarce in the neighbourhood of the settlements, the Indians of the vicinity
were stimulated to take a wider range in their hunting
expeditions; they were generally accompanied on these
expeditions by some of the traders or their dependants,
who shared in the toils and perils of the chase, and at the
same time made themselves acquainted with the best
hunting and trapping grounds, and with the remote tribes
whom they encouraged to bring their peltries to the settlements.   In this way the trade augmented and was drawn
from remote quarters to Montreal.   Every now and then
a large body of Ottowas, Hurons, and other tribes who
hunted the countries bordering on the great lakes, would
come down in a squadron of light canoes, laden with
beaver skins, and other spoils of their year's hunting.
The canoes would be unladen, taken on shore, and their
contents disposed in order.   A camp of birch bark would
be pitched outside of the town, and a kind of primitive
fair opened with that grave ceremonial so dear to the
Indians.   An audience would be demanded of the governor-general, who would hold the conference with becoming
state, seated in an elbow chair, with the Indians ranged in
semicircles before him, seated on the ground, and silently
smoking their pipes.   Speeches would be made, presents
exchanged, and the audience would break up in universal
good humour.

Now would ensue a brisk traffic with the merchants,
and all Montreal would be alive with naked Indians

running from shop to shop bargaining for arms, kettles, knives, axes, blankets, bright-coloured cloths, and other articles of use or fancy ; upon all which, says an old French writer, the merchants were sure to clear at least two hundred per cent. There was no money used in this traffic, and, after a time, all payment in spirituous liquors was prohibited, in consequence of the frantic and frightful excesses and bloody brawls which they were apt to occasion.

Their wants and caprices being supplied, they would take leave of the governor, strike their tents, launch their canoes, and ply their way up the Ottawa to the lakes.

A new and anomalous class of men gradually grew out of this trade. These were called *coureurs des bois,* rangers of the woods ; originally men who had accompanied the Indians in their hunting expeditions and made themselves acquainted with remote tracts and tribes ; and who now became, as it were, pedlers of the wilderness. These men would set out from Montreal with canoes well stocked with goods, with arms and ammunition, and would make their way up the mazy and wandering rivers that interlace the vast forests of the Canadas, coasting the most remote lakes, and creating new wants and habitudes among the natives. Sometimes they sojourned for months among them, assimilating to their tastes and habits with the happy felicity of Frenchmen ; adopting in some degree the Indian dress, and not unfrequently taking to themselves Indian wives.

Twelve, fifteen, eighteen months would often elapse without any tidings of them, when they would come sweeping their way down the Ottawa in full glee, their canoes laden down with packs of beaver skins. Now came their turn for revelry and extravagance. " You would be amazed," says an old writer, already quoted, " if you saw how lewd these pedlers are when they return, how they feast and game and how prodigal they are not only in their clothes, but upon their sweethearts. Such of them as are married have the wisdom to retire to their own houses ; but the bachelors act just as an East Indiaman and pirates are wont to do ; for they lavish, eat, drink, and play all away as long as the goods hold out ; and when these are gone, they even sell their embroidery, their lace, and their clothes.   This done they are forced upon a new voyage for subsistence."*

Many of these *coureurs des bois* became so accustomed to the Indian mode of living, and the perfect freedom of the wilderness, that they lost all relish for civilization, and identified themselves with the savages among whom they dwelt, or could only be distinguished from them by superior licentiousness.   Their conduct and example gradually corrupted the natives, and impeded the works of the Catholic missionaries, who were at this time prosecuting their pious labours in the wilds of Canada.

To check these abuses, and to protect the fur trade from various irregularities practised by these loose adventurers, an order was issued by the French government prohibiting all persons, on pain of death, from trading into the interior of the country without a licence.

These licences were granted in writing by the governor-general, and at first were given only to persons of respectability ; to gentlemen of broken fortunes ; to old officers of the army who had families to provide for ; or to their widows.   Each license permitted the fitting out of two large canoes with merchandise for the lakes, and no more than twenty-five licences were to be issued in one year. By degrees, however, private licences were also granted, and the number rapidly increased.   Those who did not choose to fit out the expeditions themselves, were permitted to sell them to the merchants ; these employed the coureurs des bois, or rangers of the woods, to undertake the long voyages on shares, and, thus the abuses of the old system were revived and continued.†

* La Hontan, v. i., let. 4.

† The following are the terms on which these expeditions were commonly undertaken.   The merchant holding the licence would fit out the two canoes with a thousand crowns worth of goods, and put them under the conduct of six coureurs des bois, to whom the goods were charged at the rate of fifteen per cent. above the ready money price in the colony.   The coureurs des bois, in their turn dealt so sharply with the savages, that they generally returned at the end of the year or so, with four canoes well laden, so as to ensure a clear profit of seven hundred per cent , insomuch that the thousand crowns invested, produced eight thousand.   Of this extravagant profit the merchant had the lion's share.   In the first place he would set aside six hun-

The pious missionaries employed by the Roman Catholic church to convert the Indians, did every thing in their power to counteract the profligacy caused and propagated by these men in the heart of the wilderness. The Catholic chapel might often be seen planted beside the trading house, and its spire surmounted by a cross, towering from the midst of an Indian village on the banks of a river or a lake. The missions had often a beneficial effect on the simple sons of the forest, but had little power over the renegades from civilization,

At length it was found necessary to establish fortified posts at the confluence of the river and lakes for the protection of the trade, and the restraint of these profligates of the wilderness. The most important of these was at Michilimackinac, situated at the strait of the same name which connects lakes Huron and Michigan. It became the great interior mart and place of deposit, and some of the regular merchants, who prosecuted the trade in person, under their licences, formed establishments here. This, too, was a rendezvous for the rangers of the woods, as well those who came up with goods from Montreal as those who returned with peltries from the interior. Here new expeditions were fitted out and took their departure for lake Michigan and the Mississippi; lake Superior and the north-west; and here the peltries brought in return were embarked for Montreal.

The French merchant at his trading post, in these primitive days of Canada, was a kind of commercial patriarch. With the lax habits and easy familiarity of his race, he had a little world of self-indulgence and misrule around him. He had his clerks, canoe-men, and retainers of all kinds, who lived with him on terms of perfect sociability, always calling him by his christain name; he had his harem of Indian beauties, and his troop of half-breed children; nor was there ever wanting a louting

dred crowns for the cost of his licence, then a thousand crowns for the cost of the original merchandise. This would leave six thousand four hundred crowns from which he would take forty per cent. for bottomry, amounting to two thousand five hundred and sixty crowns. The residue would be equally divided among six wood rangers, who would thus receive little more than six hundred crowns for all their toils and perils.

train of Indians, hanging about the establishment, eating and drinking at his expense in the intervals of their hunting expeditions.

The Canadian traders, for a long time, had troublesome competitors in the British merchants of New York, who inveigled the Indian hunters and the *coureurs des bois*, to their posts, and traded with them on more favourable terms. A still more formidable opposition was organized in the Hudson Bay Company, chartered by Charles II., in 1670, with the exclusive privilege of establishing trading houses on the shores of that bay and its tributary rivers; a privilege which they have maintained to the present day. Between this British Company and the French merchants of Canada, feuds and contests arose about alleged infringements of territorial limits, and acts of violence and bloodshed occurred between their agents.

In 1762, the French lost possession of Canada, and the trade fell principally into the hands of British subjects. For a time, however, it shrunk within narrow limits. The old *coureurs des bois* were broken up and dispersed, or, where they could be met with, were slow to accustom themselves to the habits and manners of their British employers. They missed the freedom, indulgence, and familiarity of the old French trading houses, and did not relish the sober exactness, reserve, and method of the new comers. The British traders, too, were ignorant of the country, and distrustful of the natives. They had reason to be so. The treacherous and bloody affairs of Detroit and Michilimackinac showed them the lurking hostility cherished by the savages, who had too long been taught by the French to regard them as enemies.

It was not until the year 1766, that the trade regained its old channels; but it was then pursued with much avidity and emulation by individual merchants, and soon transcended its former bounds. Expeditions were fitted out by various persons from Montreal and Michilimackinac, and rivalships and jealousies of course ensued. The trade was injured by their artifices to outbid and undermine each other; the Indians were debauched by the sale of spirituous liquors, which had been prohibited under the French rule. Scenes of drunkenness, brutality and brawl were the consequence, in the Indian villages and around the trading houses, while bloody feuds took place between rival trading parties when they happened to encounter each other in the lawless depths of the wilderness.

To put an end to these sordid and ruinous contentions, several of the principal merchants of Montreal entered into a partnership in the winter of 1783, which was augmented by amalgamation with a rival company in 1787. Thus was created the famous " North-west Company," which for a time held a lordly sway over the wintry lakes and boundless forests of the Canadas, almost equal to that of the East India Company over the voluptuous climes and magnificent realms of the Orient.

The company consisted of twenty-three share holders, or partners, but held in its employ about two thousand persons as clerks, guides, interpreters, and " voyageurs," or boatmen. These were distributed at various trading posts, established far and wide on the interior lakes and rivers, at immense distances from each other, and in the heart of trackless countries and savage tribes.

Several of the partners resided in Montreal and Quebec, to manage the main concerns of the company. These were called agents, and were personages of great weight and importance ; the other partners took their stations at the interior posts, where they remained throughout the winter, to superintend the intercourse with the various tribes of Indians. They were thence called wintering partners.

The goods destined for this wide and wandering traffic were put up at the warehouses of the company in Montreal, and conveyed in batteaux, or boats, and canoes, up the river Attawa, or Ottawa, which falls into the St. Lawrence, near Montreal, and by other rivers and portages, to lake Nipising, lake Huron, lake Superior, and thence, by several chains of great and small lakes, to lake Winipeg, lake Athabasca, and the great Slave lake. This singular and beautiful system of internal seas, which renders an immense region of wilderness so accessible to the frail bark of the Indian or the trader, was studded by the remote posts of the company, where they carried on their traffic with the surrounding tribes.

The company, as we have shown, was at first a spontaneous association of merchants; but, after it had been regularly organized, admission into it became extremely difficult. A candidate had to enter, as it were " before the mast," to undergo a long probation, and to rise slowly by his merits and services. He began, at an early age, as a clerk, and served an apprenticeship of seven years, for which he received one hundred pounds sterling, was maintained at the expense of the company, and furnished with suitable clothing and equipments. His probation was generally passed at the interior trading posts; removed for years from civilized society, leading a life almost as wild and precarious as the savages around him; exposed to the severities of a northern winter, often suffering from a scarcity of food, and sometimes destitute for a long time of both bread and salt. When his apprenticeship had expired, he received a salary according to his deserts, varying from eighty to one hundred and sixty pounds sterling, and was now eligible to the great object of his ambition, a partnership in the company; though years might yet elapse before he attained to that enviable station.

Most of the clerks were young men of good families, from the Highlands of Scotland, characterized by the perseverance, thrift, and fidelity of their country, and fitted by their native hardihood to encounter the rigorous climate of the north, and to endure the trials and privations of their lot; though it must not be concealed that the constitutions of many of them became impaired by the hardships of the wilderness, and their stomachs injured by occasional famishing, and especially by the want of bread and salt. Now and then, at an interval of years, they were permitted to come down on a visit to the establishment at Montreal, to recruit their health and to have a taste of civilized life; and these were brilliant spots in their existence.

As to the principal partners, or agents, who resided in

Montreal and Quebec, they formed a kind of commercial aristocracy, living in lordly and hospitable style. Their early associations, when clerks at the remote trading posts, and the pleasures, dangers, adventures, and mishaps, which they had shared together in their wild wood life, had linked them heartily to each other, so that they formed a convivial fraternity. Few travellers that have visited Canada some thirty years since, in the days of the M'Tavishes, the M'Gillivrays, the M'Kenzies, the Frobishers, and the other magnates of the north-west, when the company was in all its glory, but must remember the round of feasting and revelry kept up among these hyperborean nabobs.

Sometimes one or two partners, recently from the interior posts, would make their appearance in New York, in the course of a tour of pleasure and curiosity. On these occasions there was always a degree of magnificence of the purse about them, and a peculiar propensity to expenditure at the goldsmiths and jewellers, for rings, chains, brooches, necklaces, jewelled watches, and other rich trinkets, partly for their own wear, partly for presents to their female acquaintances; a gorgeous prodigality, such as was often to be noticed in former times in southern planters and West Indian creoles, when flush with the profits of their plantations.

To behold the North-west Company in all its state and grandeur, however, it was necessary to witness an annual gathering at the great interior place of conference established at Fort William, near what is called the Grand Portage, on lake Superior. Here two or three of the leading partners from Montreal proceeded once a year, to meet the partners from the various trading posts of the wilderness, to discuss the affairs of the company during the preceding year, and to arrange plans for the future.

On these occasions might be seen the change since the unceremonious times of the old French traders; now the aristocratical character of the Briton shone forth magnificently, or rather the feudal spirit of the Highlander. Every partner who had charge of an interior post, and a score of retainers at his command, felt like the chieftain of

a Highland clan, and was almost as important in the eyes
of his dependants as of himself. To him a visit to the
grand conference at Fort William was a most important
event; and he repaired there as to a meeting of parliament.

The partners from Montreal, however, were the lords of
the ascendant; coming from the midst of luxuriant and
ostentatious life, they quite eclipsed their compeers from
the woods, whose forms and faces had been battered and
hardened by hard living and hard service, and whose garments and equipments were all the worse for wear. Indeed, the partners from below considered the whole dignity of the company as represented in their persons, and
conducted themselves in suitable style. They ascended
the rivers in great state, like sovereigns making a progress:
or rather like Highland chieftains navigating their subject
lakes. They were wrapped in rich furs, their huge canoes
freighted with every convenience and luxury, and manned
by Canadian voyageurs, as obedient as Highland clans-
men. They carried up with them cooks and bakers, together with delicacies of every kind, and abundance of
choice wines for the banquet which attended this great
convocation. Happy were they, too, if they could meet
with some distinguished stranger, above all, some titled
member of the British nobility, to accompany them on
this stately occasion, and grace their high solemnities.

Fort William, the scene of this important annual meeting, was a considerable village on the banks of lake Superior. Here, in an immense wooden building, was the great
council hall, as also the banqueting chamber, decorated
with Indian arms and accoutrements, and the trophies of
the fur trade. The house swarmed at this time with
traders and voyageurs, some from Montreal, bound to the
interior posts; some from the interior posts, bound to
Montreal. The councils were held in great state, for
every member felt as if sitting in parliament, and every
retainer and dependant looked up to the assemblage with
awe, as to the house of lords. There was a vast deal of
solemn deliberation, and hard Scottish reasoning, with an
occasional swell of pompous declamation.

These grave and weighty councils were alternated by huge feasts and revels, like some of the old feasts described in Highland castles. The tables in the great banqueting-room groaned under the weight of game of all kinds ; of venison from the woods, and fish from the lakes, with hunters' delicacies, such as buffaloes' tongues, and beavers' tails ; and various luxuries from Montreal, all served up by experienced cooks brought for the purpose. There was no stint of generous wine, for it was a hard-drinking period, a time of loyal toasts, and bacchanalian songs, and brimming bumpers.

While the chiefs thus revelled in hall, and made the rafters resound with bursts of loyalty and old Scottish songs, chanted in voices cracked and sharpened by the northern blast, their merriment was echoed and prolonged by a mongrel legion of retainers, Canadian voyageurs, half breeds, Indian hunters, and vagabond hangers-on, who feasted sumptuously without on the crumbs that fell from their table, and made the welkin ring with old French ditties, mingled with Indian yelps and yellings.

Such was the North-west Company in its powerful and prosperous days, when it held a kind of feudal sway over a vast domain of lake and forest. We are dwelling too long, perhaps, upon these individual pictures, endeared to us by the associations of early life, when, as yet a stripling youth, we have sat at the hospitable boards of the " mighty North-westers," then lords of the ascendant at Montreal, and gazed with wondering and inexperienced eye at their baronial wassailing, and listened with astonished ear to their tales of hardships and adventures. It is one object of our task, however, to present scenes of the rough life of the wilderness, and we are tempted to fix these few memorials of a transient state of things fast passing into oblivion ;—for the feudal state of Fort William is at an end ; its council chamber is silent and deserted ; its banquet hall no longer echoes to the burst of loyalty, or the " auld world" ditty ; the lords of the lakes and forests have passed away ; and the hospitable magnates of Montreal—where are they !

CHAPTER II.

THE success of the North-west Company stimulated further enterprise in this opening and apparently boundless field of profit. The traffic of that company lay principally in the high northern latitudes, while there were immense regions to the south and west, known to abound with valuable peltries; but which, as yet, had been but little explored by the fur trader. A new association of British merchants was therefore formed, to prosecute the trade in this direction. The chief factory was established at the old emporium of Michilimackinac, from which place the association took its name, and was commonly called the Mackinaw Company.

While the North-westers continued to push their enterprises into the hyperborean regions from their stronghold at Fort William, and to hold almost sovereign sway over the tribes of the upper lakes and rivers, the Mackinaw Company sent forth their light perogues and barks, by Green bay, Fox river, and the Wisconsin, to that great artery of the west, the Mississippi; and down that stream to all its tributary rivers. In this way they hoped soon to monopolize the trade with all the tribes on the southern and western waters, and of those vast tracts comprised in ancient Louisiana.

The government of the United States began to view with a wary eye the growing influence thus acquired by combinations of foreigners, over the aboriginal tribes inhabiting its territories, and endeavoured to counteract it. For this purpose, as early as 1796, the government sent out agents to establish rival trading houses on the frontier, so as to supply the wants of the Indians; to link their interests and feelings with those of the people of the United

States, and to divert this important branch of trade into national channels.

The expedient, however, was unsuccessfnl, as most commercial expedients are prone to be, where the dull patronage of government is counted upon to outvie the keen activity of private enterprise. What government failed to effect, however, with all its patronage and all its agents, was at length brought about by the enterprise and perseverance of a single merchant, one of its adopted citizens; and this brings us to speak of the individual, whose enterprise is the especial subject of the following pages—a man whose name and character are worthy of being enrolled in the history of commerce, as illustrating its noblest aims and soundest maxims. A few brief anecdotes of his early life, and of the circumstances which first determined him to the branch of commerce of which we are treating, cannot but be interesting.

John Jacob Astor, the individual in question, was born in the honest little German village of Waldorf, near Heidelberg, on the banks of the Rhine. He was brought up in the simplicity of rural life, but, while yet a mere stripling, left his home, and launched himself amid the busy scenes of London, having had, from his boyhood, a singular presentiment that he would ultimately arrive at great fortune.

At the close of the American Revolution he was still in London, and scarce on the threshold of active life. An elder brother had been for some few years resident in the United States, and Mr. Astor determined to follow him, aud to seek his fortune in the rising country. Investing a small sum which he had amassed since leaving his native village, in merchandise suited to the American market, he embarked in the month of November, 1783, in a ship bound to Baltimore, and arrived in Hampton Roads in the month of January. The winter was extremely severe, and the ship, with many others, was detained by the ice in and about Chesapeake bay for nearly three months.

During this period, the passengers of the various ships used occasionally to go on shore, and mingle sociably together. In this way Mr. Astor became acquainted with a countryman of his, a furrier by trade. Having had a previous impression that this might be a lucrative trade in the new world, he made many enquiries of his new acquaintance on the subject, who cheerfully gave him all the information in his power, as to the quality and value of different furs, and the mode of carrying on the traffic. He subsequently accompanied him to New York, and, by his advice, Mr. Astor was induced to invest the proceeds of his merchandise in furs. With these he sailed from New York to London in 1784, disposed of them advantageously, made himself further acquainted with the course of the trade, and returned the same year to New York, with a view to settle in the United States.

He now devoted himself to the branch of commerce with which he had thus casually been made acquainted. He began his career, of course, on the narrowest scale; but he brought to the task a persevering industry, rigid economy, and strict integrity. To these were added an aspiring spirit that always looked upward; a genius, bold, fertile, and expansive; a sagacity quick to grasp and convert every circumstance to its advantage, and a singular and never wavering confidence of signal success."*

As yet, trade in peltries was not organized in the United States, and could not be said to form a regular line of business. Furs and skins were casually collected by the country traders in their dealings with the Indians or the white hunters, but the main supply was derived from Canada. As Mr. Astor's means increased, he made annual visits to Montreal, where he purchased furs from the houses at that place engaged in the trade. These he shipped from Canada for London, no direct trade being allowed from that colony to any but the mother country.

In 1794 or 1795, a treaty with Great Britain removed the restrictions imposed upon the trade with the colonies, and opened a direct commercial intercourse between Ca-

* An instance of this buoyant confidence, which no doubt aided to produce the success it anticipated, we have from the lips of Mr. A. himself. While yet almost a stranger in the city, and in very narrow circumstances, he passed by where a row of houses had just been erected in Broadway, and which, from the superior style of their architecture, were the talk and boast of the city. " I'll build, one day or other, a greater house than any of these, in this very street," said he to himself. He has accomplished his prediction.

nada and the United States. Mr. Astor was in London at the time, and immediately made a contract with the agents of the North-west Company for furs. He was now enabled to import them from Montreal into the United States for the home supply, and to be shipped thence to different parts of Europe, as well as to China, which has ever been the best market for the richest and finest kinds of peltry.

The treaty in question provided, likewise, that the military posts occupied by the British within the territorial limits of the United States, should be surrendered. Accordingly, Oswego, Niagara, Detroit, Michilimackinac, and other posts on the American side of the lakes, were given up. An opening was thus made for the American merchant to a trade on the confines of Canada, and within the territories of the United States. After an interval of some years, about 1807, Mr. Astor embarked in this trade on his own account. His capital and resources had by this time greatly augmented, and he had risen from small beginnings to take his place among the first merchants and financiers of the country. His genius had ever been in advance of his circumstances, prompting him to new and wide fields of enterprise beyond the scope of ordinary merchants. With all his enterprise and resources, however, he soon found the power and influence of the Michilimackinac (or Mackinaw) Company too great for him, having engrossed most of the trade within the American borders.

A plan had to be devised to enable him to enter into successful competition. He was aware of the wish of the American government, already stated, that the fur trade within its boundaries should be in the hands of American citizens, and of the ineffectual measures it had taken to accomplish that object. He now offered, if aided and protected by government, to turn the whole of that trade into American channels. He was invited to unfold his plans to government, and they were warmly approved, though the executive could give no direct aid.

Thus countenanced, however, he obtained in 1809, a charter from the legislature of the state of New York, incorporating a company under the name of " The American Fur Company," with a capital of one million of dollars, with the privilege of increasing it to two millions. The capital was furnished by himself—he, in fact, constituted the company; for, though he had a board of directors, they were merely nominal ; the whole business was conducted on his plans, and with his resources, but he preferred to do so under the imposing and formidable aspect of a corporation, rather than in his individual name, and his policy was sagacious and effective.

As the Mackinaw Company still continued its rivalry, and as the fur trade would not advantageously admit of competition, he made a new arrangement in 1811, by which, in conjunction with certain partners of the Northwest Company, and other persons engaged in the fur trade, he bought out the Mackinaw Company, and merged that and the American Fur Company into a new association, to be called " The South-west Company." This he likewise did with the privity and approbation of the American government.

By this arrangement Mr. Astor became proprietor of one half of the Indian establishments and goods which the Mackinaw Company had within the territory of the Indian country in the United States, and it was understood that the whole was to be surrendered into his hands at the expiration of five years, on condition that the American company would not trade within the British dominions.

Unluckily, the war which broke out in 1812, between Great Britain and the United States, suspended the association ; and, after the war, it was entirely dissolved ; congress having passed a law prohibiting British fur traders from prosecuting their enterprises within the territories of the United States.

CHAPTER III.

WHILE the various companies we have noticed were
pushing their enterprises far and wide in the wilds of
Canada, and along the course of the great western waters,
our adventurers, intent on the same objects, were traversing the watery wastes of the Pacific and skirting the north-
west coast of America. The last voyage of that renowned
but unfortunate discoverer, Captain Cook, had made
known the vast quantities of the sea otter to be found
along that coast, and the immense prices to be obtained
for its fur in China. It was as if a new gold coast had
been discovered. Individuals from various countries
dashed into this lucrative traffic, so that in the year 1792,
there were twenty-one vessels under different flags, plying
along the coast, and trading with the natives. The
greater part of them were American, and owned by Boston
merchants. They generally remained on the coast, and
about the adjacent sea for two years, carrying on as wandering and adventurous a commerce on the water as did
the traders and trappers on land. Their trade extended
along the whole coast from California to the high northern
latitudes. They would run in near shore, anchor, and
wait for the natives to come off in their canoes with peltries. The trade exhausted at one place, they would up
anchor and be off to another. In this way they would
consume the summer, and when autumn came on, would
run down to the Sandwich islands and winter in some
friendly and plentiful harbour. In the following year
they would resume their summer trade, commencing at
California and proceeding north; and, having in the
course of two seasons, collected a sufficient cargo of peltries, would make the best of their way to China. Here

they would sell their furs, take in teas, nankeens, and other merchandize, and return to Boston, after an absence of two or three years.

The people, however, who entered most extensively and effectually in the fur trade of the Pacific, were the Russians. Instead of making casual voyages, in transient ships, they established regular trading houses in the high latitudes, along the north-west coast of America, and upon the chain of the Aleutian islands beyond Kamtschatka and the promontory of Alaska.

To promote and protect these enterprises, a company was incorporated by the Russian government with exclusive privileges, and a capital of two hundred and sixty thousand pounds sterling; and the sovereignty of that part of the American continent, along the coast of which the posts had been established, was claimed by the Russian crown, on the plea that the land had been discovered and occupied by its subjects.

As China was the grand mart for the furs collected in these quarters, the Russians had the advantage over their competitors in the trade. The latter had to take their peltries to Canton, which, however, was a mere receiving mart, from whence they had to be distributed over the interior of the empire and sent to the northen parts, where there was the chief consumption. The Russians, on the contrary, carried their furs, by a shorter voyage, directly to the Northern parts of the Chinese empire; thus being able to afford them in the market without the additional cost of internal transportation.

We now come to the immediate field of operation of the great enterprise we have undertaken to illustrate.

Among the American ships which traded along the north-west coast in 1792, was the Columbia, Captain Gray, of Boston. In the course of her voyage she discovered the mouth of a large river in lat. 46° 19' north. Entering it with some difficulty, on account of sand bars and breakers, she came to an anchor in a spacious bay. A boat was well manned, and sent on shore to a village on the beach, but all the inhabitants fled, excepting the aged and infirm. The kind manner in which they were treated, and the presents given to them, gradually lured back the others, and a friendly intercourse took place. They had never seen a ship or a white man. When they had first descried the Columbia, they had supposed it a floating island; then some monster of the deep; but when they saw the boat putting for shore with human beings on board, they considered them cannibals, sent by the great Spirit to ravage the country and devour the inhabitants. Captain Gray did not ascend the river further than the bay in question, which continues to bear his name. After putting to sea, he fell in with the celebrated discoverer, Vancouver, and informed him of his discovery, furnishing him with a chart which he had made of the river. Vancouver visited the river, and his lieutenant, Broughton, explored it by the aid of Captain Gray's chart; ascending it upwards of one hundred miles, until within view of a snowy mountain, to which he gave the name of Mount Hood, which it still retains.

The existence of this river, however, was known long before the visits of Gray and Vancouver, but the information concerning it was vague and indefinite, being gathered from the reports of Indians. It was spoken of by travellers as the Oregon, and as the great river of the west. A Spanish ship is said to have been wrecked at its mouth, several of the crew of which lived for some time among the natives. The Columbia, however, is believed to be the first ship that made a regular discovery and anchored within its waters, and it has since generally borne the name of that vessel.

As early as 1763, shortly after the acquisition of the Canadas by Great Britain, Captain Jonathan Carver, who had been in the British provincial army, projected a journey across the continent between the forty-third and forty-sixth degrees of northen latitude, to the shores of the Pacific ocean. His objects were to ascertain the breadth of the continent at its broadest part, and to determine on some place on the shores of the Pacific, where government might establish a post to facilitate the discovery of a north west passage, or a communication between Hudson's-bay and the Pacific ocean. This place he presumed would be somewhere about the straits of Annian, at which point he supposed the Oregon disembogued itself. It was his opinion, also, that a settlement on this extremity of America would disclose new sources of trade, promote many useful discoveries, and open a more direct communication with China and the English settlements in the East Indies, than that by the Cape of Good Hope or the straits of Magellan.* This enterprising and intrepid traveller was twice baffled in individual efforts to accomplish this great journey. In 1774, he was joined in the scheme by Richard Whitworth, a member of Parliament, and a man of wealth. Their enterprise was projected on a broad and bold plan. They were to take with them fifty or sixty men, artificers and mariners. With these they were to make their way up one of the branches of the Missouri, explore the mountains for the source of the Oregon, or the river of the west, and sail down that river to its supposed exit near the straits of Annian. Here they were to erect a fort, and build the vessels necessary to carry their discoveries by sea into effect. Their plan had the sanction of the British government, and grants and other requisites were nearly completed, when the breaking out of the American revolution once more defeated the undertaking.†

The expedition of Sir Alexander Mackenzie in 1793, across the continent to the Pacific ocean, which he reached in lat. 52° 20' 48", again suggested the possibility of linking together the trade of both sides of the continent In lat. 52° 30' he had descended a river for some distance which flowed towards the south, and was called by the natives Tacoutche Tesse, and which he erroneously supposed to be the Columbia. It was afterwards acertained that it emptied itself in lat. 49°, whereas the mouth of the Columbia is about three degrees further south.

When Mackenzie some years subsequently published an account of his expeditions, he suggested the policy of opening an intercourse between the Atlantic and Pacific oceans, and forming regular establishments through the interior and at both extremes, as well as along the coasts

* Carver's Travels, Introd., p. iii. Philad. 1796.
† Carver's Travels, p. 360. Philad. 1796.

and islands. By this means, he observed, the entire command of the fur trade of North America might be obtained from latitude 48° north to the pole, excepting that portion held by the Russians, for as to the American adventurers who had hitherto enjoyed the traffic along the north-west coast, they would instantly disappear, he added, before a well regulated trade.

A scheme of this kind, however, was too vast and hazardous for individual enterprise; it could only be undertaken by a company under the sanction and protection of a government; and as there might be a clashing of claims between the Hudson's Bay and the North-west Company, the one holding by right of charter, the other by right of possession, he proposed that the two companies should coalesce in this great undertaking. The long cherished jealousies of these two companies, however, were too deep and strong to allow them to listen to such council.

In the mean time the attention of the American government was attracted to the subject, and the memorable expedition under Messrs. Lewis and Clarke, fitted out. These gentlemen, in 1804, accomplished the enterprise which had been projected by Carver and Whitworth, in 1774. They ascended the Missouri, passed through the stupendous gates of the Rocky mountains, hitherto unknown to white man; discovered and explored the upper waters of the Columbia, and followed that river down to its mouth, where their countryman, Gray, had anchored about twelve years previously. Here they passed the winter, and returned across the mountains in the following spring. The reports published by them of their expedition, demonstrated the practibility of establishing a line of communication across the continent, from the Atlantic to the Pacific ocean.

It was then that the idea presented itself to the mind of Mr. Astor, of grasping with his individual hands this great enterprise, which for years had been dubiously yet desirously contemplated by powerful associations and maternal governments. For some time he revolved the idea in his mind, gradually extending and maturing his plans as his means of executing them augmented. The main feature of his scheme was to establish a line of trading posts along the Missouri and the Columbia, to the mouth of the latter, where was to be founded the chief trading house or mart. Inferior posts would be established in the interior, and on all the tributary streams of the Columbia, to trade with the Indians; these posts would draw their supplies from the main establishment, and bring to it the peltries they collected. Coasting craft would be built and fitted out, also, at the mouth of the Columbia, to trade, at favourable seasons, all along the north-west coast and return, with the proceeds of their voyages, to this place of deposite. Thus all the Indian trade, both of the interior and the coast, would converge to this point, and thence derive its sustenance.

A ship was to be sent annually from New York to this main establishment with re-enforcements and supplies, and with merchandize suited to the trade. It would take on board the furs collected during the preceding year, carry them to Canton, invest the proceeds in the rich merchandize of China, and return thus freighted to New York.

As, in extending the American trade along the coast to the northward, it might be brought into the vicinity of the Russian Fur Company, and produce a hostile rivalry, it was part of the plan of Mr. Astor to conciliate the good will of that company by the most amicable and beneficial arrangements. The Russian establishment was chiefly dependant for its supplies upon transient trading vessels from the United States. These vessels, however, were often of more harm than advantage. Being owned by private adventurers, or casual voyagers, who cared only for present profit, and had no interest in the permanent prosperity of the trade, they were reckless in their dealings with the natives, and made no scruple of supplying them with fire-arms. In this way several fierce tribes in the vicinity of the Russian posts, or within the range of their trading excursions, were furnished with deadly means of warfare, and rendered troublesome and dangerous neighbours.

The Russian government had made representations to that of the United States of these mal-practices on the part of its citizens, and urged to have this traffic in arms prohibited ; but, as it did not infringe any municipal law, our government could not interfere. Yet still it regarded, with solicitude, a traffic which, if persisted in, might give offence to Russia, at that time almost the only power friendly to us. In this dilemma the government had applied to Mr. Astor, as one conversant in this branch of trade, for information that might point out a way to remedy the evil. This circumstance had suggested to him the idea of supplying the Russian establishment regularly by means of the annual ship that should visit the settlement at the mouth of the Columbia (or Oregon) ; by this means the casual trading vessels would be excluded from those parts of the coast where their mal-practices were so injurious to the Russians.

Such is a brief outline of the enterprise projected by Mr. Astor, but which continually expanded in his mind. Indeed it is due to him to say that he was not actuated by mere motives of individual profit. He was already wealthy beyond the ordinary desires of man, but he now aspired to that honourable fame which is awarded to men of similar scope of mind, who by their great commercial enterprises have enriched nations, peopled wildernesses, and extended the bounds of empire. He considered his projected establishment at the mouth of the Columbia as the emporium to an immense commerce ; as a colony that would form the germ of a wide civilization ; that would, in fact, carry the American population across the Rocky mountains and spread it along the shores of the Pacific, as it already animated the shores of the Atlantic.

As Mr. Astor, by the magnitude of his commercial and financial relations, and the vigour and scope of his self-taught mind, had elevated himself into the consideration of government, and the communion and correspondence with leading statesmen, he, at an early period, communicated his schemes to President Jefferson, soliciting the countenance of government. How highly they were esteemed by that eminent man, we may judge by the following passage, written by him some time afterwards to Mr. Astor.

" I remember well having invited your proposition on this subject,* and encouraged it with the assurance of every facility and protection which the government could properly afford. I considered, as a great public acquisition, the commencement of a settlement on that point of the western coast of America, and looked forward with gratification to the time when its descendants should have spread themselves through the whole length of that coast, covering it with free and independent Americans, unconnected with us but by the ties of blood and interest, and enjoying like us the rights of self-government."

The cabinet joined with Mr. Jefferson in warm approbation of the plan, and held out assurance of every protection that could, consistently with general policy, be afforded.

Mr. Astor now prepared to carry his scheme into prompt execution. He had some competition, however, to apprehend and guard against. The North-west Company, acting feebly and partially upon the suggestions of its former agent, Sir Alexander Mackenzie, had pushed one or two advanced trading posts across the Rocky mountains, into a tract of country visited by that enterprising traveller, and since named New Caledonia. This tract lay about two degrees north of the Columbia, and intervened between the territories of the United States and those of Russia. Its length was about five hundred and fifty miles, and its breadth, from the mountains to the Pacific, from three hundred to three hundred and fifty geographical miles.

Should the North-west Company persist in extending their trade in that quarter, their competition might be of a serious detriment to the plans of Mr. Astor. It is true they would contend with him to a vast disadvantage, from the checks and restrictions to which they were subjected.

* On this point Mr. Jefferson's memory was in error. The proposition alluded to was the one already mentioned, for the establishment of an American Fur Company in the Atlantic !states. The great enterprise beyond the mountains, that was to sweep the shores of the Pacific, originated in the mind of Mr. Astor, and was proposed by him to the government.

They were straitened on one side by the rivalry of the Hudson's Bay Company; then they had no good post on the Pacific where they could receive supplies by sea for their establishments beyond the mountains; nor, if they had one, could they ship their furs thence to China, that great mart for peltries; the Chinese trade being comprised in the monopoly of the East India Company. Their posts beyond the mountains had to be supplied in yearly expeditions, like caravans, from Montreal, and the furs conveyed back in the same way, by long, precarious, and expensive routes, across the continent. Mr. Astor, on the contrary, would be able to supply his proposed establishment at the mouth of the Columbia by sea, and to ship the furs collected there directly to China, so as to undersell the North-west Company in the great Chinese market.

Still, the competition of two rival companies west of the Rocky mountains could not but prove detrimental to both, and fraught with those evils, both to the trade and to the Indians, that had attended similar rivalries in the Canadas. To prevent any contest of the kind, therefore, he made known his plan to the agents of the North-west Company, and proposed to interest them to the extent of one-third, in the trade thus to be opened. Some correspondence and negotiation ensued. The company were aware of the advantages which would be possessed by Mr. Astor, should he be able to carry his scheme into effect; but they anticipated a monopoly of the trade beyond the mountains by their establishments in New Caledonia, and were loath to share it with an individual who had already proved a formidable competitor in the Atlantic trade. They hoped, too, by a timely move, to secure the mouth of the Columbia before Mr. Astor would be able to put his plans into operation; and, that key to the internal trade once in their possession, the whole country would be at their command. After some negotiation and delay, therefore, they declined the proposition that had been made to them, but subsequently dispatched a party for the mouth of the Columbia, to establish a post there before any expedition sent out by Mr. Astor might arrive.

In the mean time, Mr. Astor finding his overtures rejected, proceeded fearlessly to execute his enterprise in the face of the whole power of the North-west Company. His main establishment once planted at the mouth of the Columbia, he looked with confidence to ultimate success. Being able to reinforce and supply it amply by sea, he would push his interior posts in every direction up the rivers and along the coast; supplying the natives at a lower rate, and thus gradually obliging the North-west Company to give up the competition, relinquish New Caledonia, and retire to the other side of the mountains. He would then have possession of the trade, not merely of the Columbia and its tributaries, but of the regions farther north, quite to the Russian possessions. Such was a part of his brilliant and comprehensive plan.

He now proceeded with all diligence, to procure proper agents and coadjutors, habituated to the Indian trade and to the life of the wilderness. Among the clerks of the North-west Company were several of great capacity and experience, who had served out their probationary terms, but who, either through lack of interest and influence, or a want of vacancies, had not been promoted. They were consequently much dissatisfied, and ready for any employment in which their talents and acquirements might be turned to better account.

Mr. Astor made his overtures to several of these persons, and three of them entered into his views. One of these, Mr. Alexander M'Kay, had accompanied Sir Alexander Mackenzie in both of his expeditions to the north-west coast of America in 1789 and 1793. The other two were Duncan M'Dougal and Donald M'Kenzie. To these was subsequently added Mr. Wilson Price Hunt, of New Jersey. As this gentleman was a native born citizen of the United States, and a person of great probity and worth, he was selected by Mr. Astor to be his chief agent, and to represent him in the contemplated establishment.

On the 23d of June, 1810, articles of agreement were entered into between Mr. Astor and those four gentlemen, acting for themselves and for the several persons who had already agreed to become, or should hereafter become, associated under the firm of "The Pacific Fur Company."

According to these articles, Mr. Astor was to be at the head of the company, and to manage its affairs in New York. He was to furnish vessels, goods, provisions, arms, ammunition, and all other requisites for the enterprise at first cost and charges, provided that they did not, at any time, involve an advance of more than four hundred thousand dollars.

The stock of the company was to be divided into a hundred equal shares, with the profits accruing thereon. Fifty shares were to be at the disposition of Mr. Astor, and the other fifty to be divided among the partners and their associates. Mr. Astor was to have the privilege of introducing other persons into the connexion, as partners; two of whom, at least, should be conversant with the Indian trade, and none of them entitled to more than three shares.

A general meeting of the company was to be held annually at Columbia river, for the investigation and regulation of its affairs; at which absent members might be represented, and might vote by proxy under certain specified conditions.

The association, if successful, was to continue for twenty years; but the parties had full power to abandon and dissolve it within the first five years, should it be found unprofitable. For this term Mr. Astor covenanted to bear all the loss that might be incurred; after which it was to be borne by all the partners, in proportion to their respective shares.

The parties of the second part were to execute faithfully such duties as might be assigned to them by a majority of the company on the north-west coast, and to repair to such place or places as the majority might direct.

An agent, appointed for the term of five years, was to reside at the principal establishment on the north-west coast, and Wilson Price Hunt was the one chosen for the first term. Should the interests of the concern at any time require his absence, a person was to be appointed, in general meeting, to take his place.

Such were the leading conditions of this association. We shall now proceed to relate the various hardy and eventful expeditions, by sea and land, to which it gave rise.

CHAPTER IV.

Two expeditions set on foot—The Tonquin and her crew—Captain Thorn, his character—The partners and clerks—Canadian voyageurs, their habits, employments, dress, character, songs—Expedition of a Canadian boat and its crew by land and water—Arrival at New York—Preparation for a sea voyage—North west braggarts — Underhand precautions — Letter of instructions.

In prosecuting his great scheme of commerce and colonization, two expeditions were devised by Mr. Astor, one by sea, the other by land. The former was to carry out the people, stores, ammunition, and merchandize, requisite for establishing a fortified trading post at the mouth of Columbia river. The latter, conducted by Mr. Hunt, was to proceed up the Missouri, and across the Rocky mountains, to the same point; exploring a line of communication across the continent, and noting the places where interior trading posts might be established. The expedition by sea is the one which comes first under consideration.

A fine ship was provided called the Tonquin, of two hundred and ninety tons burthen, mounting ten guns, with a crew of twenty men. She carried an assortment of merchandise for trading with the natives of the sea board and of the interior, together with the frame of a schooner, to be employed in the coasting trade. Seeds also were provided for the cultivation of the soil, and nothing was neglected for the necessary supply of the establishment. The command of the ship was intrusted to Jonathan Thorn, of New York, a lieutenant in the United States navy, on leave of absence. He was a man of courage and firmness, who had distinguished himself in our Tripolitan war, and, from being accustomed to naval discipline, was considered by Mr. Astor as well fitted to take charge of an expedition of the kind. Four of the partners were to embark in the ship, namely, Messrs. M'Kay, M'Dougal, David Stuart, and his nephew, Robert Stuart. Mr. M'Dougal was empowered by Mr. Astor to act as his proxy in the absence of Mr. Hunt, to vote for him and in his name, on any question that might come before any meeting of the persons interested in the voyage.

Besides the partners, there were twelve clerks to go out in the ship, several of them natives of Canada, who had some experience in Indian trade. They were bound to the service of the company for five years, at the rate of one hundred dollars a year, payable at the expiration of the term, and an annual equipment of clothing to the amount of forty dollars. In case of ill conduct they were liable to forfeit their wages and be dismissed ; but, should they acquit themselves well, the confident expectation was held out to them of promotion and partnership. Their interests were thus, to some extent, identified with those of the company.

Several artisans were likewise to sail in the ship, for the supply of the colony; but the most peculiar and characteristic part of this motley embarkation consisted of thirteen Canadian " voyageurs," who had enlisted for five years. As this class of functionaries will continually recur in the course of the following narrations, and as they form one of those distinct and strongly marked castes or orders of people, springing up in this vast continent out of geographical circumstances, or the varied pursuits, habitudes, and origins of its population, we shall sketch a few of their characteristics for the information of the reader.

The " voyageurs" form a kind of confraternity in the Canadas, like arrieros, or carriers of Spain, and, like them, are employed in long internal expeditions of travel and traffic : with this difference, that the arrieros travel by land, the voyageurs by water ; the former with mules and horses, the latter with batteaux and canoes. The voyageurs may be said to have sprung up out of the fur trade, having originally been employed by the early French merchants in their trading expeditions through the labyrinth of rivers and lakes of the boundless interior. They were coeval with the *coureurs des bois*, or rangers of the woods, already noticed, and, like them, in the intervals of their long, arduous, and laborious expeditions, were prone to pass their time in idleness and revelry about the trading posts or settlements ; squandering their hard earnings in heedless conviviality, and rivalling their neighbours, the Indians, in indolent indulgence, and an impudent disregard of the morrow.

When Canada passed under British domination, and the old French trading houses were broken up, the voyageurs, like the *coureurs des bois*, were for a time disheartened and disconsolate, and with difficulty could reconcile themselves to the service of the new comers, so different in habits, manners, and language, from their former employers. By degrees, however, they became accustomed to the change, and at length came to consider the British fur traders, and especially the members of the North-west Company, as the legitimate lords of creation.

The dress of these people is generally half civilized, half savage. They wear a capot or surtout, made of a blanket a striped cotton shirt, cloth trousers, or leathern legging moccasins of deer skin, and a belt of variegated worsted, from which are suspended the knife, tobacco pouch, and other implements. Their language is of the same piebald character, being a French patois, embroidered with Indian and English words and phrases.

The lives of the voyageurs are passed in wild and extensive rovings, in the service of individuals, but more especially of the fur traders. They are generally of French descent, and inherit much of the gaiety and lightness of heart of their ancestors, being full of anecdote and song, and ever ready for the dance. They inherit, too, a fund of civility and complaisance ; and, instead of that hardness and grossness which men in laborious life are apt to indulge towards each other, they are mutually obliging and accommodating ; interchanging kind offices, yielding each other assistance and comfort in every emergency, and using the familiar appellations of " cousin" and " brother," when there is in fact no relationship. Their natural good will is probably heightened by a community of adventure and hardship in their precarious and wandering life.

No men are more submissive to their leaders and employers, more capable of enduring hardship, or more good humoured under privations. Never are they so happy as when on long and rough expeditions, toiling up rivers or coasting lakes; encamping at night on the boarders, gossiping round their fires, and bivouacking in the open air. They are dexterous boatmen, vigorous and adroit with the oar and paddle, and will row from morning unto night without a murmur. The steersman often sings an old traditionary French song, with some regular burden in which they all join, keeping time with their oars: if at any time they flag in spirits or relax in exertion, it is but necessary to strike up a song of the kind to put them all in fresh spirits and activity. The Canadian waters are vocal with these little French chansons, that have been echoed from mouth to mouth and transmitted from father to son, from the earliest days of the colony; and it has a pleasing effect, in a still golden summer evening, to see a batteau gliding across the bosom of a lake and dipping its oars to the cadence of these quaint old ditties, or sweeping along, in full chorus, on a bright sunny morning, down the transparent current of one of the Canadian rivers.

But we are talking of things that are fast fading away! The march of mechanical invention is driving every thing poetical before it. The steam-boats, which are fast dispelling the wildness and romance of our lakes and rivers, and aiding to subdue the world into common-place, are proving as fatal to the race of the Canadian voyageurs as they have been to that of the boatmen on the Mississippi. Their glory is departed. They are no longer the lords of our internal seas, and the great navigators of the wilderness. Some of them may still occasionally be seen coasting the lower lakes with their frail barks, and pitching their camps and lighting their fires upon the shores; but their range is fast contracting to those remote waters and shallow and obstructed rivers unvisited by the steam-boat. In the course of years they will gradually disappear; their songs will die away like the echoes they once

awakened, and the Canadian voyageurs will become a forgotten race, or remembered, like their associates, the
Indians, among the poetical images of past times, and as
themes for local and romantic associations.

An instance of the buoyant temperament and the pro-
fessional pride of these people was furnished in the gay
and braggart style in which they arrived at New York to
join the enterprise. They were determined to regale and
astonish the people of the "States" with the sight of a
Canadian boat and a Canadian crew. They accordingly
fitted up a large but light bark canoe, such as is used in
the fur trade; transported it in a waggon from the banks
of the St. Lawrence to the shores of lake Champlain:
traversed the lake in it, from end to end; hoisted it again
in a waggon and wheeled it off to Lansingburgh, and there
launched it upon the waters of the Hudson. Down this
river they plied their course merrily on a fine summer's day,
making its banks resound for the first time with their old
French boat songs; passing by the villages with whoop and
halloo, so as to make the honest Dutch farmers mistake
them for a crew of savages. In this way they swept, in
full song, and with regular flourish of the paddle, round
New York, in a still summer evening, to the wonder and
admiration of its inhabitants, who had never before witnessed
on their waters, a nautical apparition of the kind.

Such was the variegated band of adventurers about to
embark in the Tonquin on this arduous and doubtful
enterprise. While yet in port and on dry land, in the
bustle of preparation and the excitement of novelty, all
was sunshine and promise. The Canadians especially,
who with their constitutional vivacity, have a considerable
dash of the gascon, were buoyant and boastful, and great
braggarts as to the future; while all those who had been in
the service of the North-west Company, and engaged
in the Indian trade, plumed themselves upon their hardihood and their capacity to endure privations. If Mr. Astor
ventured to hint at the difficulties they might have to encounter, they treated them with scorn. They were
" north-westers;" men seasoned to hardships, who cared
for neither wind nor weather. They could live hard, lie

hard, sleep hard, eat dogs!—in a word they were ready to do and suffer any thing for the good of the enterprise. With all this profession of zeal and devotion, Mr. Astor was not over confident of the stability and firm faith of these mercurial beings. He had received information, also, that an armed brig from Halifax, probably at the instigation of the North-west Company, was hovering on the coast, watching for the Tonquin, with the purpose of impressing the Canadians on board of her, as British subjects, and thus interrupting the voyage. It was a time of doubt and anxiety, when the relations between the United States and Great Britain were daily assuming a more precarious aspect, and verging towards that war which shortly ensued. As a precautionary measure, therefore, he required the voyageurs, as they were about to enter into the service of an American association, and to reside within the limits of the United States, should take the oaths of naturalization as American citizens. To this they readily agreed, and shortly afterwards assured him that they had actually done so. It was not until after they had sailed that he discovered that they had entirely deceived him in the matter.

The confidence of Mr. Astor was abused in another quarter. Two of the partners, both of them Scotchmen and recently in the service of the North-west Company, had misgivings as to an enterprise which might clash with the interests and establishments protected by the British flag. They privately waited upon the British minister, Mr. Jackson, then in New York, laid open to him the whole scheme of Mr. Astor, though intrusted to them in confidence, and dependent, in a great measure, upon secrecy at the outset for its success, and inquired whether they, as British subjects, could lawfully engage in it. The reply satisfied their scruples, while the information they imparted excited the surprise and admiration of Mr. Jackson, that a private individual should have conceived and set on foot at his own risk and expense, so great an enterprise.

This step on the part of those gentlemen was not known to Mr. Astor until sometime afterwards, or it might have modified the trust and confidence reposed in them.

To guard against any interruption to the voyage by the armed brig, said to be off the harbour, Mr. Astor applied to Commodore Rodgers, at that time commanding at New York, to give the Tonquin safe convoy off the coast. The commodore having received from a high official source assurance of the deep interest which the government took in the enterprise, sent directions to Captain Hull, at that time cruising off the harbour, in the frigate Constitution, to afford the Tonquin the required protection when she should put to sea.

Before the day of embarkation, Mr. Astor addressed a letter of instruction to the four partners who were to sail in the ship. In this he enjoined them, in the most earnest manner, to cultivate harmony and unanimity, and recommended that all differences of opinions on points connected with the objects and interests of the voyage, should be discussed by the whole, and decided by a majority of votes. He, moreover, gave them especial caution as to their conduct on arriving at their destined port; exhorting them to be careful to make a favourable impression upon the wild people, among whom their lot and the fortunes of the enterprise would be cast. " If you find them kind," said he, " as I hope you will, be so to them. If otherwise, act with caution and forbearance, and convince them that you come as friends."

With the same anxious forethought he wrote a letter of instructions to Captain Thorn, in which he urged the strictest attention to the health of himself and his crew, and to the promotion of good humour and harmony on board his ship. " To prevent any misunderstanding," added he, " will require your particular good management." His letter closed with an injunction of wariness in his intercourse with the natives, a subject on which Mr. Astor was justly sensible he could not be too earnest. " I must recommend you," said he, " to be particularly careful on the coast, and not rely too much on the friendly disposition of the natives. All accidents which have as yet happened there arose from too much confidence in the Indians."

The reader will bear these instructions in mind, as

events will prove their wisdom and importance, and the disasters which ensued in consequence of the neglect of them.

CHAPTER V.

Sailing of the Tonquin—A rigid commander and a reckless crew—Landsmen on shipboard—Fresh water sailors at sea—Lubber—Nests—Ship fare—A Labrador veteran—Literary clerks—Curious travellers—Robinson Crusoe's island—Quarterdeck quarrels—Falkland islands—A wildgoosechase—Port Egmont—Epitaph hunting—"Old mortality"—Penguin shooting—Sportsmen left in the lurch—A hard pull—Further altercations—Arrival at Owyhee.

On the 8th of September, 1810, the Tonquin put to sea, where she was soon joined by the frigate Constitution. The wind was fresh and fair from the south-west, and the ship was soon out of sight of land and free from the apprehended danger of interruption. The frigate, therefore, gave her " God speed," and left her to her course.

The harmony so earnestly enjoined by Mr. Astor on this heterogeneous crew, and which had been so confidently promised in the buoyant moments of preparation, was doomed to meet with a check at the very outset.

Captain Thorn was an honest, straightforward, but somewhat dry and dictatorial commander, who having been nurtured in the system and disipline of a ship of war and in a sacred opinion of the supremacy of the quarter-deck, was disposed to be absolute lord and master on board of his ship. He appears, moreover, to have had no great opinion, from the first, of the persons embarked with him. He had stood by with surly contempt while they vaunted so bravely to Mr. Astor of all they could do and all they could undergo; how they could face all weathers, put up with all kinds of fare, and even eat dogs with a relish, when no better food was to he had. He had set them down as a set of land lubbers and braggadocios, and was disposed to treat them accordingly. Mr. Astor was, in his eyes, his only real employer, being the father of the

enterprise, who furnished all funds and bore all losses.
The others were mere agents and subordinates, who lived
at his expense.　He evidently had but a narrow idea of
the scope and nature of the enterprise, limiting his views
merely to his part of it; every thing beyond the concerns
of his ship was out of his sphere; and any thing that
interfered with the routine of his nautical duties put him
in a passion.

The partners, on the other hand, had been brought up
in the service of the North-west Company, and in a profound idea of the importance, dignity, and authority of
a partner.　They already began to consider themselves on
a par with the M‘Tavishes, the M‘Gillivrays, the Frobishers, and the other magnates of the north-west, whom they
had been accustomed to look up to as the great ones of
the earth; and they were a little disposed, perhaps, to
wear their suddenly-acquired honours with some air of
pretension.　Mr. Astor, too, had put them on their mettle
with respect to the captain, describing him as a gunpowder fellow who would command his ship in fine style,
and, if there was any fighting to do, would " blow all out
of the water."

Thus prepared to regard each other with no very cordial
eye, it is not to be wondered at that the parties soon came
into collision.　On the very first night Captain Thorn
began his man-of-war discipline by ordering the lights in
the cabin to be extinguished at eight o'clock.

The pride of the partners was immediately in arms.
This was an invasion of their rights and dignities not to be
borne.　They were on board of their own ship, and
entitled to consult their ease and enjoyment.　M‘Dougal
was the champion of their cause.　He was an active,
irritable, fuming, vainglorious little man, and elevated in
his own opinion, by being the proxy of Mr. Astor.　A
violent altercation ensued, in the course of which Thorn
threatened to put the partners in irons should they prove
refractory; upon which M‘Dougal seized a pistol and
swore to be the death of the captain should he ever offer
such an indignity.　It was some time before the irritated
parties could be pacified by the more temperate bystanders.

Such was the captain's outset with the partners. Nor did the clerks stand much higher in his good graces; indeed, he seemed to have regarded all the landsmen on board his ship as a kind of live lumber, continually in the way. The poor voyageurs, too, continually irritated his spleen by their "lubberly" and unseemly habits, so abhorrent to one accustomed to the cleanliness of a man of war. These poor fresh-water sailors, so vainglorious on shore, and almost amphibious when on lakes and rivers, lost all heart and stomach the moment they were at sea. For days they suffered the doleful rigours and retchings of seasickness, lurking below in their berths in squalid state, or emerging now and then like spectres from the hatchways, in capotes and blankets, with dirty nightcaps, grizzly beard, lantern visage and unhappy eye, shivering about the deck, and ever and anon crawling to the sides of the vessel, and offering up their tributes to the windward, to the infinite annoyance of the captain.

His letters to Mr. Astor, wherein he pours forth the bitterness of his soul, and his seamanlike impatience of what he considers the "*lubberly*" character and conduct of those around him, are before us, and are amusingly characteristic. The honest captain is full of vexation on his own account, and solicitude on account of Mr. Astor, whose property he considers at the mercy of a most heterogeneous and wasteful crew.

As to the clerks, he pronounces them mere pretenders, not one of whom had ever been among Indians, nor farther to the north-west than Montreal, nor of higher rank than bar-keeper of a tavern or marker of a billiard-table, excepting one, who had been a schoolmaster, and whom he emphatically sets down for "as foolish a pedant as ever lived."

Then as to the artisans and labourers who had been brought from Canada and shipped at such expense, the three most respectable, according to the captain's account were culprits, who had fled from Canada on account of their misdeeds; the rest had figured in Montreal as draymen, barbers, waiters, and carriole drivers, and were the most helpless, worthless beings, "that ever broke sea-biscuit."

It may easily be imagined what a series of misunderstandings and cross purposes would be likely to take place between such a crew and such a commander. The captain, in his zeal for the health and cleanliness of his ship, would make sweeping visitations to the " lubber nests" of the unlucky " voyageurs" and their companions in misery, ferret them out of their berths, make them air and wash themselves and their accoutrements, and oblige them to stir about briskly and take exercise.

Nor did his disgust and vexation cease when all hands had recovered from seasickness, and become accustomed to the ship, for now broke forth an alarming keenness of appetite that threatened havoc to the provisions. What especially irritated the captain was the daintiness of some of his cabin passengers. They were loud in their complaints of the ship's fare, though their table was served with fresh pork, hams, tongues, smoked beef, and puddings.

" When thwarted in their cravings for delicacies," said he, " they would exclaim that it was d—d hard they could not live as they pleased upon their own property, being on board their own ship, freighted with their own merchandise. And these," added he, " are the fine fellows who made such boast that they could " eat dogs. "

In his indignation at what he termed their effeminacy, he would swear that he would never take them to sea again " without having Fly-market on the forecastle, Covent-garden on the poop, and a cool spring from Canada in the maintop."

As they proceeded on their voyage and got into the smooth seas and pleasant weather of the tropics, other annoyances occurred to vex the spirit of the captain. He had been crossed by the irritable mood of one of the partners; he was now excessively annoyed by the good-humour of another. This was the elder Stuart, who was an easy soul, and of a social disposition. He had seen life in Canada, and on the coast of Labrador; had been a fur trader in the former, and a fisherman on the latter; and, in the course of his experience, had made various expeditions with voyageurs. He was accustomed, therefore, to the familiarity which prevails between that class and their superiors, and the gossipings which take place among them when seated round a fire at their encampments. Stuart was never so happy as when he could seat himself on the deck with a number of these men round him, in camping style, smoke together, passing the pipe from mouth to mouth, after the manner of the Indians, sing old Canadian boat-songs, and tell stories about their hardships and adventures, in the course of which he rivalled Sinbad in his long tales of the sea, about his fishing-exploits on the coast of Labrador.

This gossiping familiarity shocked the captain's notions of rank and subordination, and nothing was so abhorrent to him as the community of pipe between master and man and their mingling in chorus in the outlandish boat-songs.

Then there was another whimsical source of annoyance to him. Some of the young clerks, who were making their first voyage, and to whom every thing was new and strange, were, very rationally, in the habit of taking notes and keeping journals. This was a sore abomination to the honest captain, who held their literary pretensions in great contempt. "The collecting of materials for long histories of their voyage and travels," said he in his letter to Mr. Astor, "appears to engross most of their attention." We can conceive what must have been the crusty impatience of the worthy navigator, when, on any trifling occurrence in the course of the voyage, quite commonplace in his eyes, he saw these young landsmen running to record it in their journals; and what indignant glances he must have cast to right and left, as he worried about the deck, giving out his orders for the management of the ship, surrounded by singing, smoking, gossiping, scribbling groups, all, as he thought, intent upon the amusements of the passing hour, instead of the great purpose and interest of the voyage.

It is possible the captain was in some degree right in his notions. Though some of the passengers had much to gain by the voyage, none of them had any thing positively to lose. They were mostly young men in the heyday of life; and having got into fine latitudes, upon smooth seas, with a well-stored ship under them, and a fair wind in the shoulder of the sail, they seemed to have got into a holiday world, and were disposed to enjoy it. That craving desire, natural to untravelled men of fresh and lively minds, to see strange lands, and to visit scenes famous in history or fable, was expressed by some of the partners and clerks, with respect to some of the storied coasts and islands that lay within their route. The captain, however, who regarded every coast and island with a matter-of-fact eye, and had no more associations connected with them than those laid down in his sea-chart, considered all this curiosity as exceedingly idle and childish. " In the first part of the voyage," says he in his letter, " they were determined to have it said they had been in Africa, and therefore insisted on my stopping at the Cape de Verds. Next they said the ship should stop on the coast of Patagonia, for they must see the large and uncommon inhabitants of that place. Then they must go to the island where Robinson Crusoe had so long lived. And lastly, they were determined to see the handsome inhabitants of Easter island."

To all these resolves the captain opposed his peremptory veto, as " contrary to instructions." Then would break forth an unavailing explosion of wrath on the part of certain of the partners, in the course of which they did not even spare Mr. Astor for his act of supererogation in furnishing orders for the control of the ship while they were on board, instead of leaving them to be the judges, where it would be best for her to touch, and how long to remain. The choleric M'Dougal took the lead in these railings, being, as has been observed, a little puffed up with the idea of being Mr. Astor's proxy.

The captain, however, became only so much the more crusty and dogged in his adherence to his orders, and touchy and harsh in his dealings with his passengers, and frequent altercations ensued. He may in some measure have been influenced by his seamanlike impatience of the interference of landsmen, and his high notions of naval etiquette and quarterdeck authority; but he evidently had an honest, trusty concern for the interests of his employer. He pictured to himself the anxious projector of the enterprise, who had disbursed so munificently in its outfit, calculating on the zeal, fidelity and singleness of purpose of his associates and agents; while they, on the other hand, having a good ship at their disposal, and a deep pocket at home to bear them out, seemed ready to loiter on every coast, and amuse themselves in every port.

On the 4th of December they came in sight of the Falkland islands. Having been for some time on an allowance of water, it was resolved to anchor here and obtain a supply. A boat was sent into a small bay to take soundings. Mr. M'Dougal and Mr. M'Kay took this occasion to go on shore, but with a request from the captain that they would not detain the ship. Once on shore, however, they were in no haste to obey his orders, but rambled about in search of curiosities. The anchorage proving unsafe, and water difficult to be procured, the captain stood out to sea, and made repeated signals for those on shore to join the ship, but it was not until nine at night that they came on board.

The wind being adverse, the boat was again sent on shore on the following morning, and the same gentlemen again landed, but promised to come off at a moment's warning; they again forgot their promise in their eager pursuit of wild geese and sea wolves. After a time the wind hauled fair, and signals were made for the boat. Half an hour elapsed, but no boat put off. The captain reconnoitred the shore with his glass, and, to his infinite vexation, saw the loiterers in the full enjoyment of their "wildgoose-chase." Nettled to the quick, he immediately made sail. When those on shore saw the ship actually under way, they embarked with all speed, but had a hard pull of eight miles before they got on board, and then experienced but a grim reception, notwithstanding that they came well laden with the spoils of the chase.

Two days afterwards, on the 7th of December, they anchored at Port Egmont in the same island, where they remained four days taking in water and making repairs. This was a joyous time for the landsmen. They pitched

a tent on shore, had a boat at their command, and passed
their time merrily in rambling about the island, and coasting along the shore, shooting sea lions, seals, foxes, geese,
ducks, and penguins. None were keener in pursuit of
this kind of game than M'Dougal and David Stuart; the
latter was reminded of aquatic sports on the coast of Labrador, and his hunting-exploits in the north-west

In the mean time the captain addressed himself steadily
to the business of his ship, scorning the holiday spirit and
useless pursuits of his emancipated messmates, and warning them from time to time not to wander away, nor be
out of hail. They promised, as usual, that the ship should
never experience a moment's detention on their account,
but, as usual, forgot their promise.

On the morning of the 11th, the repairs being all
finished, and the water casks replenished, the signal was
given to embark, and the ship began to weigh anchor,
At this time several of the passengers were dispersed about
the island, amusing themselves in various ways. Some of
the young men had found two inscriptions, in English.
over a place where two unfortunate mariners had been
buried in this desert island. As the inscriptions were
nearly worn out by time and weather, they were playing
the part of "Old Mortality," and piously renewing them.
The signal from the ship summoned them from their labours; they saw the sails unfurled, and that it was getting under way. The two sporting partners, however, Mr.
M'Dougal and David Stuart, had strolled away to the
south of the island in pursuit of penguins. It would never
do to put off without them, as there was but one boat to
convey the whole.

While this delay took place on shore, the captain was
storming on board. This was the third time his orders
had been treated with contempt, and the ship wantonly
detained, and it should be the last; so he spread all sail
and put to sea, swearing he would leave the laggards to
shift for themselves. It was in vain that those on board
made remonstrances and entreaties, and represented the
horrors of abandoning men upon a steril and uninhabited
island : the sturdy captain was inflexible.

In the mean time the penguin hunters had joined the engravers of tombstones, but not before the ship was already out at sea. They all, to the number of eight, threw themselves into their boat, which was about twelve feet in length, and rowed with might and main. For three hours and a half did they tug anxiously and severely at the oar, swashed occasionally by the surging waves of the open sea, while the ship inexorably kept on her course, and seemed determined to leave them behind.

On board of the ship was the nephew of David Stuart, a young man of spirit and resolution. Seeing, as he thought, the captain. obstinately bent upon abandoning his uncle and the others, he seized a pistol, and in a paroxyism of wrath swore he would blow out the captain's brains, unless he put about or shortened sail.

Fortunately for all parties the wind just then came ahead, and the boat was enabled to reach the ship, otherwise disastrous circumstances might have ensued. We can hardly believe that the captain really intended to carry his threat into full effect, and rather think he meant to let the laggards off for a long pull and a hearty fright. He declared, however, in his letter to Mr. Astor, that he was serious in his threats; and there is no knowing how far such an iron man may push his notions of authority.

" Had the wind," writes he, " (unfortunately) not hauled ahead soon after leaving the harbour's mouth, I should positively have left them ; and indeed I cannot but think it an unfortunate circumstance for you that it so happened, for the first loss in this instance would, in my opinion, have proved the best, as they seem to have no idea of the value of property, nor any apparent regard for your interest, although interwoven with their own."

This, it must be confessed, was acting with a high hand, and carrying a regard to the owner's property to a dangerous length. Various petty feuds occurred also between him and the partners, in respect to the goods on board the ship, some articles of which they wished to distribute for clothing among the men, or for other purposes which they deemed essential. The captain, however, kept a mastiff watch upon the cargo, and growled and snapped if they but offered to touch box or bale. " It was contrary to orders; it would forfeit his insurance; it was out of all rule." It was in vain they insisted upon their right to do so, as part owners, and as acting for the good of the enterprise; the captain only stuck to his point the more stanchly. They consoled themselves, therefore, by declaring, that as soon as they made land they would assert their rights, and do with ship and cargo as they pleased.

Beside these feuds between the captain and the partners, there were feuds between the partners themselves, occasioned, in some measure, by jealousy of rank. M'Dougal and M'Kay began to draw plans for the fort, and other buildings of the intended establishment. They agreed very well as to the outline and dimensions, which were on a sufficiently grand scale; but when they came to arrange the details, fierce disputes arose, and they would quarrel by the hour about the distribution of the doors and windows. Many were the hard words and hard names bandied between them on these occasions, according to the captain's account. Each accused the other of endeavouring to assume unwarrantable power, and to take the lead; upon which Mr. M'Dougal would vauntingly lay down Mr. Astor's letter, constituting him his representative and proxy, a document not to be disputed.

These wordy contests, though violent, were brief; " and within fifteen minutes," says the captain, " they would be caressing each other like children."

While all this petty anarchy was agitating the little world within the Tonquin, the good ship prosperously pursued her course, doubled Cape Horn on the 25th of December, careered across the bosom of the Pacific, until, on the 11th of February, the snowy peaks of Owyhee were seen brightening above the horizon.

CHAPTER VI.

Owyhee, or Hawaii, as it is written by more exact orthographers, is the largest of the cluster, ten in number, of the Sandwich islands. It is about ninety-seven miles in length, and seventy-eight in breadth, rising gradually into three pyramidal summits or cones; the highest, Mouna Roa, being eighteen thousand feet above the level of the sea, so as to domineer over the whole Archipelago, and to be a landmark over a wide extent of ocean. It remains a lasting monument of the enterprising and unfortunate Captain Cook, who was murdered by the natives of this island.

The Sandwich islanders, when first discovered, evinced a character superior to most of the savages of the Pacific isles. They were frank and open in their deportment, friendly and liberal in their dealings, with an apt ingenuity apparent in all their rude inventions.

The tragical fate of the discoverer, which for a time brought them under the charge of ferocity, was, in fact, the result of sudden exasperation, caused by the seizure of their chief.

At the time of the visit of the Tonquin, the islanders had profited, in many respects, by occasional intercourse with white men; and had shown a quickness to observe and cultivate those arts important to their mode of living. Originally they had no means of navigating the seas by which they were surrounded, superior to light pirogues, which were little competent to contend with the storms of the broad ocean. As the islands are not in sight of each other, there could, therefore, be but casual intercourse between them. The traffic with white men had put them in

possession of vessels of superior description; they had
made themselves acquainted with their management, and
had even made rude advances in the art of ship building.

These improvements had been promoted, in a great
measure, by the energy and sagacity of one man, the
famous Tamaahmaah. He had originally been a petty
eri, or chief; but, being of an intrepid and aspiring nature,
he had risen in rank, and, availing himself of the superior
advantages now afforded in navigation, had brought the
whole Archipelago in subjection to his arms. At the time
of the arrival of the Tonquin he had about forty schooners,
of from twenty to thirty tons burthen, and one old American ship. With these he maintained undisputed sway
over his insular domains, and carried on an intercourse
with the chiefs or governors whom he had placed in command of the several islands.

The situation of this group of islands, far in the bosom
of the vast Pacific, and their abundant fertility, rendered
them important stopping places on the highway to China,
or to the north-west coast of America. Here the vessels
engaged in the fur trade touched to make repairs and procure provisions; and here they often sheltered themselves
during the winters that occurred in their long coasting
expeditions.

The British navigators were, from the first, aware of the
value of these islands to the purposes of commerce; and
Tamaahmaah, not long after he had attained the sovereign
sway, was persuaded by Vancouver, the celebrated discoverer, to acknowledge on behalf of himself and subjects,
allegiance to the king of Great Britain. The reader cannot but call to mind the visit which the royal family and
court of the Sandwich islands was, in late years, induced
to make to the court of St. James's; and the serio-comic
ceremonials and mock parade which attended that singular
travesty of monarchal style.

It was a part of the wide and comprehensive plan of
Mr. Astor to establish a friendly intercourse between these
islands and his intended colony, which might, for a time,
have occasion to draw supplies thence; and he even had
a vague idea of, some time or other, getting possession of

one of their islands as a rendezvous for his ships, and a link in the chain of his commercial establishments.

On the evening of the 12th of February the Tonquin anchored in the bay of Karakakooa, in the island of Owyhee. The surrounding shores were wild and broken, with overhanging cliffs and precipices of black volcanic rock. Beyond these, however, the country was fertile and well cultivated, with enclosures of yams, plantains, sweet potatoes, sugar-canes, and other productions of warm climates and teeming soils ; and the numerous habitations of the natives were pleasantly sheltered beneath clumps of cocoa-nut and bread-fruit trees, which afforded both food and shade. This mingled variety of garden and grove swept gradually up the sides of the mountains, until succeeded by dense forests, which in turn gave place to naked and craggy rocks, until the summits rose into the regions of perpetual snow.

The royal residence of Tamaahmaah was at this time at another island named Woahoo. The island of Owyhee was under the command of one of his eris, or chiefs, who resided at the village of Tocaigh, situated on a different part of the coast from the bay of Karakakooa.

On the morning after her arrival, the ship was surrounded by canoes and pirogues, filled with the islanders of both sexes, bringing off supplies of fruits and vegetables, bananas, plantain, watermelons, yams, cabbages, and taro. The captain was desirous, however, of purchasing a number of hogs, but there were none to be had. The trade in pork was a royal monopoly, and no subject of the great Tamaahmaah dared to meddle with it. Such provisions as they could furnish, however, were brought by the natives in abundance, and a lively intercourse was kept up during the day, in which the women mingled in the kindest manner.

The islanders are a comely race, of a copper complexion. The men are tall and well made, with forms indicating strength and activity ; the women with regular and occasionally handsome features, and a lascivious expression, characteristic of their temperament. Their style of dress was nearly the same as in the days of Captain Cook.

The men wore the maro, a band one foot in width and several feet in length, swathed round the loins, and formed of tappa, or cloth of bark; the kihei, or mantle, about six feet square, tied in a knot over one shoulder, passed under the opposite arm, so as to leave it bare, and falling in graceful folds before and behind to the knee, so as to bear some resemblance to a Roman toga.

The female dress consisted of the pau, a garment formed of a piece of tappa, several yards in length, and one in width, wrapped round the waist, and reaching like a petticoat to the knees. Over this the kihei or mantle, larger than that of the men, sometimes worn over both shoulders, like a shawl, sometimes over one only. These mantles were seldom worn by either sex during the heat of the day, when the exposure of their persons was at first very revolting to a civilized eye.

Towards evening several of the partners and clerks went on shore, where they were well received and hospitably entertained. A dance was performed for their amusement, in which nineteen young women and one man figured very gracefully, singing in concert, and moving to the cadence of their song.

All this, however, was nothing to the purpose in the eyes of Captain Thorn, who, being disappointed in his hope of obtaining a supply of pork, or finding good water, was anxious to be off. This it was not so easy to effect. The passengers, once on shore, were disposed, as usual, to profit by the occasion. The partners had many inquiries to make relative to the island, with a view to business; while the young clerks were delighted with the charms and graces of the dancing damsels.

To add to their gratifications, an old man offered to conduct them to the spot were Captain Cook was massacred. The proposition was eagerly accepted, and all hands set out on a pilgrimage to the place. The veteran islander performed his promise faithfully, and pointed out the very spot where the unfortunate discoverer fell. The rocks and cocoa-trees around bore record of the fact, in the marks of the balls fired from the boats upon the savages. The pilgrims gathered round the old man, and drew from him all the particulars he had to relate respecting this memorable event; while the honest captain stood by and bit his nails with impatience. To add to his vexation, they employed themselves in knocking off pieces of the rocks, and cutting off the bark of the trees marked by the balls, which they conveyed back to the ship as precious relics.

Right glad, therefore, was he to get them and their treasures fairly on board, when he made sail from this unprofitable place, and steered for the bay of Tocaigh, the residence of the chief or governor of the island, where he hoped to be more successful in obtaining supplies. On coming to anchor the captain went on shore, accompanied by Mr. M'Dougal and Mr. M'Kay, and paid a visit to the governor. This dignitary proved to be an old sailor, by the name of John Young; who, after being tossed about the seas like another Sinbad, had, by one of the whimsical freaks of fortune, been elevated to the government of a savage island. He received his visiters with more hearty familiarity than personages in his high station are apt to indulge, but soon gave them to understand that provisions were scanty at Tocaigh, and that there was no good water; no rain having fallen in the neighbourhood in three years.

The captain was immediately for breaking up the conference and departing, but the partners were not so willing to part with the nautical governor, who seemed disposed to be extremely communicative, and from whom they might be able to procure some useful information. A long conversation accordingly ensued, in the course of which they made many inquiries about the affairs of the islands, their natural productions, and the possibility of turning them to advantage in the way of trade; nor did they fail to inquire into the individual history of John Young, and how he came to be governor. This he gave with great condescension, running through the whole course of his fortunes " even from his boyish days."

He was a native of Liverpool, in England, and had followed the sea from his boyhood, until, by dint of good conduct, he had risen so far in his profession as to be boatswain of an American ship called the Eleanor, commanded by Captain Metcalf. In this vessel he had sailed in 1789, on one of those casual expeditions to the north-west coast, in quest of furs. In the course of the voyage, the captain left a small schooner named the Fair American, at Nootka, with a crew of five men, commanded by his son, a youth of eighteen. She was to follow on in the track of the Eleanor.

In February, 1790, Captain Metcalf touched at the island of Mowee, one of the Sandwich group. While anchored here, a boat which was astern of the Eleanor was stolen, and a seaman who was in it was killed. The natives generally disclaimed the outrage, and brought the shattered remains of the boat and the dead body of the seaman to the ship. Supposing that they had thus appeased the anger of the captain, they thronged, as usual, in great numbers about the vessel to trade. Captain Metcalf, however, determined on a bloody revenge. The Eleanor mounted ten guns; all these he ordered to be loaded with musket-balls, nails, and pieces of old iron, and then fired them, and the small arms of the ship, among the natives. The havoc was dreadful; more than a hundred, according to Young's account, were slain.

After this signal act of vengence, Captain Metcalf sailed from Mowee, and made for the island of Owyhee, where he was well received by Tamaahmaah. The fortunes of this warlike chief were at that time on the rise. He had originally been of inferior rank, ruling over only one or two districts in Owyhee, but had gradually made himself sovereign of his native island.

The Eleanor remained some few days at anchor here, and an apparently friendly intercourse was kept up with the inhabitants. On the 17th of March, John Young obtained permission to pass the night on shore. On the following morning a signal gun summoned him to return on board.

He went to the shore to embark, but found all the canoes hauled up on the beach and rigorously tabooed, or interdicted. He would have launched one himself, but was informed by Tamaahmaah that if he presumed to do so, he would be put to death.

Young was obliged to submit, and remained all day in great perplexity to account for this mysterious taboo, and fearful that some hostility was intended. In the evening he learned the cause of it, and his uneasiness was increased. It appeared that the vindictive act of Captain Metcalf had recoiled upon his own head. The schooner, Fair American, commanded by his son, following in his track, had fallen into the hands of the natives to the southward of Tocaigh bay, and young Metcalf and four of the crew had been massacred.

On receiving intelligence of this event, Tamaahmaah had immediately tabooed all the canoes, and interdicted all intercourse with the ship, lest the captain should learn the fate of the schooner, and take his revenge upon the island. For the same reason he prevented Young from rejoining his countrymen. The Eleanor continued to fire signals from time to time for two days, and then sailed ; concluding, no doubt, that the boatswain had deserted.

John Young was in despair when he saw the ship make sail, and found himself abandoned among savages ;—and savages, too, sanguinary in their character, and inflamed by acts of hostility. He was agreeably disappointed, however, in experiencing nothing but kind treatment from Tamaahmaah and his people. It is true he was narrowly watched whenever a vessel came in sight, lest he should escape, and relate what had passed; but at other times he was treated with entire confidence and great distinction. He became a prime favourite, cabinet counsellor, and active coadjutor of Tamaahmaah, attending him in all excursions, whether of business or pleasure, and aiding in his warlike and ambitious enterprises. By degrees he rose to the rank of a chief, espoused one of the beauties of the island, and became habituated and reconciled to his new way of life; thinking it better, perhaps, to rule among savages than serve among white men ; to be a feathered chief than a tarpauling boatswain. His favour with Tamaahmaah never declined ; and when that sagacious, intrepid, and aspiring chieftain had made himself sovereign over the whole group of islands, and removed his residence to Woahoo, he left his faithful adherent John Young in command of Owyhee.

Such is an outline of the history of Governor Young, as furnished by himself; and we regret that we are not able to give any account of the state maintained by this sea-faring worthy, and the manner in which he discharged his high functions; though it is evident he had more of the hearty familiarity of the forecastle than the dignity of the gubernatorial office.

These long conferences were bitter trials to the patience of the captain, who had no respect either for the governor or his island, and was anxious to push on in quest of provisions and water. As soon as he could get his inquisitive partners once more on board, he weighed anchor, and made sail for the island of Woahoo, the royal residence of Tamaahmaah.

This is the most beautiful island of the Sandwich group. It is forty-six miles in length, and twenty-three in breadth. A ridge of volcanic mountains extends through the centre, rising into lofty peaks, and skirted by undulating hills and rich plains, where the cabins of the natives peep out from beneath groves of cocoa-nut and other luxuriant trees.

On the 21st of February the Tonquin cast anchor in the beautiful bay before the village of Waititi (pronounced Whyteetee), the abode of Tamaahmaah. This village contained about two hundred habitations, composed of poles set in the ground, tied together at the ends, and thatched with grass, and was situated in an open grove of cocoa-nuts. The royal palace of Tamaahmaah was a large house of two stories; the lower of stone, the upper of wood. Round this his body-guard kept watch, composed of twenty-four men, in long blue cassocks turned up with yellow, and each armed with a musket.

While at anchor in this place, much ceremonious visiting and long conferences took place between the potentate of the islands and the partners in the company. Tamaahmaah came on board of the ship in royal style, in his double pirogue. He was between fifty and sixty years of age, above the middle size, large and well made, though some-what corpulent. He was dressed in an old suit of regi-mentals, with a sword by his side, and seemed somewhat embarrassed by his magnificent attire. Three of his wives accompanied him. They were almost as tall, and quite as corpulent; but by no means to be compared with him in grandeur of habiliments, wearing no other garb than the pau. With him also came his great favourite and confi-dential counsellor, Kraimaker; who, from holding a post equivalent to that of prime minister, had been familiarly named Billy Pitt by the British visiters to the islands.

The sovereign was received with befitting ceremonial. The American flag was displayed, four guns were fired, and the partners appeared in scarlet coats, and conducted their illustrious guests to the cabin, where they were re-galed with wine. In this interview the partners endea-voured to impress the monarch with a sense of their im-portance, and of the importance of the association to which they belonged. They let him know that they were eris, or chiefs, of a great company about to be established on the north-west coast, and talked of the probability of opening a trade with his islands, and of sending ships there occasionally. All this was gratifying and interesting to him, for he was aware of the advantages of trade, and de-sirous of promoting frequent intercourse with white men. He encouraged Europeans and Americans to settle in his islands, and intermarry with his subjects. There were between twenty and thirty white men at that time resident in the island, but many of them were mere vagabonds, who remained there in hopes of leading a lazy and an easy life. For such Tamaahmaah had a great con-tempt; those only had his esteem and countenance who knew some trade or mechanic art, and were sober and in-dustrious.

On the day subsequent to the monarch's visit, the part-ners landed and waited upon him in return. Knowing the effect of show and dress upon men in savage life, and wishing to make a favourable impression as the *eris*, or chiefs, of the great American Fur Company, some of them appeared in Highland plaids and kelts, to the great admiration of the natives.

While visits of ceremony and grand diplomatic conferences were going on between the partners and the king, the captain in his plain matter-of-fact way, was pushing what he considered a far more important negociation—the purchase of a supply of hogs. He found that the king had profited in more ways than one by his intercourse with white men. Above all other arts he had learned the art of driving a bargain. He was a magnanimous monarch, but a shrewd pork merchant; and perhaps thought he could not do better with his future allies, the American Fur Company, than to begin by close dealing. Several interviews were requisite, and much bargaining, before he could be brought to part with a bristle of his bacon, and then he insisted upon being paid in hard Spanish dollars; giving as a reason that he wanted money to purchase a frigate from his brother George, as he affectionately termed the king of England.*

At length the royal bargain was concluded; the necessary supply of hogs obtained, besides several goats, two sheep, a quantity of poultry, and vegetables in abundance. The partners now urged to recruit their forces from the natives of this island. They declared they had never seen watermen equal to them, even among the voyageurs of the north-west; and, indeed, they are remarkable for

---

* It appears, from the accounts of subsequent voyagers, that Tamaahmaah afterwards succeeded in his wish of purchasing a large ship. In this he sent a cargo of sandal wood to Canton, having discovered that the foreign merchants trading with him made large profits on this wood, shipped by them from the islands to the Chinese markets. The ship was manned by natives, but the officers were Englishmen. She accomplished her voyage, and returned in safety to the islands, with the Hawaiian flag floating gloriously in the breeze. The king hastened on board; expecting to find his sandal wood converted into crapes and damasks, and other rich stuffs of China, but found, to his astonishment, by the legerdemain of traffic, his cargo had all disappeared, and, in place of it, remained a bill of charges amounting to *three thousand dollars*. It was some time before he could be made to comprehend certain of the most important items of the bill, such as pilotage, anchorage, and custom-house fees; but when he discovered that maritime states in other countries derived large revenues in this manner, to the great cost of the merchant, "Well," cried he, "then I will have harbour fees also." He established them accordingly. Pilotage a dollar a foot on the draft of each vessel. Anchorage from sixty to seventy dollars. In this way he greatly increased the royal revenue, and turned his China speculation to account.

their skill in managing their light craft, and can swim and dive like waterfowl. The partners were inclined, therefore, to take thirty or forty with them to the Columbia, to be employed in the service of the company. The captain, however, objected that there was not room in his vessel for the accommodation of such a number. Twelve only were therefore enlisted for the company, and as many more for the service of the ship. The former engaged to serve for the term of three years, during which they were to be fed and clothed ; and at the expiration of the time were to receive one hundred dollars in merchandise.

And now, having embarked his live stock, fruits, vegetables, and water, the captain made ready to sail. How much the honest man had suffered in spirit by what he considered the freaks and vagaries of his passengers, and how little he had understood their humours and intentions, is amusingly shown in a letter written to Mr. Astor from Woahoo, which contains his comments on the scenes we have described.

" It would be difficult," he writes, " to imagine the frantic gambols that are daily played off here; sometimes dressing in red coats, and otherwise very fantastically, and collecting a number of ignorant natives around them, telling them that they are the great *eares* of the northwest, and making arrangements for sending three or four vessels yearly to them from the coast with spars, &c. ; while those very natives cannot even furnish a hog to the ship. Then dressing in Highland plaids and kelts, and making similar arrangements, with presents of rum, wine, or any thing that is at hand. Then taking a number of clerks and men on shore to the very spot on which Captain Cook was killed, and each fetching off a piece of the rock or tree that was touched by the shot. Then setting down with some white man or some native who can be a little understood, and collecting the history of those islands, of Tamaahmaah's wars, the curiosities of the islands, &c., preparatory to the histories of their voyages ; and the collection is indeed ridiculously contemptible. To enumerate the thousand instances of ignorance, filth, &c., or

to particularize all the frantic gambols that are daily practised, would require volumes."

Before embarking, the great eris of the American Fur
Company took leave of their illustrious ally in due style,
with many professions of lasting friendship and promises
of future intercourse; while the matter-of-fact captain
anathematized him in his heart for a grasping, trafficking
savage, as shrewd and sordid in his dealings as a white
man. As one of the vessels of the company will, in the
course of events, have to appeal to the justice and mag-
nanimity of this island potentate, we shall see how far the
honest captain was right in his opinion.

CHAPTER VII.

Departure from the Sandwich islands—Misunderstandings—Miseries of a
suspicious man—Arrival at Colombia—Dangerous service—Gloomy apprehensions—Bars and breakers—Perils of the ship—Disasters of a boat's
crew—Burial of a Sandwich islander.

It was on the 28th of February that the Tonquin set
sail from the Sandwich islands. For two days the wind
was contrary, and the vessel was detained in their neighbourhood; at length a favourable breeze sprang up, and
in a little while the rich groves, green hills, and snowy
peaks of those happy islands, one after another, sank from
sight, or melted into the blue distance, and the Tonquin
ploughed her course towards the sterner regions of the
Pacific.

The misunderstandings between the captain and his
passengers still continued, or, rather, increased in gravity.
By his altercations and his moody humours, he had cut
himself off from all community of thought, or freedom of
conversation with them. He disdained to ask any questions as to their proceedings, and could only guess at the
meaning of their movements, and in so doing indulged in
conjectures and suspicions, which produced the most
whimsical self-torment.

Thus, in one of his disputes with them, relative to the goods on board, some of the packages of which they wished to open, to take out articles of clothing for the men or presents for the natives, he was so harsh and peremptory that they lost all patience, and hinted that they were the strongest party, and might reduce him to a very ridiculous dilemma, by taking from him the command.

A thought now flashed across the captain's mind that they really had a design to depose him, and that, having picked up some information at Owyhee, possibly of war between the United States and England, they meant to alter the destination of the voyage; perhaps to seize upon ship and cargo for their own use.

Once having conceived this suspicion, every thing went to foster it. They had distributed fire-arms among some of their men, a common precaution among the fur traders when mingling with the natives. This, however, looked like preparation. Then several of the partners and clerks and some of the men, being Scotsmen, were acquainted with the Gaelic, and held long conversations together in that language. These conversations were considered by the captain of a " mysterious and unwarrantable nature," and related, no doubt, to some foul conspiracy that was brewing among them. He frankly avows such suspicions, in his letter to Mr. Astor, but intimates that he stood ready to resist any treasonous outbreak; and seems to think that the evidence of preparation on his part had an effect in overawing the conspirators.

The fact is, as we have since been informed by one of the parties, it was a mischievous pleasure with some of the partners and clerks, who were young men, to play upon the suspicious temper and splenetic humours of the captain. To this we may ascribe many of their whimsical pranks and absurd propositions, and, above all, their mysterious colloquies in Gaelic.

In this sore and irritable mood did the captain pursue his course, keeping a wary eye on every movement, and bristling up whenever the detested sound of the Gaelic language grated upon his ear. Nothing occurred, however, materially to disturb the residue of the voyage excepting a violent storm; and, on the 22d of March, the Tonquin arrived at the mouth of the Oregon, or Columbia river.

The aspect of the river and the adjacent coast was wild and dangerous. The mouth of the Columbia is upwards of four miles wide, with a peninsular and promontory on one side, and a long low spit of land on the other; between which a sand bar and chain of breakers almost block up the entrance. The interior of the country rises into successive ranges of mountains, which, at the time of the arrival of the Tonquin, were covered with snow.

A fresh wind from the north-west sent a rough tumbling sea upon the coast, which broke upon the bar in furious surges, and extended a sheet of foam almost across the mouth of the river. Under these circumstances the captain did not think it prudent to approach within three leagues, until the bar should be sounded and the channel ascertained. Mr. Fox, the chief mate, was ordered to this service in the whale-boat, accompanied by John Martin, an old seaman, who had formerly visited the river, and by three Canadians. Fox requested to have regular sailors to man the boat, but the captain would not spare them from the service of the ship, and supposed the Canadians, being expert boatmen on lakes and rivers, were competent to the service, especially when directed and aided by Fox and Martin. Fox seems to have lost all firmness of spirit on the occasion, and to have regarded the service with a misgiving heart. He came to the partners for sympathy, knowing their differences with the captain, and the tears were in his eyes as he represented his case. " I am sent off," said he, " without seamen to man my boat, in boisterous weather, and on the most dangerous part of the north-west coast. My uncle was lost a few years ago on this same bar, and I am now going to lay my bones alongside of his." The partners sympathized in his apprehensions, and remonstrated with the captain. The latter, however, was not to be moved. He had been displeased with Mr. Fox in the earlier part of the voyage, considering him indolent and inactive; and probably thought his present repugance arose from a want of true nautical spirit. The interference of the partners in the business of the ship, also was not calculated to have a favourable effect on a stickler for authority like himself, especially in his actual state of feeling towards them.

At one o'clock, P. M., therefore, Fox and his comrades set off in the whale-boat, which is represented as small in size, and crazy in condition. All eyes were strained after the little bark as it pulled for shore, rising and sinking with the huge rolling waves, until it entered, a mere speck, among the foaming breakers, and was soon lost to view. Evening set in, night succeeded and passed away, and morning returned, but without the return of the boat.

As the wind had moderated, the ship stood near to the land, so as to command a view of the river's mouth. Nothing was to be seen but a wild chaos of tumbling waves breaking upon the bar, and apparently forming a foaming barrier from shore to shore. Towards night the ship again stood out to gain sea-room, and a gloom was visible in every countenance. The captain himself shared in the general anxiety, and probably repented of his peremptory orders. Another weary and watchful night succeeded, during which the wind subsided, and the weather became serene.

On the following day, the ship having drifted near the land, anchored in fourteen fathoms water, to the northward of the long peninsula or promontory, which forms the north side of the entrance, and is called Cape Disappointment. The pinnace was then manned, and two of the partners, Mr. David Stuart and Mr. M'Kay, set off in the hope of learning something of the fate of the whale-boat. The surf, however, broke with such violence along the shore, that they could find no landing place. Several of the natives appeared on the beach, and made signs to them to row round the cape, but they thought it most prudent to return to the ship.

The wind now springing up, the Tonquin got under way, and stood in to seek the channel, but was again deterred, by the frightful aspect of the breakers, from venturing within a league. Here she hove to; and Mr. Mumford, the second mate, was despatched with four hands, in the pinnace, to sound across the channel until he should find four fathoms depth. The pinnace entered among the breakers, but was near being lost, and with difficulty got back to the ship. The captain insisted that Mr. Mumford had steered too much to the southward. He now turned to Mr. Aiken, an able mariner, destined to command the schooner intended for the coasting trade, and ordered him, together with John Coles, sail-maker, Stephen Weeks, armourer, and two Sandwich islanders, to proceed ahead and take soundings, while the ship should follow under easy sail. In this way they proceeded until Aiken had ascertained the channel, when signal was given from the ship for him to return on board. He was then within pistol shot; but so furious was the current, and tumultuous the breakers, that the boat became unmanageable, and was hurried away, the crew crying out piteously for assistance. In a few moments she could not be seen from the ship's deck. Some of the passengers climbed to the mizen top, and beheld her still struggling to reach the ship; but shortly after she broached broadside to the waves, and her case seemed desperate. The attention of those on board of the ship was now called to their own safety. They were in shallow water; the vessel struck repeatedly, the waves broke over her, and there was danger of her foundering. At length she got into seven fathoms water, and the wind lulling, and the night coming on, cast anchor. With the darkness their anxieties increased. The wind whistled, the sea roared, the gloom was only broken by the ghastly glare of the foaming breakers, the minds of the seamen were full of dreary apprehensions, and some of them fancied they heard the cries of their lost comrades mingling with the uproar of the elements. For a time, too, the rapidly ebbing tide threatened to sweep them from their precarious anchorage. At length the reflux of the tide, and the springing up of the wind, enabled them to quit their dangerous situation, and take shelter in a small bay within Cape Disappointment, where they rode in safety during the residue of a stormy night, and enjoyed a brief interval of refreshing sleep.

With the light of day returned their cares and anxieties. They looked out from the mast-head over a wild coast, and wilder sea, but could discover no trace of the two boats and their crews that were missing. Several of the natives came on board with peltries, but there was no disposition to trade. They were interrogated by signs after the lost boats, but could not understand the inquiries.

Parties now went on shore and scoured the neighbourhood. One of these was headed by the captain. They had not proceeded far when they beheld a person at a distance in civilized garb. As he drew near he proved to be Weekes, the armourer. There was a burst of joy, for it was hoped his comrades were near at hand. His story, however, was one of disaster. He and his companions had found it impossible to govern their boat, having no rudder, and being beset by rapid and whirling currents and boisterous surges. After long struggling, they had let her go at the mercy of the waves, tossing about, sometimes with her bow, sometimes with her broadside to the surges, threatened each instant with destruction, yet repeatedly escaping, until a huge sea broke over and swamped her. Weekes was overwhelmed by the boiling waves, but, emerging above the surface, looked round for his companions. Aiken and Coles were not to be seen; near him were the two Sandwich islanders, stripping themselves of their clothing that they might swim more freely. He did the same, and the boat floating near to him he seized hold of it. The two islanders joined him, and, uniting their forces, they succeeded in turning the boat upon her keel; then bearing down her stern and rocking her, they forced out so much water that she was able to bear the weight of a man without sinking. One of the islanders now got in, and in a little while baled out the water with his hands. The other swam about and collected the oars, and they all three got once more on board.

By this time the tide had swept them beyond the breakers, and Weekes called on his companions to row for land. They were so chilled and benumbed by the cold, however, that they lost all heart, and absolutely refused. Weekes was equally chilled, but had superior sagacity and self-command. He counteracted the tendency to drowsiness and stupor which cold produces by keeping himself in constant exercise; and seeing that the vessel was advancing, and that every thing depended upon himself, he set to work to scull the boat clear of the bar, and into quiet water.

Towards midnight one of the poor islanders expired: his companion threw himself on his corpse, and could not be persuaded to leave him. The dismal night wore away amidst these horrors: as the day dawned, Weekes found himself near the land. He steered directly for it, and at length, with the aid of the surf, ran his boat high upon a sandy beach.

Finding that one of the Sandwich islanders yet gave signs of life, he aided him to leave the boat, and set out with him towards the adjacent woods. The poor fellow, however, was too feeble to follow him, and Weekes was soon obliged to abandon him to his fate and provide for his own safety. Falling upon a beaten path, he pursued it, and after a few hours, came to a part of the coast, where, to his surprise and joy, he beheld the ship at anchor, and was met by the captain and his party.

After Weekes had related his adventures, three parties were despatched to beat up the coast in search of the unfortunate islander. They returned at night without success, though they had used the utmost diligence. On the following day the search was resumed, and the poor fellow was at length discovered lying beneath a group of rocks, his legs swollen, his feet torn and bloody from walking through bushes and briars, and himself half dead with cold, hunger, and fatigue. Weekes and this islander were the only survivors of the crew of the jolly-boat, and no trace was ever discovered of Fox and his party. Thus eight men were lost on the first approach to the coast; a commencement that cast a gloom over the spirits of the whole party, and was regarded by some of the superstitious as an omen that boded no good to the enterprise.

Towards night the Sandwich islanders went on shore, to bury the body of their unfortunate countryman who had perished in the boat. On arriving at the place where it had been left, they dug a grave in the sand, in which they deposited the corpse, with a biscuit under one of the arms, some lard under the chin, and a small quantity of tobacco, as provisions for its journey in the land of spirits. Having covered the body with sand and flints, they kneeled along the grave in a double row, with their faces turned to the east, while one who officiated as a priest sprinkled them with water from a hat. In so doing he recited a kind of prayer or invocation, to which, at intervals, the others made responses. Such were the simple rites performed by these poor savages at the grave of their comrade on the shores of a strange land ; and when these were done, they rose and returned in silence to the ship, without once casting a look behind.

CHAPTER VIII.

Mouth of the Columbia—The native tribes—Their fishing—Their canoes—Bold navigators—Equestrian Indians and piscatory Indians, difference in their physical organization — Search for a trading site—Expedition of M'Dougal and David Stuart—Comcomly, the one-eyed chieftain—Influence of wealth in savage life—Slavery among the natives—An aristocracy of flatheads—Hospitality among the Chinooks—Comcomly's daughter, her conquest.

THE Columbia, or Oregon, for the distance of thirty or forty miles from its entrance into the sea, is, properly speaking, a mere estuary, indented by deep bays so as to vary from three to seven miles in width ; and is rendered extremely intricate and dangerous by shoals reaching nearly from shore to shore, on which, at times, the winds and currents produce foaming and tumultuous breakers. The mouth of the river proper is but about half a mile wide, formed by the contracting shores of the estuary.

The entrance from the sea, as we have already observed, is bounded on the south side by a flat sandy spit of land, stretching into the ocean. This is commonly called Point Adams. The opposite, or northern side, is Cape Disappointment; a kind of peninsula, terminating in a steep knoll or promontory crowned with a forest of pine trees, and connected with the main land by a low and narrow neck. Immediately within this cape is a wide, open bay, terminating at Chinook point, so called from a neighbouring tribe of Indians. This was called Baker's bay, and here the Tonquin was anchored.

The natives inhabiting the lower part of the river, and with whom the company was likely to have the most frequent intercourse, were divided at this time into four tribes, the Chinooks, Clatsops, Wahkiacums, and Cathlamahs. They resembled each other in person, dress, language, and manner; and were probably from the same stock, but broken into tribes, or rather hordes, by those feuds and schisms frequent among Indians.

These people generally live by fishing. It is true they occasionally hunt the elk and deer, and ensnare the waterfowl of the ponds and rivers, but these are casual luxuries. Their chief subsistence is derived from the salmon and other fish which abound in the Columbia and its tributary streams, aided by roots and herbs, especially the wappatoo, which is found on the islands of the river.

As the Indians of the plains who depend upon the chase are bold and expert riders, and pride themselves upon their horses, so these piscatory tribes of the coast excel in the management of canoes, and are never more at home than when riding upon the waves. Their canoes vary in form and size. Some are upwards of fifty feet long, cut out of a single tree, either fir or white cedar, and capable of carrying thirty persons. They have thwart pieces from side to side about three inches thick, and their gunwales flare outwards, so as to cast off the surges of the waves. The bow and stern are decorated with grotesque figures of men and animals, sometimes five feet in height.

In managing their canoes, they kneel two and two along the bottom, sitting on their heels, and wielding paddles from four to five feet long, while one sits on the stern and steers with a paddle of the same kind. The women are equally expert with the men in managing the canoe, and generally take the helm.

It is surprising to see with what fearless unconcern these savages venture in their light barks upon the roughest and most tempestuous seas. They seem to ride upon the waves like seafowl. Should a surge throw the canoe upon its side and endanger its overturn, those to windward lean over the upper gunwale, thrust their paddles deep into the wave, apparently catch the water and force it under the canoe, and by this action, not merely regain an equilibrium, but give their bark a vigorous impulse forward.

The effect of different modes of life upon the human frame and human character . is strikingly instanced in the contrast between the hunting Indians of the prairies, and the piscatory Indians of the seacoast. The former, continually on horseback scouring the plains, gaining their food by hardy exercise, and subsisting chiefly on flesh, are generally tall, sinewy, meagre, but well-formed, and of bold and fierce deportment; the latter, lounging about the river banks, or squatting and curved up in their canoes, are generally low in stature, ill-shaped, with crooked legs, thick ankles, and broad flat feet. They are inferior also in muscular power and activity, and in *game* qualities and appearance to their hard-riding brethren of the prairies.

Having premised these few particulars concerning the neighbouring Indians, we will return to the immediate concerns of the Tonquin and her crew.

Further search was made for Mr. Fox and his party, but with no better success, and they were at length given up as lost. In the meantime, the captain and some of the partners explored the river for some distance in a large boat, to select a suitable place for the trading post. Their old jealousies and differences continued; they never could coincide in their choice, and the captain objected altogether to any site so high up the river. They all returned, therefore, to Baker's bay in no very good-humour. The partners proposed to examine the opposite shore, but the captain was impatient of any further delay. His eagerness to " get on" had increased upon him. He thought all these excursions a sheer loss of time, and was resolved to land at once, build a shelter for the reception of that part of his cargo destined for the use of the settlement, and, having cleared his ship of it and of his irksome shipmates, to depart upon the prosecution of his coasting voyage, according to orders.

On the following day, therefore, without troubling himself to consult the partners, he landed in Baker's bay, and proceeded to erect a shed for the reception of the rigging, equipments, and stores of the schooner, that was to be built for the use of the settlement.

This dogged determination on the part of the sturdy captain gave high offence to Mr. M'Dougal, who now considered himself at the head of the concern, as Mr. Astor's representative and proxy. He set off the same day (April 5th), accompanied by Mr. David Stuart, for the southern shore, intending to be back by the seventh. Not having the captain to contend with, they soon pitched upon a spot which appeared to them favourable for the intended establishment. It was on a point of land called Point George, having a very good harbour, where vessels, not exceeding two hundred tons burthen, might anchor within fifty yards of the shore.

After a day thus profitably spent, they recrossed the river, but landed on the northern shore, several miles above the anchoring ground of the Tonquin, in the neighbourhood of Chinook, and visited the village of that tribe. Here they were received with great hospitality by the chief, who was named Comcomly, a shrewd old savage, with but one eye, who will occasionally figure in this narrative. Each village forms a petty sovereignty, governed by its own chief, who, however, possesses but little authority, unless he be a man of wealth and substance; that is to say, possessed of canoes, slaves, and wives. The greater number of these, the greater is the chief. How many wives this one-eyed potentate maintained we are not told, but he certainly possessed great sway, not merely over his own tribe, but over the neighbourhood.

Having mentioned slaves, we would observe, that slavery exists among several of the tribes beyond the Rocky mountains. The slaves are well treated while in good health, but occupied in all kinds of drudgery. Should they become useless, however, by sickness or old age, they are totally neglected, and left to perish; nor is any respect paid to their bodies after death.

A singular custom prevails, not merely among the Chinooks, but among most of the tribes about this part of the coast, which is the flattening of the forehead. The process by which this deformity is effected commences immediately after birth. The infant is laid in a wooden trough, by way of cradle. The end on which the head reposes is higher than the rest. A padding is placed on the forehead of the infant, with a piece of bark above it, and is pressed down by cords, which pass through holes on each side of the trough. As the tightening of the padding and the pressing of the head to the board is gradual, the process is said not to be attended with much pain. The appearance of the infant, however, while in this state of compression, is whimsically hideous, and "its little black eyes," we are told, "being forced out by the tightness of the bandages, resemble those of a mouse choaked in a trap."

About a year's pressure is sufficient to produce the desired effect; at the end of which time the child emerges from its bandages a complete flathead, and continues so through life. It must be noted, however, that this flattening of the head has something in it of aristocratical significancy, like the crippling of the feet among the Chinese ladies of quality. At any rate it is a sign of freedom. No slave is permitted to bestow this enviable deformity upon his child; all the slaves therefore are roundheads.

With this worthy tribe of Chinooks the two partners passed a part of a day very agreeably. M'Dougal, who was somewhat vain of his official rank, had given it to be understood that they were two chiefs of a great trading

company, about to be established here, and the quick-
sighted, though one-eyed chief, who was somewhat practised in traffic with white men, immediately perceived the
policy of cultivating the friendship of two such important
visiters. He regaled them, therefore, to the best of his
ability, with abundance of salmon and wappatoo. The
next morning, March 7th, they prepared to return to the
vessel, according to promise. They had eleven miles of
open bay to traverse; the wind was fresh, the waves ran
high. Comcomly remonstrated with them on the hazard
to which they would be exposed. They were resolute,
however, and launched their boat, while the wary chieftain
followed at some short distance in his canoe. Scarce had
they rowed a mile, when a wave broke over their boat and
upset it. They were in imminent peril of drowning, especially Mr. M'Dougal, who could not swim. Comcomly,
however, came bounding over the waves in his light canoe,
and snatched them from a watery grave.

They were taken on shore and a fire made, at which
they dried their clothès, after which Comcomly conducted
them back to his village. Here every thing was done that
could be devised for their entertainment during three days
that they were detained by bad weather. Comcomly
made his people perform antics before them; and his
wives and daughters endeavoured, by all the soothing and
endearing arts of women, to find favour in their eyes.
Some even painted their bodies with red clay, and anointed
themselves with fish oil, to give additional lustre to
their charms. Mr. M'Dougal seems to have had a heart
susceptible to the influence of the gentler sex. Whether
or no it was first touched on this occasion we do not learn;
but it will be found, in the course of this work, that one of
the daughters of the hospitable Comcomly eventually made
a conquest of the great eris of the American Fur Company.

When the weather had moderated and the sea became
tranquil, the one-eyed chief of the Chinooks manned his
state canoe, and conducted his guests in safety to the
ship, where they were welcomed with joy, for apprehen-

sions had been felt for their safety. Comcomly and his people were then entertained on board of the Tonquin, and liberally rewarded for their hospitality and services. They returned home highly satisfied, promising to remain faithful friends and allies of the white men.

CHAPTER IX.

Point George—Founding of Astoria—Indian visiters—Their reception—The Captain taboo's the ship—Departure of the Tonquin—Comments on the conduct of Captain Thorn.

FROM the report made by the two exploring partners, it was determined that point George should be the site of the trading house. These gentlemen, it is true, were not perfectly satisfied with the place, and were desirous of continuing their search; but Captain Thorn was impatient to land his cargo and continue his voyage, and protested against any more of what he termed "sporting excursions."

Accordingly, on the 12th of April, the launch was freighted with all things necessary for the purpose, and sixteen persons departed in her to commence the establishment, leaving the Tonquin to follow as soon as the harbour could be sounded.

Crossing the wide mouth of the river, the party landed, and encamped at the bottom of a small bay within point George. The situation chosen for the fortified post was on an elevation facing to the north, with the wide estuary, its sand bars, and tumultuous breakers spread out before it, and the promontory of Cape Disappointment, fifteen miles distant, closing the prospect to the left. The surrounding country was in all the freshness of spring; the trees were in the young leaf, the weather was superb, and every thing looked delightful to men just emancipated from long confinement on shipboard. The Tonquin shortly afterwards made her way through the intricate channel, and came to anchor in the little bay, and was saluted from the encampment with three volleys of musketry and three cheers. She returned the salute with three cheers and three guns.

All hands now set to work cutting down trees, clearing away thickets, and marking out the place for the residence, storehouse, and powder magazine, which were to be built of logs, and covered with bark. Others landed the timbers intended for the frame of the coasting vessel, and proceeded to put them together; while others prepared a garden spot, and sowed the seeds of various vegetables.

The next thought was to give a name to the embryo metropolis: the one that naturally presented itself was that of the projector and supporter of the whole enterprise. It was accordingly named ASTORIA.

The neighbouring Indians now swarmed about the place. Some brought a few land-otter and sea-otter skins to barter, but in very scanty parcels; the greater number came prying about to gratify their curiosity, for they are said to be impertinently inquisitive, while not a few came with no other design than to pilfer, the laws of *meum* and *tuum* being but slightly respected among them. Some of them beset the ship in their canoes, among whom was the Chinook chief Comcomly, and his liege subjects. These were well received by Mr. M'Dougal, who was delighted with an opportunity of entering upon his functions, and acquiring importance in the eyes of his future neighbours. The confusion thus produced on board, and the derangement of the cargo caused by this petty trade, stirred the spleen of the captain, who had a sovereign contempt for the one-eyed chieftain and all his crew. He complained loudly of having his ship lumbered by a host of "Indian ragamuffins," who had not a skin to dispose of, and at length put his positive interdict upon all trafficking on board. Upon this Mr. M'Dougal was fain to land, and establish his quarters at the encampment, where he could exercise his rights and enjoy his dignities without control.

The feud, however, between these rival powers still continued, but was chiefly carried on by letter. Day

after day, and week after week elapsed, yet the store-
houses requisite for the reception of the cargo were not
completed, and the ship was detained in port; while
the captain was teased by frequent requisitions for various
articles for the use of the establishment, or the trade with
the natives. An angry correspondence took place, in
which he complained bitterly of the time wasted in
" smoking and sporting parties," as he termed the re-
connoitering expeditions, and in clearing and preparing
meadow ground and turnip patches, instead of dispatching
his ship. At length all these jarring matters were adjusted, if not to the satisfaction, at least to the acquiescence of all parties. The part of the cargo destined for
the use of Astoria was landed, and the ship left free to
proceed on her voyage.

As the Tonquin was to coast to the north, to trade for
peltries at the different harbours, and to touch at Astoria
on her return in the autumn, it was unanimously declared
that Mr. M'Kay should go in her as supercargo, taking
with him Mr. Lewis as ship's clerk. On the 1st of June
the ship got under way, and dropped down to Baker's
bay, where she was detained for a few days by a head
wind; but early in the morning of the 5th, stood out to
sea with a fine breeze and swelling canvass, and swept off
gaily on her fatal voyage, from which she was never to
return !

On reviewing the conduct of Captain Thorn, and ex-
amining his peevish and somewhat whimsical correspondence, the impression left upon our mind is, upon the
whole, decidedly in his favour. While we smile at the
simplicity of his heart and the narrowness of his views,
which made him regard every thing out of the direct path
of his daily duty, and the rigid exigencies of the service,
as trivial and impertinent, which inspired him with contempt for the swelling vanity of some of his coadjutors,
and the literary exercises and curious researches of others,
we cannot but applaud that strict and conscientious devotion to the interests of his employer, and to what he considered the true objects of the enterprise in which he was
engaged. He certainly was to blame occasionally for the

asperity of his manners, and the arbitrary nature of his measures, yet much that is exceptionable in this part of his conduct may be traced to rigid notions of duty, acquired in that tyrannical school, a ship of war, and to the construction given by his companions to the orders of Mr. Astor, so little in conformity with his own. His mind, too, appears to have become almost diseased by the suspicions he had formed as to the loyalty of his associates, and the nature of their ultimate designs; yet on this point there were circumstances to, in some measure, justify him. The relations between the United States and Great Britain were at that time in a critical state; in fact, the two countries were on the eve of a war. Several of the partners were British subjects, and might be ready to desert the flag under which they acted, should a war take place. Their application to the British minister at New York shows the dubious feeling with which they had embarked in the present enterprise. They had been in the employ of the North-west Company, and might be disposed to rally again under that association, should events threaten the prosperity of this embryo establishment of Mr. Astor. Beside, we have the fact, averred to us by one of the partners, that some of them, who were young and heedless, took a mischievous and unwarrantable pleasure in playing upon the jealous temper of the captain, and affecting mysterious consultations and sinister movements.

These circumstances are cited in palliation of the doubts and surmises of Captain Thorn, which might otherwise appear strange and unreasonable. That most of the partners were perfectly upright and faithful in the discharge of the trust reposed in them, we are fully satisfied; still the honest captain was not invariably wrong in his suspicions; and that he formed a pretty just opinion of the integrity of that aspiring personage, Mr. M'Dougal, will be substantially proven in the sequel.

CHAPTER X.

WHILE the Astorians were busily occupied in completing their factory and fort, a report was brought to them, by an Indian from the upper part of the river, that a party of thirty white men had appeared on the banks of the Columbia, and were actually building houses at the second rapids. This information caused much disquiet. We have already mentioned that the North-west Company had established posts to the west of the Rocky mountains, in a district called by them New Caledonia, which extended from lat. 52° to 55° north, being within the British territories. It was now apprehended that they were advancing within the American limits, and were endeavouring to seize upon the upper part of the river, and forestal the American Fur Company in the surrounding trade ; in which case, bloody feuds might be anticipated, such as had prevailed between the rival fur companies in former days.

A reconnoitring party was sent up the river to ascertain the truth of the report. They ascended to the foot of the first rapid, about two hundred miles, but could hear nothing of any white men being in the neighbourhood.

Not long after their return, however, further accounts were received, by two wandering Indians, which established the fact, that the North-west Company had actually erected a trading house on the Spokan river, which falls into the north branch of the Columbia.

What rendered this intelligence the more disquieting, was the inability of the Astorians, in their present reduced state as to numbers, and the exigencies of their new establishment, to furnish detachments to penetrate the country in different directions, and fix the posts necessary to secure the interior trade.

It was resolved, however, at any rate, to advance a counter check to this post on the Spokan, and one of the partners, Mr. David Stuart, prepared to set out for the purpose with eight men and a small assortment of goods. He was to be guided by the two Indians, who knew the country, and promised to take him to a place not far from the Spokan river, and in a neighbourhood abounding with beaver. Here he was to establish himself and to remain for a time, provided he found the situation advantageous and the natives friendly.

On the 15th of July, when Mr. Stuart was nearly ready to embark, a canoe made its appearance, standing for the harbour, and manned by nine white men. Much speculation took place who these strangers could be, for it was too soon to expect their own people, under Mr. Hunt, who were to cross the continent. As the canoe drew near, the British standard was distinguished : on coming to land, one of the crew stepped on shore, and announced himself as Mr. David Thompson, astronomer, and partner of the North-west Company. According to his account, he had set out in the preceding year with a tolerable strong party, and a supply of Indian goods, to cross the Rocky mountains. A part of his people, however, had deserted him on the eastern side, and returned with the goods to the nearest north-west post. He had persisted in crossing the mountain with eight men, who remained true to him. They had traversed the higher regions, and ventured near the source of the Columbia, where, in the spring, they had constructed a cedar canoe, the same in which they had reached Astoria.

This, in fact, was the party dispatched by the North-west Company to anticipate Mr. Astor in his intention of effecting a settlement at the mouth of the Columbia river. It appears, from information subsequently derived from other sources, that Mr. Thompson had pushed on his course with great haste, calling at all the Indian villages in his march, presenting them with British flags, and even planting them at the forks of the rivers, proclaiming formally that he took possession of the country in the name of the king of Great Britain for the North-west Company.

As his original plan was defeated by the desertion of his people, it is probable that he descended the river simply to reconnoitre, and ascertain whether an American settlement had been commenced.

Mr. Thompson was, no doubt, the first white man who descended the northern branch of the Columbia from so near its source. Lewis and Clarke struck the main body of the river at the forks, about four hundred miles from its mouth. They entered it from Lewis river, its southern branch, and thence descended.

Though Mr. Thompson could be considered as little better than a spy in the camp, he was received with great cordiality by Mr. M'Dougal, who had a lurking feeling of companionship and good will for all the North-west Company. He invited him to head quarters, where he and his people were hospitably entertained. Nay, further, being somewhat in extremity, he was furnished by Mr. M'Dougal with goods and provisions for his journey back, across the mountains, much against the wishes of Mr. David Stuart, who did not think the object of his visit entitled him to any favour.

On the 23rd of July, Mr. Stuart set out upon his expedition to the interior. His party consisted of four of the clerks, Messrs. Pillett, Ross, M'Lennon, and Montigny, two Canadian voyageurs, and two natives of the Sandwich islands. They had three canoes well laden with provisions, and with goods and necessaries for a trading establishment.

Mr. Thompson and his party set out in company with them, it being his intention to proceed direct to Montreal. The partners at Astoria forwarded by him a short letter to Mr. Astor, informing him of their safe arrival at the mouth of the Columbia, and that they had not yet heard of Mr. Hunt. The little squadron of canoes set sail with a favourable breeze, and soon passed Tongue point, a long, high, and rocky promontory, covered with trees, and stretching far into the river. Opposite to this, on the northern shore, is a deep bay, where the Columbia anchored at the time of the discovery, and which is still called Gray's bay, from the name of her commander.

From hence the general course of the river, for about seventy miles, was nearly south-east; varying in breadth according to its bays and indentations, and navigable for vessels of three hundred tons. The shores were in some places high and rocky, with low marshy islands at their feet, subject to innundation, and covered with willows, poplars, aud other trees that love an alluvial soil. Sometimes the mountains receded, and gave place to beautiful plains and noble forests. While the river margin was richly fringed with trees of deciduous foliage, the rough uplands were crowned by majestic pines, and firs of gigantic size, some towering to the height of between two and three hundred feet, with proportionate circumference. Out of these the Indians wrought their great canoes and pirogues.

At one part of the river they passed, on the northern side, an isolated rock, about one hundred and fifty feet high, rising from a low, marshy soil, and totally disconnected with the adjacent mountains. This was held in great reverence by the neighbouring Indians, being one of their principal places of sepulture. The same provident care for the deceased that prevails among the hunting tribes of the prairies is observable among the piscatory tribes of the rivers and seacoast.

Among the former, the favorite horse of the hunter is buried with him in the same funereal mound, and his bow and arrows are laid by his side, that he may be perfectly equipped for the "happy hunting grounds" of the land of spirits. Among the latter, the Indian is wrapped in his mantle of skins, laid in his canoe, with his paddle, his fishing spear, and other implements beside him, and placed aloft on some rock or eminence overlooking the river, or bay, or lake, that he has frequented. He is thus fitted out to launch away upon those placid streams and sunny lakes stocked with all kinds of fish and water fowl, which are prepared in the next world for those who have acquitted themselves as good sons, good fathers, good husbands, and, above all, good fishermen, during their mortal sojourn.

The isolated rock in question presented a spectacle of

the kind, numerous dead bodies being deposited in canoes on its summit; while on poles around were trophies, or rather funereal offerings of trinkets, garments, baskets of roots, and other articles for the use of the deceased. A reverential feeling protects these sacred spots from robbery or insult. The friends of the deceased, especially the women, repair here at sunrise and sunset for some time after his death, singing his funeral dirge, and uttering loud wailings and lamentations.

From the number of dead bodies in canoes observed upon this rock by the first explorers of the river, it received the name of Mount Coffin, which it continues to bear.

Beyond this rock they passed the mouth of a river on the right bank of the Columbia, which appeared to take its rise in a distant mountain, covered with snow. The Indian name of this river was Cowleskee. Some miles further on they came to the great Columbian valley, so called by Lewis and Clarke. It is sixty miles in width, and extends far to the south-south-east, between parallel ridges of mountains, which bound it on the east and west. Through the centre of this valley flowed a large and beautiful stream, called the Wallamot,* which came wandering, for several hundred miles, through a yet unexplored wilderness. The sheltered situation of this immense valley had an obvious effect upon the climate. It was a region of great beauty and luxuriance, with lakes and pools, and green meadows shaded by noble groves. Various tribes were said to reside in this valley, and along the banks of the Wallamot.

About eight miles above the mouth of the Wallamot, the little squadron arrived at Vancouver's point, so called in honour of that celebrated voyager by his lieutenant (Broughton) when he explored the river. This point is said to present one of the most beautiful scenes on the Columbia : a lovely meadow, with a silver sheet of limpid water in the centre, enlivened by wild fowl; a range of hills crowned by forests, while the prospect is closed by Mount Hood, a magnificent mountain rising into a lofty

* Pronounced Wallámot, the accent being upon the second syllable.

peak, and covered with snow ; the ultimate landmark of the first explorers of the river.

Point Vancouver is about one hundred miles from Astoria.   Here the reflux of the tide ceases to be perceptible. To this place vessels of two and three hundred tons burthen may ascend.   The party under the command of Mr. Stuart had been three or four days in reaching it, though we have forborne to notice their daily progress and nightly encampments.

From point Vancouver the river turned towards the north-east, and became more contracted and rapid, with occasional islands and frequent sand-banks.   These islands are furnished with a number of ponds, and, at certain seasons, abound with swan, geese, brandts, cranes, gulls, plover, and other wild fowl.   The shores, too, are low, and closely wooded, with such an undergrowth of vines and rushes as to be almost impassable.

About thirty miles above point Vancouver the mountains again approach on both sides of the river, which is bordered by stupendous precipices, covered with the fir and the white cedar, and enlivened occasionally by beautiful cascades leaping from a great height, and sending up wreaths of vapour.   One of these precipices, or cliffs, is curiously worn by time and weather, so as to have the appearance of a ruined fortress, with towers and battlements, beetling high above the river; while two small cascades, one hundred and fifty feet in height, pitch down from the fissures of the rocks.

The turbulence and rapidity of the current continually augmenting as they advanced, gave the voyagers intimation that they were approaching the great obstructions of the river; and at length they arrived at Strawberry Island, so called by Lewis and Clarke, which lies at the foot of the first rapid.   As this part of the Columbia will be repeatedly mentioned in the course of this work, being the scene of some of its incidents, we shall give a general description of it in this place.

The falls or rapids of the Columbia are situated about one hundred and eighty miles above the mouth of the river.   The first is a perpendicular cascade of twenty feet,

after which there is a swift descent for a mile, between islands of hard black rock, to another pitch of eight feet divided
by two rocks. About two and a half miles below this the
river expands into a wide basin, seemingly dammed up
by a perpendicular ridge of black rock. A current, however, sets diagonally to the left of this rocky barrier,
where there is a chasm forty-five yards in width. Through
this the whole body of the river roars along, swelling, and
whirling, and boiling for some distance in the wildest confusion. Through this tremendous channel the intrepid
explorers of the river, Lewis and Clarke, passed safely in
their boats; the danger being, not from the rocks, but
from the great surges and whirlpools.

At the distance of a mile and a half from the foot of
this narrow channel is a rapid, formed by two rocky
islands; and two miles beyond is a second great fall, over
a ledge of rocks twenty feet high, extending nearly from
shore to shore. The river is again compressed into a
channel from fifty to a hundred feet wide, worn through
a rough bed of hard black rock, along which it boils and
roars with great fury for the distance of three miles.
This is called "the Long Narrows."

Here is the great fishing place of the Columbia. In
the spring of the year, when the water is high, the salmon
ascend the river in incredible numbers. As they pass
through this narrow strait, the Indians, standing on the
rocks, or on the end of wooden stages projecting from the
banks, scoop them up with small nets distended on hoops
and attached to long handles, and cast them on shore.

They are then cured and packed in a peculiar manner.
After having been disembowelled, they are exposed to the
sun on scaffolds erected on the river banks. When sufficiently dry, they are pounded fine between two stones,
pressed into the smallest compass, and packed in baskets
or bales of grass matting, about two feet long and one in
diameter, lined with the cured skin of a salmon. The top
is likewise covered with fish skins, secured by cords passing through holes in the edge of the basket. Packages
are then made, each containing twelve of these bales,
seven at bottom, five at top, pressed close to each other,

with the corded side upward, wrapped in mats and corded. These are placed in dry situations, and again covered with matting. Each of these packages contain from ninety to a hundred pounds of dried fish, which in this state will keep sound for several years.*

We have given this process at some length, as furnished by the first explorers, because it marks a practised ingenuity in preparing articles of traffic for a market, seldom seen among our aboriginals. For like reasons we would make especial mention of the village of Wish-ram, at the head of the Long Narrows, as being a solitary instance of an aboriginal trading mart, or emporium. Here the salmon caught in the neighbouring rapids were " warehoused," to await customers. Hither the tribes from the mouth of the Columbia repaired with the fish of the seacoast, the roots, berries, and especially the wappatoo, gathered in the lower parts of the river, together with goods and trinkets obtained from the ships which casually visited the coast. Hither also the tribes from the Rocky Mountains brought down horses, bear grass, quamash, and other commodities of the interior. The merchant fishermen at the falls acted as middlemen or factors, and passed the objects of traffic, as it were, cross-handed; trading away part of the wares received from the mountain tribes to those of the river and the plains, and *vice versá*: their packages of pounded salmon entered largely into the system of barter, and, being carried off in opposite directions, found their way to the savage hunting camps far in the interior, and to the casual white traders who touched upon the coast.

We have already noticed certain contrarieties of character between the Indian tribes, produced by their diet and mode of life ; and no where are they more apparent than about the falls of Columbia. The Indians of this great fishing mart are represented by the earliest explorers as sleeker and fatter, but less hardy and active, than the tribes of the mountains and the prairies, who live by hunting, or of the upper parts of the river, where fish is scanty, and the inhabitants must eke out their subsistence by digging

* Lewis and Clarke, vol. ii., p. 32.

roots or chasing the deer. Indeed, whenever an Indian of the upper country is too lazy to hunt, yet is fond of good living, he repairs to the falls, to live in abundance without labour.

" By such worthless dogs as these," says an honest trader in his journal, which now lies before us, " by such worthless dogs as these are these noted fishing places peopled, which, like our great cities, may with propriety be called the head-quarters of vitiated principles."

The habits of trade and the avidity of gain have their corrupting effects even in the wilderness, as may be instanced in the members of the aboriginal emporium ; for the same journalist denounces them as " saucy, impudent rascals, who will steal when they can, and pillage whenever a weak party falls in their power."

That he does not belie them will be evidenced hereafter, when we have occasion again to touch at Wish-ram, and navigate the rapids. In the present instance the travellers effected the laborious ascent of this part of the river, with all its various portages, without molestation, and once more launched away in smooth water above the high falls.

The two parties continued together, without material impediment, for three or four hundred miles further up the Columbia; Mr. Thompson appearing to take great interest in the success of Mr. Stuart, and pointing out places favourable, as he said, to the establishment of his contemplated trading post.

Mr. Stuart, who distrusted his sincerity, at length pretended to adopt his advice, and, taking leave of him, remained as if to establish himself, while the other proceeded on his course towards the mountains. No sooner, however, had he fairly departed, than Mr. Stuart again pushed forward, under guidance of the two Indians, nor did he stop until he had arrived within about one hundred and forty miles of the Spokan river, which he considered near enough to keep the rival establishment in check.

The place which he pitched upon for his trading post was a point of land about three miles in length and two in breadth, formed by the junction of the Oakinagan with the Columbia. The former is a river which has its source in a considerable lake about a hundred and fifty miles west of the point of junction. The two rivers, about the place of their confluence, are bordered by immense prairies covered with herbage, but destitute of trees. The point itself was ornamented with wild flowers of every hue, in which innumerable humming-birds were "banqueting nearly the livelong day."

The situation of this point appeared to be well adapted for a trading post. The climate was salubrious, the soil fertile, the rivers well stocked with fish, the natives peaceable and friendly. There were easy communications with the interior by the upper waters of the Columbia and the lateral stream of the Oakinagan, while the downward current of the Columbia furnished a highway to Astoria.

Availing himself, therefore, of the driftwood which had collected in quantities in the neighbouring bends of the river, Mr. Stuart and his men set to work to erect a house, which in a little while was sufficiently completed for their residence; and thus was established the first interior post of the company. We will now return to notice the progress of affairs at the mouth of the Columbia.

CHAPTER XI.

Alarm at Astoria—Rumour of Indian hostilities—Preparations for defence—
Tragical fate of the Tonquin.

THE sailing of the Tonquin, and the departure of Mr. David Stuart and his detachment, had produced a striking effect on affairs at Astoria. The natives who had swarmed about the place began immediately to drop off, until at length not an Indian was to be seen. This, at first, was attributed to the want of peltries with which to trade; but in a little while the mystery was explained in a more alarming manner. A conspiracy was said to be on foot among the neighbouring tribes to make a combined attack upon the white men, now that they were so reduced in number. For this purpose there had been a gathering of warriors in a neighbouring bay, under the pretext of fishing for sturgeon; and fleets of canoes were expected to join them from the north and south. Even Comcomly, the one-eyed chief, notwithstanding his professed friendship for Mr. M'Dougal, was strongly suspected of being concerned in this general combination.

Alarmed at rumours of this impending danger, the Astorians suspended their regular labour, and set to work with all haste to throw up temporary works for refuge and defence. In the course of a few days they surrounded their dwelling-house and magazines with a picket fence ninety feet square, flanked by two bastions, on which were mounted four four-pounders. Every day they exercised themselves in the use of their weapons, so as to qualify themselves for military duty, and at night they ensconced themselves in their fortress, and posted sentinels to guard against surprise. In this way they hoped, even in case of attack, to be able to hold out until the arrival of the party to be conducted by Mr. Hunt across the Rocky mountains, or until the return of the Tonquin. The latter dependance, however, was doomed soon to be destroyed. Early in August, a wandering band of savages from the strait of Juan de Fuca made their appearance at the mouth of the Columbia, where they came to fish for sturgeon. They brought disastrous accounts of the Tonquin, which were at first treated as mere fables, but which were too sadly confirmed by a different tribe that arrived a few days subsequently. We shall relate the circumstances of this melancholy affair as correctly as the casual discrepancies in the statements that have reached us will permit.

We have already stated that the Tonquin set sail from the mouth of the river on the 5th of June. The whole number of persons on board amounted to twenty-three. In one of the outer bays they picked up, from a fishing canoe, an Indian named Lamazee, who had already made two voyages along the coast, and knew something of the languages of the various tribes. He agreed to accompany them as interpreter.

Steering to the north, Captain Thorn arrived in a few

days at Vancouver's island, and anchored in the harbour of Neweetee, very much against the advice of his Indian interpreter, who warned him against the perfidious character of the natives of this part of the coast. Numbers of canoes soon came off, bringing sea-otter skins to sell. It was too late in the day to commence a traffic, but Mr. M'Kay, accompanied by a few of the men, went on shore to a large village to visit Wicananish, the chief of the surrounding territory, six of the natives remaining on board as hostages. He was received with great professions of friendship, entertained hospitably, and a couch of sea-otter skins was prepared for him in the dwelling of the chieftain, where he was prevailed upon to pass the night.

In the morning, before Mr. M'Kay had returned to the ship, great numbers of the natives came off in their canoes to trade, headed by two sons of Wicananish. As they brought abundance of sea-otter skins, and there was every appearance of a brisk trade, Captain Thorn did not wait for the return of Mr. M'Kay, but spread out his wares upon the deck, making a tempting display of blankets, cloths, knives, beads, and fish-books, expecting a prompt and profitable sale. The Indians, however, were not so eager and simple as he had supposed, having learned the art of bargaining and the value of merchandise from the casual traders along the coast. They were guided, too, by a shrewd old chief named Nookamis, who had grown gray in traffic with New England skippers, and prided himself upon his acuteness. His opinion seemed to regulate the market. When Captain Thorn made what he considered a liberal offer for an otter skin, the wily old Indian treated it with scorn, and asked more than double. His comrades all took their cue from him, and not an otter skin was to be had at a reasonable rate.

The old fellow, however, overshot his mark, and mistook the character of the man he was treating with. Thorn was a plain straightforward sailor, who never had two minds nor two prices in his dealings, was deficient in patience and pliancy, and totally wanting in the chicanery of traffic. He had a vast deal of stern, but honest pride in his nature, and, moreover, held the whole savage race in sovereign contempt. Abandoning all further attempts, therefore, to bargain with his shuffling customers, he thrust his hands into his pockets, and paced up and down the deck in sullen silence. The cunning old Indian followed him to and fro, holding out a sea-otter skin to him at every turn, and pestering him to trade. Finding other means unavailing, he suddenly changed his tone, and began to jeer and banter him upon the mean prices he offered. This was too much for the patience of the captain, who was never remarkable for relishing a joke, especially when at his own expense. Turning suddenly upon his persecutor, he snatched the proffered otter skin from his hands, rubbed it in his face, and dismissed him over the side of the ship with no very complimentary application to accelerate his exit. He then kicked the peltries to the right and left about the deck, and broke up the market in the most ignominious manner. Old Nookamis made for shore in a furious passion, in which he was joined by Shewish, one of the sons of Wicananish, who went off breathing vengeance, and the ship was soon abandoned by the natives.

When Mr. M'Kay returned on board, the interpreter related what had passed, and begged him to prevail upon the captain to make sail, as, from his knowledge of the temper and pride of the people of the place, he was sure they would resent the indignity offered to one of their chiefs. Mr. M'Kay, who himself possessed some experience of Indian character, went to the captain, who was still pacing the deck in moody humour, represented the danger to which his hasty act had exposed the vessel, and urged him to weigh anchor. The captain made light of his councils, and pointed to his cannon and fire-arms as a sufficient safeguard against naked savages. Further remonstrances only provoked taunting replies and sharp altercations. The day passed away without any signs of hostility, and at night the captain retired as usual to his cabin, taking no more than the usual precautions.

On the following morning, at daybreak, while the captain and Mr. M'Kay were yet asleep, a canoe came alongside in which were twenty Indians, commanded by young

Shewish. They were unarmed, their aspect and demeanour
friendly, and they held up otter skins, and made signs
indicative of a wish to trade The caution enjoined by
Mr. Astor, in respect to the admission of Indians on board
of the ship, had been neglected for some time past; and
the officer of the watch, perceiving those in the canoe to
be without weapons, and having received no orders to the
contrary, readily permitted them to mount the deck.
Another canoe soon succeeded, the crew of which was
likewise admitted. In a little while other canoes came
off, and Indians were soon clambering into the vessel on
all sides.

The officer of the watch now felt alarmed, and called
to Captain Thorn and Mr. M'Kay. By the time they
came on deck, it was thronged with Indians. The interpreter noticed to Mr. M'Kay that many of the natives
wore short mantles of skins, and intimated a suspicion that
they were secretly armed. Mr. M'Kay urged the captain
to clear the ship and get under way. He again made light
of the advice; but the augmented swarm of canoes about
the ship, and the numbers still putting off from shore, at
length awakened his distrust, and he ordered some of the
crew to weigh anchor, while some were sent aloft to make
sail.

The Indians now offered to trade with the captain on
his own terms, prompted, apparently, by the approaching
departure of the ship. Accordingly, a hurried trade was
commenced. The main articles sought by the savages in
barter were knives; as fast as some were supplied they
moved off, and others succeeded. By degrees they were
thus distributed about the deck, and all with weapons.

The anchor was now nearly up, the sails were loose,
and the captain, in a loud and peremptory tone, ordered
the ship to be cleared. In an instant a signal yell was
given: it was echoed on every side, knives and war-clubs
were brandished in every direction, and the savages rushed
upon their marked victims.

The first that fell was Mr. Lewis, the ship's clerk. He
was leaning, with folded arms, over a bale of blankets,

engaged in bargaining, when he received a deadly stab in the back, and fell down the companionway.

Mr. M'Kay, who was seated on the taffrail, sprang on his feet, but was instantly knocked down with a war-club, and flung backwards into the sea, where he was despatched by the women in the canoes.

In the mean time, Captain Thorn made desperate fight against fearful odds. He was a powerful as well as resolute man, but he had come upon deck without weapons. Shewish, the young chief, singled him out as his peculiar prey, and rushed upon him at the first outbreak. The captain had barely time to draw a clasp-knife, with one blow of which he laid the young savage dead at his feet. Several of the stoutest followers of Shewish now set upon him. He defended himself vigorously, dealing crippling blows to right and left, and strewing the quarter-deck with the slain and wounded. His object was, to fight his way to the cabin, where there were fire-arms; but he was hemmed in with foes, covered with wounds, and faint with loss of blood. For an instant he leaned upon the tiller-wheel, when a blow from behind, with a war-club, felled him to the deck, where he was despatched with knives and thrown overboard.

While this was transacting upon the quarter-deck, a chance medley fight was going on throughout the ship. The crew fought desperately with knives, handspikes, and whatever weapon they could seize upon in the moment of surprise. They were soon, however, overpowered by numbers, and mercilessly butchered.

As to the seven who had been sent aloft to make sail, they contemplated with horror the carnage that was going on below. Being destitute of weapons, they let themselves down by the running rigging, in hopes of getting between decks. One fell in the attempt, and was instantly despatched; another received a death-blow in the back as he was descending; a third, Stephen Weekes, the armourer, was mortally wounded as he was getting down the hatchway.

The remaining four made good their retreat into the cabin, where they found Mr. Lewis still alive, though mortally wounded. Barricading the cabin door, they broke holes through the companionway, and, with the muskets and ammunition which were at hand, opened a brisk fire that soon cleared the deck.

Thus far the Indian interpreter, from whom these particulars are derived, had been an eye-witness of the deadly conflict. He had taken no part in it, and had been spared by the natives as being of their race. In the confusion of the moment he took refuge with the rest, in the canoes. The survivors of the crew now sallied forth, and discharged some of the deck guns, which did great execution among the canoes, and drove all the savages to shore.

For the remainder of the day no one ventured to put off to the ship, deterred by the effects of the fire-arms. The night passed away without any further attempt on the part of the natives. When the day dawned, the Tonquin still lay at anchor in the bay, her sails all loose and flapping in the wind, and no one apparently on board of her. After a time, some of the canoes ventured forth to reconnoitre, taking with them the interpreter. They paddled about her, keeping cautiously at a distance, but growing more and more imboldened at seeing her quiet and lifeless. One man at length made his appearance on the deck, and was recognised by the interpreter as Mr. Lewis. He made friendly signs, and invited them on board. It was long before they ventured to comply. Those who mounted the deck met with no opposition ; no one was to be seen on board ; for Mr. Lewis, after inviting them, had disappeared. Other canoes now pressed forward to board the prize ; the decks were soon crowded, and the sides covered with clambering savages, all intent on plunder. In the midst of their eagerness and exultation, the ship blew up with a tremendoes explosion. Arms, legs, and mutilated bodies were blown into the air, and dreadful havoc was made in the surrounding canoes. The interpreter was in the main chains at the time of the explosion, and was thrown unhurt into the water, where he succeeded in getting into one of the canoes. According to his statement, the bay presented an awful spectacle after the catastrophe. The ship had disappeared, but the bay was covered with fragments of the wreck, with shattered canoes, and Indians swimming for their lives, or struggling in the agonies of death; while those who had escaped the danger remained aghast and stupified, or made with frantic panic for the shore. Upwards of a hundred savages were destroyed by the explosion, many more were shockingly mutilated, and for days afterwards the limbs and bodies of the slain were thrown upon the beach.

The inhabitants of Neweetee were overwhelmed with consternation at this astounding calamity, which had burst upon them in the very moment of triumph. The warriors sat mute and mournful, while the women filled the air with loud lamentations. Their weeping and wailing, however, was suddenly changed into yells of fury at the sight of four unfortunate white men, brought captive into the village. They had been driven on shore in one of the ship's boats, and taken at some distance along the coast.

The interpreter was permitted to converse with them. They proved to be the four brave fellows who had made such desperate defence from the cabin. The interpreter gathered from them some of the particulars already related. They told him further, that, after they had beaten off the enemy, and cleared the ship, Lewis advised that they should slip the cable and endeavour to get to sea. They declined to take his advice, alleging that the wind set too strongly into the bay, and would drive them on shore. They resolved, as soon as it was dark, to put off quietly in the ship's boat, which they would be able to do unperceived, and to coast along back to Astoria. They put their resolution into effect; but Lewis refused to accompany them, being disabled by his wound, hopeless of escape, and determined on a terrible revenge. On the voyage out, he had repeatedly expressed a presentiment that he should die by his own hands; thinking it highly probable that he should be engaged in some contest with the natives, and being resolved, in case of extremity, to commit suicide, rather than be made a prisoner. He now declared his intention to remain on board of the ship until daylight, to decoy as many of the savages on

board as posible, then to set fire to the powder magazine,
and terminate his life by a signal act of vengeance. How
well, he succeeded has been shown. His companions
bade him a melancholy adieu, and set off on their precarious expedition. They strove with might and main to
get out of the bay, but found it impossible to weather a
point of land, and were at length compelled to take shelter in a small cove, where they hoped to remain concealed
until the wind should be more favourable. Exhausted by
fatigue and watching, they fell into a sound sleep, and in
that state were surprised by the savages. Better had it
been for those unfortunate men had they remained with
Lewis, and shared his heroic death : as it was, they perished in a more lingering and protracted manner, being
sacrificed by the natives to the manes of their friends with
all the lingering tortures of savage cruelty. Some time
after their death, the interpreter, who had remained a
kind of prisoner at large, effected his escape, and brought
the tragical tidings to Astoria.

Such is the melancholy story of the Tonquin, and such
was the fate of her brave but headstrong commander, and
her adventurous crew. It is a catastrophe that shows the
importance, in all enterprises of moment, to keep in mind
the general instructions of the sagacious heads which devise them. Mr. Astor was well aware of the perils to
which ships were exposed on this coast from quarrels
with the natives, and from perfidious attempts of the
latter to surprise and capture them in unguarded moments. He had repeatedly enjoined it upon Captain
Thorn, in conversation, and at parting, in his letter of
instructions, to be courteous and kind in his dealings with
the savages, but by no means to confide in their apparent
friendship, *nor to admit more than a few on board of his
ship at a time.*

Had the deportment of Captain Thorn been properly
regulated, the insult so wounding to savage pride would
never have been given. Had he enforced the rule to
admit but a few at a time, the savages would not have
been able to get the mastery. He was too irritable, however, to practise the necessary self-command, and, having

been nurtured in a proud contempt of danger, thought it beneath him to manifest any fear of a crew of unarmed savages.

With all his faults and foibles, we cannot but speak of him with esteem, and deplore his untimely fate; for we remember him well in early life, as a companion in pleasant scenes and joyous hours. When on shore, among his friends, he was a frank, manly, soundhearted sailor. On board ship he evidently assumed the hardness of deportment and sternness of demeanour which many deem essential to naval service. Throughout the whole of the expedition, however, he showed himself loyal, single-minded, straightforward, and fearless; and if the fate of his vessel may be charged to his harshness and imprudence, we should recollect that he paid for his error with his life.

The loss of the Tonquin was a grievous blow to the infant establishment of Astoria, and one that threatened to bring after it a train of disasters. The intelligence of it did not reach Mr. Astor until many months afterwards, He felt it in all its force, and was aware that it must cripple, if not entirely defeat, the great scheme of his ambition. In his letters, written at the time, he speaks of it as "a calamity, the length of which he could not foresee." He indulged, however, in no weak and vain lamentation, but sought to devise a prompt and efficient remedy. The very same evening he appeared at the theatre, with his usual serenity of countenance. A friend, who knew the disastrous intelligence he had received, expressed his astonishment that he could have calmness of spirit sufficient for such a scene of light amusement. "What would you have me to do?" was his characteristic reply: "would you have me stay at home and weep for what I cannot help?"

CHAPTER XII.

THE tidings of the loss of the Tonquin, and massacre of her crew, struck dismay into the hearts of the Astorians. They found themselves a mere handful of men, on a savage coast, surrounded by hostile tribes, who would doubtless be incited and encouraged to deeds of violence by the late fearful catastrophe. In this juncture Mr. M'Dougal, we are told, had recourse to a stratagem by which to avail himself of the ignorance and credulity of the savages, and which certainly does credit to his ingenuity.

The natives of the coast, and, indeed, of all the regions west of the mountains, had an extreme dread of the small-pox; that terrific scourge having, a few years previously, appeared among them, and almost swept off entire tribes. Its origin and nature were wrapped in mystery, and they conceived it an evil inflicted upon them by the Great Spirit, or brought among them by the white men. The last idea was seized upon by Mr. M'Dougal. He assembled several of the chieftains whom he believed to be in the conspiracy. When they were all seated around, he informed them that he had heard of the treachery of some of their northern brethren towards the Tonquin, and was determined on vengeance. "The white men among you," said he, "are few in number, it is true, but they are mighty in medicine. See here," continued he, drawing forth a small bottle and holding it before their eyes; "in this bottle I hold the smallpox, safely corked up: I have but to draw the cork, and let loose the pestilence, to sweep man, woman, and child, from the face of the earth!"

The chiefs were struck with horror and alarm. They implored him not to uncork the bottle, since they and all their people were firm friends of the white men, and would always remain so; but should the smallpox be once let out, it would run like wildfire throughout the country, sweeping off the good as well as the bad; and surely he would not be so unjust as to punish his friends for crimes committed by his enemies.

Mr. M'Dougal pretended to be convinced by their reasoning, and assured them that, so long as the white people should be unmolested, and the conduct of their Indian neighbours friendly and hospitable, the phial of wrath should remain sealed up; but on the least act of hostility, the fatal cork should be drawn.

From this time, it is added, he was much dreaded by the natives as one who held their fate in his hands, and was called, by way of pre-eminence, " the Great Smallpox Chief."

All this while, the labours at the infant settlement went on with unremitting assiduity; and by the 26th of September, a commodious mansion, spacious enough to accommodate all hands, was completed. It was built of stone and clay, there being no calcarious stone in the neighbourhood from which lime for mortar could be procured. The schooner was also finished, and launched, with the accustomed ceremony, on the 2d of October, and took her station below the fort. She was named the Dolly, and was the first American vessel launched on this coast.

On the 5th of October, in the evening, the little community of Astoria was enlivened by the unexpected arrival of a detachment from Mr. David Stuart's post on the Oakinagan. It consisted of two of the clerks and two of the privates. They brought favourable accounts of the new establishment, but reported that, as Mr. Stuart was apprehensive there might be a difficulty of subsisting his whole party throughout the winter, he had sent one half back to Astoria, retaining with him only Ross, Montigny, and two others. Such is the hardihood of the Indian trader. In the heart of a savage and unknown country, seven hundred miles from the main body of his fellow-adventurers, Stuart had dismissed half of his little number, and was prepared with the residue to brave all the perils of the wilderness, and the rigours of a long and dreary winter.

With the return party came a Canadian creole named Regis Brugiere, and an Iroquois hunter, with his wife and two children. As these two personages belong to certain classes which have derived their peculiar characteristics from the fur-trade, we deem some few particulars concerning them pertinent to the nature of this work.

Brugiere was of a class of beaver-trappers and hunters technically called freemen, in the language of the traders. They are generally Canadians by birth, and of French descent, who have been employed for a term of years by some fur company, but their term being expired, continue to hunt and trap on their own account, trading with the company like the Indians. Hence they derive their appellation of freemen, to distinguish them from the trappers, who are bound for a number of years, and receive wages, or hunt on shares.

Having passed their early youth in the wilderness, separated almost entirely from civilized man, and in frequent intercourse with the Indians, they lapse, with a facility common to human nature, into the habitudes of savage life. Though no longer bound by engagements to continue in the interior, they have become so accustomed to the freedom of the forest and the prairie, that they look back with repugnance upon the restraints of civilization. Most of them intermarry with the natives, and, like the latter, have often a plurality of wives. Wanderers of the wilderness, according to the vicissitudes of the seasons, the migrations of animals, and the plenty or scarcity of game, they lead a precarious and unsettled existence; exposed to sun and storm, and all kinds of hardships, until they resemble the Indians in complexion as well as in tastes and habits. From time to time they bring the peltries they have collected to the trading houses of the company in whose employ they have been brought up. Here they traffick them away for such articles of merchandise or ammunition as they may stand in need of. At the time when Montreal was the great emporium of the fur trader, one of these freemen of the wilderness would suddenly return, after an absence of many years, among his old friends and comrades. He would be greeted as one risen from the dead ; and with the greater welcome, as he returned flush of money. A short time, however, spent in revelry, would be sufficient to drain his purse and sate him with civilized life, and he would return with new relish to the unshackled freedom of the forest.

Numbers of men of this class were scattered throughout the north-west territories. Some of them retained a little of the thrift and forethought of the civilized man, and became wealthy among their improvident neighbours: their wealth being chiefly displayed in large bands of horses, which covered the prairies in the vicinity of their abodes. Most of them, however, were prone to assimilate to the red man in their heedlessness of the future.

Such was Regis Brugiere, a freeman and rover of the wilderness. Having been brought up in the service of the North-west Company, he had followed in the train of one of its expeditions across the Rocky mountains, and undertaken to trap for the trading post established on the Spokan river. In the course of his hunting excursions he had accidentally, or designedly, found his way to the post of Mr. Stuart, and been prevailed upon to descend the Columbia, and " try his luck" at Astoria.

Ignace Shonowane, the Iroquois hunter, was a specimen of a different class. He was one of those aboriginals of Canada who had partially conformed to the habits of civilization, and the doctrines of Christianity, under the influence of the French colonists and the Catholic priests, who seem generally to have been more successful in conciliating, taming, and converting the savages, than their English and Protestant rivals. These half-civilized Indians retained some of the good, and many of the evil qualities of their original stock. They were first-rate hunters, and dextrous in the management of the canoe. They could undergo great privations, and were admirable for the service of the rivers, lakes, and forests, provided they could be kept sober, and in proper subordination ; but, once inflamed with liquor, to which they were madly addicted, all the dormant passions inherent in their nature were prone to break forth, and to hurry them into the most vindictive and bloody acts of violence.

Though they generally professed the Roman Catholic religion, yet it was mixed, occasionally, with some of their ancient superstitions, and they retained much of the Indian belief in charms and omens. Numbers of these men were employed by the North-west Company as trappers, hunters, and canoe men, but on lower terms than were allowed to white men. Ignace Shonowane had, in this way, followed the enterprise of the company to the banks of the Spokan, being, probably, one of the first of his tribe that had traversed the Rocky mountains.

Such were some of the motley populace of the wilderness, incident to the fur trade, who were gradually attracted to the new settlement of Astoria.

The month of October now began to give indications of approaching winter. Hitherto, the colonists had been well pleased with the climate. The summer had been temperate, the mercury never rising above eighty degrees. Westerly winds had prevailed during the spring and the early part of summer, and been succeeded by fresh breezes from the north-west. In the month of October the southerly winds set in, bringing with them frequent rain.

The Indians now began to quit the borders of the ocean, and to retire to their winter quarters in the sheltered bosom of the forests, or along the small rivers and brooks. The rainy season, which commences in October, continues, with little intermission, until April; and though the winters are generally mild, the mercury seldom sinking below the freezing point, yet the tempests of wind and rain are terrible. The sun is sometimes obscured for weeks, the brooks swell into roaring torrents, and the country is threatened with a deluge.

The departure of the Indians to their winter quarters gradually rendered provisions scanty, and obliged the colonists to send out foraging expeditions in the Dolly. Still, the little handful of adventurers kept up their spirits in their lonely fort at Astoria, looking forward to the time when they should be animated and reinforced by the party under Mr. Hunt, that was to come to them across the Rocky mountains.

The year gradually wore away. The rain, which had poured down almost incessantly since the 1st of October, cleared up towards the evening of the 31st of December, and the morning of the 1st of January ushered in a day of sunshine.

The hereditary French holiday-spirit of the Canadian voyageurs is hardly to be depressed by any adversities; and they can manage to get up a *fête* in the most squallid situations, and under the most untoward circumstances. An extra allowance of rum, and a little flour to make cakes and puddings, constitute a "regale," and they forget all their toils and troubles in the song and the dance.

On the present occasion, the partners endeavoured to celebrate the new year with some effect. At sunrise the drums beat to arms, the colours were hoisted, with three rounds of small arms, and three discharges of cannon. The day was devoted to games of agility and strength, and other amusements; and grog was temperately distributed, together with bread, butter, and cheese. The best dinner their circumstances could afford was served up at mid-day. At sunset the colours were lowered with another discharge of artillery. The night was spent in dancing; and, though there was a lack of female partners to excite their gallantry, the voyageurs kept up the ball, with true French spirit, until three o'clock in the morning. So passed the new-year festival of 1812 at the infant colony of Astoria.

CHAPTER XIII.

WE have followed up the fortunes of the maritime part
of this enterprise to the shores of the Pacific, and have
conducted the affairs of the embryo establishment to the
opening of the new year; let us now turn back to the
adventurous band to whom was intrusted the land expedition, and who were to make their way to the mouth of the
Columbia, up vast rivers, across trackless plains, and
over the rugged barriers of the Rocky mountains.

The conduct of this expedition, as has been already
mentioned, was assigned to Mr. Wilson Price Hunt, of
Trenton, New Jersey, one of the partners of the company,
who was ultimately to be at the head of the establishment
at the mouth of the Columbia. He is represented as a
man ;scrupulously upright and faithful in his dealings,
amiable in his disposition, and of most accommodating
manners; and his whole conduct will be found in unison
with such a character. He was not practically experienced
in the Indian trade; that is to say, he had never made
any expeditions of traffic into the heart of the wilderness;
but he had been engaged in commerce at St. Louis, then
a frontier settlement on the Mississippi, where the chief
branch of his business had consisted in furnishing Indian
traders with goods and equipments. In this way, he had
acquired much knowledge of the trade at second hand, and
of the various tribes, and the interior country over which it
extended.

Another of the partners, Mr. Donald M‘Kenzie, was
associated with Mr. Hunt in the expedition, and excelled
on those points in which the other was deficient; for he

had been ten years in the interior, in the service of the North-west Company, and valued himself on his knowledge of " woodcraft," and the strategy of Indian trade and Indian warfare. He had a frame seasoned to toils and hardships; a spirit not to be intimidated, and was reputed to be a " remarkable shot ;" which of itself was sufficient to give him renown upon the frontier.

Mr. Hunt and his coadjutor repaired, about the latter part of July, 1810, to Montreal, the ancient emporium of the fur trade, where every thing requisite for the expedition could be procured. One of the first objects was to recruit a complement of Canadian voyageurs from the disbanded herd usually to be found loitering about the place. A degree of jockeyship, however, is required for this service, for a Canadian voyageur is as full of latent tricks and vice as a horse; and when he makes the greatest external promise, is prone to prove the greatest " take in." Beside, the North-west Company, who maintained a long established control at Montreal, and knew the qualities of every voyageur, secretly interdicted the prime hands from engaging in this new service ; so that, although liberal terms were offered, few presented themselves but such as were not worth having.

From these, Mr. Hunt engaged a number sufficient, as he supposed, for present purposes ; and, having laid in a supply of ammunition, provisions, and Indian goods, embarked all on board of one of those great canoes at that time universally used by the fur traders for navigating the intricate and often obstructed rivers. The canoe was between thirty and forty feet long, and several feet in width ; constructed of birch bark, sewed with fibres of the roots of the spruce-tree, and daubed with resin of the pine, instead of tar. The cargo was made up in packages, weighing from ninety to one hundred pounds each, for the facility of loading and unloading, and of transportation at portages. The canoe itself, though capable of sustaining a freight of upwards of four tons, could readily be carried on men's shoulders. Canoes of this size are generally managed by eight or ten men, two of whom are picked veterans, who receive double wages, and are stationed, one at the bow and the other at the stern, to keep a look out, and to steer. They are termed the foreman and the steersman. The rest, who ply the paddles, are called middle men. When there is a favourable breeze, the canoe is occasionally navigated with a sail.

The expedition took its regular departure, as usual, from St. Anne's, near the extremity of the island of Montreal, the great starting place of traders to the interior. Here stood the ancient chapel of St. Anne, the patroness of the Canadian voyageurs; where they made confession and offered up their vows, previous to departing on any hazardous expedition. The shrine of the saint was decorated with relics and votive offerings hung up by these superstitious beings, either to propitiate her favour, or in gratitude for some signal deliverance in the wilderness. It was the custom, too, of these devout vagabonds, after leaving the chapel, to have a grand carouse, in honour of the saint and for the prosperity of the voyage. In this part of their devotions the crew of Mr. Hunt proved themselves by no means deficient. Indeed, he soon discovered that his recruits, enlisted at Montreal, were fit to vie with the ragged regiment of Falstaff. Some were able-bodied, but inexpert; others were expert, but lazy; while a third class were expert and willing, but totally worn out, being broken down veterans, incapable of toil.

With this inefficient crew he made his way up the Ottawar river, and by the ancient route of the fur traders, along a succession of small lakes and rivers, to Michilimackinac. Their progress was slow and tedious. Mr. Hunt was not accustomed to the management of " voyageurs," and he had a crew admirably disposed to play the old soldier, and balk their work; and ever ready to come to a halt, land, make a fire, put on the great pot, and smoke, and gossip, and sing by the hour.

It was not until the 22nd of July that they arrived at Mackinaw, situated on the island of the same name, at the confluence of lakes Huron and Michigan. This famous old French trading post continued to be a rallying point for a multifarious and motley population. The inhabitants were amphibious in their habits, most of them being, or having been, voyageurs or canoe-men. It was the great place of arrival and departure of the south-west fur trade. Here the Mackinaw Company had established its principal post, from whence it communicated with the interior and with Montreal. Hence its various traders and trappers set out for their respective destinations about lake Superior and its tributary waters, or for the Mississippi, the Arkansas, the Missouri, and the other regions of the west. Here, after the absence of a year or more, they returned with their peltries, and settled their accounts; the furs rendered in by them being transmitted, in canoes, from hence to Montreal. Mackinaw was, therefore, for a great part of the year, very scantily peopled; but at certain seasons the traders arrived from all points, with their crews of voyageurs, and the place swarmed like a hive.

Mackinaw, at that time, was a mere village, stretching along a small bay, with a fine broad beach in front of its principal row of houses, and dominated by the old fort, which crowned an impending height. The beach was a kind of public promenade, where were displayed all the vagaries of a seaport on the arrival of a fleet from a long cruise. Here voyageurs frolicked away their wages, fiddling and dancing in the booths and cabins, buying all kinds of knick-knacks, dressing themselves out finely, and parading up and down, like arrant braggarts and coxcombs. Sometimes they met with rival coxcombs in the young Indians from the opposite shore, who would appear on the beach painted and decorated in fantastic style, and would saunter up and down to be gazed at and admired, perfectly satisfied that they eclipsed their pale-faced competitors.

Now and then a chance party of " North-westers" appeared at Mackinaw from the rendezvous at fort William. These held themselves up as the chivalry of the fur trade. They were men of iron ; proof against cold weather, hard fare, and perils of all kinds. Some would wear the northwest button, and a formidable dirk, and assume something of a military air. They generally wore feathers in their hats, and affected the " brave." " Je suis un homme du

nord!"—" I am a man of the north," one of these swelling fellows would exclaim, sticking his arms akimbo, and
ruffling by the south-westers, whom he regarded with
great contempt, as men softened by mild climates and the
luxurious fare of bread and bacon, and whom he stigmatized with the inglorious name of pork-eaters. The superiority assumed by these vainglorious swaggerers was in
general tacitly admitted. Indeed, some of them had acquired great notoriety for deeds of hardihood and courage;
for the fur trade had its heroes, whose names resounded
throughout the wilderness.

Such was Mackinaw at the time of which we are treating. It now, doubtless, presents a totally different aspect.
The fur companies no longer assemble there; the navigation of the lakes is carried on by steam-boats and various
shipping, and the race of traders, and trappers, and voyageurs, and Indian dandies, have vapoured out their brief
hour and disappeared. Such changes does the lapse of a
handful of years make in this ever-changing country.

At this place Mr. Hunt remained for some time, to
complete his assortment of Indian goods, and to increase
his number of voyageurs, as well as to engage some of a
more efficient character than those enlisted at Montreal.

And now commenced another game of jockeyship.
There were able and efficient men in abundance at Mackinaw, but for several days not one presented himself.
If offers were made to any, they were listened to with a
shake of the head. Should any one seem inclined to en-
list, there were officious idlers and busy-bodies of that
class, who are ever ready to dissuade others from any enterprise in which they themselves have no concern.
These would pull him by the sleeve, take him on one
side, and murmur in his ear, or would suggest difficulties
outright.

It was objected that the expedition would have to navigate unknown rivers, and pass through howling wildernesses infested by savage tribes, who had already cut off
the unfortunate voyageurs that had ventured among them.
That it was to climb the Rocky mountains and descend

into desolate and famished regions, where the traveller was often obliged to subsist on grasshoppers and crickets, or to kill his own horse for food.

At length one man was hardy enough to engage, and he was used like a "stool pigeon," to decoy others; but several days elapsed before any more could be prevailed upon to join him. A few then came to terms. It was desirable to engage them for five years, but some refused to engage for more than three. Then they must have part of their pay in advance, which was readily granted. When they had pocketed the amount, and squandered it in regales or in outfits, they began to talk of pecuniary obligations at Mackinaw, which must be discharged before they would be free to depart; or engagements with other persons, which were only to be cancelled by a "reasonable consideration."

It was in vain to argue or remonstrate. The money advanced had already been sacked and spent, and must be lost and the recruits left behind, unless they could be freed from their debts and engagements. Accordingly, a fine was paid for one; a judgment for another; a tavern bill for a third; and almost all had to be bought off from some prior engagement either real or pretended.

Mr. Hunt groaned in spirit at the incessant aud unreasonable demands of these worthies upon his purse; yet, with all this outlay or funds, the number recruited was but scanty, and many of the most desirable still held themselves aloof, and were not to be caught by a golden bait. With these he tried another temptation. Among the recruits who had enlisted he distributed feathers and ostrich plumes. These they put in their hats, and thus figured about Mackinaw, assuming airs of vast importance, as "voyageurs in a new company that was to eclipse the North-west." The effect was complete. A French Canadian is too vain and mercurial a being to withstand the finery and ostentation of the feather. Numbers immediately pressed into the service. One must have an ostrich feather; another a white feather with a red end; a third, a bunch of cocks' tails. Thus all paraded about, in vainglorious style, more delighted with the feathers in their hats than with the money in their pockets; and considering themselves fully equal to the boastful "men of the north."

While thus recruiting the number of rank and file, Mr. Hunt was joined by a person whom he had invited, by letter, to engage as a partner in the expedition. This was Mr. Ramsay Crooks, a young man, a native of Scotland, who had served under the North-west Company, and been engaged in trading expeditions upon his individual account among the tribes of the Missouri. Mr. Hunt knew him personally, and had conceived a high and merited opinion of his judgment, enterprise, and integrity: he was rejoiced, therefore, when the latter consented to accompany him. Mr. Crooks, however, drew from experience a picture of the dangers to which they would be subjected, and urged the importance of going with a considerable force. In ascending the upper Missouri they would have to pass through the country of the Sioux Indians, who had manifested repeated hostility to the white traders, and rendered their expeditions extremely perilous; firing upon them from the river banks as they passed beneath in their boats, and attacking them in their encampments. Mr. Crooks himself, when voyaging in company with another trader of the name of M'Lellan, had been interrupted by those marauders, and had considered himself fortunate in escaping down the river without loss of life or property, but with a total abandonment of his trading voyage.

Should they be fortunate enough to pass through the country of the Sioux without molestation, they would have another tribe still more savage and warlike beyond, and deadly foes of the white men. These were the Blackfeet Indians, who ranged over a wide extent of country which they would have to traverse.

Under all these circumstances, it was thought advisable to augment the party considerably. It already exceeded the number of thirty, to which it had originally been limited; but it was determined, on arriving at St. Louis, to increase it to the number of sixty.

These matters being arranged, they prepared to em-

bark; but the embarkation of a crew of Canadian voyageurs, on a distant expedition, is not so easy a matter as
might be imagined; especially of such a set of vainglorious fellows with money in both pockets, and cocks' tails
in their hats. Like sailors, the Canadian voyageurs generally preface a long cruise with a carouse. They have
their cronies, their brothers, their cousins, their wives,
their sweethearts, all to be entertained at their expense.
They feast, they fiddle, they drink, they sing, they dance,
they frolic and fight, until they are all as mad as so many
drunken Indians. The publicans are all obedience to
their commands, never hesitating to let them run up
scores without limit, knowing that, when their own money
is expended, the purses of their employers must answer for
the bill, or the voyage must be delayed. Neither was it
possible, at that time, to remedy the matter at Mackinaw.
In that amphibious community there was always a propensity to wrest the laws in favour of riotous or mutinous
boatmen. It was necessary, also, to keep the recruits in
good humour, seeing the novelty and danger of the service into which they were entering, and the ease with
which they might at any time escape it, by jumping into
a canoe and going down the stream.

Such were the scenes that beset Mr. Hunt, and gave
him a foretaste of the difficulties of his command. The
little cabarets and suttlers' shops along the bay resounded
with the scraping of fiddles, with snatches of old French
songs, with Indian whoops and yelps; while every plumed
and feathered vagabond had his troop of loving cousins
and comrades at his heels. It was with the utmost difficulty they could be extricated from the clutches of the
publicans, and the embraces of their pot companions, who
followed them to the water's edge with many a hug, a kiss
on each cheek, and a maudlin benediction in Canadian
French.

It was about the 12th of August that they left Mackinaw, and pursued the usual route by Green bay, Fox
and Wisconsin rivers, to Prairie du Chien, and thence
down the Mississippi to St. Louis, where they landed on
the 3d of September.

CHAPTER XIV.

St. Louis, which is situated on the right bank of the Mississippi river, a few miles below the mouth of the Missouri, was, at that time, a frontier settlement, and the last fitting out place for the Indian trade of the southwest. It possessed a motley population, composed of the creole descendants of the original French colonists ; the keen traders from the Atlantic states ; the backwoodmen of Kentucky and Tennessee ; the Indians and half-breeds of the prairies ; together with a singular aquatic race that had grown up from the navigation of the rivers—the "boatmen of the Mississippi;" who possessed habits, manners, and almost a language, peculiarly their own, and strongly technical. They, at that time, were extremely numerous, and conducted the chief navigation and commerce of the Ohio and the Mississippi, as the voyageurs did of the Canadian waters ; but, like them, their consequence and characteristics are rapidly vanishing before the all-pervading intrusion of steam-boats.

The old French houses engaged in the Indian trade had gathered round them a train of dependants, mongrel Indians, and mongrel Frenchmen, who had intermarried with Indians. These they employed in their various expeditions by land and water. Various individuals of other countries had, of late years, pushed the trade further into the interior, to the upper waters of the Missouri, and had swelled the number of these hangers on. Several of these traders had, two or three years previously, formed themselves into a company, composed of twelve partners, with a capital of about forty thousand dollars, called the Missouri Fur Company ; the object of which was, to establish posts along the upper part of that river, and monopolize the trade. The leading partner of this company was Mr. Manuel Lisa, a Spaniard by birth, and a man of bold and enterprising character, who had ascended the Missouri almost to its source, and made himself well acquainted and popular with several of its tribes. By his exertions, trading posts had been established, in 1808, in the Sioux country, and among the Aricara and Mandan tribes; and a principal one, under Mr. Henry, one of the partners, at the forks of the Missouri. This company had in its employ about two hundred and fifty men, partly American hunters, and partly creoles and Canadian voyageurs.

All these circumstances combined to produce a population at St. Louis even still more motley than that at Mackinaw. Here were to be seen about the river banks, the hectoring, extravagant, bragging boatmen of the Mississippi, with the gay, grimacing, singing, good-humoured Canadian voyageurs. Vagrant Indians of various tribes loitered about the streets. Now and then, a stark Kentucky hunter, in leathern hunting-dress, with rifle on shoulder and knife in belt, strode along. Here and there were new brick houses and shops, just set up by bustling, driving, and eager men of traffic, from the Atlantic states; while, on the other hand, the old French mansions, with open casements, still retained the easy, indolent air of the original colonists; and now and then the scraping of a fiddle, a strain of an ancient French song, or the sound of billiard-balls, showed that the happy Gallic turn for gaiety and amusement still lingered about the place.

Such was St. Louis at the time of Mr. Hunt's arrival there; and the appearance of a new fur company, with ample funds at its command, produced a strong sensation among the Indian traders of the place, and awakened keen jealousy and opposition on the part of the Missouri Company. Mr. Hunt proceeded to strengthen himself against all competition. For this purpose he secured to the interests of the association another of those enterprising men, who had been engaged in individual traffic with the tribes of the Missouri. This was a Mr. Joseph Miller, a gentleman well educated and well informed, and of a respectable family of Baltimore. He had been an officer in the army of the United States, but had resigned in disgust, on being refused a furlough, and had taken to trapping beaver and trading among the Indians. He was easily induced by Mr. Hunt to join as a partner, and was considered by him, on account of his education and acquirements, and his experience in Indian trade, a valuable addition to the company.

Several additional men were likewise enlisted at St. Louis; some as boatmen, and others as hunters. These last were engaged, not merely to kill game for provisions, but also, and indeed chiefly, to trap beaver and other animals of rich furs, valuable in the trade. They enlisted on different terms. Some were to have a fixed salary of three hundred dollars; others were to be fitted out and maintained at the expense of the company, and were to hunt and trap on shares.

As Mr. Hunt met with much opposition on the part of rival traders, especially the Missouri Fur Company, it took him some weeks to complete his preparations. The delays which he had previously experienced at Montreal, Mackinaw, and on the way, added to those at St. Louis, had thrown him much behind his original calculations, so that it would be impossible to effect his voyage up the Missouri in the present year. This river, flowing from high and cold latitudes, and through wide and open plains, exposed to chilling blasts, freezes early. The winter may be dated from the 1st of November; there was every prospect, therefore, that it would be closed with ice long before Mr. Hunt could reach its upper waters. To avoid, however, the expense of wintering at St. Louis, he determined to push up the river as far as possible, to some point above the settlements, where game was plenty, and where his whole party could be subsisted by hunting, until the breaking up of the ice in the spring should permit them to resume their voyage.

Accordingly, on the 21st of October he took his departure from St. Louis. His party was distributed in three boats. One was the barge which he had brought from Mackinaw; another was of a larger size, such as was formerly used in navigating the Mohawk river, and

known by the generic name of the Schenectady barge;
the other was a large keel-boat, at that time the grand
conveyance on the Mississippi.

In this way they set out from St. Louis, in buoyant
spirits, and soon arrived at the mouth of the Missouri.
This vast river, three thousand miles in length, and which,
with its tributary streams, drains such an immense extent
of country, was as yet but casually and imperfectly navigated by the adventurous bark of the fur trader.   A
steam-boat had never yet stemmed its turbulent current.
Sails were but of casual assistance, for it required a strong
wind to conquer the force of the stream.   The main dependance was on bodily strength and manual dexterity.
The boats in general had to be propelled by oars and
setting poles, or drawn by the hand, and by grappling
hooks from one root or overhanging tree to another; or
towed by the long cordelle, or towing-line, where the
shores were sufficiently clear of woods and thickets to
permit the men to pass along the banks.

During this long and tedious progress, the boat would
be exposed to frequent danger from floating trees and
great masses of driftwood, or to be empaled upon snags
and sawyers; that is to say, sunken trees, presenting a
jagged or pointed end above the surface of the water.   As
the channel of the river frequently shifted from side to
side, according to the bends and sandbanks, the boat had,
in the same way, to advance in a zigzag course.   Often a
part of the crew would have to leap into the water at the
shallows, and wade along with the towing-line, while their
comrades on board toilfully assisted with oar and setting
pole.   Sometimes the boat would seem to be retained
motionless, as if spell bound, opposite some point round
which the current set with violence, and where the utmost
labour scarce effected any visible progress.   On these
occasions it was that the merits of the Canadian voyageurs
came into full action.   Patient of toil, not to be disheartened by impediments and disappointments, fertile in
expedients, and versed in every mode of humouring and
conquering the wayward current, they would ply every
exertion, sometimes in the boat, sometimes on shore, some-

times in the water, however cold; always alert, always in
good humour; and, should they at any time flag or grow
weary, one of their popular boat-songs, chanted by a
veteran oarsman, and responded to in chorus, acted as a
never-failing restorative.

By such assiduous and persevering labour they made
their way about four hundred and fifty miles up the Missouri, by the 16th of November, to the mouth of the
Nodowa. As this was a good hunting country, and as
the season was rapidly advancing, they determined to
establish their winter quarters at this place; and, in fact,
two days after they had come to a halt, the river closed
just above their encampment. The party had not been
long at this place when they were joined by Mr. Robert
M'Lellan, another trader of the Missouri; the same who
had been associated with Mr. Crooks in the unfortunate
expedition in which they had been intercepted by the
Sioux Indians, and obliged to make a rapid retreat down
the river.

M'Lellan was a remarkable man. He had been a par-
tisan under General Wayne in his Indian wars, where he
had distinguished himself by his fiery spirit and reckless
daring, and marvellous stories were told of his exploits.
His appearance answered to his character. His frame was
meagre, but muscular; showing strength, activity, and
iron firmness. His eyes were dark, deep set, and piercing.
He was restless, fearless, but of impetuous and sometimes ungovernable temper. He had been invited by Mr.
Hunt to enrol himself as a partner, and gladly consented;
being pleased with the thoughts of passing, with a powerful force, through the country of the Sioux, and perhaps having an opportunity of revenging himself upon
that lawless tribe for their past offences.

Another recruit that joined the camp of Nodowa deserves equal mention. This was John Day, a hunter from
the backwoods of Virginia, but who had been several
years on the Missouri in the service of Mr. Crooks, and of
other traders. He was about forty years of age, six feet
two inches high, straight as an Indian, with an elastic
step as if he trod on springs, and a handsome, open,

manly countenance. It was his boast that, in his younger days, nothing could hurt or daunt him; but he had "lived too fast," and injured his constitution by his excesses. Still he was strong of hand, bold of heart, a prime wood-man, and an almost unerring shot. He had the frank spirit of a Virginian, and the rough heroism of a pioneer of the west.

The party were now brought to a halt for several months. They were in a country abounding with deer and wild turkeys, so that there was no stint of provisions, and every one appeared cheerful and contented. Mr. Hunt determined to avail himself of this interval to return to St. Louis and obtain a reinforcement. He wished to procure an interpreter, acquainted with the language of the Sioux; as, from all accounts, he apprehended diffi-culties in passing through the country of that nation. He felt the necessity, also, of having a greater number of hunters, not merely to keep up a supply of provisions throughout their long and arduous expedition, but also as a protection and defence in case of Indian hostilities. For such service the Canadian voyageurs were little to be de-pended upon, fighting not being a part of their profession. The proper kind of men were American hunters, expe-rienced in savage life and savage warfare, and possessed of the true game spirit of the west.

Leaving, therefore, the encampment in charge of the other partners, Mr. Hunt set off on foot on the 1st of January, 1810, for St. Louis. He was accompanied by eight men as far as fort Osage, about one hundred and fifty miles below Nodawa. Here he procured a couple of horses, and proceeded on the remainder of his journey with two men, sending the other six back to the encamp-ment. He arrived at St. Louis on the 20th of January.

CHAPTER XV.

Opposition of the Missouri Fur Company—Blackfeet Indians—Pierre Dorion, a half-breed interpreter—Old Dorion and his hybrid progeny—Family quarrels—Cross purposes between Dorion and Lisa—Renegadoes from Nodowa—Perplexities of a commander—Messrs. Bradbury and Nuttall join the expedition—Legal embarrassments of Pierre Dorion—Departure from St. Louis—Conjugal discipline of a half-breed—Annual swelling of the rivers—Daniel Boon, the patriarch of Kentucky—John Colter—His adventures among the Indians—Rumours of danger ahead—Port Osage—An Indian war-feast—Troubles in the Dorion family—Buffaloes and Turkey-buzzards.

On this his second visit to St. Louis, Mr. Hunt was again impeded in his plans by the opposition of the Missouri Fur Company. The affairs of that company were, at this time, in a very dubious state. During the preceding year, their principal establishment at the forks of the Missouri had been so much harassed by the Blackfeet Indians, that its commander, Mr. Henry, one of the partners, had been compelled to abandon the post and cross the Rocky mountains, with the intention of fixing himself upon one of the upper branches of the Columbia. What had become of him and his party was unknown. The most intense anxiety was felt concerning them, and apprehensions that they might have been cut off by the savages. At the time of Mr. Hunt's arrival at St. Louis, the Missouri Company were fitting out an expedition to go in quest of Mr. Henry. It was to be conducted by Mr. Manuel Lisa, the enterprising partner already mentioned.

There being thus two expeditions on foot at the same moment, an unusual demand was occasioned for hunters and voyageurs, who accordingly profited by the circumstance, and stipulated for high terms. Mr. Hunt found a keen and subtle competitor in Lisa, and was obliged to secure his recruits by liberal advances of pay, and by other pecuniary indulgences.

The greatest difficulty was to procure the Sioux interpreter. There was but one man to be met with at St. Louis who was fitted for the purpose, but to secure him would require much management. The individual in question was a half-breed, named Pierre Dorion; and, as he figures hereafter in this narrative, and is, withal, a striking specimen of the hybrid race on the frontier, we shall give a few particulars concerning him. Pierre was the son of Dorion, the French interpreter, who accompanied Messrs. Lewis and Clarke in their famous exploring expedition across the Rocky mountains. Old Dorion was one of those French creoles, descendants of the ancient Canadian stock, who abound on the western frontier, and amalgamate or cohabit with the savages. He had sojourned among various tribes, and perhaps left progeny among them all; but his regular, or habitual wife, was a Sioux squaw. By her he had a hopeful brood of half-breed sons, of whom Pierre was one. The domestic affairs of old Dorion were conducted on the true Indian plan. Father and sons would occasionally get drunk together, and then the cabin was a scene of ruffian brawl and fighting, in the course of which the old Frenchman was apt to get soundly belaboured by his mongrel offspring. In a furious scuffle of the kind, one of the sons got the old man upon the ground, and was upon the point of scalping him. " Hold ! my son," cried the old fellow, in imploring accents, " you are too brave, too *honourable* to scalp your father !" This last appeal touched the French side of the half-breed's heart, so he suffered the old man to wear his scalp unharmed.

Of this hopeful stock was Pierre Dorion, the man whom it was now the desire of Mr. Hunt to engage as an interpreter. He had been employed in that capacity by the Missouri Fur Company during the preceding year, and had conducted their traders in safety through the different tribes of the Sioux. He had proved himself faithful and serviceable while sober ; but the love of liquor, in which he had been nurtured and brought up, would occasionally break out, and with it the savage side of his character.

It was this love of liquor which had embroiled him with the Missouri Company. While in their service at fort

Mandan, on the frontier, he had been seized with a whiskey mania ; and, as the beverage was only to be procured
at the company's store, it had been charged in his account
at the rate of ten dollars a quart.   This item had ever
remained unsettled, and a matter of furious dispute, the
mere mention of which was sufficient to put him in a
passion.

The moment it was discovered by Mr. Lisa that Pierre
Dorion was in treaty with the new and rival association,
he endeavoured, by threats as well as promises, to prevent
his engaging in their service.   His promises might, perhaps, have prevailed ; but his threats, which related to
the whiskey debt, only served to drive Pierre into the opposite ranks.   Still, he took advantage of this competition
for his services to stand out with Mr. Hunt on the most
advantageous terms, and, after a negotiation of nearly two
weeks, capitulated to serve in the expedition, as hunter
and interpreter, at the rate of three hundred dollars a
year, two hundred of which were to be paid in advance.

When Mr. Hunt had got every thing ready for leaving
St. Louis, new difficulties arose.   Five of the American
hunters, from the encampment at Nodowa, suddenly
made their appearance.   They alleged that they had been
ill treated by the partners at the encampment, and had
come off clandestinely, in consequence of a dispute.   It was
useless at the present moment, and under present circumstances, to attempt any compulsory measures with these
deserters.   Two of them Mr. Hunt prevailed upon, by
mild means, to return with him.   The rest refused ; nay,
what was worse, they spread such reports of the hardships
and dangers to be apprehended in the course of the expedition, that they struck a panic into those hunters who
had recently engaged at St. Louis, and, when the hour of
departure arrived, all but one refused to embark.   It was
in vain to plead or remonstrate ; they shouldered their
rifles and turned their back upon the expedition, and Mr.
Hunt was fain to put off from the shore with the single
hunter and a number of voyageurs whom he had engaged.
Even Pierre Dorion, at the last moment, refused to enter
the boat until Mr. Hunt consented to take his squaw and

two children on board also. But the tissue of perplexities, on account of this worthy individual, did not end here.

Among the various persons who were about to proceed up the Missouri with Mr. Hunt, were two scientific gentlemen: one Mr. John Bradbury, a man of mature age, but great enterprise and personal activity, who had been sent out by the Linnean Society of Liverpool, to make a collection of American plants; the other a Mr. Nuttall, likewise an Englishman, younger in years, who has since made himself known as the author of " Travels in Arkansas," and a work on the " Genera of American Plants." Mr. Hunt had offered them the protection and facilities of his party, in their scientific researches up the Missouri. As they were not ready to depart at the moment of embarkation, they put their trunks on board of the boat, but remained at St. Louis until the next day, for the arrival of the post, intending to join the expedition at St. Charles, a short distance above the mouth of the Missouri.

The same evening, however, they learned that a writ had been issued against Pierre Dorion for his whiskey debt, by Mr. Lisa, as agent of the Missouri Company, and that it was the intention to entrap the mongrel linguist on his arrival at St. Charles. Upon hearing this, Mr. Bradbury and Mr. Nuttall set off a little after midnight, by land, got ahead of the boat as it was ascending the Missouri, before its arrival at St. Charles, and gave Pierre Dorion warning of the legal toil prepared to ensnare him. The knowing Pierre immediately landed and took to the woods, followed by his squaw laden with their papooses, and a large bundle containing their most precious effects; promising to rejoin the party some distance above St. Charles. There seemed little dependence to be placed upon the promises of a loose adventurer of the kind, who was at the very time playing an evasive game with his former employers; who had already received two-thirds of his year's pay, and had his rifle on his shoulder, his family and worldly fortune at his heels, and the wild woods before him. There was no alternative, however, and it was hoped his pique against his old employers would render him faithful to his new ones.

The party reached St. Charles in the afternoon, but the harpies of the law looked in vain for their expected prey. The boats resumed their course on the following morning, and had not proceeded far when Pierre Dorion made his appearance on the shore. He was gladly taken on board, but he came without his squaw. They had quarrelled in the night; Pierre had administered the Indian discipline of the cudgel, whereupon she had taken to the woods, with their children and all their worldly goods. Pierre evidently was deeply grieved and disconcerted at the loss of his wife and his knapsack, wherefore Mr. Hunt despatched one of the Canadian voyageurs in search of the fugitive; and the whole party, after proceeding a few miles further, encamped on an island to await his return. The Canadian rejoined the party, but without the squaw: and Pierre Dorion passed a solitary and anxious night, bitterly regretting his indiscretion in having exercised his conjugal authority so near home. Before daybreak, however, a well-known voice reached his ears from the opposite shore. It was his repentant spouse, who had been wandering the woods all night in quest of the party, and at length descried it by its fires. A boat was despatched for her, the interesting family was once more united, and Mr. Hunt now flattered himself that his perplexities with Pierre Dorion were at an end.

Bad weather, very heavy rains, and an unusually early rise in the Missouri, rendered the ascent of the river toilsome, slow, and dangerous. The rise of the Missouri does not generally take place until the month of May or June: the present swelling of the river must have been caused by a freshet in some of its more southern branches. It could not have been the great annual flood, as the higher branches must still have been ice-bound.

And here we cannot but pause, to notice the admirable arrangement of nature, by which the annual swellings of the various great rivers which empty themselves into the Mississippi, have been made to precede each other at considerable intervals. Thus, the flood of the Red river precedes that of the Arkansas by a month. The Arkansas, also, rising in a much more southern latitude than the

Missouri, takes the lead of it in its annual excess, and its superabundant waters are disgorged and disposed of long before the breaking up of the icy barriers of the north; otherwise, did all these mighty streams rise simultaneously, and discharge their vernal floods into the Mississippi, an inundation would be the consequence, that would submerge and devastate all the lower country.

On the afternoon of the third day, January 17th, the boats touched at Charette, one of the old villages founded by the original French colonists. Here they met with Daniel Boon, the renowned patriarch of Kentucky, who had kept in the advance of civilization, and on the borders of the wilderness, still leading a hunter's life, though now in his eighty-fifth year. He had but recently returned from a hunting and trapping expedition, and had brought nearly sixty beaver skins as trophies of his skill. The old man was still erect in form, strong in limb, and unflinching in spirit; and as he stood on the river bank, watching the departure of an expedition destined to traverse the wilderness to the very shores of the Pacific, very probably felt a throb of his old pioneer spirit, impelling him to shoulder his rifle and join the adventurous band. Boon flourished several years after this meeting, in a vigorous old age, the Nestor of hunters and backwoodmen; and died, full of sylvan honour and renown, in 1818, in his ninety-second year.

The next morning early, as the party were yet encamped at the mouth of a small stream, they were visited by another of these heroes of the wilderness, one John Colter, who had accompanied Lewis and Clarke in their memorable expedition. He had recently made one of those vast internal voyages so characteristic of this fearless class of men, and of the immense regions over which they hold their lonely wanderings; having come from the head waters of the Missouri to St. Louis in a small canoe. This distance of three thousand miles he had accomplished in thirty days. Colter kept with the party all the morning. He had many particulars to give them concerning the Blackfeet Indians, a restless and predatory tribe, who had conceived an implacable hostility to the white men, in

consequence of one of their warriors having been killed by
Captain Lewis, while attempting to steal horses. Through
the country infested by these savages the expedition would
have to proceed, and Colter was urgent in reiterating the
precautions that ought to be observed respecting them.
He had himself experienced their vindictive cruelty, and
his story deserves particular citation, as showing the hair-
breadth adventures to which these solitary rovers of the
wilderness are exposed.

Colter, with the hardihood of a regular trapper, had
cast himself loose from the party of Lewis and Clarke in
the very heart of the wilderness, and had remained to
trap beaver alone on the head waters of the Missouri.
Here he fell in with another lonely trapper, like himself,
named Potts, and they agreed to keep together. They
were in the very region of the terrible Blackfeet, at that
time thirsting to revenge the death of their companion,
and knew that they had to expect no mercy at their hands.
They were obliged to keep concealed all day in the woody
margins of the rivers, setting their traps after nightfall,
and taking them up before daybreak. It was running a
fearful risk for the sake of a few beaver skins; but such
is the life of the trapper.

They were on a branch of the Missouri called Jefferson's Fork, and had set their traps at night, about six
miles up a small river that emptied itself into the fork.
Early in the morning they ascended the river in a canoe,
to examine the traps. The banks on each side were high
and perpendicular, and cast a shade over the stream. As
they were softly paddling along, they heard the trampling
of many feet upon the banks. Colter immediately gave
the alarm of " Indians!" and was for instant retreat.
Potts scoffed at him for being frightened by the trampling
of a herd of buffaloes. Colter checked his uneasiness, and
paddled forward. They had not gone much further when
frightful whoops and yells burst forth from each side of
the river, and several hundred Indians appeared on either
bank. Signs were made to the unfortunate trappers to
come on shore. They were obliged to comply. Before
they could get out of their canoe, a savage seized the rifle

belonging to Potts. Colter sprang on shore, wrested the weapon from the hands of the Indian, and restored it to his companion, who was still in the canoe, and immediately pushed into the stream. There was the sharp twang of a bow, and Potts cried out that he was wounded. Colter urged him to come on shore and submit, as his only chance for life; but the other knew there was no prospect of mercy, and determined to die game. Levelling his rifle, he shot one of the savages dead on the spot. The next moment he fell himself, pierced with innumerable arrows.

The vengeance of the savages now turned upon Colter. He was stripped naked, and, having some knowledge of the Blackfoot language, overheard a consultation as to the mode of despatching him, so as to derive the greatest amusement from his death. Some were for setting him up as a mark, and having a trial of skill at his expense. The chief, however, was for nobler sport. He seized Colter by the shoulder, and demanded if he could run fast. The unfortunate trapper was too well acquainted with Indian customs not to comprehend the drift of the question. He knew he was to run for his life, to furnish a kind of human hunt to his persecutors. Though in reality he was noted among his brother hunters for swiftness of foot, he assured the chief that he was a very bad runner. His stratagem gained him some vantage ground. He was led by the chief into the prairie, about four hundred yards from the main body of the savages, and then turned loose, to save himself if he could. A tremendous yell let him know that the whole pack of bloodhounds were off in full cry. Colter flew, rather than ran; he was astonished at his own speed; but he had six miles of prairie to traverse before he should reach the Jefferson fork of the Missouri; how could he hope to hold out such a distance with the fearful odds of several hundred to one against him! The plain, too, abounded with the prickly pear, which wounded his naked feet. Still he fled on, dreading each moment to hear the twang of a bow, and to feel an arrow quivering at his heart. He did not even dare to look round, lest he should lose an inch of that distance on which his life depended. He had run nearly half way across the plain when the sound of pursuit grew somewhat fainter, and he ventured to turn his head. The main body of his pursuers were a considerable distance behind; several of the faster runners were scattered in the advance; while a swift-footed warrior, armed with a spear, was not more than a hundred yards behind him.

Inspired with new hope, Colter redoubled his exertions, but strained himself to such a degree, that the blood gushed from his mouth and nostrils, and streamed down his breast. He arrived within a mile of the river. The sound of footsteps gathered upon him. A glance behind showed his pursuer within twenty yards, and preparing to launch his spear. Stopping short, he turned round and spread out his arms. The savage, confounded by this sudden action, attempted to stop and to hurl his spear, but fell in the very act. His spear stuck in the ground, and the shaft broke in his hand. Colter plucked up the pointed part, pinned the savage to the earth, and continued his flight. The Indians, as they arrived at their slaughtered companion, stopped to howl over him. Colter made the most of this precious delay, gained the skirt of cotton-wood bordering the river, dashed through it, and plunged into the stream. He swam to a neighbouring island, against the upper end of which the driftwood had lodged in such quantities as to form a natural raft; under this he dived, and swam below water until he succeeded in getting a breathing place between the floating trunks of trees, whose branches and bushes formed a covert several feet above the level of the water. He had scarcely drawn breath after all his toils, when he heard his pursuers on the river bank, whooping and yelling like so many fiends. They plunged in the river, and swam to the raft. The heart of Colter almost died within him as he saw them, through the chinks of his concealment, passing and repassing, and seeking for him in all directions. They at length gave up the search, and he began to rejoice in his escape, when the idea presented itself that they might set the raft on fire. Here was a new source of horrible apprehension, in which he remained until nightfall. Fortunately, the idea did not suggest itself to the Indians. As soon as it was dark, finding by the silence around that his pursuers had departed, Colter dived again, and came up beyond the raft. He then swam silently down the river for a considerable distance, when he landed, and kept on all night, to get as far off as possible from this dangerous neighbourhood.

By daybreak he had gained sufficient distance to relieve him from the terrors of his savage foes; but now new sources of inquietude presented themselves. He was naked and alone, in the midst of an unbounded wilderness; his only chance was to reach a trading post of the Missouri Company, situated on a branch of the Yellowstone river. Even should he elude his pursuers, days must elapse before he could reach this post, during which he must traverse immense prairies destitute of shade, his naked body exposed to the burning heat of the sun by day, and the dews and chills of the night season, and his feet lacerated by the thorns of the prickly pear. Though he might see game in abundance around him, he had no means of killing any for his sustenance, and must depend for food upon the roots of the earth. In defiance of these difficulties he pushed resolutely forward, guiding himself in his trackless course by those signs and indications known only to Indians and backwoodmen; and, after braving dangers and hardships, enough to break down any spirit but that of a western pioneer, arrived safe at the solitary post in question.*

Such is a sample of the rugged experience which Colter had to relate of savage life; yet, with all these perils and terrors fresh in his recollection, he could not see the present band on their way to those regions of danger and adventure, without feeling a vehement impulse to join them. A western trapper is like a sailor; past hazards only stimulate him to further risks. The vast prairie is to the one what the ocean is to the other, a boundless field of enterprise and exploit. However he may have suffered in his late cruise, he is always ready to join a new expe-

* Bradbury. Travels in America, p. 17.

dition; and the more adventurous its nature, the more attractive is it to his vagrant spirit.

Nothing seems to have kept Colter from continuing with the party to the shores of the Pacific, but the circumstance of his having recently married. All the morning he kept with them, balancing in his mind the charms of his bride against those of the Rocky mountains; the former, however, prevailed, and after a march of several miles, he took a reluctant leave of the travellers, and turned his face homeward.

Continuing their progress up the Missouri, the party encamped on the evening of the 21st of March, in the neighbourhood of a little frontier village of French creoles. Here Pierre Dorion met with some of his old comrades, with whom he had a long gossip, and returned to the camp with rumours of bloody feuds between the Osages and the Ioways, or Ayaways, Potowatomies, Sioux, and Sawkees. Blood had already been shed, and scalps been taken. A war party, three hundred strong, were prowling in the neighbourhood; others might be met with higher up the river; it behoved the travellers, therefore, to be upon their guard against robbery or surprise, for an Indian war party on the march is prone to acts of outrage.

In consequence of this report, which was subsequently confirmed by further intelligence, a guard was kept up at night round the encampment, and they all slept on their arms. As they were sixteen in number, and well supplied with weapons and ammunition, they trusted to be able to give any marauding party a warm reception. Nothing occurred, however, to molest them on their voyage, and on the 8th of April they came in sight of fort Osage. On their approach the flag was hoisted on the fort, and they saluted it by a discharge of fire-arms. Within a short distance of the fort was an Osage village, the inhabitants of which, men, women, and children, thronged down to the water side to witness their landing. One of the first persons they met on the river bank was Mr. Crooks, who had come down in a boat with nine men, from the winter encampment at Nodowa, to meet them.

They remained at fort Osage a part of three days,

during which they were hospitably entertained at the garrison by Lieutenant Brownson, who held a temporary command. They were regaled also with a war-feast at the village; the Osage warriors having returned from a successful foray against the Ioways, in which they had taken seven scalps. These were paraded on poles about the village, followed by the warriors decked out in all their savage ornaments, and hideously painted as if for battle.

By the Osage warriors, Mr. Hunt and his companions were again warned to be on their guard in ascending the river, as the Sioux tribe meant to lie in wait and attack them.

On the 10th of April they again embarked, their party being now augmented to twenty-six, by the addition of Mr. Crooks and his boat's crew. They had not proceeded far, however, when there was a great outcry from one of the boats; it was occasioned by a little domestic discipline in the Dorion family. The squaw of the worthy interpreter, it appeared, had been so delighted with the scalp-dance, and other festivities of the Osage village, that she had taken a strong inclination to remain there. This had been as strongly opposed by her liege lord, who had compelled her to embark. The good dame had remained sulky ever since; whereupon Pierre, seeing no other mode of exorcising the evil spirit out of her, and being perhaps a little inspired by whiskey, had resorted to the Indian remedy of the cudgel, and, before his neighbours could interfere, had belaboured her so soundly, that there is no record of her having shown any refractory symptoms throughout the remainder of the expedition.

For a week they continued their voyage, exposed to almost incessant rains. The bodies of drowned buffaloes floated past them in vast numbers; many had drifted upon the shore, or against the upper ends of the rafts and islands. These had attracted great flights of turkey-buzzards: some were banqueting on the carcases, others were soring far aloft in the sky, and others were perched on the trees, with their backs to the sun, and their wings stretched out to dry, like so many vessels in harbour, spreading their sails after a shower.

The turkey-buzzard (*vultur aura*, or golden vulture), when on the wing, is one of the most specious and imposing of birds. Its flight in the upper regions of the air is really sublime, extending its immense wings, and wheeling slowly and majestically to and fro, seemingly without exerting a muscle or fluttering a feather, but moving by mere volition, and sailing on the bosom of the air, as a ship upon the ocean. Usurping the empyreal realm of the eagle, he assumes for a time the port and dignity of that majestic bird, and often is mistaken for him by ignorant crawlers upon earth. It is only when he descends from the clouds to pounce upon carrion that he betrays his low propensities, and reveals his caitiff character. Near at hand he is a disgusting bird, ragged in plumage, base in aspect, and of loathsome odour.

On the 17th of April, Mr. Hunt arrived with his party at the station near the Nodowa river, where the main body had been quartered during the winter.

CHAPTER XVI.

Return of spring—Appearance of snakes—Great flights of wild pigeons—Renewal of the voyage—Night encampments—Platte river—Ceremonials on passing it—Signs of Indian war parties—Magnificent prospect at Papillion Creek—Desertion of two hunters—An irruption into the camp of Indian desperadoes—Village of the Omahas—Anecdotes of the tribe—Feudal wars of the Indians—Story of Blackbird, the famous Omaha chief.

THE weather continued rainy and ungenial for some days after Mr. Hunt's return to Nodowa; yet spring was rapidly advancing, and vegetation was putting forth with all its early freshness and beauty. The snakes began to recover from their torpor and crawl forth into day, and the neighbourhood of the wintering house seems to be much infested with them. Mr. Bradbury, in the course of his botanical researches, found a surprising number in a half torpid state, under flat stones upon the banks which overhung the cantonment, and narrowly escaped being struck by a rattlesnake, which darted at him from a cleft in the rock, but fortunately gave him warning by its rattle.

The pigeons, too, were filling the woods in vast migratory flocks. It is almost incredible to describe the prodigious flights of these birds in the western wildernesses. They appear absolutely in clouds, and move with astonishing velocity, their wings making a whistling sound as they fly. The rapid evolutions of these flocks, wheeling and shifting suddenly, as if with one mind and one impulse; the flashing changes of colour they present, as their backs, their breasts, or the under part of their wings, are turned to the spectator, are singularly pleasing. When they alight, if on the ground, they cover whole acres at a time; if upon trees, the branches often break beneath their weight. If suddenly startled while feeding in the midst of a forest, the noise they make in getting on the wing is like the roar of a cataract or the sound of distant thunder.

A flight of this kind, like an Egyptian flight of locusts, devours every thing that serves for its food as it passes along. So great were the numbers in the vicinity of the camp, that Mr. Bradbury, in the course of a morning's excursion, shot nearly three hundred with a fowling-piece. He gives a curious, though apparently a faithful account of the kind of discipline observed in these immense flocks, so that each may have a chance of picking up food. As the front ranks must meet with the greatest abundance, and the rear ranks must have scanty pickings, the instant a rank finds itself the hindmost, it rises in the air, flies over the whole flock, and takes its place in the advance. The next rank follows in its course, and thus the last is continually becoming first, and all by turns have a front place at the banquet.

The rains having at length subsided, Mr. Hunt broke up the encampment, and resumed his course up the Missouri.

The party now consisted of nearly sixty persons; of whom five were partners; one, John Reed, was a clerk; forty were Canadian "voyageurs," or "engagés," and there were several hunters. They embarked in four boats, one of them was of a large size, mounting a swivel and two howitzers. All were furnished with masts and sails, to be used when the wind was sufficiently favourable and strong to overpower the current of the river. Such was the case for the first four or five days, when they were wafted steadily up the stream by a strong south-easter.

Their encampments at night were often pleasant and picturesque—on some beautiful bank, beneath spreading trees, which afforded them shelter and fuel. The tents were pitched, the fires made, and the meals prepared by the voyageurs, and many a story was told, and joke passed, and song sung, round the evening fire. All, however, were asleep at an early hour. Some under the tents, others wrapped in blankets before the fire, or beneath the trees ; and some few in the boats and canoes.

On the 28th, they breakfasted on one of the islands which lie at the mouth of the Nebraska, or Platte river ; the largest tributary of the Missouri, and about six hundred miles above its confluence with the Mississippi. This broad but shallow stream flows for an immense distance through a wide and verdant valley, scooped out of boundless prairies. It draws its main supplies, by several forks or branches, from the Rocky mountains. The mouth of this river is established as the dividing point between the upper and lower Missouri; and the earlier voyageurs, in their toilsome ascent, before the introduction of steamboats, considered one half of their labours accomplished when they reached this place. The passing of the mouth of the Nebraska, therefore, was equivalent among boatmen to the crossing of the line among sailors, and was celebrated with like ceremonials of a rough and waggish nature, practised upon the uninitiated ; among which was the old nautical joke of shaving. The river deities, however, like those of the sea, were to be propitiated by a bribe, and the infliction of these rude honours to be parried by a treat to the adepts.

At the mouth of the Nebraska new signs were met with of war parties which had recently been in the vicinity. There was the frame of a skin canoe, in which the warriors had traversed the river. At night, also, the lurid reflection of immense fires hung in the sky, showing the conflagration of great tracts of the prairies. Such fires not being made by hunters so late in the season, it was supposed they were caused by some wandering war parties. These often take the precaution to set the prairies on fire behind them to conceal their traces from their enemies. This is chiefly done when the party has been unsuccessful and is on the retreat, and apprehensive of pursuit. At such time it is not safe even for friends to fall in with them, as they are apt to be in savage humour, and disposed to vent their spleen in capricious outrage. These signs, therefore, of a band of marauders on the prowl, called for some degree of vigilance on the part of the travellers.

After passing the Nebraska, the party halted for part of two days on the bank of the river, a little above Papillion Creek, to supply themselves with a stock of oars and poles from the tough wood of the ash, which is not met with higher up the Missouri. While the voyageurs were thus occupied, the naturalists rambled over the adjacent country to collect plants. From the summit of a range of bluffs on the opposite side of [the river, above two hundred and fifty feet high, they had one of those vast and magnificent prospects which sometimes unfold themselves in those boundless regions. Below them was the valley of the Missouri, about seven miles in breadth, clad in the fresh verdure of spring; enamelled with flowers and interspersed with clumps and groves of noble trees, between which the mighty river poured its turbulent and turbid stream. The interior of the country presented a singular scene ; the immense waste being broken up by innumerable green hills, not above eighty feet in height, but extremely steep, and acutely pointed at their summits. A long line of bluffs extended for upwards of thirty miles parallel to the Missouri, with a shallow lake stretching along their base, which had evidently once formed a bed of the river. The surface of this lake was covered with aquatic plants, on the broad leaves of which numbers of water-snakes, drawn forth by the genial warmth of spring, were basking in the sunshine.

On the 2d of May, at the usual hour of embarking, the camp was thrown into some confusion by two of the hunters, named Harrington, expressing their intention to abandon the expedition and return home. One of these had joined the party in the preceding autumn, having been hunting for two years on the Missouri; the other had engaged at St. Louis, in the following March, and had come up from thence with Mr. Hunt. He now declared that he had enlisted merely for the purpose of following his brother and persuading him to return; having been enjoined to do so by his mother, whose anxiety had been awakened by the idea of his going on such a wild and distant expedition.

The loss of two stark hunters and prime riflemen was a serious affair to the party, for they were approaching the region where they might expect hostilities from the Sioux; indeed, throughout the whole of their perilous journey, the services of such men would be all important, for little reliance was to be placed upon the valour of the Canadians in case of attack. Mr. Hunt endeavoured by arguments, expostulations, and entreaties, to shake the determination of the two brothers. He represented to them that they were between six and seven hundred miles above the mouth of the Missouri; that they would have four hundred miles to go before they could reach the habitation of a white man, throughout which they would be exposed to all kinds of risks; since, he declared, if they persisted in abandoning him and breaking their faith, he would not furnish them with a single round of ammunition. All was in vain; they obstinataly persisted in their resolution; whereupon Mr. Hunt, partly incited by indignation, partly by the policy of deterring others from desertion, put his threat in execution, and left them to find their way back to the settlements without, as he supposed, a single bullet or a charge of powder.

The boats now continued their slow and toilsome course for several days against the current of the river. The late signs of roaming war parties caused a vigilant watch to be kept up at night when the crews encamped on shore; nor was this vigilance superfluous; for, on the night of the 7th instant, there was a wild and fearful yell, and eleven Sioux warriors, stark naked, with tomahawks in their hands, rushed into the camp. They were instantly surrounded and seized, whereupon their leader called out to his followers to desist from any violence, and pretended to be perfectly pacific in his intentions. It proved, however, that they were a part of the war party, the skeleton of whose canoe had been seen at the mouth of the river Platte, and the reflection of whose fires had been descried in the air. They had been disappointed or defeated in their foray, aad in their rage and mortification these eleven warriors had " devoted their clothes to the medicine." This is a desperate act of Indian braves when foiled in war, and in dread of scoffs and sneers. In such case they sometimes throw off their clothes and ornaments, devote themselves to the Great Spirit, and attempt some reckless exploit with which to cover their disgrace. Woe to any defenceless party of white men that may then fall in their way!

Such was the explanation given by Pierre Dorian, the half-breed interpreter, of this wild intrusion into the camp; and the party were so exasperated when apprized of the sanguinary intentions of the prisoners, that they were for shooting them on the spot. Mr. Hunt, however, exerted his usual moderation and humanity, and ordered that they should be conveyed across the river, in one of the boats, threatening them, however, with certain death, if again caught in any hostile act.

On the 10th of May the party arrived at the Omaha (pronounced Omawhaw) village, about eight hundred and thirty miles above the mouth of the Missouri, and encamped in its neighbourhood. The village was situated under a hill on the bank of the river, and consisted of about eighty lodges. These were of a circular and conical form, and about sixteen feet in diameter; being mere tents of dressed buffalo skins, sewed together and stretched on long poles, inclined towards each other so as to cross at about half their height. Thus the naked tops of the poles diverge in such a manner that, if they were covered with skins like the lower ends, the tent would be shaped like an hour-glass, and present the appearance of one cone inverted on the apex of another.

The forms of Indian lodges are worthy of attention, each tribe having a different mode of shaping and arranging them, so that it is easy to tell, on seeing a lodge or an encampment at a distance, to what tribe the inhabitants belong. The exterior of the Omaha lodges have often a gay and fanciful appearance, being painted with undulating bands of red or yellow, or decorated with rude figures of horses, deer, and buffaloes, and with human faces, painted like full moons, four and five feet broad.

The Omahas were once one of the numerous and powerful tribes of the prairies, vying in warlike might and prowess with the Sioux, the Pawnees, the Sauks, the Konzas, and the Iatans. Their wars with the Sioux, however, had thinned their ranks, and the smallpox in 1802 had swept off two-thirds of their number. At the time of Mr. Hunt's visit they still boasted about two hundred warriors and hunters, but they are now fast melting away, and, before long, will be numbered among those extinguished nations of the west that exist but in tradition.

In his correspondence with Mr. Astor, from this point of his journey, Mr. Hunt gives a sad account of the Indian tribes bordering on the river. They were in continual war with each other, and their wars were of the most harassing kind ; consisting not merely of main conflicts and expeditions of moment, involving the sackings, burnings, and massacres of towns and villages, but of individual acts of treachery, murder, and cold-blooded cruelty ; or of vaunting and foolhardy exploits of single warriors, either to avenge some personal wrong, or gain the vainglorious trophy of a scalp. The lonely hunter, the wandering wayfarer, the poor squaw cutting wood or gathering corn, was liable to be surprised and slaughtered. In this way tribes were either swept away at once, or gradually thinned out, and savage life was surrounded with constant horrors and alarms. That the race of red men should diminish from year to year, and so few should survive of the numerous nations which evidently once peopled the vast regions of the west, is nothing surprising ; it is rather a matter of surprise that so many should survive ; for the existence of a savage in these parts seems little better than a prolonged and all-besetting death. It is, in fact, a caricature of the boasted romance of feudal times; chivalry in its native and uncultured state, and knight-errantry run wild.

In their more prosperous days, the Omahas looked upon themselves as the most powerful and perfect of human beings, and considered all created things as made for their peculiar use and benefit. It is this tribe of whose chief, the famous Wash-ing-guh-sah-ba, or Blackbird, such savage and romantic stories are told. He had died about ten years previous to the arrival of Mr. Hunt's party, but his name was still remembered with awe by his people. He was one of the first among the Indian chiefs on the Missouri to deal with the white traders, and showed great sagacity in levying his royal dues. When a trader arrived in his village, he caused all his goods to be brought into his lodge and opened. From these he selected whatever suited his sovereign pleasure—blankets, tobacco, whiskey, powder, ball, beads, and red paint; and laid the articles on one side, without deigning to give any compensation. Then, calling to him his herald or crier, he would order him to mount on top of the lodge and summon all the tribe to bring in their peltries, and trade with the white man. The lodge would soon be crowded with Indians bringing bear, beaver, otter, and other skins. No one was allowed to dispute the prices fixed by the white trader upon his articles, who took care to indemnify himself five times over for the goods set apart by the chief. In this way the Blackbird enriched himself, and enriched the white men, and became exceedingly popular among the traders of the Missouri. His people, however, were not equally satisfied by a regulation of trade which worked so manifestly against them, and began to show signs of discontent. Upon this a crafty and unprincipled trader revealed a secret to the Blackbird, by which he might acquire unbounded sway over his ignorant and superstitious subjects. He instructed him in the poisonous qualities of arsenic, and furnished him with an ample supply of that baneful drug. From this time the Blackbird seemed endowed with supernatural powers, to possess the gift of prophecy, and to hold the disposal of life and death within his hands. Woe to any one who questioned his authority, or dared to dispute his commands ! The Blackbird prophesied his death within a certain time, and he had the secret means of verifying his prophecy. Within the fated period the offender was smitten with strange and sudden disease, and perished from the face of the earth. Every one stood aghast at these multiplied examples of his superhuman might, and dreaded to displease so omnipotent and vindictive a being ; and the Blackbird enjoyed a wide and undisputed sway.

It was not, however, by terror alone that he ruled his people ; he was a warrior of the first order, and his exploits in arms were the theme of young and old. His career had begun by hardships, having been taken prisoner by the Sioux in early youth. Under his command, the Omahas obtained great character for military prowess, nor did he permit an insult or injury to one of his tribe to pass unrevenged. The Pawnee republicans had inflicted a gross indignity on a favourite and distinguished Omaha brave. The Blackbird assembled his warriors, led them against the Pawnee town, attacked it with irresistible fury, slaughtered a great number of its inhabitants, and burnt it to the ground. He waged fierce and bloody war against the Ottoes for many years, until peace was effected between them by the mediation of the whites. Fearless in battle, and fond of signalizing himself, he dazzled his followers by his daring acts. In attacking a Kanza village, he rode singly round it, loading and discharging his rifle at the inhabitants as he galloped past them. He kept up in war the same idea of mysterious and supernatural power. At one time, when pursuing a war party by their tracks across the prairies, he repeatedly discharged his rifle into the prints made by their feet and by the hoofs of their horses, assuring his followers that he would thereby cripple the fugitives, so that they would easily be overtaken. He, in fact, did overtake them, and destroyed them almost to a man ; and his victory was considered miraculous, both by friend and foe. By these and similar exploits, he made himself the pride and boast of his people, and became popular among them, notwithstanding his death-denouncing fiat.

With all his savage and terrific qualities, he was sensible of the power of female beauty, and capable of love. A war party of the Poncas had made a foray into the lands of the Omahas, and carried off a number of women and horses. The Blackbird was roused to fury, and took the field with all his braves, swearing to " eat up the Ponca nation,"—the Indian threat of exterminating war. The Poncas, sorely pressed, took refuge behind a rude bulwark of earth ; but the Blackbird kept up so galling a fire, that he seemed likely to execute his menace. In their extremity they sent forth a herald, bearing the calumet or pipe of peace, but he was shot down by order of the Blackbird. Another herald was sent forth in similar guise, but he shared a like fate. The Ponca chief then, as a last hope, arrayed his beautiful daughter in her finest ornaments, and sent her forth with a calumet to sue for peace. The charms of the Indian maid touched the stern heart of the Blackbird ; he accepted the pipe at her hand, smoked it, and from that time a peace took place between the Poncas and the Omahas.

This beautiful damsel, in all probability, was the favourite wife whose fate makes so tragic an incident in the story of the Blackbird. Her youth and beauty had gained an absolute sway over his rugged heart, so that he distinguished her above all his other wives. The habitual gratification of his vindictive impulses, however, had taken away from him all mastery over his passions, and rendered him liable to the most furious transports of rage. In one of these his beautiful wife had the misfortune to offend him, when, suddenly drawing his knife, he laid her dead at his feet with a single blow.

In an instant his frenzy was at an end. He gazed for a time in mute bewilderment upon his victim ; then drawing his buffalo robe over his head, he sat down beside the corpse, and remained brooding over his crime and his loss. Three days elapsed, yet the chief continued silent and motionless, tasting no food and apparently sleepless. It was apprehended that he intended to starve himself to death ; his people approached him in trembling awe, and entreated him once more to uncover his face and be comforted ; but he remained unmoved. At length one of his warriors brought in a small child, and, laying it on the ground, placed the foot of the Blackbird upon its neck. The heart of the gloomy savage was touched by this appeal : he threw aside his robe ; made an harangue upon what he had done ; and from that time forward seemed to have thrown the load of grief and remorse from his mind.

He still retained his fatal and mysterious secret, and with it his terrific power ; but, though able to deal death to his enemies, he could not avert it from himself or his friends. In 1802 the smallpox, that dreadful pestilence, which swept over the land like a fire over the prairies, made its appearance in the village of the Omahas. The poor savages saw with dismay the ravages of a malady, loathsome and agonizing in its details, and which set the skill and experience of their conjurers and medicine-men at defiance. In a little while, two-thirds of the population were swept from the face of the earth, and the doom of the rest seemed sealed. The stoicism of the warriors was at an end ; they became wild and desperate ; some set fire to the village as a last means of checking the pestilence ; others, in a frenzy of despair, put their wives and children to death, that they might be spared the agonies of an inevitable disease, and that they might all go to some better country.

When the general horror and dismay was at its height, the Blackbird himself was struck down with the malady. The poor savages, when they saw their chief in danger, forgot their own miseries, and surrounded his dying bed. His dominant spirit and his love for the white men, were evinced in his latest breath, with which he designated his place of sepulture. It was to be on a hill or promontory, upwards of four hundred feet in height, overlooking a great extent of the Missouri, from whence he had been accustomed to watch for the barks of the white men. The Missouri washes the base of the promontory, and, after winding and doubling in many links and mazes in the plain below, returns to within nine hundred yards of its starting place; so that for thirty miles navigating with sail and oar, the voyageur finds himself continually near to this singular promontory as if spell-bound.

It was the dying command of the Blackbird that his tomb should be upon the summit of this hill, in which he should be interred, seated on his favourite horse, that he might overlook his ancient domain, and behold the barks of the white men as they came up the river to trade with his people.

His dying orders were faithfully obeyed. His corpse was placed astride of his war-steed, and a mound raised over them on the summit of the hill. On the top of the mound was erected a staff, from which fluttered the banner of the chieftain, and the scalps that he had taken in battle. When the expedition under Mr. Hunt visited that part of the country, the staff still remained with the fragments of the banner; and the superstitious rite of placing food from time to time on the mound, for the use of the deceased, was still observed by the Omahas. That rite has since fallen into disuse, for the tribe itself is almost extinct. Yet the hill of the Blackbird continues an object of veneration to the wandering savage, and a landmark to the voyager of the Missouri; and as the civilized traveller comes within sight of its spell-bound crest, the mound is pointed out to him from afar, which still encloses the grim skeletons of the Indian warrior and his horse.

CHAPTER XVII.

Rumours of danger from the Sioux Tetons—Ruthless character of those savages—Pirates of the Missouri—Their affair with Crooks and Mr. M'Lellan —A trading expedition broken up—M'Lellan's vow of vengeance—Uneasiness in the camp—Desertions—Departure from the Omaha village—Meeting with Jones and Carson, two adventurous trappers —Scientific pursuits of Messrs. Bradbury and Nuttall—Zeal of a botanist—Adventure of Mr. Bradbury with a Ponca Indian—Expedient of the pocket compass and microscope—A messenger from Lisa—Motives for pressing forward.

WHILE Mr. Hunt and his party were sojourning at the village of the Omahas, three Sioux Indians of the Yankton Ahna tribe arrived, bringing unpleasant intelligence. They reported that certain bands of the Sioux Tetons, who inhabited a region many leagues further up the Missouri, were near at hand, awaiting the approach of a party, with the avowed intention of opposing their progress.

The Sioux Tetons were at that time a sort of pirates of the Missouri, who considered the well-freighted bark of the American trader fair game. They had their own traffic with the British merchants of the north-west, who brought them regular supplies of merchandise by way of the river St. Peter. Being thus independent of the Missouri traders for their supplies, they kept no terms with them, but plundered them whenever they had an opportunity. It has been insinuated that they were prompted to these outrages by the British merchants, who wished to keep off all rivals in the Indian trade; but others allege another motive, and one savouring of a deeper policy. The Sioux, by their intercourse with the British traders, had acquired the use of fire-arms, which had given them vast superiority over other tribes higher up the Missouri. They had made themselves also, in a manner, factors for the upper tribes, supplying them at second hand, and at greatly advanced prices, with goods derived from the white men. The Sioux, therefore, saw with jealousy the American traders pushing their way up the Missouri; foreseeing that the upper tribes would thus be relieved from all dependance on them for supplies; nay, what was worse, would be furnished with fire-arms, and elevated into formidable r vals.

We have already alluded to a case in which Mr. Crooks and Mr. M'Lellan had been interrupted in a trading voyage by these ruffians of the river; and, as it is in some degree connected with circumstances hereafter to be related, we shall specify it more particularly.

About two years before the time of which we are treating, Crooks and M'Lellan were ascending the river in boats with a party of about forty men, bound on one of their trading expeditions to the upper tribes. In one of the bends of the river, where the channel made a deep curve under the impending banks, they suddenly heard yells and shouts above them, and beheld the cliffs overhead covered with armed savages. It was a band of Sioux warriors, upwards of six hundred strong. They brandished their weapons in a menacing manner, and ordered the boats to turn back and land lower down the river. There was no disputing these commands, for they had the power to shower destruction upon the white men, without risk to themselves. Crooks and M'Lellan, therefore, turned back with feigned alacrity; and, landing, had an interview with the Sioux. The latter forbade them, under pain of exterminating hostility, from attempting to proceed up the river, but offered to trade peacefully with them if they would halt where they were. The party, being principally composed of voyageurs, was too weak to contend with so superior a force, and one so easily augmented; they pretended, therefore, to comply cheerfully with their arbitrary dictation, and immediately proceeded to cut down trees and erect a trading house. The warrior band departed for their village, which was about twenty miles distant, to collect objects of traffic; they left six or eight of their number, however, to keep watch upon the white men, and scouts were continually passing to and fro with intelligence.

Mr. Crooks saw that it would be impossible to prosecute his voyage without the danger of having his boats plundered, and a great part of his men massacred; he determined, however, not to be entirely frustrated in the objects of his expedition. While he continued, therefore, with great apparent earnestness and assiduity, the construction of the trading house, he despatched the hunters and trappers of his party in a canoe, to make their way up the river to the original place of destination, there to busy themselves in trapping and collecting peltries, and to await his arrival at some future period.

As soon as the detachment had had sufficient time to ascend the hostile country of the Sioux, Mr. Crooks suddenly broke up his feigned trading establishment, embarked his men and effects, and, after giving the astonished rear-guard of savages a galling and indignant message to take to their countrymen, pushed down the river with all speed, sparing neither oar nor paddle, day nor night, until fairly beyond the swoop of these river hawks.

What increased the irritation of Messrs. Crooks and M'Lellan at this mortifying check to their gainful enterprise, was the information that a rival trader was at the bottom of it; the Sioux, it is said, having been instigated to this outrage by Mr. Manuel Lisa, the leading partner and agent of the Missouri Fur Company, already mentioned. This intelligence, whether true or false, so roused the fiery temper of M'Lellan, that he swore, if ever he fell in with Lisa in the Indian country, he would shoot him on the spot; a mode of redress perfectly in unison with the character of the man, and the code of honour prevalent beyond the frontier.

If Crooks and M'Lellan had been exasperated by the insolent conduct of the Sioux Tetons, and the loss which it had occasioned, those freebooters had been no less indignant at being outwitted by the white men, and disappointed of their anticipated gains, and it was apprehended they would be particularly hostile against the present expedition, when they should learn that these gentlemen were engaged in it.

All these causes of uneasiness were concealed as much as possible from the Canadian voyageurs, lest they should become intimidated; it was impossible, however, to prevent the rumours brought by the Indians from leaking out, and they became subjects of gossiping and exaggeration. The chief of the Omahas, too, on returning from a hunting excursion, reported that two men had been killed some

distance above, by a band of Sioux.   This added to the
fears that already began to be excited.   The voyageurs
pictured to themselves bands of fierce warriors stationed
along each bank of the river, by whom they would be exposed to be shot down in their boats ; or lurking hordes,
who would set on them at night, and massacre them in their
encampments.   Some lost heart, and proposed to return,
rather than fight their way, and, in a manner, run the
gauntlet through the country of these piratical marauders.
In fact, three men deserted while at this village.   Luckily,
their place was supplied by three others who happened to
be there, and who were prevailed on to join the expedition
by promises of liberal pay, and by being fitted out and
equipped in complete style.

The irresolution and discontent visible among some of
his people, arising at times almost to mutiny, and the occasional desertions which took place while thus among
friendly tribes, and within reach of the frontiers, added
greatly to the anxieties of Mr. Hunt, and rendered him
eager to press forward and leave a hostile tract behind
him, so that it would be as perilous to return as to keep
on, and no one would dare to desert.

Accordingly, on the 15th of May he departed from the
village of the Omahas, and set forward towards the country of the formidable Sioux Tetons.   For the first five
days, they had a fair and fresh breeze, and the boats made
good progress.   The wind then came ahead, and the river
beginning to rise, and to increase in rapidity, betokened
the commencement of the annual flood, caused by the
melting of the snow on the Rocky mountains, and the
vernal rains of the upper prairies.

As they were now entering a region where foes might
be lying in wait on either bank, it was determined, in
hunting for game, to confine themselves principally to the
islands, which sometimes extend to considerable length,
and are beautifully wooded, affording abundant pasturage
and shade.   On one of these they killed three buffaloes
and two elks, and, halting on the edge of a beautiful
prairie, made a sumptuous hunter's repast.   They had not
long resumed their boats and pulled along the river banks,

when they descried a canoe approaching navigated by two men, whom, to their surprise, they ascertained to be white men. They proved to be two of those strange and fearless wanderers of the wilderness, the trappers. Their names were Benjamin Jones and Alexander Carson. They had been for two years past hunting and trapping near the head of the Missouri, and were thus floating for thousands of miles in a cockle-shell, down a turbulent stream, through regions infested with savage tribes, yet apparently as easy and unconcerned as if navigating securely in the midst of civilization.

The acquisition of two such hardy, experienced, and dauntless hunters, was peculiarly desirable at the present moment. They needed but little persuasion. The wilderness is the home of the trapper; like the sailor, he cares but little to which point of the compass he steers; and Jones and Carson readily abandoned their voyage to St. Louis, and turned their faces towards the Rocky mountains and the Pacific.

The two naturalists, Mr. Bradbury and Mr. Nuttall, who had joined the expedition at St. Louis, still accompanied it, and pursued their researches on all occasions. Mr. Nuttall seems to have been exclusively devoted to his scientific pursuits. He was a zealous botanist, and all his enthusiasm was awakened at beholding a new world, as it were, opening upon him in the boundless prairies, clad in the vernal and variegated robe of unknown flowers. Whenever the boats landed at meal times, or for any temporary purpose, he would spring on shore and set out on a hunt for new specimens. Every plant or flower of a rare or unknown species was eagerly seized as a prize. Delighted with the treasures spreading themselves out before him, he went groping and stumbling along among a wilderness of sweets, forgetful of every thing but his immediate pursuit, and had often to be sought after when the boats were about to resume their course. At such times he would be found far off in the prairies, or up the course of some petty stream laden with plants of all kinds.

The Canadian voyageurs, who are a class of people

that know nothing out of their immediate line, and with constitutional levity make a jest of any thing they cannot understand, were extremely puzzled by this passion for collecting what they considered mere useless weeds. When they saw the worthy botanist coming back heavy laden with his specimens, and treasuring them up as carefully as a miser would his hoard, they used to make merry among themselves at his expense, regarding him as some whim-sical kind of madman.

Mr. Bradbury was less exclusive in his tastes and habits, and combined the hunter and sportsman with the natural-ist. He took his rifle or fowling-piece with him in his geological researches, conformed to the hardy and rugged habits of the men around him, and of course gained favour in their eyes. He had a strong relish for incident and adventure, was curious in observing savage manners and savage life, and ready to join any hunting or other excur-sion. Even now, that the expedition was proceeding through a dangerous neighbourhood, he could not check his propensity to ramble. Having observed, on the even-ing of the 22nd of May, that the river ahead made a great bend which would take up the navigation of the follow-ing day, he determined to profit by the circumstance. On the morning of the 22nd, therefore, instead of embarking, he filled his shot-pouch with parched corn, for provisions, and set off to cross the neck on foot and meet the boats in the afternoon at the opposite side of the bend. Mr. Hunt felt uneasy at his venturing thus alone, and reminded him that he was in an enemy's country; but Mr. Bradbury made light of the danger, and started off cheerily upon his ramble. His day was passed pleasantly in traversing a beautiful track, making botanical and geological researches, and observing the habits of an extensive village of prairie dogs, at which he made several ineffectual shots, without considering the risk he run of attracting the attention of any savages that might be lurking in the neighbourhood. In fact, he had totally forgotten the Sioux Tetons, and all the perils of the country, when, about the middle of the afternoon, as he stood near the river bank, and was look-ing out for the boat, he suddenly felt a hand laid on his

shoulder. Starting and turning round, he beheld a naked
savage with a bow bent, and the arrow pointed at his
breast. In an instant his gun was levelled and his hand
upon the lock. The Indian drew his bow still further,
but forbore to launch the shaft. Mr. Bradbury, with admirable presence of mind, reflected that the savage, if
hostile in his intents, would have shot him without giving
him a chance of defence; he paused, therefore, and held
out his hand. The other took it in sign of friendship,
and demanded in the Osage language whether he was a
Big Knife, or American. He answered in the affirmative,
and inquired whether the other were a Sioux. To his
great relief he found that he was a Ponca. By this time
two other Indians came running up, and all three laid
hold of Mr. Bradbury, and seemed disposed to compel him
to go off with them among the hills. He resisted, and
sitting down on a sand hill, contrived to amuse them with
a pocket-compass. When the novelty of this was exhausted they again seized him, but he now produced
a small microscope. This new wonder again fixed the
attention of the savages, who have far more curiosity
than it has been the custom to allow them. While thus
engaged, one of them suddenly leaped up and gave a
war-whoop. The hand of the hardy naturalist was again
on his gun, and he was prepared to make battle, when the
Indian pointed down the river and revealed the true
cause of his yell. It was the mast of one of the boats
appearing above the low willows which bordered the
stream. Mr. Bradbury felt infinitely relieved by the sight.
The Indians on their part now showed signs of apprehension, and were disposed to run away; but he assured them
of good treatment and something to drink if they would
accompany him on board of the boats. They lingered for
a time, but disappeared before the boats came to land.

On the following morning they appeared at the camp
accompanied by several of their tribe. With them came
also a white man, who announced himself as a messenger
bearing missives for Mr. Hunt. In fact he brought a letter from Mr. Manuel Lisa, partner and agent of the
Missouri Fur Company. As has already been mentioned,

this gentleman was going in search of Mr. Henry and his party, who had been dislodged from the forks of the Missouri by the Blackfeet Indians, and had shifted his post somewhere beyond the Rocky mountains. Mr. Lisa had left St. Louis three weeks after Mr. Hunt, and having heard of the hostile intentions of the Sioux, had made the greatest exertions to overtake him, that they might pass through the dangerous part of the river together. He had twenty stout oarsmen in his service, and they plied their oars so vigorously, that he had reached the Omaha village just four days after the departure of Mr. Hunt. From this place he despatched the messenger in question, trusting to his overtaking the barges as they toiled up against the stream, and were delayed by the windings of the river. The purport of his letter was to entreat Mr. Hunt to wait until he could come up with him, that they might unite their forces and be a protection to each other in their perilous course through the country of the Sioux. In fact, as it was afterwards ascertained, Lisa was apprehensive that Mr. Hunt would do him some ill office with the Sioux bands, securing his own passage through their country by pretending that he with whom they were accustomed to trade, was on his way to them with a plentiful supply of goods. He feared, too, that Crooks and M'Lellan would take this opportunity to retort upon him the perfidy which they accused him of having used two years previously among these very Sioux. In this respect, however, he did them signal injustice. There was no such thing as covert design or treachery in their thought; but M'Lellan, when he heard that Lisa was on his way up the river, renewed his open threat of shooting him the moment he met him on Indian land.

The representations made by Crooks and M'Lellan of the treachery they had experienced, or fancied, on the part of Lisa, had great weight with Mr. Hunt, especially when he recollected the obstacles that had been thrown in his own way by that gentleman at St. Louis. He doubted, therefore, the fair dealing of Lisa, and feared that, should they enter the Sioux country together, the latter might make use of his influence with that tribe, as he had in the case of Crooks and M'Lellan, and instigate them to oppose his progress up the river.

He sent back, therefore, an answer calculated to beguile Lisa, assuring him that he would wait for him at the Poncas village, which was but a little distance in advance; but no sooner had the messenger departed, than he pushed forward with all diligence, barely stopping at the village to procure a supply of dried buffalo meat, and hastening to leave the other party as far behind as possible, thinking there was less to be apprehended from the open hostility of Indian foes, than from the quiet strategy of an Indian trader.

CHAPTER XVIII.

Camp gossip—Deserters—Recruits—Kentucky hunters—A veteran woodman —Tidings of Mr. Henry—Danger from the Blackfeet—Alteration of plans— Scenery of the river—Buffalo roads—Iron ore—Country of the Sioux—A land of danger—Apprehensions of the voyageurs—Indian scouts—Threatened hostilities—A council of war—An array of battle—A parley—The pipe of peace—Speech-making.

IT was about noon when the party left the Poncas village, about a league beyond which they passed the mouth of the Quicourt, or Rapid river (called, in the original French, *l'Eau Qui Court*). After having proceeded some distance further, they landed, and encamped for the night. In the evening camp, the voyageurs gossiped, as usual, over the events of the day; and especially over intelligence picked up among the Poncas. These Indians had confirmed the previous reports of the hostile intentions of the Sioux, and had assured them that five tribes, or bands, of that fierce nation were actually assembled higher up the river, and waiting to cut them off. This evening gossip, and the terrific stories of Indian warfare to which it gave rise, produced a strong effect upon the imaginations of the irresolute; and on the morning it was discovered that the two men, who had joined the party at the Maha village, and been so bounteously fitted out, had deserted in the course of the night, carrying with them all their equipments. As it was known that one of them could not swim, it was hoped that the banks of the Quicourt river would bring them to a halt. A general pursuit was therefore instituted, but without success.

On the following morning (May 26th), as they were all on shore, breakfasting on one of the beautiful banks of the river, they observed two canoes descending along the opposite side. By the aid of spy-glasses, they ascertained that there were two white men in one of the canoes, and one in the other. A gun was discharged, which called the attention of the voyageurs, who crossed over. They proved to be three Kentucky hunters, of the true "dreadnought" stamp. Their names were Edward Robinson, John Hoback, and Jacob Rizner. Robinson was a veteran backwoodman, sixty-six years of age. He had been one of the first settlers of Kentucky, and engaged in many of the conflicts of the Indians on "The Bloody Ground." In one of these battles he had been scalped, and he still wore a handkerchief bound round his head to protect the part. These men had passed several years in the upper wilderness. They had been in the service of the Missouri Company under Mr. Henry, and had crossed the Rocky mountains with him in the preceding year, when driven from his post on the Missouri, by the hostilities of the Blackfeet. After crossing the mountains, Mr. Henry had established himself on one of the head branches of the Colombia river. There they had remained with him for some months, hunting and trapping, until, having satisfied their wandering propensities, they felt disposed to return to their families and comfortable homes which they had left in Kentucky. They had accordingly made their way back across the mountains, and down the rivers, and were in full career for St. Louis, when thus suddenly interrupted. The sight of a powerful party of traders, trappers, hunters, and voyageurs, well armed and equipped, furnished at all points, in high health and spirits, and banqueting lustily on the green margin of the river, was a spectacle equally stimulating to these veteran backwoodmen with the glorious array of a campaigning army to an old soldier; but when they learned the grand scope and extent of the enterprise in hand, it was irresistible: homes and families, and all the charms of green Kentucky, vanished from their thoughts; they cast loose their canoes to drift down the stream, and joyfully enlisted in the band of adventurers. They engaged on similar terms with some of the other hunters. The company was to fit them out, and keep them supplied with the requisite equipments and munitions, and they were to yield one half of the produce of their hunting and trapping.

The addition of three such stanch recruits was extremely acceptable at this dangerous part of the river. The knowledge of the country which they had acquired, also, in their journeys, and hunting excursions along the rivers and among the Rocky mountains, was all-important; in fact, the information derived from them induced Mr. Hunt to alter his future course. He had hitherto intended to proceed by the route taken by Lewis and Clarke in their famous exploring expedition, ascending the Missouri to its forks, and thence going, by land, across the mountains. These men informed him, however, that on taking that course he would have to pass through the country infested by the savage tribe of the Blackfeet, and would be exposed to their hostilities; they being, as has already been observed, exasperated to deadly animosity against the whites, on account of the death of one of their tribe by the hands of Captain Lewis. They advised him rather to pursue a route more to the southward, being the same by which they had returned. This would carry them over the mountains about where the head waters of the Platte and the Yellowstone take their rise, at a place much more easy and practicable than that where Lewis and Clarke had crossed. In pursuing this course, also, he would pass through a country abounding with game, where he would have a better chance of procuring a constant supply of provisions than by the other route, and would run less risk of molestation from the Blackfeet. Should he adopt this advice, it would be better for him to abandon the river at the Aricara town, at which he would arrive in the course of a few days. As the Indians of that town possessed horses in abundance, he might purchase a sufficient number of them for his great journey overland, which would commence at that place.

After reflecting on this advice, and consulting with his associates, Mr. Hunt came to the determination to follow the route thus pointed out, in which the hunters engaged to pilot him.

The party continued their voyage with delightful May weather. The prairies bordering on the river were gaily painted with innumerable flowers, exhibiting the motley confusion of colours of a Turkey carpet. The beautiful islands also, on which they occasionally halted, presented the appearance of mingled grove and garden. The trees were often covered with clambering grape vines in blossom, which perfumed the air. Between the stately masses of the groves were grassy lawns and glades, studded with flowers, or interspersed with rose bushes in full bloom. These islands were often the resort of the buffalo, the elk, and the antelope, who had made innumerable paths among the trees and thickets, which had the effect of the mazy walks and alleys of parks and shrubberies. Sometimes, where the river passed between high banks and bluffs, the roads, made by the tramp of buffaloes for many ages along the face of the heights, looked like so many well-travelled highways. At other places, the banks were banded with great veins of iron ore, laid bare by the abrasion of the river. At one place the course of the river was nearly in a straight line for about fifteen miles. The banks sloped gently to its margin, without a single tree, but bordered with grass and herbage of a vivid green. Along each bank, for the whole fifteen miles, extended a stripe, one hundred yards in breadth, of a deep rusty brown, indicating an inexhaustible bed of iron, through the centre of which the Missouri had worn its way. Indications of the continuance of this bed were afterwards observed higher up the river. It is, in fact, one of the mineral magazines which nature has provided in the heart of this vast realm of fertility, and which, in connexion with the immense beds of coal on the same river, seem garnered up as the elements of the future wealth and power of the mighty west.

The sight of these mineral treasures greatly excited the curiosity of Mr. Bradbury, and it was tantalizing to him to be checked in his scientific researches, and obliged to forego his usual rambles on shore ; but they were now entering the fated country of the Sioux Tetons, in which it was dangerous to wander about unguarded.

This country extends for some days' journey along the river, and consists of vast prairies, here and there diversified by swelling hills, and cut up by ravines, the channels of turbid streams in the rainy seasons, but almost destitute of water during the heats of summer. Here and there, on the sides of the hills, or along the alluvial borders and bottoms of the ravines, are groves and skirts of forests ; but for the most part the country presented to the eye a boundless waste, covered with herbage, but without trees.

The soil of this immense region is strongly impregnated with sulphur, copperas, alum, and glauber salts ; its various earths impart a deep tinge to the streams which drain it, and these, with the crumbling of the banks along the Missouri, give to the waters of that river much of the colouring matter with which they are clouded.

Over this vast track the roving bands of the Sioux Tetons hold their vagrant sway ; subsisting by the chase of the buffalo, the elk, the deer, and the antelope, and waging ruthless warfare with other wandering tribes.

As the boats made their way up the stream bordered by this land of danger, many of the Canadian voyageurs, whose fears had been awakened, would regard with a distrustful eye the boundless waste extending on each side. All, however, was silent, and apparently untenanted by a human being. Now and then a herd of deer would be seen feeding tranquilly among the flowery herbage, or a line of buffaloes, like a caravan on its march, moving across the distant profile of the prairie. The Canadians, however, began to apprehend an ambush in every thicket, and to regard the broad tranquil plain as a sailor eyes some shallow and perfidious sea, which, though smooth and safe to the eye, conceals the lurking rock or treacherous shoal. The very name of a Sioux became a watchword of terror. Not an elk, a wolf, or any other animal, could appear on the hills, but the boats resounded with exclamations from stem to stern, "*Voilà les Sioux!*" "*voilà les Sioux!*" (There are the Sioux! There are the Sioux!) Whenever it was practicable, the night encampment was on some island in the centre of the stream.

On the morning of the 31st of May, as the travellers were breakfasting on the right bank of the river, the usual alarm was given, but with more reason, as two Indians actually made their appearance on a bluff on the opposite or north-east side, and harangued them in a loud voice. As it was impossible at that distance to distinguish what they said, Mr. Hunt, after breakfast, crossed the river with Pierre Dorion, the interpreter, and advanced boldly to converse with them, while the rest remained watching in mute suspense the movements of the parties. As soon as Mr. Hunt landed, one of the Indians disappeared behind the hill, but shortly reappeared on horseback, and went scouring off across the heights. Mr. Hunt held some conference with the remaining savage, and then recrossed the river to his party.

These two Indians proved to be spies or scouts of a large war party encamped about a league off, and numbering two hundred and eighty lodges, or about six hundred warriors, of three different tribes of Sioux; the Yangtons Ahna, the Tetons Bois-brulé, and the Tetons Min-na-kine-azzo. They expected daily to be reinforced by two other tribes, and had been waiting eleven days for the arrival of Mr. Hunt's party, with a determination to oppose their progress up the river; being resolved to prevent all trade with the white men with their enemies the Aricaras, Mandans, and Minatarees. The Indian who had galloped off on horseback had gone to give notice of the approach of the party, so that they might now look out for some fierce scenes with those piratical savages, of whom they had received so many formidable accounts.

The party braced up their spirits to the encounter, and,

re-embarking, pulled resolutely up the stream.   An island
for some time intervened between them and the opposite
side of the river; but on clearing the upper end, they
came in full view of the hostile shore.   There was a ridge
of hills down which the savages were pouring in great
numbers, some on horseback, and some on foot.   Reconnoitring them with the aid of glasses, they perceived that
they were all in warlike array, painted and decorated for
battle.   Their weapons were bows and arrows, and a few
short carbines, and most of them had round shields.   Altogether, they had a wild and gallant appearance, and,
taking possession of a point which commanded the river,
ranged themselves along the bank as if prepared to dispute
the passage.

At sight of this formidable front of war, Mr. Hunt and
his companions held council together.   It was plain that
the rumours they had heard were correct, and the Sioux
were determined to oppose their progress by force of arms.
To attempt to elude them and continue along the river
was out of the question.   The strength of the mid-current
was too violent to be withstood, and the boats were obliged
to ascend along the river banks.   These banks were often
high and perpendicular, affording the savages frequent
stations, from whence, safe themselves, and almost unseen,
they might shower down their missiles upon the boats
below, and retreat at will without danger from pursuit.
Nothing apparently remained, therefore, but to fight or
turn back.   The Sioux far outnumbered them, it is true,
but their own party was about sixty strong, well armed
and supplied with ammunition; and beside their guns and
rifles, they had a swivel and two howitzers mounted in
the boats.   Should they succeed in breaking this Indian
force by one vigorous assault, it was likely they would
be deterred from making any future attack of consequence.   The fighting alternative was, therefore, instantly adopted, and the boats pulled to shore nearly opposite to the hostile force.   Here the arms were all examined and put in order.   The swivel and howitzers were
then loaded with powder and discharged, to let the savages know by the report how formidably they were pro-

vided. The noise echoed along the shores of the river, and must have startled the warriors, who were only accustomed to the sharp reports of rifles. The same pieces were then loaded with as many bullets as they would probably bear; after which the whole party embarked, and pulled across the river. The Indians remained watching them in silence, their painted forms and visages glaring in the sun, and their feathers fluttering in the breeze. The poor Canadians eyed them with rueful glances, and now and then a fearful ejaculation would escape them. " Parblue! this is a sad scrape we are in, brother!" would one mutter to the next oarsman. " Ay, ay," the other would reply, " we are not going to a wedding, my friend!"

When the boats arrived within rifle shot, the hunters and other fighting personages on board seized their weapons, and prepared for action. As they rose to fire, a confusion took place among the savages. They displayed their buffalo robes, raised them with both hands above their heads, and then spread them before them on the ground. At sight of this, Pierre Dorion eagerly cried out to the party not to fire, as this movement was a peaceful signal, and an invitation to a parley. Immediately about a dozen of the principal warriors, separating from the rest, descended to the edge of the river, lighted a fire, seated themselves in a semicircle round it, and, displaying the calumet, invited the party to land. Mr. Hunt now called a council of the partners on board of his boat. The question was, whether to trust the amicable overtures of these ferocious people? It was determined in the affirmative; for, otherwise, there was no alternative but to fight them. The main body of the party were ordered to remain on board of the boats, keeping within shot, and prepared to fire in case of any signs of treachery; while Mr. Hunt and the other partners (M'Kenzie, Crooks, and M'Lellan), proceeded to land, accompanied by the interpreter and Mr. Bradbury. The chiefs, who awaited them on the margin of the river, remained seated in their semicircle, without stirring a limb or moving a muscle, motionless as so many statues. Mr. Hunt and his companions advanced without hesitation, and took their seats on the sand so as to complete the circle. The band of warriors who lined the banks above stood looking down in silent groups and clusters, some ostentatiously equipped and decorated, others entirely naked, but fantastically painted, and all variously armed.

The pipe of peace was now brought forward with due cere-mony. The bowl was of a species of red stone resembling porphyry : the stem was six feet in length, decorated with tufts of horsehair dyed red. The pipebearer stepped within the circle, lighted the pipe, held it towards the sun, then towards the different points of the compass, after which he handed it to the principal chief. The latter smoked a few whiffs, then, holding the head of the pipe in his hand, of-fered the other end to Mr. Hunt, and to each one succes-sively in the circle. When all had smoked, it was consi-dered that an assurance of good faith and amity had been interchanged. Mr. Hunt now made a speech in French, which was interpreted as he proceeded by Pierre Dorion. He informed the Sioux of the real object of the expedition of himself and his companions, which was, not to trade with any of the tribes up the river, but to cross the moun-tains to the great salt lake in the west, in search of some of their brothers, whom they had not seen for eleven months. That he had heard of the intention of the Sioux to oppose his passage, and was prepared, as they might see, to effect it at all hazards ; nevertheless, his feelings towards the Sioux were friendly, in proof of which he had brought them a present of tobacco and corn. So saying, he ordered about fifteen carottes of tobacco, and as many bags of corn, to be brought from the boat and laid in a heap near the council fire.

The sight of these presents mollified the chieftain, who had doubtless been previously rendered considerate by the resolute conduct of the white men, the judicious disposi-tion of their little armament, the completeness of their equipments, and the compact array of battle which they presented. He made a speech in reply, in which he stated the object of their hostile assemblage, which had been merely to prevent supplies of arms and ammunition from going to the Aricaras, Mandans, and Minatarees, with whom they were at war; but being now convinced that the party were carrying no supplies of the kind, but merely proceeding in quest of their brothers beyond the mountains, they would not impede them in their voyage. He concluded by thanking them for their present, and advising them to encamp on the opposite side of the river, as he had some young men among his warriors for whose discretion he could not be answerable, and who might be troublesome.

Here ended the conference: they all arose, shook hands, and parted. Mr. Hunt and his companions re-embarked, and the boats proceeded on their course unmolested.

END OF THE FIRST VOLUME.

VOLUME THE SECOND.

CHAPTER I.

The great bend of the Missouri—Crooks and M'Lellan meet with two of their Indian opponents—Wanton outrage of a white man the cause of Indian hostility —Dangers and precautions—An Indian war party—Dangerous situation of Mr. Hunt—A friendly encampment feasting and dancing— Approach of Manuel Lisa and his party—A grim meeting between old rivals —Pierre Dorion in a fury—A burst of chivalry.

On the afternoon of the following day (June 1st) they arrived at the great bend, where the river winds for about thirty miles round a circular peninsula, the neck of which is not above two thousand yards across. On the succeeding morning, at an early hour, they descried two Indians standing on a high bank of the river, waving and spreading their buffalo robes in signs of amity. They immediately pulled to shore and landed. On approaching the savages, however, the latter showed evident symptoms of alarm, spreading out their arms horizontally, according to their mode of supplicating clemency. The reason was soon explained. They proved to be two chiefs of the very war party that had brought Messrs. Crooks and M'Lellan to a stand two years before, and obliged them to escape down the river. They ran to embrace these gentlemen, as if delighted to meet with them; yet they evidently feared some retaliation of their past misconduct, nor were they quite at ease until the pipe of peace had been smoked.

Mr. Hunt having been informed that the tribe to which these men belonged had killed three white men during the preceding summer, reproached them with the crime,

and demanded their reasons for such savage hostility.
" We kill white men," replied one of the chiefs, " because
white men kill us. That very man," added he, pointing
to Carson, one of the new recruits, " killed one of our
brothers last summer. The three white men were slain to
avenge his death."

The chief was correct in his reply. Carson admitted
that, being with a party of Aricaras on the banks of the
Missouri, and seeing a war party of Sioux on the opposite side, he had fired with his rifle across. It was a
random shot, made without much expectation of effect,
for the river was full half a mile in breadth. Unluckily it
brought down a Sioux warrior, for whose wanton destruction threefold vengeance had been taken, as had been
stated. In this way outrages are frequently committed
on the natives by thoughtless or mischievous white men ;
the Indians retaliate according to a law of their code,
which requires blood for blood; their act, of what with
them is pious vengeance, resounds throughout the land,
and is represented as wanton and unprovoked ; the neighbourhood is roused to arms ; a war ensues, which ends in
the destruction of half the tribe, the ruin of the rest, and
their expulsion from their hereditary homes. Such is too
often the real history of Indian warfare, which in general
is traced up only to some vindictive act of a savage;
while the outrage of the scoundrel white man that provoked it is sunk in silence.

The two chiefs, having smoked their pipe of peace
and received a few presents, departed well satisfied. In a
little while two others appeared on horseback, and rode
up abreast of the boats. They had seen the presents
given to their comrades, but were dissatisfied with them,
and came after the boats to ask for more. Being somewhat peremptory and insolent in their demands, Mr. Hunt
gave them a flat refusal, and threatened, if they or any of
their tribe followed him with similar demands, to treat
them as enemies. They turned and rode off in a furious
passion. As he was ignorant what force these chiefs
might have behind the hills, and as it was very possible
they might take advantage of some pass of the river to

attack the boats, Mr. Hunt called all stragglers on board,
and prepared for such emergency. It was agreed that
the large boat commanded by Mr. Hunt should ascend
along the north-east side of the river, and the three smaller
boats along the south side. By this arrangement each
party would command a view of the opposite heights
above the heads and out of the sight of their companions,
and could give the alarm should they perceive any Indians
lurking there. The signal of alarm was to be two shots
fired in quick succession.

The boats proceeded for the greater part of the day
without seeing any signs of an enemy. About four
o'clock in the afternoon, the large boat, commanded by
Mr. Hunt, came to where the river was divided by a long
sand bar, which apparently, however, left a sufficient
channel between it and the shore along which they were
advancing. He kept up this channel, therefore, for some
distance until the water proved too shallow for the boat.
It was necessary, therefore, to put about, return down
the channel, and pull round the lower end of the sand
bar into the main stream. Just as he had given orders to
this effect to his men, two signal guns were fired from the
boats on the opposite side of the river. At the same moment a file of savage warriors was observed pouring down
from the impending bank, and gathering on the shore at
the lower end of the bar. They were evidently a war
party, being armed with bows and arrows, battle-clubs
and carbines, and round bucklers of buffalo hide, and
their naked bodies were painted with black and white
stripes. The natural inference was, that they belonged
to the two tribes of Sioux which had been expected by
the great war party, and that they had been invited to
hostility by the two chiefs who had been enraged by the
refusal and the menace of Mr. Hunt. Here then was a
fearful predicament. Mr. Hunt and his crew seemed
caught as it were in a trap. The Indians, to the number
of about a hundred, had already taken possession of a
point near which the boat would have to pass; others
kept pouring down the bank, and it was probable that
some would remain posted on the top of the height.

The hazardous situation of Mr. Hunt was perceived by those in the other boats, and they hastened to his assistance. They were at some distance above the sand bar, however, and on the opposite side of the river, and saw, with intense anxiety, the number of savages continually augmenting, at the lower end of the channel, so that the boat would be exposed to a fearful attack before they could render them any assistance. Their anxiety increased as they saw Mr. Hunt and his party descending the channel, and dauntlessly approaching the point of danger; but it suddenly changed into surprise on beholding the boat pass by the savage hoard unmolested, and steer out safely into the broad river.

The next moment the whole band of warriors was in motion. They ran along the banks until they were opposite to the boats, then, throwing by their weapons and buffalo robes, plunged into the river, waded and swam off to the boats, and surrounded them in crowds, seeking to shake hands with every individual on board; for the Indians have long since found this to be the white man's token of amity, and they carry it to an extreme.

All uneasiness was now at an end. The Indians proved to be a war party of Aricaras, Mandans, and Minatarees, consisting of three hundred warriors, and bound on a foray against the Sioux. Their war plans were abandoned for the present, and they determined to return to the Aricara town, where they hoped to obtain from the white men arms and ammunition that would enable them to take the field with advantage over their enemies.

The boats now sought the first convenient place for encamping. The tents were pitched; the warriors fixed their camp at about a hundred yards distant; provisions were furnished from the boats sufficient for all parties; there was hearty though rude feasting in both camps, and in the evening the red warriors entertained their white friends with dances and songs, that lasted until after midnight.

On the following morning (July 3), the travellers reembarked, and took a temporary leave of their Indian

friends, who intended to proceed immediately for the Aricara town, where they expected to arrive in three days,
long before the boats could reach there.   Mr. Hunt had
not proceeded far before the chief came galloping along
the shore, and made signs for a parley.   He said his
people could not go home satisfied unless they had something to take with them to prove that they had met with
the white men.   Mr. Hunt understood the drift of the
speech, and made the chief a present of a cask of powder,
a bag of balls, and three dozen of knives, with which he
was highly pleased.   While the chief was receiving these
presents, an Indian came running along the shore and announced that a boat, filled with white men, was coming up
the river.   This was by no means agreeable tidings to Mr.
Hunt, who directly concluded it to be the boat of Mr.
Manuel Lisa ; and he was vexed to find that alert and
adventurous trader upon his heels, whom he had hoped to
have out manœuvred, and left far behind.   Lisa, however,
was too much experienced in the wiles of Indian trade to
be lulled by the promise of waiting for him at the Poncas
village ; on the contrary, he had allowed himself no repose, and had strained every nerve to overtake the rival
party, and, availing himself of the moonlight, had even
sailed during a considerable part of the night.   In this
he was partly prompted by his apprehensions of the Sioux,
having met a boat which had probably passed Mr. Hunt's
party in the night, and which had been fired into by these
savages.

On hearing that Lisa was so near at hand, Mr. Hunt
perceived that it was useless to attempt any longer to evade
him ; after proceeding a few miles further, therefore, he
came to a halt, and waited for him to come up.   In a
little while the barge of Lisa made its appearance.   It
came sweeping gently up the river, manned by his twenty
stout oarsmen, and armed by a swivel mounted at the
bow.   The whole number on board amounted to twenty-
six men ; among whom was Mr. Henry Brackenbridge,
then a young, enterprising man, who was a mere passenger,
tempted by notions of curiosity to accompany Mr. Lisa.

He has since made himself known by various writings, among which may be noted a narrative of this very voyage.

The approach of Lisa, while it was regarded with uneasiness by Mr. Hunt, roused the ire of M'Lellan; who, calling to mind old grievances, began to look round for his rifle, as if he really intended to carry his threat into execution, and shoot him on the spot; and it was with some difficulty that Mr. Hunt was enabled to restrain his ire, and prevent a scene of outrage and confusion.

The meeting between the two leaders, thus mutually distrustful, could not be very cordial; and as to Messrs. Crooks and M'Lellan, though they refrained from any outbreak, yet they regarded in grim defiance their old rival and underplotter. In truth, a general distrust prevailed throughout the party concerning Lisa and his intentions. They considered him artful and slippery, and secretly anxious for the failure of their expedition. There being now nothing more to be apprehended from the Sioux, they suspected that Lisa would take advantage of his twenty-oared barge to leave them and get first among the Aricaras. As he had traded with those people, and possessed great influence over them, it was feared he might make use of it to impede the business of Mr. Hunt and his party. It was resolved, therefore, to keep a sharp look out upon his movements; and M'Lellan swore that if he saw the least sign of treachery on his part, he would instantly put his old threat into execution.

Notwithstanding these secret jealousies and heart-burnings, the two parties maintained an outward appearance of civility, and for two days continued forward in company with some degree of harmony. On the third day, however, an explosion took place, and it was produced by no less a personage than Pierre Dorion, the half-breed interpreter. It will be recollected that this worthy had been obliged to steal a march from St. Louis, to avoid being arrested for an old whiskey debt which he owed to the Missouri Fur Company, and by which Mr. Lisa had hoped to prevent his enlisting in Mr. Hunt's expedition. Dorion, since the arrival of Lisa, had kept aloof, and regarded him with a sullen and dogged aspect. On the 5th of July the two parties were brought to a halt by a heavy rain, and remained encamped about a hundred yards apart. In the course of the day Lisa undertook to tamper with the faith of Pierre Dorion, and, inviting him on board of his boat, regaled him with his favourite whiskey. When he thought him sufficiently mellowed, he proposed to him to quit the service of his new employers, and return to his old allegiance. Finding him not to be moved by soft words, he called to mind his old debt to the company, and threatened to carry him off by force, in payment of it. The mention of this debt always stirred up the gall of Pierre Dorion, bringing with it the remembrance of the whiskey extortion. A violent quarrel arose between him and Lisa, and he left the boat in high dudgeon. His first step was to repair to the tent of Mr. Hunt, and reveal the attempt that had been made to shake his faith. While he was yet talking, Lisa entered the tent, under the pretext of coming to borrow a towing line. High words instantly ensued between him and Dorion, which ended by the half-breed's dealing him a blow. A quarrel in the " Indian country," however, is not to be settled with fisticuffs. Lisa immediately rushed to his boat for a weapon. Dorion snatched up a pair of pistols belonging to Mr. Hunt, and placed himself in battle array. The noise had roused the camp, and every one pressed to know the cause. Lisa now reappeared upon the field with a knife stuck in his girdle. Mr. Breckenridge, who had tried in vain to mollify his ire, accompanied him to the scene of action. Pierre Dorion's pistols gave him the advantage, and he maintained a most warlike attitude. In the mean time, Crooks and M'Lellan had learnt the cause of the affray, and were each eager to take the quarrel into their own hands. A scene of uproar and hubbub ensued that defies description. M'Lellan would have brought his rifle into play, and settled all old and new grudges by a pull of the trigger, had he not been restrained by Mr. Hunt. That gentleman acted as moderator, endeavouring to prevent a general mêlée; in the midst of the brawl, however, an expression was made use of by Lisa derogatory to his own honour. In an instant, the tranquil spirit of Mr. Hunt was in a flame. He now became as eager to fight as any one on the ground, and challenged Lisa to settle the dispute on the spot with pistols. Lisa repaired to his boat to arm himself for the deadly feud. He was followed by Messrs. Bradbury and Breckenridge, who, novices in Indian life and the " chivalry" of the frontier, had no relish for scenes of blood and brawl. By their earnest mediation, the quarrel was with great difficulty brought to a close without bloodshed; but the two leaders of the rival camps separated in anger, and all personal intercourse ceased between them.

CHAPTER II.

Features of the wilderness—Herds of buffalo—Antelopes—Their varieties and habits—John Day—His hunting stratagem—Interview with three Aricaras —Negotiations between the rival parties—The Lefthanded and the Big Man, two Aricara chiefs—Aricara village—Its inhabitants—Ceremonials on landing—A council lodge—Grand conference—Speech of Lisa—Negotiation for horses—Shrewd suggestion of Gray Eyes, an Aricara chief—Encampment of the trading parties.

THE rival parties now coasted along the opposite sides of the river, within sight of each other; the barges of Mr. Hunt always keeping some distance in the advance, lest Lisa should push on and get first to the Aricara village. The scenery and objects, as they proceeded, gave evidence that they were advancing deeper and deeper into the domains of savage nature. Boundless wastes kept extending to the eye, more and more animated by herds of buffalo. Sometimes these unwieldy animals were seen moving in long procession across the silent landscape; at other times they were scattered about, singly or in groups, on the broad enamelled prairies and green acclivities, some cropping the rich pasturage, others reclining amidst the flowery herbage; the whole scene realizing in a manner the old scriptural descriptions of the vast pastoral countries of the Orient, with " cattle upon a thousand hills."

At one place the shores seemed absolutely lined with buffaloes; many were making their way across the stream, snorting, and blowing, and floundering. Numbers, in spite of every effort, were borne by the rapid current within shot of the boats, and several were killed. At another place a number were descried on the beach of a small island, under the shade of the trees, or standing in the water, like cattle, to avoid the flies and the heat of the day.

Several of the best marksmen stationed themselves in the bow of a barge, which advanced slowly and silently, stemming the current with the aid of a broad sail and a fair breeze. The buffaloes stood gazing quietly at the barge as it approached, perfectly unconscious of their danger. The fattest of the herd was selected by the hunters, who all fired together and brought down their victim.

Besides the buffaloes they saw abundance of deer, and frequent gangs of stately elks, together with light troops of sprightly antelopes, the fleetest and most beautiful inhabitants of the prairies.

There are two kinds of antelopes in these regions, one nearly the size of the common deer, the other not much larger than a goat. Their colour is a light gray, or rather dun, slightly spotted with white; and they have small horns like those of the deer, which they never shed. Nothing can surpass the delicate and elegant finish of their limbs, in which lightness, elasticity, and strength are wonderfully combined. All the attitudes and movements of this beautiful animal are graceful and picturesque, and it is altogether a fit subject for the fanciful uses of the poet, as the oft sung gazelle of the east.

Their habits are shy and capricious; they keep on the open plains, are quick to take the alarm, and bound away with a fleetness that defies pursuit. When thus skimming across a prairie in the autumn, their light gray or dun colour blends with the hue of the withered herbage, the swiftness of their motion baffles the eye, and they almost seem unsubstantial forms, driven like gossamer before the wind.

While they thus keep to the open plain and trust to their speed, they are safe ; but they have a prurient curiosity that sometimes betrays them to their ruin.   When they have scud for some distance and left their pursuer behind, they will suddenly stop and turn to gaze at the object of their alarm.   If the pursuit is not followed up they will, after a time, yield to their inquisitive hankering, and return to the place from whence they have been frightened.

John Day, the veteran hunter already mentioned, displayed his experience and skill in entrapping one of these beautiful animals.   Taking advantage of its well known curiosity, he laid down flat among the grass, and putting his handkerchief on the end of his ramrod, waved it gently in the air.   This had the effect of the fabled facination of the rattlesnake.   The antelope gazed at the mysterious object for some time at a distance, then approached timidly, pausing and reconnoitring with increased curiosity; moving round the point of attraction in a circle, but still drawing nearer and nearer, until, being within the range of the deadly rifle, he fell a victim to his curiosity.

On the 10th of June, as the party were making brisk progress with a fine breeze, they met a canoe with three Indians descending the river.   They came to a parley, and brought news from the Aracara village.   The war party, which had caused such sad alarm at the sand bar, had reached the village some days previously, announced the approach of a party of traders, and displayed with great ostentation the presents they had received from them.   On further conversation with these three Indians, Mr. Hunt learned the real danger which he had run, when hemmed up within the sand bar.   The Mandans, who were of the war party, when they saw the boat so completely entrapped and apparently within their power, had been eager for attacking it, and securing so rich a prize.   The Minatarees, also, were nothing loth, feeling in some measure committed in hostility to the whites, in consequence of their tribe having killed two white men above the fort of the Missouri Fur Company.   Fortunately, the Aracaras, who formed the majority of the war party, proved true in their friendship to the whites, and prevented any hostile act, otherwise a bloody affray, and perhaps a horrible massacre, might have ensued.

On the 11th of June, Mr. Hunt and his companions encamped near an island about six miles below the Aricara village. Mr. Lisa encamped, as usual, at no great distance; but the same sullen and jealous reserve, and non-intercourse continued between them. Shortly after pitching the tents, Mr. Breckenridge made his appearance as an ambassador from the rival camp. He came on behalf of his companions, to arrange the manner of making their entrance into the village and of receiving the chiefs ; for every thing of the kind is a matter of grave ceremonial among the Indians.

The partners now expressed frankly their deep distrust of the intentions of Mr. Lisa, and their apprehensions, that out of the jealousy of trade, and resentment of recent disputes, he might seek to instigate the Aricaras against them. Mr. Breckenridge assured them that their suspicions were entirely groundless, and pledged himself that nothing of the kind should take place. He found it difficult, however, to remove their distrust ; the conference, therefore, ended without producing any cordial understanding ; and M'Lellan recurred to his old threat of shooting Lisa the instant he discovered any thing like treachery in his proceedings.

That night the rain fell in torrents, accompanied by thunder and lightning. The camp was deluged, and the bedding and baggage drenched. All hands embarked at an early hour, and set forward for the village. About nine o'clock, when about half way, they met a canoe, on board of which were two Aricara dignataries. One, a fine looking man, much above the common size, was hereditary chief of the village : he was called the Left-handed, on account of a personal peculiarity. The other, a ferocious looking savage, was the war-chief, or generalissimo ; he was known by the name of the Big Man, an appellation he well deserved from his size, for he was of a gigantic frame. Both were of fairer complexion than is usual with savages.

They were accompanied by an interpreter, a French creole, one of those haphazard wights of Gallic origin, who abound upon our frontier, living among the Indians, like one of their own race. He had been twenty years among the Aracaras, had a squaw and a troop of piebald children, and officiated as interpreter to the chiefs. Through this worthy organ the two dignitaries signified to Mr. Hunt their sovereign intention to oppose the further progress of the expedition up the river, unless a boat were left to trade with them. Mr. Hunt, in reply, explained the object of his voyage, and his intention of debarking at their village, and proceeding thence by land; and that he would willingly trade with them for a supply of horses for his journey. With this explanation they were perfectly satisfied; and, putting about, steered for their village to make preparations for the reception of the strangers.

The village of the Rikaras, Aricaras, or Ricarees, for the name is thus variously written, is between the 46th and 47th parallels of north latitude, and fourteen hundred and thirty miles above the mouth of the Missouri. The party reached it about ten o'clock in the morning, but landed on the opposite side of the river, where they spread out their baggage and effects to dry. From hence they commanded an excellent view of the village. It was divided into two portions, about eighty yards apart, being inhabited by two distinct bands. The whole extended about three quarters of a mile along the river bank, and was composed of conical lodges, that looked like so many small hillocks, being wooden frames intertwined with osier, and covered with earth. The plain beyond the village swept up into hills of considerable height, but the whole country was nearly destitute of trees. While they were regarding the village, they beheld a singular fleet coming down the river. It consisted of a number of canoes, each made of a single buffalo hide stretched on sticks, so as to form a kind of circular trough. Each one was navigated by a single squaw, who knelt in the bottom and paddled, towing after her frail bark a bundle of floating wood intended for firing. This kind of canoe is in frequent use among the Indians; the buffalo hide being easily made up into a bundle and transported on horseback : it is very serviceable in conveying baggage across the rivers.

The great number of horses grazing around the village, and scattered over the neighbouring hills and valleys, bespoke the equestrian habits of the Aricaras, who are admirable horsemen. Indeed, in the number of his horses consists the wealth of an Indian of the prairies ; who resembles an Arab in his passion for this noble animal, and in his adroitness in the management of it.

After a time, the voice of the sovereign chief, " the Lefthanded," was heard across the river, announcing that the council lodge was preparing, and inviting the white men to come over. The river was half a mile in width, yet every word uttered by the chieftain was heard. This may be partly attributed to the distinct manner in which every syllable of the compound words in the Indian languages is articulated and accented ; but in truth, a savage warrior might often rival Achilles himself for force of lungs.*

Now came the delicate point of management ; how the two rival parties were to conduct their visit to the village with proper circumspection and due decorum. Neither of the leaders had spoken to each other since their quarrel. All communication had been by ambassadors. Seeing the jealousy entertained of Lisa, Mr. Breckenridge, in his negotiation, had arranged that a deputation from each party should cross the river at the same time, so that neither would have the first access to the ear of the Ari caras.

The distrust of Lisa, however, had increased in proportion as they approached the sphere of action, and M'Lellan, in particular, kept a vigilant eye upon his motions, swearing to shoot him if he attempted to cross the river first.

About two o'clock the large boat of Mr. Hunt was manned, and he stepped on board, accompanied by Messrs. M'Kenzie and M'Lellan ; Lisa at the same time embarked in his barge ; the two deputations amounted in

* Bradbury, p. 110.

all to fourteen persons, and never was any movement of rival potentates conducted with more wary exactness.

They landed amidst a rabble crowd, and were received on the bank by the lefthanded chief, who conducted them into the village with grave courtesy; driving to the right and left the swarms of old squaws, imp-like boys, and vagabond dogs, with which the place abounded. They wound their way between the cabins, which looked like dirt-heaps huddled together without any plan, and surrounded by old palisades; all filthy in the extreme, and redolent of villanous smells.

At length they arrived at the council lodge. It was somewhat spacious, and formed of four forked trunks of trees placed upright, supporting cross beams and a frame of poles interwoven with osiers, and the whole covered with earth. A hole sunken in the centre formed the fire-place, and immediately above was a circular hole in the apex of the lodge, to let out the smoke and let in the day-light. Around the lodge were recesses for sleeping, like the berths on board ships, screened from view by curtains of dressed skins. At the upper end of the lodge was a kind of hunting and warlike trophy consisting of two buf-falo heads, garishly painted, surmounted by shields, bows, quivers of arrows, and other weapons.

On entering the lodge the chief pointed to mats or cushions which had been placed around for the strangers, and on which they seated themselves, while he placed himself on a kind of stool. An old man then came for-ward with the pipe of peace or good fellowship, lighted and handed it to the chief, and then falling back, squatted himself near the door. The pipe was passed from mouth to mouth, each one taking a whiff, which is equivalent to the inviolable pledge of faith, of taking salt together among the ancient Britons. The chief then made a sign to the old pipe-bearer, who seemed to fill, likewise, the station of herald, seneschal, and public crier, for he ascended to the top of the lodge to make proclamation. Here he took his post beside the aperture for the emission of smoke, and the admission of light; the chief dictated from within what he was to proclaim, and he bawled it forth with a force of lungs that resounded over all the village.   In this way he summoned the warriors and great men to council ; every now and then reporting progress to his chief through the hole in the roof.

In a little while the braves and sages began to enter one by one as their names were called or announced, emerging from under the buffalo robe suspended over the entrance instead of a door, stalking across the lodge to the skins placed on the floor, and crouching down on them in silence. In this way twenty entered and took their seats, forming an assemblage worthy of the pencil ; for the Aricaras are a noble race of men, large and well formed, and maintain a savage grandeur and gravity of demeanour in their solemn ceremonials.

All being seated, the old seneschal prepared the pipe of ceremony or council, and having lit it, handed it to the chief.   He inhaled the sacred smoke, gave a puff upward to the heaven, then downward to the earth, then towards the east; after this it was as usual passed from mouth to mouth, each holding it respectfully until his neighbour had taken several whiffs ; and now the grand council was considered as opened in due form.

The chief made an harangue welcoming the white men to his village, and expressing his happiness in taking them by the hand as friends ; but at the same time complaining of the poverty of himself and his people; the usual prelude among Indians to begging or hard bargaining.

Lisa rose to reply, and the eyes of Hunt and his companions were eagerly turned upon him, those of M'Lellan glaring like a basilisk's.   He began by the usual expressions of friendship, and then proceeded to explain the object of his own party.   Those persons, however, said he, pointing to Mr. Hunt and his companions, are of a different party, and are quite distinct in their views ; but, added he, though we are separate parties, we make but one common cause when the safety of either is concerned. Any injury or insult offered to them I shall consider as done to myself, and will resent it accordingly.   I trust, therefore, that you will treat them with the same friendship that you have always manifested for me, doing every thing in your power to serve them and to help them on their way.   The speech of Lisa, delivered with an air of frankness and sincerity, agreeably surprised and disappointed the rival party.

Mr. Hunt then spoke, declaring the object of his journey to the great Salt lake beyond the mountains, and that he should want horses for the purpose, for which he was ready to trade, having brought with him plenty of goods.   Both he and Lisa concluded their speeches by making presents of tobacco.

The lefthanded chieftain in reply promised his friendship and aid to the new comers, and welcomed them to his village.   He added that he had not the number of horses to spare that Mr. Hunt required, and expressed a doubt whether they should be able to part with any. Upon this, another chieftain, called Gray Eyes, made a speech, and declared that they could readily supply Mr. Hunt with all the horses he might want, since if they had not enough in the village, they could easily steal more. This honest expedient immediately removed the main difficulty; but the chief deferred all trading for a day or two, until he should have time to consult with his subordinate chiefs, as to market rates ; for the principal chief of a village, in conjunction with his council, usually fixes the prices at which articles shall be bought and sold, and to them the village must conform.

The council now broke up.   Mr. Hunt transferred his camp across the river at a little distance below the village, and the lefthanded chief placed some of his warriors as a guard to prevent the intrusion of any of his people.   The camp was pitched on the river bank just above the boats. The tents and the men wrapt in their blankets and bivouacking on skins in the open air, surrounded the baggage at night.   Four sentinels also kept watch within sight of each other outside of the camp until midnight, when they were relieved by four others, who mounted guard until daylight.   Mr. Lisa encamped near to Mr. Hunt, between him and the village.

The speech of Mr. Lisa in the council had produced a

pacific effect in the encampment. Though the sincerity of his friendship and good will towards the new company still remained matter of doubt, he was no longer suspected of an intention to play false. The intercourse between the two leaders was, therefore, resumed, and the affairs of both parties went on harmoniously.

CHAPTER III.

An Indian horse fair—Love of the Indians for horses—Scenes in the Aricara village—Indian hospitality—Duties of Indian women—Game habits of the men—Their indolence—Love of gossiping—Rumours of lurking enemies—Scouts—An alarm—A sallying forth—Indian dogs—Return of a horse-stealing party—An Indian deputation—Fresh alarms—Return of a successful war party—Dress of the Aricaras—Indian toilet—Triumphal entry of the war party—Meetings of relations and friends—Indian sensibility—Meeting of a wounded warrior and his mother—Festivities and lamentations.

A TRADE now commenced with the Aricaras under the regulation and supervision of their two chieftains. Lisa sent a part of his goods to the lodge of the lefthanded dignitary, and Mr. Hunt established his mart in the lodge of the Big Man. The village soon presented the appearance of a busy fair; and as horses were in demand, the purlieus and the adjacent plain were like the vicinity of a Tartar encampment; horses were put through all their paces, and horsemen were careering about with that dexterity and grace for which the Aricaras are noted. As soon as a horse was purchased, his tail was cropped, a sure mode of distinguishing him from the horses of the tribe; for the Indians disdain to practise this absurd, barbarous, and indecent mutilation, invented by some mean and vulgar mind, insensible to the merit and perfections of the animal. On the contrary, the Indian horses are suffered to remain in every respect the superb and beautiful animals which nature formed them.

The wealth of an Indian of the far west consists principally in his horses, of which each chief and warrior possesses a great number, so that the plains about an Indian village or encampment are covered with them. These form objects of traffic, or objects of depredation, and in this way pass from tribe to tribe over great tracts of country. The horses owned by the Aricaras are, for the most part, of the wild stock of the prairies; some, however, had been obtained from the Poncas, Pawnees, and other tribes to the south-west, who had stolen them from the Spaniards in the course of horse-stealing expeditions into the Mexican territories. These were to be known by being branded; a Spanish mode of marking horses not practised by the Indians.

As the Aricaras were meditating another expedition against their enemies the Sioux, the articles of traffic most in demand were guns, tomahawks, scalping-knives, powder, ball, and other munitions of war. The price of a horse, as regulated by the chiefs, was commonly ten dollars' worth of goods at first cost. To supply the demand thus suddenly created, parties of young men and braves had sallied forth on expeditions to steal horses; a species of service among the Indians which takes precedence of hunting, and is considered a department of honourable warfare.

While the leaders of the expedition were actively engaged in preparing for the approaching journey, those who had accompanied it for curiosity or amusement, found ample matter for observation in the village and its inhabitants. Wherever they went they were kindly entertained. If they entered a lodge, the buffalo robe was spread before the fire for them to sit down; the pipe was brought, and while the master of the lodge conversed with his guests, the squaw put the earthen vessel over the fire, well filled with dried buffalo meat and pounded corn; for the Indian in his native state, before he has mingled much with white men, and acquired their sordid habits, has the hospitality of the Arab; never does a stranger enter his door without having food placed before him; and never is the food thus furnished made a matter of traffic.

The life of an Indian when at home in his village is a life of indolence and amusement. To the woman is consigned the labours of the household and the field; she arranges the lodge; brings wood for the fire; cooks; jerks venison and buffalo meat; dresses the skins of the animals killed in the chase; cultivates the little patch of maize, pumpkins, and pulse, which furnishes a great part of their provisions. Their time for repose and recreation is at sunset, when the labours of the day being ended, they gather together to amuse themselves with petty games, or to hold gossiping convocations on the tops of their lodges.

As to the Indian, he is a game animal, not to be degraded by useful or menial toil. It is enough that he exposes himself to the hardships of the chase and the perils of war; that he brings home food for his family, and watches and fights for its protection. Every thing else is beneath his attention. When at home, he attends only to his weapons and his horses, preparing the means of future exploit. Or he engages with his comrades in games of dexterity, agility, and strength; or in gambling games in which every thing is put at hazard, with a recklessness seldom witnessed in civilized life.

A great part of the idle leisure of the Indians when at home is passed in groups, squatted together on the bank of a river, on the top of a mound on the prairie, or on the roof of one of their earth-covered lodges, talking over the news of the day, the affairs of the tribe, the events and exploits of their last hunting or fighting expedition, or listening to the stories of old times told by some veteran chronicler; resembling a group of our village quidnuncs and politicians, listening to the prosings of some superannuated oracle, or discussing the contents of an ancient newspaper.

As to the Indian women, they are far from complaining of their lot. On the contrary, they would despise their husbands could they stoop to any menial office, and would think it conveyed an imputation upon their own conduct. It is the worst insult one virago can cast upon another in a moment of altercation. "Infamous woman!" will she cry, "I have seen your husband carrying wood into his lodge to make the fire. Where was his squaw, that he should be obliged to make a woman of himself?"

Mr. Hunt and his fellow travellers had not been many days at the Aricara village, when rumours began to circulate that the Sioux had followed them up, and that a war party, four or five hundred in number, were lurking somewhere in the neighbourhood. These rumours produced much embarrassment in the camp. The white hunters were deterred from venturing forth in quest of game, neither did the leaders think it proper to expose them to such risk. The Aricaras, too, who had suffered greatly in their wars with this cruel and ferocious tribe, were roused to increased vigilance, and stationed mounted scouts upon the neighbouring hills. This, however, is a general precaution among the tribes of the prairies. Those immense plains present a horizon like the ocean, so that any object of importance can be descried afar, and information communicated to a great distance. The scouts are stationed on the hills, therefore, to look out both for game and for enemies, and are, in a manner, living telegraphs conveying their intelligence by concerted signs. If they wish to give notice of a herd of buffalo in the plain beyond, they gallop backwards and forwards abreast, on the summit of the hill. If they perceive an enemy at hand, they gallop to and fro, crossing each other; at sight of which, the whole village flies to arms.

Such an alarm was given in the afternoon of the 15th. Four scouts were seen crossing and recrossing each other at full gallop, on the summit of a hill about two miles distant down the river. The cry was up that the Sioux were coming. In an instant the village was in an uproar. Men, women, and children were all brawling and shouting; dogs barking, yelping, and howling. Some of the warriors ran for the horses, to gather and drive them in from the prairie, some for their weapons. As fast as they could arm and equip they sallied forth; some on horseback, some on foot. Some hastily arrayed in their war dress, with coronets of fluttering feathers, and their bodies smeared with paint; others naked, and only furnished with the weapons they had snatched up. The women and children gathered on the tops of the lodges, and heightened the confusion of the scene by their vociferation. Old men who could no longer bear arms took similar stations, and harangued the warriors as they passed, exhorting them to valorous deeds. Some of the veterans took arms themselves, and sallied forth with tottering steps. In this way, the savage chivalry of the village, to the number of five hundred, poured forth, helter-skelter, riding and running, with hideous yells and war-whoops, like so many bedlamites or demoniacs let loose.

After a while the tide of war rolled back, but with far less uproar. Either it had been a false alarm, or the enemy had retreated on finding themselves discovered, and quiet was restored to the village. The white hunter continuing to be fearful of ranging this dangerous neighbourhood, fresh provisions began to be scarce in the camp. As a substitute, therefore, for venison and buffalo meat, the travellers had to purchase a number of dogs to be shot and cooked for the supply of the camp. Fortunately, however chary the Indians might be of their horses, they were liberal of their dogs. In fact, these animals swarm about an Indian village as they do about a Turkish town. Not a family but has two or three dozen belonging to it, of all sizes and colours; some, of a superior breed, are used for hunting; others, to draw the sledge, while others, of a mongrel breed, and idle vagabond nature, are fattened for food. They are supposed to be descended from the wolf, and retain something of his savage but cowardly temper, howling rather than barking; showing their teeth and snarling on the slightest provocation, but sneaking away on the least attack.

The excitement of the village continued from day to day. On the day following the alarm just mentioned, several parties arrived from different directions, and were met and conducted by some of the braves to the council lodge, where they reported the events and success of their expeditions, whether of war or hunting; which news was afterwards promulgated throughout the village, by certain old men who acted as heralds or town criers. Among the parties which arrived was one that had been among the Snake nation stealing horses, and returned crowned with success. As they passed in triumph through the village they were cheered by the men, women, and children, collected as usual on the tops of the lodges, and were exhorted by the Nestors of the village to be generous in their dealings with the white men.

The evening was spent in feasting and rejoicing among the relations of the successful warriors; but sounds of grief and wailing were heard from the hills adjacent to the village; the lamentations of women who had lost some relative in the foray.

An Indian village is subject to continual agitations and excitements. The next day arrived a deputation of braves from the Cheyenne or Shienne nation; a broken tribe, cut up, like the Aricaras, by wars with the Sioux, and driven to take refuge among the Black hills, near the sources of the Cheyenne river, from which they derive their name. One of these deputies was magnificently arrayed in a buffalo robe, on which various figures were fancifully embroidered with split quills dyed red and yellow; and the whole was fringed with the slender hoofs of young fawns, that rattled as he walked.

The arrival of this deputation was the signal for another of those ceremonials which occupy so much of Indian life; for no being is more courtly and punctilious, and more observant of etiquette and formality, than an American savage.

The object of the deputation was to give notice of an intended visit of the Shienne (or Cheyenne) tribe to the Aricara village in the course of fifteen days. To this visit Mr. Hunt looked forward, to procure additional horses for his journey; all his bargaining being ineffectual in obtaining a sufficient supply from the Aricaras. Indeed nothing could prevail upon the latter to part with their prime horses, which had been trained to buffalo hunting.

As Mr. Hunt would have to abandon his boats at this place, Mr. Lisa now offered to purchase them, and such of his merchandise as was superfluous, and to pay him in horses, to be obtained at a fort belonging to the Missouri Fur Company situated at the Mandan villages, about a

hundred and fifty miles further up the river.   A bargain
was promptly made, and Mr. Lisa and Mr. Crooks, with
several companions, set out for the fort to procure the
horses.   They returned, after upwards of a fortnight's
absence, bringing with them the stipulated number of
horses.   Still the cavalry was not sufficiently numerous to
convey the party and the baggage and merchandise, and
a few days more were required to complete the arrangements for the journey.

On the 9th of July, just before daybreak, a great noise
and vociferation was heard in the village.   This being the
usual Indian hour of attack and surprise, and the Sioux
being known to be in the neighbourhood, the camp was
instantly on the alert.   As the day broke, Indians were
descried in considerable number on the bluffs, three or
four miles down the river.   The noise and agitation in the
village continued.   The tops of the lodges were crowded
with the inhabitants, all earnestly looking towards the
hills, and keeping up a vehement chattering.   Presently
an Indian warrior galloped past the camp towards the
village, and in a little while the legions began to pour
forth.

The truth of the matter was now ascertained.   The Indians upon the distant hills were three hundred Aricara
braves, returning from a foray.   They had met the war
party of Sioux who had been so long hovering about the
neighbourhood, had fought with them the day before,
killed several, and defeated the rest, with the loss of but
two or three of their own men and about a dozen wounded; and they were now halting at a distance until their
comrades in the village should come forth to meet them,
and swell the parade of their triumphal entry.   The warrior
who had galloped past the camp was the leader of the
party hastening home to give tidings of his victory.

Preparations were now made for this great martial ceremony.   All the finery and equipments of the warriors
were sent forth to them, that they might appear to the
greatest advantage.   Those, too, who had remained at
home, tasked their wardrobes and toilets to do honour to
the procession.

The Aricaras generally go naked, but, like all savages, they have their gala dress, of which they are not a little vain. This usually consists of a gay surcoat and leggings of the dressed skin of the antelope, resembling chamois leather, and embroidered with porcupine quills brilliantly dyed. A buffalo robe is thrown over the right shoulder, and across the left is slung a quiver of arrows. They wear gay coronets of plumes, particularly those of the swan; but the feathers of the black eagle are considered the most worthy, being a sacred bird among the Indian warriors. He who has killed an enemy in his own land, is entitled to drag at his heels a fox-skin attached to each mocassin; and he who has slain a grizzly bear, wears a necklace of his claws, the most glorious trophy that a hunter can exhibit.

An Indian toilet is an operation of some toil and trouble; the warrior often has to paint himself from head to foot, and is extremely capricious and difficult to please, as to the hideous distribution of streaks and colours. A great part of the morning, therefore, passed away before there were any signs of the distant pageant. In the mean time a profound stillness reigned over the village. Most of the inhabitants had gone forth; others remained in mute expectation. All sports and occupations were suspended, excepting that in the lodges the painstaking squaws were silently busied preparing the repasts for the warriors.

It was near noon that a mingled sound of voices and rude music, faintly heard from a distance, gave notice that the procession was on the march. The old men and such of the squaws as could leave their employments hastened forth to meet it. In a little while it emerged from behind a hill, and had a wild and picturesque appearance as it came moving over the summit in measured step, and to the cadence of songs and savage instruments; the warlike standards and trophies flaunting aloft, and the feathers, and paint, and silver ornaments of the warriors glaring and glittering in the sunshine.

The pageant had really something chivalrous in its arrangement. The Aricaras are divided into several bands, each bearing the name of some animal or bird, as the buffalo, the bear, the dog, the pheasant. The present party consisted of four of these bands, one of which was the dog, the most esteemed in war, being composed of young men under thirty, and noted for prowess. It is engaged on the most desperate occasions. The bands marched in separate bodies under their several leaders. The warriors on foot came first, in platoons of ten or twelve abreast; then the horsemen. Each band bore as an ensign a spear or bow decorated with beads, porcupine quills, and painted feathers. Each bore its trophies of scalps, elevated on poles, their long black locks streaming in the wind. Each was accompanied by its rude music and minstrelsy. In this way the proceesion extended nearly a quarter of a mile. The warriors were variously armed, some few with guns, others with bows and arrows, and war-clubs, all had shields of buffalo hide, a kind of defence generally used by the Indians of the open prairies, who have not the covert of trees and forests to protect them. They were painted in the most savage style. Some had a stamp of a red hand across their mouths, a sign that they had drunk the life-blood of a foe !

As they drew near to the village the old men and women began to meet them, and now a scene ensued that proved the fallacy of the old fable of Indian apathy and stoicism. Parents and children, husbands and wives, brothers and sisters, met with the most rapturous expressions of joy; while wailings and lamentations were heard from the relatives of the killed and wounded. The procession, however, continued on with slow and measured step, in cadence to the solemn chant, and the warriors maintained their fixed and stern demeanour.

Between two of the principal chiefs rode a young warrior, who had distinguished himself in the battle. He was severely wounded, so as with difficulty to keep on his horse ; but he preserved a serene and steadfast countenance, as if perfectly unharmed. His mother had heard of his condition. She broke through the throng, and rushing up, threw her arms around him and wept aloud. He kept up the spirit and demeanour of a warrior to the last, but expired shortly after he had reached his home.

The village was now a scene of the utmost festivity and triumph. The banners, and trophies, and scalps, and painted shields were elevated on poles near the lodges. There were war-feasts, and scalp-dances, with warlike songs and savage music; all the inhabitants were arrayed in their festal dresses; while the old heralds went round from lodge to lodge, promulgating with loud voices the events of the battle and the exploits of the various warriors.

Such was the boisterous revelry of the village; but sounds of another kind were heard on the surrounding hills; piteous wailing of the women, who had retired thither to mourn in darkness and solitude for those who had fallen in battle. There the poor mother of the youthful warrior who had returned home in triumph but to die, gave full vent to the anguish of a mother's heart. How much does this custom of the Indian women of repairing to the hill tops in the night, and pouring forth their wailings for the dead, call to mind the beautiful and affecting passage of scripture: " In Rama was there a voice heard, lamentation, and weeping, and great mourning, Rachael weeping for her children, and would not be comforted, because they are not !"

CHAPTER IV.

Wilderness of the far west—Great American desert—Parched seasons—Black hills—Rocky mountains—Wandering and predatory hordes—Speculations on what may be the future population—Apprehended dangers—A plot to desert—Rose, the interpreter—His sinister character—Departure from the Aricara village.

WHILE Mr. Hunt was deligently preparing for his arduous journey, some of his men began to lose heart at the perilous prospect before them; but, before we accuse them of want of spirit, it is proper to consider the nature of the wilderness into which they were about to adventure. It was a region almost as vast and trackless as the ocean, and, at the time of which we treat, but little known, excepting through the vague accounts of Indian hunters. A part of their route would lay across an immense tract stretching north and south for hundreds of miles along the foot of the Rocky mountains, and drained by the tributary streams of the Missouri and the Mississippi. This region, which resembles one of the immeasurable steppes of Asia, has not inaptly been termed " the great American desert." It spreads forth into undulating and treeless plains, and desolate sandy wastes, wearisome to the eye from their extent and monotony, and which are supposed by geologists, to have formed the ancient floor of the ocean, countless ages since, when its primeval waves beat against the granite bases of the Rocky mountains.

It is a land where no man permanently abides ; for, in certain seasons of the year, there is no food either for the hunter or his steed. The herbage is parched and withered ; the brooks and streams are dried up ; the buffalo, the elk, and deer have wandered to distant parts, keeping within the verge of expiring verdure, and leaving behind them a vast uninhabited solitude, seamed by ravines, the beds of former torrents, but now serving only to tantalize and increase the thirst of the traveller.

Occasionally the monotony of this vast wilderness is interrupted by mountainous belts of sand and limestone, broken into confused masses ; with precipitous cliffs and yawning ravines, looking like the ruins of a world ; or is traversed by lofty and barren ridges of rock, almost impassable, like those denominated the Black hills. Beyond these rise the stern barriers of the Rocky mountains, the limits, as it were, of the Atlantic world. The rugged defiles and deep valleys of this vast chain form sheltering places for restless and ferocious bands of savages, many of them the remnants of tribes, once inhabitants of the prairies, but broken up by war and violence, and who carry into their mountain haunts the fierce passions and reckless habits of desperadoes.

Such is the nature of this immense wilderness of the far west ; which apparently defies cultivation, and the habitation of civilized life. Some portions of it along the rivers may partially be subdued by agriculture, others may form vast pastoral tracts, like those of the east; but it is to be feared that a great part of it will form a lawless interval between the abodes of civilized man, like the wastes of the ocean or the deserts of Arabia; and, like them, be subject to the depredations of the marauder. Here may spring up new and mongrel races, like new formations in geology, the amalgamation of the " debris" and " abrasians" of former races, civilized and savage; the remains of broken and almost extinguished tribes; the descendants of wandering hunters and trappers; of fugitives from the Spanish and American frontiers; of adventurers and desperadoes of every class and country, yearly ejected from the bosom of society into the wilderness. We are contributing incessantly to swell this singular and heterogeneous cloud of wild population that is to hang about our frontier, by the transfer of whole tribes of savages from the east of the Mississippi to the great wastes of the far west. Many of these bear with them the smart of real or fancied injuries; many consider themselves expatriated beings wrongfully exiled from their hereditary homes, and the sepulchres of their fathers, and cherish a deep and abiding animosity against the race that has dispossessed them. Some may gradually become pastoral hordes, like those rude and migratory people, half shepherd, half warrior, who, with their flocks and herds, roam the plains of upper Asia; but others, it is to be apprehended, will become predatory bands, mounted on the fleet steeds of the prairies, with the open plains for their marauding grounds, and the mountains for their retreats and lurking places. Here they may resemble those great hordes of the north, " Gog and Magog with their bands," that haunted the gloomy imaginations of the prophets. " A great company and a mighty host, all riding upon horses, and warring upon those nations which were at rest, and dwelt peaceably, and had gotten cattle and goods."

The Spaniards changed the whole character and habits of the Indians when they brought the horse among them. In Chili, Tucuman, and other parts, it has converted

them, we are told, into Tartar-like tribes, and enabled them to keep the Spaniards out of their country,
and even to make it dangerous for them to venture far
from their towns and settlements.   Are we not in danger
of producing some such state of things in the boundless
regions of the far west?   That these are not mere fanciful
and extravagant suggestions we have sufficient proofs in
the dangers already experienced by the traders to the
Spanish mart of Santa Fé, and to the distant posts of the
fur companies.   These are obliged to proceed in armed
caravans, and are subject to murderous attacks from bands
of Pawnees, Camanches, and Blackfeet, that come scouring upon them in their weary march across the plains, or
lie in wait for them among the passes of the mountains.

We are wandering, however, into excursive speculations,
when our intention was merely to give an idea of the
nature of the wilderness which Mr. Hunt was about to
traverse, and which at that time was far less known than
at present; though it still remains in a great measure an
unknown land.   We cannot be surprised, therefore, that
some of the least resolute of his party should feel dismay
at the thoughts of adventuring into this perilous wilderness under the uncertain guidance of three hunters, who
had merely passed once through the country and might
have forgotten the landmarks.   Their apprehensions were
aggravated by some of Lisa's followers, who, not being
engaged in the expedition, took a mischievous pleasure in
exaggerating its dangers.   They painted in strong colours,
to the poor Canadian voyageurs, the risk they run of
perishing with hunger and thirst; of being cut off by war
parties of the Sioux who scoured the plains; of having
their horses stolen by the Upsarokas or Crows, who infested the skirts of the Rocky mountains; or of being
butchered by the Blackfeet, who lurked among the defiles.
In a word, there was little chance of their getting alive
across the mountains; and even if they did, those three
guides knew nothing of the howling wilderness that lay
beyond.

The apprehensions thus awakened in the minds of some
of the men came well nigh proving detrimental to the

expedition. Some of them determined to desert, and to make their way back to St. Louis. They accordingly purloined several weapons and a barrel of gunpowder, as ammunition for their enterprise, and buried them in the river bank, intending to seize one of the boats and make off in the night. Fortunately their plot was overheard by John Day, the Kentuckian, and communicated to the partners, who took quiet and effectual means to frustrate it.

The dangers to be apprehended from the Crow Indians had not been overrated by the camp gossips. These savages, through whose mountain haunts the party would have to pass, were noted for daring and excursive habits, and great dexterity in horse-stealing. Mr. Hunt, therefore, considered himself fortunate in having met with a man who might be of great use to him in any intercourse he might have with the tribe. This was a wandering individual named Edward Rose, whom he had picked up somewhere on the Missouri—one of those anomalous beings found on the frontier, who seemed to have neither kin nor country. He had lived some time among the Crows, so as to become acquainted with their language and customs; and was, withal, a dogged, sullen, silent fellow, with a sinister aspect, and more of the savage than the civilized man in his appearance. He was engaged to serve in general as a hunter, but as guide and interpreter when they should reach the country of the Crows.

On the 18th of July, Mr. Hunt took up his line of march by land from the Aricara village, leaving Mr. Lisa and Mr. Nuttall there, where they intended to await the expected arrival of Mr. Henry from the Rocky mountains. As to Messrs. Bradbury and Breckenridge, they had departed some days previously, on a voyage down the river to St. Louis, with a detachment from Mr. Lisa's party. With all his exertions, Mr. Hunt had been unable to obtain a sufficient number of horses for the accommodation of all his people. His cavalcade consisted of eighty-two horses, most of them heavily laden with Indian goods, beaver traps, ammunition, Indian corn, corn meal, and other necessaries. Each of the partners was

mounted, and a horse was allotted to the interpreter,
Pierre Dorion, for the transportation of his luggage and
his two children. His squaw, for the most part of the
time, trudged on foot, like the residue of the party;
nor did any of the men show more patience and fortitude than this resolute woman in enduring fatigue and
hardship.

The veteran trappers and voyageurs of Lisa's party
shook their heads as their comrades set out, and took
leave of them as of doomed men ; and even Lisa himself
gave it as his opinion, after the travellers had departed,
that they would never reach the shores of the Pacific, but
would either perish with hunger in the wilderness, or be
cut off by the savages.

CHAPTER V.

Summer weather of the Prairies—Purity of the atmosphere—Canadians on
the march—Sickness in the camp—Big river—Vulgar nomenclature—Suggestions about the original Indian names—Camp of Cheyennes—Trade for
horses — Character of the Cheyennes—Their horsemanship—Historical
anecdotes of the tribe.

THE course taken by Mr. Hunt was at first to the north-
west, but soon turned and kept generally to the south-
west, to avoid the country infested by the Blackfeet. His
rout took him across some of the tributary streams of the
Missouri, and over immense prairies, bounded only by the
horizon, and destitute of trees. It was now the height of
summer, and these naked plains would be intolerable to
the traveller were it not for the breezes which sweep over
them during the fervour of the day, bringing with them
tempering airs from the distant mountains. To the preva-
lence of these breezes, and to the want of all leafy covert,
may we also attribute the freedom from those flies and
other insects so tormenting to man and beast during the
summer months, in the lower plains, which are bordered
and interspersed with woodland.

The monotony of these immense landscapes, also, would be as wearisome as that of the ocean, were it not relieved in some degree by the purity and elasticity of the atmosphere, and the beauty of the heavens. The sky has that delicious blue for which the sky of Italy is renowned; the sun shines with a splendour, unobscured by any cloud or vapour, and a starlight night on the prairies is glorious. This purity and elasticity of atmosphere increases as the traveller approaches the mountains, and gradually rises into the more elevated prairies.

On the second day of the journey, Mr. Hunt arranged the party into small and convenient messes, distributing among them the camp kettles. The encampments at night were as before; some sleeping under tents, and others bivouacking in the open air. The Canadians proved as patient of toil and hardship on the land as on the water; indeed, nothing could surpass the patience and good humour of these men upon the march. They were the cheerful drudges of the party, loading and unloading the horses, pitching the tents, making the fires, cooking; in short, performing all those household and menial offices which the Indians usually assign to the squaws; and, like the squaws, they left all the hunting and fighting to others. A Canadian has but little affection for the exercise of the rifle.

The progress of the party was but slow for the first few days. Some of the men were indisposed; Mr. Crooks, especially, was so unwell that he could not keep on his horse. A rude kind of litter was, therefore, prepared for him, consisting of two long poles, fixed, one on each side of two horses, with a matting between them, on which he reclined at full length, and was protected from the sun by a canopy of boughs.

On the evening of the 23rd (July) they encamped on the banks of what they term Big river; and here we cannot but pause to lament the stupid, commonplace, and often ribald names entailed upon the rivers, and other features of the great west, by traders and settlers. As the aboriginal tribes of these magnificent regions are yet in existence, the Indian names might easily be recovered; which, besides

being in general more sonorous and musical, would remain
mementoes of the primitive lords of the soil, of whom in a
little while scarce any traces will be left.   Indeed, it is to
be wished that the whole of our country could be rescued,
as much as possible, from the wretched nomenclature inflicted upon it, by ignorant and vulgar minds; and this
might be done, in a great degree, by restoring the Indian
names, wherever significant and euphonious.   As there
appears to be a spirit of research abroad in respect to our
aboriginal antiquities, we would suggest, as a worthy object
of enterprise, a map, or maps, of every part of our country, giving the Indian names wherever they could be ascertained.   Whoever achieves such a task worthily, will
leave a monument to his own reputation.

To return from this digression.   As the travellers were
now in a country abounding with buffalo, they remained
for several days encamped upon the banks of Big river,
to obtain a supply of provisions, and to give the invalids
time to recruit.

On the second day of their sojourn, as Ben Jones, John
Day, and others of the hunters were in pursuit of game,
they came upon an Indian camp on the open prairie, near
to a small stream which ran through a ravine.   The tents
or lodges were of dressed buffalo skins, sewn together and
stretched on tapering pine-poles, joined at top, but ra-
diating at bottom, so as to form a circle capable of admit-
ing fifty persons.   Numbers of horses were grazing in the
neighbourhood of the camp, or straying at large in the
prairie; a sight most acceptable to the hunters.   After
reconnoitring the camp for some time, they ascertained it
to belong to a band of Cheyenne Indians, the same that
had sent a deputation to the Aricaras.   They received the
hunters in the most friendly manner; invited them to their
lodges, which were more cleanly than Indian lodges are
prone to be, and set food before them with true uncivilized
hospitality.   Several of them accompanied the hunters
back to the camp, when a trade was immediately opened.
The Cheyennes were astonished and delighted to find a
convoy of goods and trinkets thus brought into the very
heart of the prairie; while Mr. Hunt and his companions

were overjoyed to have an opportunity of obtaining a further supply of horses from these equestrian savages.

During a fortnight that the travellers lingered at this place, their encampment was continually thronged by the Cheyennes. They were a civil, well-behaved people, cleanly in their persons, and decorous in their habits. The men were tall, straight, and vigorous, with aquiline noses, and high cheek bones. Some were almost as naked as ancient statues, and might have stood as models for a statuary; others had leggins and mocassins of deer-skin, and buffalo robes, which they threw gracefully over their shoulders. In a little while, however, they began to appear in more gorgeous array, tricked out in the finery obtained from the white men; bright cloths; brass rings; beads of various colours; and happy was he who could render himself hideous with vermilion.

The travellers had frequent occasion to admire the skill and grace with which these Indians managed their horses. Some of them made a striking display when mounted; themselves and their steeds decorated in gala style: for the Indians often bestow more finery upon their horses than upon themselves. Some would hang round the necks, or rather on the breasts of their horses, the most precious ornaments they had obtained from the white men; others interwove feathers in their manes and tails. The Indian horses, too, appear to have an attachment to their riders; and, indeed, it is said that the horses of the prairies readily distinguish an Indian from a white man by the smell, and give a preference to the former. Yet the Indians, in general, are hard riders, and, however they may value their horses, treat them with great roughness and neglect. Occasionally the Cheyennes joined the white hunters in pursuit of the elk and buffalo; and when in the ardour of the chase, spared neither themselves nor their steeds, scouring the prairies at full speed, and plunging down precipices and frightful ravines that threatened the necks of both horse and horseman. The Indian steed, well trained to the chase, seems as mad as his rider, and pursues the game as eagerly as if it were his natural prey, on the flesh of which he was to banquet.

The history of the Cheyennes is that of many of those wandering tribes of the prairies. They were the remnant of a once powerful people called the Shaways, inhabiting a branch of the Red river which flows into Lake Winnipeg. Every Indian tribe has some rival tribe with which it wages implacable hostility. The deadly enemies of the Shaways were the Sioux, who, after a long course of warfare, proved too powerful for them, and drove them across the Missouri. They again took root near the Warricanne creek, and established themselves there in a fortified village.

The Sioux still followed them with deadly animosity; dislodged them from their village, and compelled them to take refuge in the Black hills, near the upper waters of the Sheyenne or Cheyenne river. Here they lost even their name, and became known among the French colonists by that of the river they frequented.

The heart of the tribe was now broken; its numbers were greatly thinned by their harassing wars. They no longer attempted to establish themselves in any permanent abode that might be an object of attack to their cruel foes. They gave up the cultivation of the fruits of the earth, and became a wandering tribe, subsisting by the chase, and following the buffalo in its migrations.

Their only possessions were horses, which they caught on the prairies, or reared, or captured on predatory incursions into the Mexican territories, as has already been mentioned. With some of these they repaired once a year to the Aricara villages, exchanged them for corn, beans, pumpkins, and articles of European merchandise, and then returned into the heart of the prairies.

Such are the fluctuating fortunes of these savage nations. War, famine, pestilence, together or singly, bring down their strength and thin their numbers. Whole tribes are rooted up from their native places, wander for a time about these immense regions, become amalgamated with other tribes, or disappear from the face of the earth. There appears to be a tendency to extinction among all the savage nations; and this tendency would seem to have been in operation among the aboriginals of this country long before the advent of the white men, if we may judge from the traces and traditions of ancient populousness in regions which were silent and deserted at the time of the discovery; and from the mysterious and perplexing vestiges of unknown races, predecessors of those found in actual possession, and who must long since have become gradually extinguished or been destroyed. The whole history of the aboriginal population of this country, however, is an enigma, and a grand one—will it ever be solved?

CHAPTER VI.

New distribution of horses—Secret information of treason in the camp—Rose the interpreter, his perfidious character—His plots—Anecdotes of the Crow Indians—Notorious horse-stealers—Some account of Rose—A desperado of the frontier.

On the 6th of August, the travellers bade farewell to the friendly band of Cheyennes, and resumed their journey. As they had obtained thirty-six additional horses by their recent traffic, Mr. Hunt made a new arrangement. The baggage was made up in smaller loads. A horse was allotted to each of the six prime hunters, and others were distributed among the voyageurs, a horse for every two, so that they could ride and walk alternately. Mr. Crooks being still too feeble to mount the saddle, was carried on a litter.

Their march this day lay among singular hills and knolls of an indurated red earth, resembling brick, about the bases of which were scattered pumice stones and cinders, the whole bearing traces of the action of fire. In the evening they encamped on a branch of Big river.

They were now out of the tract of country infested by the Sioux, and had advanced such a distance into the interior, that Mr. Hunt no longer felt apprehensive of the desertion of any of his men. He was doomed, however, to experience new cause of anxiety. As he was seated in his tent after nightfall, one of the men came to him privately, and informed him that there was mischief brewing in the camp. Edward Rose, the interpreter, whose sinister looks we have already mentioned, was denounced by this secret informer as a designing, treacherous scoundrel, who was tampering with the fidelity of certain of the men, and instigating them to a flagrant piece of treason. In the course of a few days they would arrive at the mountainous district infested by the Upsarokas or Crows, the tribe among which Rose was to officiate as interpreter. His plan was, that several of the men should join with him, when in that neighbourhood, in carrying off a number of the horses with their packages of goods, and deserting to those savages. He assured them of good treatment among the Crows, the principal chiefs and warriors of whom he knew; they would soon become great men among them, and have the finest women, and the daughters of the chiefs for wives; and the horses and goods they carried off would make them rich for life.

The intelligence of this treachery on the part of Rose gave much disquiet to Mr. Hunt, for he knew not how far it might be effective among his men. He had already had proofs that several of them were disaffected to the enterprise, and loath to cross the mountains. He knew also that savage life had charms for many of them, especially Canadians, who were prone to intermarry and domesticate themselves among the Indians.

And here a word or two concerning the Crows may be of service to the reader, as they will figure occasionally in the succeeding narration.

The tribe consists of four bands, which have their nestling places in fertile, well-wooded valleys, lying among the Rocky mountains, and watered by the Big Horse river and its tributary streams; but, though these are properly their homes, where they shelter their old people, their wives, and their children, the men of the tribe are almost continually on the foray and the scamper. They are, in fact, notorious marauders and horsestealers;

crossing and recrossing the mountains, robbing on the one side, and conveying their spoils to the other. Hence, we are told, is derived their name, given to them on account of their unsettled and predatory habits; winging their flight like the crows, from one side of the mountains to the other, and making free booty of every thing that lies in their way. Horses, however, are the especial objects of their depredations, and their skill and audacity in stealing them are said to be astonishing. This is their glory and delight; an accomplished horsestealer fills up their idea of a hero. Many horses are obtained by them, also, in barter from tribes in and beyond the mountains. They have an absolute passion for this noble animal; besides which he is with them an important object of traffic. Once a year they make a visit to the Mandans, Minatarees, and other tribes of the Missouri, taking with them droves of horses which they exchange for guns, ammunition, trinkets, vermilion, cloths of bright colours, and various other articles of European manufacture. With these they supply their own wants and caprices, and carry on the internal trade for horses already mentioned.

The plot of Rose to rob and abandon his countrymen when in the heart of the wilderness, and to throw himself into the hands of a horde of savages, may appear strange and improbable to those unacquainted with the singular and anomalous characters that are to be found about the borders. This fellow, it appears, was one of those desperadoes of the frontiers outlawed by their crimes, who combine the vices of civilized and savage life, and are ten times more barbarous than the Indians with whom they consort. Rose had formerly belonged to one of the gangs of pirates who infested the islands of the Mississippi, plundering boats as they went up and down the river, and who sometimes shifted the scene of their robberies to the shore, waylaying travellers as they returned by land from New Orleans with the proceeds of their downward voyage, plundering them of their money and effects, and often perpetrating the most atrocious murders.

These hordes of villains being broken up and dispersed, Rose had betaken himself to the wilderness, and associated himself with the Crows, whose predatory habits were congenial with his own, had married a woman of the tribe, and, in short, had identified himself with those vagrant savages.

Such was the worthy guide and interpreter, Edward Rose. We give his story, however, not as it was known to Mr. Hunt and his companions at the time, but as it has been subsequently ascertained. Enough was known of the fellow and his dark and perfidious character to put Mr. Hunt upon his guard : still, as there was no knowing how far his plans might have succeeded, and as any rash act might blow the mere smouldering sparks of treason into a sudden blaze, it was thought advisable by those with whom Mr. Hunt consulted, to conceal all knowledge or suspicion of the meditated treachery, but to keep up a vigilant watch upon the movements of Rose, and a strict guard upon the horses at night.

CHAPTER VII.

Substitute for fuel on the prairies—Fossil trees—Fierceness of the buffaloes when in heat—Three hunters missing—Signal fires and smokes—Uneasiness concerning the lost men—A plan to forestal a rogue—New arrangement with Rose—Return of the wanderers.

THE plains over which the travellers were journeying continued to be destitute of tress or even shrubs ; insomuch that they had to use the dung of the buffalo for fuel, as the Arabs of the desert use that of the camel. This substitute for fuel is universal among the Indians of these upper prairies, and is said to make a fire equal to that of turf. If a few chips are added, it throws out a cheerful and kindly blaze.

These plains, however, had not always been equally destitute of wood, as was evident from the trunks of trees which the travellers repeatedly met with, some still standing, others lying about in broken fragments, but all in a fossil state, having flourished in times long past.   In these singular remains, the original grain of the wood was still so distinct that they could be ascertained to be the ruins of oak trees. Several pieces of the fossil wood were selected by the men to serve as whetstones.

In this part of the journey there was no lack of provisions, for the prairies were covered with immense herds of buffalo. These, in general, are animals of peaceable demeanour, grazing quietly like domestic cattle; but this was the season when they are in heat, and when the bulls are unusually fierce and pugnacious. There was accordingly a universal restlessness and commotion throughout the plain; and the amorous herds gave utterance to their feelings in low bellowings that resounded like distant thunder. Here and there fierce duellos took place between rival enamorados; butting their huge shagged fronts together, goring each other with their short black horns, and tearing up the earth with their feet in perfect fury.

In one of the evening halts, Pierre Dorion, the interpreter, together with Carson and Gardpie, two of the hunters, were missing, nor had they returned by morning. As it was supposed they had wandered away in pursuit of buffalo, and would readily find the track of the party, no solicitude was felt on their account. A fire was left burning, to guide them by its column of smoke, and the travellers proceeded on their march. In the evening a signal fire was made on a hill adjacent to the camp, and in the morning it was replenished with fuel so as to last throughout the day. These signals are usual among the Indians, to give warnings to each other, or to call home straggling hunters; and such is the transparency of the atmosphere in those elevated plains, that a slight column of smoke can be discerned from a distance, particularly in the evenings. Two or three days elapsed, however, without the reappearance of the three hunters; and Mr. Hunt slackened his march to give them time to overtake him.

A vigilant watch continued to be kept upon the movements of Rose, and of such of the men as were considered doubtful in their loyalty; but nothing occurred to excite immediate apprehensions. Rose evidently was not a

favourite among his comrades, and it was hoped that he
had not been able to make any real partisans.

On the 10th of August they encamped among hills, on
the highest peak of which Mr. Hunt caused a huge pyre
of pine wood to be made, which soon sent up a great
column of flame that might be seen far and wide over the
prairies. This fire blazed all night, and was amply replenished at daybreak; so that the towering pillar of
smoke could not but be descried by the wanderers if
within the distance of a day's journey.

It is a common occurrence in these regions, where the
features of the country so much resemble each other, for
hunters to lose themselves and wander for many days, before they can find their way back to the main body of their
party. In the present instance, however, a more than
common solicitude was felt in consequence of the distrust awakened by the sinister designs of Rose.

The route now became excessively toilsome over a ridge
of steep rocky hills, covered with loose stones. These
were intersected by deep valleys, formed by two branches
of Big river, coming from the south of west, both of which
they crossed. These streams were bordered by meadows,
well stock with buffaloes. Loads of meat were brought in
by the hunters; but the travellers were rendered dainty
by profusion, and would cook only the choice pieces.

They had now travelled for several days at a very slow
rate, and had made signal fires and left traces of their
route at every stage, yet nothing was heard or seen of the
lost men. It began to be feared that they might have
fallen into the hands of some lurking band of savages. A
party numerous as that of Mr. Hunt, with a long train of
pack-horses, moving across open plains or naked hills, is
discoverable at a great distance by Indian scouts, who
spread the intelligence rapidly to various points, and assemble their friends to hang about the skirts of the travellers, steal their horses, or cut off any stragglers from the
main body.

Mr. Hunt and his companions were more and more
sensible how much it would be in the power of this sullen
and daring vagabond Rose, to do them mischief, when

they should become entangled in the defiles of the mountains, with the passes of which they were wholly unacquainted, and which were infested by his freebooting friends, the Crows. There, should he succeed in seducing some of the party into his plans, he might carry off the best horses and effects, throw himself among his savage allies, and set all pursuit at defiance. Mr. Hunt resolved, therefore, to frustrate the knave, divert him by management from his plans, and make it sufficiently advantageous for him to remain honest. He took occasion, accordingly, in the course of conversation, to inform Rose that, having engaged him chiefly as a guide and interpreter through the country of the Crows, they would not stand in need of his services beyond. Knowing, therefore, his connexion by marriage with that tribe, and his predilection for a residence among them, they would put no constraint upon his will, but, whenever they met with a party of that people, would leave him at liberty to remain among his adopted brethren. Furthermore that, in thus parting with him, they would pay him half a year's wages in consideration of his past services, and would give him a horse, three beaver traps, and sundry other articles calculated to set him up in the world.

This unexpected liberality, which made it nearly as profitable and infinitely less hazardous for Rose to remain honest than to play the rogue, completely disarmed him. From that time his whole deportment underwent a change. His brow cleared up and appeared more cheerful ; he left off his sullen, skulking habits, and made no further attempts to tamper with the faith of his comrades.

On the 13th of August Mr. Hunt varied his course and inclined westward, in hopes of falling in with the three lost hunters; who, it was now thought, might have kept to the right hand of Big river. This course soon brought him to a fork of the Little Missouri, about a hundred yards wide, and resembling the great river of the same name in the strength of its current, its turbid water, and the frequency of drift wood and sunken trees.

Rugged mountains appeared ahead, crowding down to the water edge, and offering a barrier to further progress

on the side they were ascending. Crossing the river,
therefore, they encamped on its north-west bank, where
they found good pasturage and buffalo in abundance.
The weather was overcast and rainy, and a general gloom
pervaded the camp; the voyageurs sat moping in groups,
with their shoulders as high as their heads, croaking their
forebodings, when suddenly towards evening a shout of
joy gave notice that the lost men were found. They came
slowly lagging into the camp, with weary looks, and horses
jaded and wayworn. They had, in fact, been for several
days incessantly on the move. In their hunting excursion
on the prairies they had pushed so far in pursuit of buffalo, as to find it impossible to retrace their steps over
plains trampled by innumerable herds; and were baffled
by the monotony of the landscape in their attempts to
recall landmarks. They had ridden to and fro until they
had almost lost the points of the compass, and became
totally bewildered; nor did they ever perceive any of the
signal fires and columns of smoke made by their comrades. At length, about two days previously, when almost spent by anxiety and hard riding, they came, to their
great joy, upon the " trail" of the party, which they had
since followed up steadily.

Those only who have experienced the warm cordiality
that grows up between comrades in wild and adventurous
expeditions of the kind, can picture to themselves the
hearty cheering with which the stragglers were welcomed
to the camp. Every one crowded round them to ask
questions, and to hear the story of their mishaps; and
even the squaw of the moody half-breed, Pierre Dorion,
forgot the sternness of his domestic rule, and the conjugal discipline of the cudgel, in her joy at his safe
return.

CHAPTER VIII.

MR. HUNT and his party were now on the skirts of the Black hills, or Black mountains, as they are sometimes called; an extensive chain, lying about a hundred miles east of the Rocky mountains, and stretching in a north-east direction from the south fork of the Nebraska, or Platte river, to the great north bend of the Missouri. The Sierra or ridge of the Black hills, in fact, forms the dividing line between the waters of the Missouri and those of the Arkansas and the Mississippi, and gives rise to the Cheyenne, the Little Missouri, and several tributary streams of the Yellowstone.

The wild recesses of these hills, like those of the Rocky mountains, are retreats and lurking places for broken and predatory tribes, and it was among them that the remnant of the Cheyenne tribe took refuge, as has been stated, from their conquering enemies, the Sioux.

The Black hills are chiefly composed of sand stone, and in many places are broken into savage cliffs and precipices, and present the most singular and fantastic forms; sometimes resembling towns and castellated fortresses. The ignorant inhabitants of plains are prone to clothe the mountains that bound their horizon with fanciful and superstitious attributes. Thus the wandering tribes of the prairies, who often behold clouds gathering round the summits of these hills, and lightning flashing, and thunder pealing from them, when all the neighbouring plains are serene and sunny, consider them the abode of the genii or thunder spirits, who fabricate storms and tempests. On entering their defiles, therefore, they often hang offerings on the trees, or place them on the rocks, to

propitiate the invisible " lords of the mountains," and procure good weather and successful hunting ; and they attach
unusual significance to the echoes which haunt the precipices.   This superstition may also have arisen, in part,
from a natural phenomenon of a singular nature.   In the
most calm and serene weather, and at all times of the day
or night, successive reports are now and then heard among
these mountains, resembling the discharge of several
pieces of artillery.   Similar reports were heard by Messrs.
Lewis and Clarke in the Rocky mountains, which, they
say, were attributed by the Indians to the bursting of
the rich mines of silver contained in the bosom of the
mountains.

In fact, these singular explosions have received fanciful
explanations from learned men, and have not been satis-
factorily accounted for even by philosophers.   They are
said to occur frequently in Brazil.   Vasconcelles, a Jesuit
father, describes one which he heard in the Sierra, or
mountain region of Piratininga, and which he compares to
the discharges of a park of artillery.   The Indians told him
that it was an explosion of stones.   The worthy father had
soon a satisfactory proof of the truth of their information,
for the very place was found where a rock had burst and
exploded from its entrails a stony mass, like a bomb-shell,
and of the size of a bull's heart.   This mass was broken
either in the ejection or its fall, and wonderful was the
internal organization revealed.   It had a shell harder even
than iron ; within which were arranged, like the seeds of
a pomegranite, jewels of various colours; some transparent as crystal, others of a fine red, and others of mixed
hues.   The same phenomenon is said to occur occasionally in the adjacent province of Guayra, where stones of
the bigness of a man's hand are exploded, with a loud
noise, from the bosom of the earth, and scatter about
glittering and beautiful fragments that look like precious
gems, but are of no value.

The Indians of the Orellanna, also, tell of horrible
noises heard occasionally in the Paraguaxo, which they
consider the throes and groans of the mountain endeavouring to cast forth the precious stones hidden within its

entrails. Others have endeavoured to account for these discharges of " mountain artillery" on humbler principles; attributing them to the loud reports made by the disruption and fall of great masses of rock, reverberated and prolonged by the echoes; others, to the disengagement of hydrogen, produced by subterraneous beds of coal in a state of ignition. In whatever way this singular phenomenon may be accounted for, the existence of it appears to be well established. It remains one of the lingering mysteries of nature, which throw something of a supernatural charm over her wild mountain solitudes; and we doubt whether the imaginative reader will not rather join with the poor Indian in attributing it to the thunder spirits, or the guardian genii of unseen treasures, than to any commonplace physical cause.

Whatever might be the supernatural influences among these mountains, the travellers found their physical difficulties hard to cope with. They made repeated attempts to find a passage through, or over the chain, but were as often turned back by impassable barriers. Sometimes a defile seemed to open a practicable path, but it would terminate in some wild chaos of rocks and cliffs, which it was impossible to climb. The animals of these solitary regions were different from those they had been accustomed to. The black-tailed deer would bound up the ravines on their approach, and the bighorn would gaze fearlessly down upon them from some impending precipice, or skip playfully from rock to rock. These animals are only to be met with in mountainous regions. The former is larger than the common deer, but its flesh is not equally esteemed by hunters. It has very large ears, and the tip of the tail is black, from which it derives its name.

The bighorn is so named from its horns, which are of a great size, and twisted like those of a ram. It is called by some the argali, by others, the ibex, though differing from both of these animals. The Mandans call it the ahsahta, a name much better than the clumsy appellation which it generally bears. It is of the size of a small elk, or large deer, and of a dun colour, excepting the belly and round the tail, where it is white. In its habits it resembles the goat, frequenting the rudest precipices; cropping the herbage from their edges; and, like the chamois, bounding lightly and securely among dizzy heights, where the hunter dares not venture. It is difficult, therefore, to get within shot of it. Ben Jones the hunter, however, in one of the passes of the Black hills, succeeded in bringing down a bighorn from the verge of a precipice, the flesh of which was pronounced by the gourmands of the camp to have the flavour of excellent mutton.

Baffled in his attempts to traverse this mountain chain, Mr. Hunt skirted along it to the south-west, keeping it on the right; and still in hope of finding an opening. At an early hour one day, he encamped in a narrow valley on the banks of a beautifully clear but rushy pool; surrounded by thickets bearing abundance of wild cherries, currants, and yellow and purple gooseberries.

While the afternoon's meal was in preparation, Mr. Hunt and Mr. M'Kenzie ascended to the summit of the nearest hill, from whence, aided by the purity and transparency of the evening atmosphere, they commanded a vast prospect on all sides. Below them extended a plain, dotted with innumerable herds of buffalo. Some were lying down among the herbage, others roaming in their unbounded pastures, while many were engaged in fierce contests like those already described, their low bellowings reaching the ear like the hoarse murmurs of the surf on a distant shore.

Far off in the west they descried a range of lofty mountains printing the clear horizon, some of them evidently capped with snow. These they supposed to be the Bighorn mountains, so called from the animal of that name, with which they abound. They are a spur of the great Rocky chain. The hill from whence Mr. Hunt had this prospect was, according to his computation, about two hundred and fifty miles from the Aricara village.

On returning to the camp, Mr. Hunt found some uneasiness prevailing among the Canadian voyageurs. In straying among the thickets they had beheld tracks of grizzly bears in every direction; doubtless attracted thither by the fruit. To their dismay they now found that they had encamped in one of the favourite resorts of this dreaded animal. The idea marred all the comfort of the encampment. As night closed, the surrounding thickets were peopled with terrors; insomuch that, according to Mr. Hunt, they could not help starting at every little breeze that stirred the bushes.

The grizzly bear is the only really formidable quadruped of our continent. He is the favourite theme of the hunters of the far west, who describe him as equal in size to a common cow, and of prodigious strength. He makes battle if assailed, and often, if pressed by hunger, is the assailant. If wounded, he becomes furious, and will pursue the hunter. His speed exceeds that of a man, but is inferior to that of a horse. In attacking he rears himself on his hind legs, and springs the length of his body. Woe to horse or rider that comes within the sweep of his terrific claws, which are sometimes nine inches in length, and tear every thing before them!

At the time we are treating of, the grizzly bear was still frequent on the Missouri, and in the lower country, but, like some of the broken tribes of the prairies, he has gradually fallen back before his enemies, and is now chiefly to be found in the upland regions, in rugged fastnesses like those of the Black hills and the Rocky mountains. Here he lurks in caverns, or holes which he has digged in the sides of hills, or under the roots and trunks of fallen trees. Like [the common bear, he is fond of fruits, and mast, and roots, the latter of which he will dig up with his fore claws. He is carnivorous also, and will even attack and conquer the lordly buffalo, dragging his huge carcass to the neighbourhood of his den, that he may prey upon it at his leisure.

The hunters, both white and red men, consider this the most heroic game. They prefer to hunt him on horseback, and will venture so near as sometimes to singe his hair with the flash of the rifle. The hunter of the grizzly bear, however, must be an experienced hand, and know where to aim at a vital part; for of all quadrupeds, he is the most difficult to be killed. He will receive repeated wounds without flinching, and rarely is a shot mortal unless through the head or heart.

That the dangers apprehended from the grizzly bear, at this night encampment, were not imaginary, was proved on the following morning. Among the hired men of the party was one William Cannon, who had been a soldier at one of the frontier posts, and entered into the employ of Mr. Hunt at Mackinaw. He was an inexperienced hunter and a poor shot, for which he was much bantered by his more adroit comrades. Piqued at their raillery, he had been practising ever since he had joined the expedition, but without success. In the course of the present afternoon, he went forth by himself to take a lesson in venerie, and, to his great delight, had the good fortune to kill a buffalo. As he was a considerable distance from the camp, he cut out the tongue and some of the choice bits, made them into a parcel, and, slinging them on his shoulders by a strap passed round his forehead, as the voyageurs carry packages of goods, set out all glorious for the camp, anticipating a triumph over his brother hunters. In passing through a narrow ravine, he heard a noise behind him, and looking round beheld, to his dismay, a grizzly bear in full pursuit, apparently attracted by the scent of the meat. Cannon had heard so much of the invulnerability of this tremendous animal, that he never attempted to fire, but, slipping the strap from his forehead, let go the buffalo meat and ran for his life. The bear did not stop to regale himself with the game, but kept on after the hunter. He had nearly overtaken him when Cannon reached a tree, and, throwing down his rifle, scrambled up it. The next instant Bruin was at the foot of the tree; but, as this species of bear does not climb, he contented himself with turning the chase into a blockade. Night came on. In the darkness Cannon could not perceive whether or not the enemy maintained his station; but his fears pictured him rigorously mounting guard. He passed the night, therefore, in the tree, a prey to dismal fancies. In the morning the bear was gone. Cannon warily descended the tree, gathered up his gun, and made the best of his way back to the camp, without venturing to look after his buffalo meat.

While on this theme we will add another anecdote of an

adventure with a grizzly bear, told of John Day, the Kentucky hunter, but which happened at a different period of the expedition. Day was hunting in company with one of the clerks of the company, a lively youngster, who was a great favourite with the veteran, but whose vivacity he had continually to keep in check. They were in search of deer, when suddenly a huge grizzly bear emerged from a thicket about thirty yards distant, rearing himself upon his hind legs with a terrific growl, and displaying a hideous array of teeth and claws. The rifle of the young man was levelled in an instant, but John Day's iron hand was quickly upon his arm. "Be quiet, boy! be quiet!" exclaimed the hunter, between his clenched teeth, and without turning his eyes from the bear. They remained motionless. The monster regarded them for a time, then, lowering himself on his fore paws, slowly withdrew. He had not gone many paces before he again turned, reared himself on his hind legs, and repeated his menace. Day's hand was still on the arm of his young companion, he again pressed it hard, and kept repeating between his teeth, "Quiet, boy!—keep quiet!—keep quiet!"—though the latter had not made a move since his first prohibition. The bear again lowered himself on all fours, retreated some twenty yards further, and again turned, reared, showed his teeth and growled. This third menace was too much for the game spirit of John Day. "By Jove!" exclaimed he, "I can stand this no longer!" and in an instant a ball from his rifle whizzed into the foe. The wound was not mortal; but, luckily, it dismayed instead of enraging the animal, and he retreated into the thicket.

Day's young companion reproached him for not practising the caution which he enjoined upon others. "Why, boy," replied the veteran, "caution is caution, but one must not put up with too much even from a bear. Would you have me suffer myself to be bullied all day by a varmint?"

CHAPTER IX.

Indian trail—Rough mountain travelling—Sufferings from hunger and thirst
—Powder river—Game in abundance—A hunter's paradise—Mountain peak
seen at a great distance—One of the Big Horn chain—Rocky mountains—
Extent—Appearance—Height—The Great American Desert—Various characteristics of the mountains—Indian superstitions concerning them—
Land of souls—Towns of the free and generous spirits—Happy hunting
grounds.

For the two following days the travellers pursued a
westerly course for thirty-four miles, along a ridge of
country dividing the tributary waters of the Missouri and
the Yellowstone.   As landmarks they guided themselves
by the summits of the far distant mountains, which they
supposed to belong to the Big Horn chain.   They were
gradually rising into a higher temperature, for the weather
was cold for the season, with a sharp frost in the night,
and ice of an eighth of an inch in thickness.

On the twenty-second of August, early in the day, they
came upon the trail of a numerous band.   Rose and the
other hunters examined the foot-prints with great attention, and determined it to be the trail of a party of Crows,
returning from an annual trading visit to the Mandans.
As this trail afforded more commodious travelling, they
immediately struck into it, and followed it for two days.
It led them over rough hills, and through broken gullies,
during which time they suffered great fatigue from the
ruggedness of the country.   The weather, too, which had
recently been frosty, was now oppressively warm, and
there was great scarcity of water, insomuch that a valuable dog belonging to Mr. M'Kenzie died of thirst.

At one time they had twenty-five miles of painful travel, without a drop of water, until they arrived at a small
running stream.   Here they eagerly slaked their thirst;
but, this being allayed, the calls of hunger became equally
importunate.   Ever since they had got among these barren and arid hills, where there was a deficiency of grass,
they had met with no buffaloes; those animals keeping in

the grassy meadows near the streams. They were obliged therefore to have recourse to their corn meal, which they reserved for such emergencies. Some, however, were lucky enough to kill a wolf, which they cooked for supper, and pronounced excellent food.

The next morning they resumed their wayfaring, hungry and jaded, and had a dogged march of eighteen miles among the same kind of hills. At length they emerged upon a stream of clear water, one of the forks of Powder river, and to their great joy beheld once more wide grassy meadows, stocked with herds of buffalo. For several days they kept about the banks of this river, ascending it about eighteen miles. It was a hunter's paradise; the buffaloes were in such abundance that they were enabled to kill as many as they pleased, and to jerk a sufficient supply of meat for several day's journeying. Here, then, they revelled and reposed after their hungry and weary travel, hunting and feasting, and reclining upon the grass. Their quiet, however, was a little marred by coming upon traces of Indians, who, they concluded, must be Crows; they were therefore obliged to keep a more vigilant watch than ever upon their horses. For several days they had been directing their march towards the lofty mountain descried by Mr. Hunt and Mr. M'Kenzie on the 17th of August, the height of which rendered it a landmark over a vast extent of country. At first it had appeared to them solitary and detached; but as they advanced towards it, it proved to be the principal summit of a chain of mountains. Day by day it varied in form, or rather its lower peaks, and the summits of others of the chain emerged above the clear horizon, and finally the inferior line of hills which connected most of them rose to view. So far, however, are objects discernible in the pure atmosphere of these elevated plains, that, from the place where they first descried the main mountain, they had to travel a hundred and fifty miles before they reached its base. Here they encamped on the thirtieth of August, having come nearly four hundred miles since leaving the Aricara village.

The mountain which now towered above them was one

of the Big Horn chain, bordered by a river of the same name, and extending for a long distance rather east of north and west of south. It was a part of the great system of granite mountains which forms one of the most important and striking features of North America, stretching parallel to the coast of the Pacific from the Isthmus of Panama almost to the Arctic ocean; and presenting a corresponding chain to that of the Andes in the southern hemisphere. This vast range has acquired from its rugged and broken character, and its summits of naked granite, the appellation of the Rocky mountains, a name by no means distinctive, as all elevated ranges are rocky. Among the early explorers it was known as the range of Chippewyan mountains, and this Indian name is the one it is likely to retain in poetic usage. Rising from the midst of vast plains and prairies, traversing several degrees of latitude, dividing the waters of the Atlantic and the Pacific, and seeming to bind with diverging ridges the level regions on its flanks, it has been figuratively termed the backbone of the northern continent.

The Rocky mountains do not present a range of uniform elevation, but rather groups and occasionally detached peaks. Though some of these rise to the region of perpetual snows, and are upwards of eleven thousand feet in real altitude, yet their height from their immediate bases is not so great as might be imagined, as they swell up from elevated plains, several thousand feet above the level of the ocean. These plains are often of a desolate sterility, mere sandy wastes, formed of the detritus of the granite heights, destitute of trees and herbage, scorched by the ardent and reflected rays of the summer's sun, and, in winter, swept by chilling blasts from the snow-clad mountains. Such is a great part of that vast region extending north and south along the mountains, several hundred miles in width, which has not improperly been termed the Great American Desert. It is a region that almost discourages all hope of cultivation, and can only be traversed with safety by keeping near the streams which intersect it. Extensive plains likewise occur among the higher regions of the mountains, of considerable fertility.

Indeed, these lofty plats of table land seem to form a peculiar feature in the American continents. Some occur among the Cordilleras of the Andes, where cities and towns, and cultivated farms, are to be seen eight thousand feet above the level of the sea.

The Rocky mountains, as we have already observed, occur sometimes singly or in groups, and occasionally in collateral ridges. Between these are deep valleys, with small streams winding through them, which find their way into the lower plains, augmenting as they proceed, and ultimately discharging themselves into those vast rivers, which traverse the prairies like great arteries, and drain the continent.

While the granitic summits of the Rocky mountains are bleak and bare, many of the inferior ridges are scantily clothed with scrubbed pines, oaks, cedar, and furze. Various parts of the mountains also bear traces of volcanic action. Some of the interior valleys are strewed with scoria and broken stones, evidently of volcanic origin; the surrounding rocks bear the like character, and vestiges of extinguished craters are to be seen on the elevated heights.

We have already noticed the superstitious feelings with which the Indians regard the Black hills; but this immense range of mountains, which divides all that they know of the world, and give birth to such mighty rivers, is still more an object of awe and veneration. They call it " The crest of the world," and think that Wacondah, or the master of life, as they designate the Supreme Being, has his residence among these aerial heights. The tribes on the eastern prairies call them the mountains of the setting sun. Some of them place the " happy hunting grounds," their ideal paradise, among the recesses of these mountains; but say that they are invisible to living men. Here also is the " Land of souls," in which are the " towns of the free and generous spirits," where those who have pleased the master of life while living, enjoy after death all manner of delights.

Wonders are told of these mountains by the distant tribes, whose warriors or hunters have ever wandered in their neighbourhood. It is thought by some that, after death, they will have to travel these mountains, and ascend one of their highest and most rugged peaks, among rocks and snows and tumbling torrents. After many moons of painful toil they will reach the summit, from whence they will have a view over the land of souls. There they will see the happy hunting grounds, with the souls of the brave and good living in tents in green meadows, by bright running streams, or hunting the herds of buffalo, and elks, and deer, which have been slain on earth. There, too, they will see the villages or towns of the free and generous spirits brightening in the midst of delicious prairies. If they have acquitted themselves well while living, they will be permitted to descend, and enjoy this happy country; if otherwise, they will but be tantalised with this prospect of it, and then hurled back from the mountain, to wander about the sandy plains, and endure the eternal pangs of unsatisfied thirst and hunger.

CHAPTER X.

Region of the Crow Indians—Scouts on the look-out—Visit from a crew of hard riders—A Crow camp—Presents to the Crow chief—Bargaining—Crow bullies—Rose among his Indian friends—Parting with the Crows—Perplexities among the mountains—More of the Crows—Equestrian children—Search after stragglers.

THE travellers had now arrived in the vicinity of the mountain regions infested by the Crow Indians. These restless marauders, as has already been observed, are apt to be continually on the prowl about the skirts of the mountains; and even when encamped in some deep and secluded glen, they keep scouts upon the cliffs and promontories, who, unseen themselves, can discern every living thing that moves over the subjacent plains and valleys. It was not to be expected that our travellers could pass unseen through a region thus vigilantly sentinelled; accordingly, in the edge of the evening, not long after they had encamped at the foot of the Big Horn Sierra, a couple of wild-looking beings, scantily clad in skins, but well armed, and mounted on horses as wild-looking as themselves, were seen approaching with great caution from among the rocks. They might have been mistaken for two of the evil spirits of the mountains, so formidable in Indian fable.

Rose was immediately sent out to hold a parley with them, and invite them to the camp. They proved to be two scouts from the same band that had been tracked for some days past, and which was now encamped at some distance, in the folds of the mountain. They were easily prevailed upon to come to the camp, where they were well received, and, after remaining there until late in the evening, departed, to make a report of all they had seen and experienced, to their companions.

The following day had scarce dawned, when a troop of these wild mountain scamperers came galloping with whoops and yells into the camp, bringing an invitation from their chief for the white men to visit him. The tents were accordingly struck, the horses laden, and the party were soon on the march. The Crow horsemen, as they escorted them, appeared to take a pride in showing off their equestrian skill and hardihood; careering at full speed on their half-savage steeds, and dashing among rocks and crags, and up and down the most rugged and dangerous places with perfect ease and unconcern.

A ride of sixteen miles brought them, in the afternoon, in sight of the Crow camp. It was composed of leathern tents, pitched in a meadow, on the border of a small clear stream, at the foot of the mountain. A great number of horses were grazing in the vicinity, many of them doubtless captured in marauding excursions.

The Crow chieftain came forth to meet his guests, with great professions of friendship, and conducted them to his tents, pointing out, by the way, a convenient place where they might fix their camp. No sooner had they done so, than Mr. Hunt opened some of the packages, and made the chief a present of a scarlet blanket, and a quantity of powder and ball; he gave him also some knives, trinkets, and tobacco, to be distributed among his warriors; with all which the grim potentate seemed, for the time, well pleased. As the Crows, however, were reputed to be perfidious in the extreme, and as errant freebooters as the bird after which they were so worthily named, and as their general feelings towards the whites were known to be by no means friendly, the intercourse with them was conducted with great circumspection.

The following day was passed in trading with the Crows for buffalo robes and skins, and in bartering galled and jaded horses for others that were in good condition. Some of the men also purchased horses on their own account, so that the number now amounted to one hundred and twenty-one, most of them sound and active, and fit for mountain service.

Their wants being supplied, they ceased all further traffic, much to the dissatisfaction of the Crows, who became extremely urgent to continue the trade, and, finding their importunities of no avail, assumed an insolent and menacing tone. All this was attributed by Mr. Hunt and his associates to the perfidious instigations of Rose, the interpreter, who they suspected of the desire to foment ill will between them and the savages, for the promotion of his nefarious plans. M'Lellan, with his usual *tranchant* mode of dealing out justice, resolved to shoot the desperado on the spot in case of any outbreak. Nothing of the kind, however, occurred. The Crows were probably daunted by the resolute, though quiet, demeanour of the white men, and the constant vigilance and armed preparation which they maintained; and Rose, if he really still harboured his knavish designs, must have perceived that they were suspected, and, if attempted to be carried into effect, might bring ruin on his own head.

The next morning, bright and early, Mr. Hunt proposed to resume his journeying. He took a ceremonious leave of the Crow chieftain, and his vagabond warriors, and, according to previous arrangements, consigned to their cherishing friendship and fraternal adoption, their worthy confederate, Rose; who, having figured among the water pirates of the Mississippi, was well fitted to rise to distinction among the land pirates of the Rocky mountains.

It is proper to add that the ruffian was well received among the tribe, and appeared to be perfectly satisfied with the compromise he had made; feeling much more at his ease among savages than among white men. It is outcasts from civilization, fugitives from justice, and heartless desperadoes of this kind, who sow the seeds of enmity and bitterness among the unfortunate tribes of the frontier. There is no enemy so implacable against a country or a community as one of its own people, who has rendered himself an alien by his crimes.

Right glad to be relieved from this treacherous companion, Mr. Hunt pursued his course along the skirts of the mountain in a southern direction, seeking for some practicable defile by which he might pass through it; none such presented, however, in the course of fifteen miles, and he encamped on a small stream, still on the outskirts. The green meadows which border these mountain streams are generally well stocked with game, and the hunters soon killed several fat elks, which supplied the camp with fresh meat. In the evening the travellers were surprised by an unwelcome visit from several Crows, belonging to a different band from that which they had recently left, and who said their camp was among the mountains. The consciousness of being environed by such dangerous neighbours, and of being still within the range of Rose and his fellow ruffians, obliged the party to be continually on the alert, and to maintain weary vigils throughout the night, lest they should be robbed of their horses.

On the 3d of September, finding that the mountain still stretched onwards, presenting a continued barrier, they endeavoured to force a passage to the westward, but soon became entangled among rocks and precipices which set all their efforts at defiance. The mountain seemed for the most part rugged, bare, and steril; yet here and there it was clothed with pines, and with shrubs and flowering plants, some of which were in bloom. In toiling among

these weary places, their thirst became excessive, for no
water was to be met with.   Numbers of the men wandered off into rocky dells and ravines, in hopes of finding
some brook or fountain; some of whom lost their way,
and did not rejoin the main party.

After half a day of painful and fruitless scrambling,
Mr. Hunt gave up the attempt to penetrate in this direction, and, returning to the little stream on the skirts of
the mountain, pitched his tents within six miles of his
encampment of the preceding night.   He now ordered
that signals should be made for the stragglers in quest of
water, but the night passed away without their return.

The next morning, to their surprise, Rose made his
appearance at the camp, accompanied by some of his
Crow associates.   His unwelcome visit revived their suspicions, but he announced himself as a messenger of
good-will from the chief, who, finding they had taken a
wrong road, had sent Rose and his companions to guide
them to a nearer and better one across the mountain.

Having no choice, being themselves utterly at fault,
they set out under this questionable escort.   They had
not gone far before they fell in with the whole party of
Crows, who, they now found, were going the same road
with themselves.   The two cavalcades of white and red
men, therefore, pushed on together, and presented a wild
and picturesque spectacle, as, equipped with various
weapons and in various garbs, with trains of packhorses,
they wound in long lines through the rugged defiles, and
up and down the crags and steeps of the mountain.

The travellers had again an opportunity to see and
admire the equestrian habitudes and address of this hard-
riding tribe.   They were all mounted, man, woman, and
child; for the Crows have horses in abundance, so that no
one goes on foot. The children are perfect imps on horseback.   Among them was one so young that he could not
yet speak.   He was tied on a colt of two years old, but
managed the reins as if by instinct, and plied the whip
with true Indian prodigality.   Mr. Hunt inquired the age
of this infant jockey, and was answered that " he had
seen two winters."

This is almost realizing the fable of the centaurs ; nor can we wonder at the equestrian adroitness of these savages, who are thus in a manner cradled in the saddle, and become in infancy almost identified with the animal they bestride.

The mountain defiles were exceedingly rough and broken, and the travelling painful to the burdened horses. The party, therefore, proceeded but slowly, and were gradually left behind by the band of Crows, who had taken the lead. It is more than probable that Mr. Hunt loitered in his course, to get rid of such fellow-travellers. Certain it is that he felt a sensation of relief as he saw the whole crew, the renegade Rose and all, disappear among the windings of the mountain, and heard the last yelp of the savages die away in the distance.

When they were fairly out of sight and out of hearing, he encamped on the head waters of the little stream of the preceding day, having come about sixteen miles. Here he remained all the succeeding day, as well to give time for the Crows to get in the advance, as for the stragglers, who had wandered away in quest of water two days previously, to rejoin the camp. Indeed, considerable uneasiness began to be felt concerning these men, lest they should become utterly bewildered in the defiles of the mountains, or should fall into the hands of some marauding band of savages. Some of the most experienced hunters were sent in search of them; others, in the mean time, employed themselves in hunting. The narrow valley in which they encamped being watered by a running stream, yielded fresh pasturage, and, though in the heart of the Big Horn mountains, was well stocked with buffalo. Several of these were killed, as also a grizzly bear. In the evening, to the satisfaction of all parties, the stragglers made their appearance, and provisions being in abundance, there was hearty good cheer in the camp.

CHAPTER XI.

RESUMING their course on the following morning, Mr. Hunt and his companions continued on westward through a rugged region of hills and rocks, but diversified in many places by grassy little glens, with springs of water, bright sparkling brooks, clumps of pine trees, and a profusion of flowering plants, which were in full bloom, although the weather was frosty. These beautiful and verdant recesses, running through and softening the rugged mountains, were cheering and refreshing to the wayworn travellers.

In the course of the morning, as they were entangled in a defile, they beheld a small band of savages, as wild looking as the surrounding scenery, who reconnoitred them warily from the rocks before they ventured to advance. Some of them were mounted on horses rudely caparisoned, with bridles or halters of buffalo hide, one end trailing after them on the ground. They proved to be a mixed party of Flatheads and Shoshonies, or Snakes; and as these tribes will be frequently mentioned in the course of this work, we shall give a few introductory particulars concerning them.

The Flatheads in question are not to be confounded with those of the name who dwell about the lower waters of the Columbia ; neither do they flatten their heads, as the others do. They inhabit the banks of a river on the west side of the mountains, and are described as simple, honest, and hospitable. Like all people of similar character, whether civilized or savage, they are prone to be imposed upon ; and are especially maltreated by the ruthless Blackfeet, who harass them in their villages, steal their horses by night, or openly carry them off in the face of day, without provoking pursuit or retaliation.

The Shoshonies are a branch of the once powerful and

prosperous tribe of the Snakes, who possessed a glorious hunting country about the upper forks of the Missouri, abounding in beaver and buffalo. Their hunting ground was occasionally invaded by the Blackfeet, but the Snakes battled bravely for their domains, and a long and bloody feud existed, with variable success. At length the Hudson's Bay Company, extending their trade into the interior, had dealings with the Blackfeet, who were nearest to them, and supplied them with fire-arms. The Snakes, who occasionally traded with the Spaniards, endeavoured, but in vain, to obtain similar weapons; the Spanish traders wisely refused to arm them so formidably.

The Blackfeet had now a vast advantage, and soon dispossessed the poor Snakes of their favourite hunting grounds, their land of plenty, and drove them from place to place, until they were fain to take refuge in the wildest and most desolate recesses of the Rocky mountains. Even here they are subjected to occasional visits from their implacable foes, as long as they have horses, or any other property to tempt the plunderer. Thus by degrees the Snakes have become a scattered, broken-spirited, impoverished people; keeping about lonely rivers and mountain streams, and subsisting chiefly upon fish. Such of them as still possess horses, and occasionally figure as hunters, are called Shoshonies; but there is another class, the most abject and forlorn, who are called Shuckers, or more commonly Diggers and Root-eaters. These are a shy, secret, solitary race, who keep in the most retired parts of the mountains, lurking like gnomes in caverns and clefts of the rocks, and subsisting in a great measure on the roots of the earth. Sometimes, in passing through a solitary mountain valley, the traveller comes perchance upon the bleeding carcass of a deer or buffalo that has just been slain. He looks round in vain for the hunter; the whole landscape is lifeless and deserted: at length he perceives a thread of smoke, curling up from among the crags and cliffs, and scrambling to the place, finds some forlorn and skulking brood of Diggers, terrified at being discovered.

The Shoshonies, however, who, as has been observed,

have still " horse to ride and weapon to wear," are somewhat bolder in their spirit, and more open and wide in
their wanderings.   In the autumn, when salmon disappear
from the rivers, and hunger begins to pinch, they even
venture down into their ancient hunting grounds, to make
a foray among the buffaloes.   In this perilous enterprise
they are occasionally joined by the Flatheads, the perse-
cutions of the Blackfeet having produced a close alliance
and co-operation between these luckless and maltreated
tribes.   Still, notwithstanding their united force, every
step they take within the debateable ground, is taken in
fear and trembling, and with the utmost precaution : and
an Indian trader assures us, that he has seen at least five
hundred of them, armed and equipped for action, and
keeping watch upon the hill tops, while about fifty were
hunting in the prairie.   Their excursions are brief and
hurried : as soon as they have collected and jerked sufficient buffalo meat for winter provisions, they pack their
horses, abandon the dangerous hunting grounds, and
hasten back to the mountains, happy if they have not the
terrible Blackfeet rattling after them.

Such a confederate band of Shoshonies and Flatheads
was the one met by our travellers.   It was bound on a
visit to the Arapahoes, a tribe inhabiting the banks of the
Nebraska.   They were armed to the best of their scanty
means, and some of the Shoshonies had bucklers of buffalo hide, adorned wtth feathers and leathern fringes, and
which have a charmed virtue in their eyes, from having
been prepared, with mystic ceremonies, by their conjurers.

In company with this wandering band our travellers
proceeded all day.   In the evening they encamped near
to each other in a defile of the mountains, on the borders
of a stream running north, and falling into Bighorn river.
In the vicinity of the camp, they found gooseberries,
strawberries, and currants, in great abundance.   The defile bore traces of having been a thoroughfare for countless
herds of buffaloes, though not one was to be seen.   The
hunters succeeded in killing an elk and several black-
tailed deer.

They were now in the bosom of the second Bighorn ridge, with another lofty and snow-crowned mountain full in view to the west. Fifteen miles of western course brought them, on the following day, down into an intervening plain, well stocked with buffalo. Here the Snakes and Flatheads joined with the white hunters in a successful hunt, that soon filled the camp with provisions.

On the morning of the 9th of September, the travellers parted company with their Indian friends, and continued on their course to the west. A march of thirty miles brought them, in the evening, to the banks of a rapid and beautifully clear stream about a hundred yards wide. It is the north fork or branch of the Bighorn river, but bears its peculiar name of the Wind river, from being subject in the winter season to a continued blast which sweeps its banks and prevents the snow from lying on them. This blast is said to be caused by a narrow gap or funnel in the mountains through which the river forces its way between perpendicular precipices, resembling cut rocks.

This river gives its name to a whole range of mountains consisting of three parallel chains, eighty miles in length, and about twenty or twenty-five broad. One of its peaks is probably fifteen thousand feet above the level of the sea, being one of the highest of the Rocky Sierra. These mountains give rise, not merely to the Wind or Bighorn river, but to several branches of the Yellowstone and the Missouri on the east, and of the Columbia and Colorado on the west; thus dividing the sources of these mighty streams.

For five succeeding days, Mr. Hunt and his party continued up the course of the Wind river, to the distance of about eighty miles, crossing and recrossing it, according to its windings, and the nature of its banks; sometimes passing through valleys, at other times scrambling over rocks and hills. The country in general was destitute of trees, but they passed through groves of wormwood, eight and ten feet in height, which they used occasionally for fuel, and they met with large quantities of wild flax.

The mountains were destitute of game; they came in sight of two grizzly bears, but could not get near enough for a shot; provisions therefore began to be scanty. They saw large flights of the kind of thrush commonly called the robin, and many smaller birds of migratory species; but the hills in general appeared lonely and with few signs of animal life. On the evening of the 14th September, they encamped on the forks of the Wind, or Bighorn river. The largest of these forks came from the range of Wind river mountains.

The hunters who served as guides to the party in this part of their route, had assured Mr. Hunt that, by following up Wind river, and crossing a single mountain ridge, he would come upon the waters of the Columbia. The scarcity of game, however, which already had been felt to a pinching degree, and which threatened them with famine among the steril heights which lay before them, admonished them to change their course. It was determined, therefore, to make for a stream, which, they were informed, passed through the neighbouring mountains, to the south of west, on the grassy banks of which it was probable they would meet with buffalo. Accordingly, about three o'clock on the following day, meeting with a beaten Indian road which led in the proper direction, they struck into it, turning their backs upon Wind river.

In the course of the day, they came to a height that commanded an almost boundless prospect. Here one of the guides paused, and, after considering the vast landscape attentively, pointed to three mountain peaks glistening with snow, which rose, he said, above a fork of Columbia river. They were hailed by the travellers with that joy with which a beacon on a seashore is hailed by mariners after a long and dangerous voyage. It is true there was many a weary league to be traversed before they should reach these landmarks: for, allowing for their evident height, and the extreme transparency of the atmosphere, they could not be much less than a hundred miles distant. Even after reaching them, there would yet remain hundreds of miles of their journey to be accomplished. All these matters were forgotten in the joy at seeing the first landmarks of the Columbia, that river which formed the bourn of the expedition. These remarkable peaks are known to some travellers as the Tetons: as they had been guiding points for many days to **Mr.** Hunt, he gave them the name of the Pilot Knobs.

The travellers continued their course to the south of west for about forty miles, through a region so elevated that patches of snow lay on the highest summi ts, and on the northern declivities. At length they came to the desired stream, the object of their search, the waters of which flowed to the west. It was, in fact, a branch of the Colorado, which falls into the gulf of California, and had received from the hunters the name of Spanish river, from information given by the Indians, that Spaniards resided upon its lower waters.

The aspect of this river and its vicinity was cheering to the wayworn and hungry travellers. Its banks were green, and there were grassy valleys running from it in various directions, into the heart of the rugged mountains, with herds of buffalo quietly grazing. The hunters sallied forth with keen alacrity, and soon returned laden with provisions.

In this part of the mountains Mr. Hunt met with three different kinds of gooseberries. The common purple, on a low and very thorny bush ; a yellow kind, of an excellent flavour, growing on a stalk free from thorns ; and a deep purple, of the size and taste of our winter grape, with a thorny stalk. There were also three kinds of currants, one very large, and well tasted, of a purple colour, and growing on a bush eight or nine feet high. Another of a yellow colour, and of the size and taste of the large red currant, the bush four or five feet high ; and the third a beautiful scarlet, resembling the strawberry in sweetness, though rather insipid, and growing on a low bush.

On the 17th, they continued down the course of the river, making fifteen miles to the south-west. The river abounded with geese and ducks, and there were signs of its being inhabited by beaver and otters ; indeed they were now approaching regions where these animals, the great object of the fur trade, are said to abound. They encamped for the night opposite the end of a mountain in the west, which was probably the last chain of the Rocky mountains. On the following morning they abandoned the main course of Spanish river, and taking a north-west direction for eight miles, came upon one of its little tributaries, issuing out of the bosom of the mountains, and running through green meadows, yielding pasturage to herds of buffalo. As these were probably the last of that animal they would meet with, they encamped on the grassy banks of the river, determined to spend several days in hunting, so as to be able to jerk sufficient meat to supply them until they should reach the waters of the Columbia, where they trusted to find fish enough for their support. A little repose, too, was necessary for both men and horses, after their rugged and incessant marching ; having in the course of the last seventeen days, traversed two hundred and sixty miles of rough and, in many parts, steril mountain country.

CHAPTER XII.

A plentiful hunting camp—Shoshonie hunters—Hoback's river—Mad river— Encampment near the Pilot Knobs—A consultation—Preparations for a perilous voyage.

FIVE days were passed by Mr. Hunt and his companions in the fresh meadows watered by the bright little mountain stream. The hunters made great havoc among the buffaloes, and brought in quantities of meat ; the voyageurs busied themselves about the fires, roasting and stewing for present purposes, or drying provisions for the journey ; the packhorses, eased of their burdens, rolled in the grass, or grazed at large about the ample pastures ; those of the party who had no call upon their services, indulged in the luxury of perfect relaxation, and the camp presented a picture of rude feasting and revelry, of mingled bustle and repose, characteristic of a halt in a fine hunting country. In the course of one of their excursions, some of the men came in sight of a small party of Indians, who instantly fled in great apparent consternation. They immediately returned to camp with the intelligence; upon which Mr. Hunt and four others flung themselves upon their horses, and sallied forth to reconnoitre. After riding for about eight miles, they came upon a wild mountain scene. A lonely green valley stretched before them, surrounded by rugged heights. A herd of buffalo were careering madly through it, with a troop of savage horsemen in full chase, plying them with their bows and arrows. The appearance of Mr. Hunt and his companions put an abrupt end to the hunt; the buffalo scuttled off in one direction, while the Indians plied their lashes and galloped off in another, as fast as their steeds could carry them. Mr. Hunt gave chase; there was a sharp scamper, though of short continuance. Two young Indians, who were indifferently mounted, were soon overtaken. They were terribly frightened, and evidently gave themselves up for lost. By degrees their fears were allayed by kind treatment; but they continued to regard the strangers with a mixture of awe and wonder; for it was the first time in their lives they had ever seen a white man.

They belonged to a party of Snakes who had come across the mountains on their autumnal hunting excursion to provide buffalo meat for the winter. Being persuaded of the peaceable intentions of Mr. Hunt and his companions, they willingly conducted them to their camp. It was pitched in a narrow valley on the margin of a stream. The tents were of dressed skins, some of them fantastically painted; with horses grazing about them. The approach of the party caused a transient alarm in the camp, for these poor Indians were ever on the look-out for cruel foes. No sooner, however, did they recognise the garb and complexion of their visiters than their apprehensions were changed into joy; for some of them had dealt with white men, and knew them to be friendly, and to abound with articles of singular value. They welcomed them, therefore, to their tents, set food before them, and entertained them to the best of their power.

They had been successful in their hunt, and their camp was full of jerked buffalo meat; all of the choicest kind,

and extremely fat.   Mr. Hunt purchased enough of them,
in addition to what had been killed and cured by his own
hunters, to load all the horses excepting those reserved
for the partners and the wife of Pierre Dorion.   He
found also a few beaver skins in their camp, for which
he paid liberally, as an inducement for them to hunt for
more ; informing them that some of his party intended to
live among the mountains, and trade with the native
hunters for their peltries.   The poor Snakes soon compre-
hended the advantages thus held out to them, and promised to exert themselves to procure a quantity of beaver
skins for future traffic.

Being now well supplied with provisions, Mr. Hunt
broke up his encampment on the 24th of September, and
continued on to the west.   A march of fifteen miles, over
a mountain ridge, brought them to a stream about fifty feet
in width, which Hoback, one of their guides, who had
traped about the neighbourhood when in the service of
Mr. Henry, recognised for one of the head waters of
the Columbia.   The travellers hailed it with delight, as
the first stream they had encountered tending toward
their point of destination.   They kept along it for two
days, during which, from the contribution of many rills
and brooks, it gradually swelled into a small river.   As
it meandered among rocks and precipices, they were frequently obliged to ford it, and such was its rapidity, that
the men were often in danger of being swept away.   Sometimes the banks advanced so close upon the river, that they
were obliged to scramble up and down their rugged promontories, or to skirt along their bases where there was
scarce a foothold.   Their horses had dangerous falls in
some of these passes.   One of them rolled, with his load,
nearly two hundred feet down hill into the river,
but without receiving any injury.   At length they
emerged from these stupendous defiles, and continued for several miles along the bank of Hoback's
river, through one of the stern mountain valleys.   Here
it was joined by a river of greater magnitude and swifter
current, and their united waters swept off through the
valley in one impetuous stream, which, from its rapidity
and turbulence, had received the name of Mad river.   At

the confluence of these streams the travellers encamped. An important point in their arduous journey had been obtained : a few miles from their camp rose the three vast snowy peaks called the Tetons, or the Pilot Knobs, the great landmarks of the Columbia, by which they had shaped their course through this mountain wilderness. By their feet flowed the rapid current of Mad river, a stream ample enough to admit of the navigation of canoes, and down which they might possibly be able to steer their course to the main body of the Columbia. The Canadian voyageurs rejoiced at the idea of once more launching themselves upon their favourite element ; of exchanging their horses for canoes, and of gliding down the bosoms of rivers, instead of scrambling over the backs of mountains. Others of the party, also inexperienced in this kind of travelling, considered their toils and troubles as drawing to a close. They had conquered the chief difficulties of this great rocky barrier, and now flattered themselves with the hope of an easy downward course for the rest of their journey. Little did they dream of the hardships and perils by land and water, which were yet to be encountered in the frightful wilderness that intervened between them and the shores of the Pacific.

CHAPTER XIII.

A consultation whether to proceed by land or water—Preparations for boatbuilding—An exploring party—A party of trappers detached—Two Snake visiters—Their report concerning the river—Confirmed by the exploring party—Mad river abandoned—Arrival at Henry's fort—Detachment of Robinson, Hoback, and Rezner to trap—Mr. Miller resolves to accompany them—Their departure.

On the banks of Mad river Mr. Hunt held a consultation with the other parties as to their future movements. The wild and impetuous current of the river rendered him doubtful whether it might not abound with impediments lower down, sufficient to render the navigation of it slow

and perilous, if not impracticable.   The hunters, who had
acted as guides, knew nothing of the character of the river
below ; what rocks, and shoals, and rapids might obstruct
it, or through what mountains and deserts it might pass.
Should they then abandon their horses, cast themselves
loose in fragile barks upon this wild, doubtful, and unknown river ? or should they continue their more toilsome
and tedious, but, perhaps, more certain wayfaring by
land ?

The vote, as might have been expected, was almost
unanimous for embarkation ; for when men are in difficulties, every change seems to be for the better.   The
difficulty now was, to find timber of sufficient size for the
construction of canoes, the trees in these high mountain
regions being chiefly a scrubbed growth of pines and
cedars, aspens, haws, and service berries, and a small
kind of cotton tree, with a leaf resembling that of the
willow.   There was a species of large fir, but so full of
knots, as to endanger the axe in hewing it.   After searching for some time, a growth of timber, of sufficient size,
was found lower down the river, whereupon the encampment was moved to the vicinity.

The men were now set to work to fell trees, and the
mountains echoed to the unwonted sound of their axes.
While preparations were thus going on for a voyage down
the river, Mr, Hunt, who still entertained doubts of its
practicability, despatched an exploring party, consisting
of John Reed the clerk, John Day the hunter, and Pierre
Dorion the interpreter, with orders to proceed several
days' march along the stream, and notice its course and
character.

After their departure, Mr. Hunt turned his thoughts to
another object of importance.   He had now arrived at
the head waters of the Columbia, which were among the
main points [embraced by the enterprise of Mr. Astor.
These upper streams were reputed to abound in beaver,
and had as yet been unmolested by the white trapper.
The numerous signs of beaver met with during the recent
search for timber, gave evidence that the neighbourhood
was a good " trapping ground."   Here, then, it was pro-

per to begin to cast loose those leashes of hardy trappers, that are detached from trading parties, in the very heart of the wilderness. The men detached in the present instance were Alexander Carson, Louis St. Michel, Pierre Detayé, and Pierre Delaunay. Trappers generally go in pairs ,that they may assist, protect, and comfort each other in their lonely and perilous occupations. Thus Carson and St. Michel formed one couple, and Detayé and Delaunay another. They were fitted out with traps, arms, ammunition, horses, and every other requisite, and were to trap upon the upper part of Mad river, and upon the neighbouring streams of the mountains. This would probably occupy them for some months; and, when they should have collected a sufficient quantity of peltries, they were to pack them upon their horses, and make the best of their way to the mouth of Columbia river, or to any intermediate post which might be established by the company. They took leave of their comrades, and started off on their several courses with stout hearts and cheerful countenances; though these lonely cruisings into a wild and hostile wilderness seem to the uninitiated equivalent to being cast adrift in the ship's yawl in the midst of the ocean.

Of the perils that attend the lonely trapper, the reader will have sufficient proof, when he comes, in the after part of this work, to learn the hard fortunes of these poor fellows in the course of their wild peregrinations.

The trappers had not long departed, when two Snake Indians wandered into the camp. When they perceived that the stangers were fabricating canoes, they shook their heads, and gave them to understand that the river was not navigable. Their information, however, was scoffed at by some of the party, who were obstinately bent on embarkation, but was confirmed by the exploring party, who returned after several days' absence. They had kept along the river with great difficulty for two days, and found it a narrow, crooked, turbulent stream, confined in a rocky channel, with many rapids, and occasionally overhung with precipices. From the summit of one of these they had caught a bird's eye view of its boisterous career, for a great distance, through the heart of the mountain, with impending rocks and cliffs. Satisfied, from this view, that it was useless to follow its course, either by land or water, they had given up all further investigation.

These concurring reports determined Mr. Hunt to abandon Mad river, and seek some more navigable stream. This determination was concurred in by all his associates excepting Mr. Miller, who had become impatient of the fatigue of land travel, and was for immediate embarkation at all hazards. This gentleman had been in a gloomy and irritated state of mind for some time past, being troubled with a bodily malady that rendered travelling on horseback extremely irksome to him, and being, moreover, discontented with having a smaller share in the expedition than his comrades. His unreasonable objections to a further march by land were overruled, and the party prepared to decamp.

Robinson, Hoback, and Rezner, the three hunters who had hitherto served as guides among the mountains, now stepped forward, and advised Mr. Hunt to make for the post established during the preceding year by Mr. Henry, of the Missouri Fur Company. They had been with Mr. Henry, and, as far as they could judge by the neighbouring landmarks, his post could not be very far off. They presumed there could be but one intervening ridge of mountains, which might be passed without any great difficulty. Henry's post, or fort, was on an upper branch of the Columbia, down which they made no doubt it would be easy to navigate in canoes.

The two Snake Indians being questioned in the matter, showed a perfect knowledge of the situation of the post, and offered with great alacrity to guide them to the place. Their offer was accepted, greatly to the displeasure of Mr. Miller, who seemed obstinately bent upon braving the perils of the Mad river.

The weather for a few days past had been stormy, with rain and sleet. The Rocky mountains are subject to tempestuous winds from the west; these sometimes come in flaws or currents, making a path through the forests many yards in width, and whirling off trunks and branches to a great distance. The present storm subsided on the 3d of October, leaving all the surrounding heights covered with snow; for, while rain had fallen in the valley, it had snowed on the hill tops.

On the 4th, they broke up their encampment, and crossed the river, the water coming up to the girths of their horses. After travelling four miles, they encamped at the foot of the mountain, the last, as they hoped, which they should have to traverse. Four days more took them across it, and over several plains, watered by beautiful little streams, tributaries of Mad river. Near one of their encampments there was a hot spring continually emitting a cloud of vapour. These elevated plains, which give a peculiar character to the mountains, are frequented by large gangs of antelopes, fleet as the wind.

On the evening of the 8th October, after a cold wintry day, with gusts of westerly wind and flurries of snow, they arrived at the sought for post of Mr. Henry. Here he had fixed himself, after being compelled by the hostilities of the Blackfeet, to abandon the upper waters of the Missouri. The post, however, was deserted, for Mr. Henry had left it in the course of the preceding spring, and, as it afterwards appeared, had fallen in with Mr. Lisa, at the Aricara village on the Missouri, some time after the separation of Mr. Hunt and his party.

The weary travellers gladly took possession of the deserted log-huts which had formed the post, and which stood on the bank of a stream upwards of a hundred yards wide, on which they intended to embark. There being plenty of suitable timber in the neighbourhood, Mr. Hunt immediately proceeded to construct canoes. As he would have to leave his horses and their accoutrements here, he determined to make this a trading post, where the trappers and hunters, to be distributed about the country, might repair; and where the traders might touch on their way through the mountains to and from the establishment at the mouth of the Columbia. He informed the two Snake Indians of this determination, and engaged them to remain in that neighbourhood, and take care of the horses until the white men should return, promising them ample rewards for their fidelity. It may seem a desperate chance to trust to the faith and honesty of two such vagabonds ; but, as the horses would have, at all events, to be abandoned, and would otherwise become the property of the first vagrant horde that should encounter them, it was one chance in favour of their being regained.

At this place another detachment of hunters prepared to separate from the party for the purpose of trapping beaver. Three of these had already been in this neighbourhood, being the veteran Robinson and his companions, Hoback and Rezner, who had accompanied Mr. Henry across the mountains, and who had been picked up by Mr. Hunt on the Missouri, on their way home to Kentucky. According to agreement, they were fitted out with horses, traps, ammunition, and every thing requisite for their undertaking, and were to bring in all the peltries they should collect, either to this trading post, or to the establishment at the mouth of Columbia river. Another hunter, of the name of Cass, was associated with them in their enterprise. It is in this way that small knots of trappers and hunters are distributed about the wilderness by the fur companies, and, like cranes and bitterns, haunt its solitary streams. Robinson the Kentuckian, the veteran of the "bloody ground," who, as has already been noted, had been scalped by the Indians in his younger days, was the leader of this little band. When they were about to depart, Mr. Miller called the partners together, and threw up his share in the company, declaring his intention of joining the party of trappers.

This resolution struck every one with astonishment, Mr. Miller being a man of education and of cultivated habits, and little fitted for the rude life of a hunter. Beside, the precarious and slender profits arising from such a life were beneath the prospects of one who held a share in the general enterprise. Mr. Hunt was especially concerned and mortified at his determination, as it was through his advice and influence he had entered into the concern. He endeavoured, therefore, to dissuade him from this sudden resolution; representing its rashness and the hardships and perils to which it would expose him. He earnestly advised him, however he might feel dissatisfied with the enterprise, still to continue on in company until they should reach the mouth of Columbia river. There they would meet the expedition that was to come by sea; when, should he still feel disposed to relinquish the undertaking, Mr. Hunt pledged himself to furnish him a passage home in one of the vessels belonging to the company.

To all this, Miller replied abruptly, that it was useless to argue with him, as his mind was made up. They might furnish him, or not, as they pleased, with the necessary supplies, but he was determined to part company here, and set off with the trappers. So saying, he flung out of their presence without vouchsafing any further conversation.

Much as this wayward conduct gave them anxiety, the partners saw it was in vain to remonstrate. Every attention was paid to fit him out for his headstrong undertaking. He was provided with four horses, and all the articles he required. The two Snakes undertook to conduct him and his companions to an encampment of their tribe, lower down among the mountains, from whom they would receive information as to the best trapping grounds. After thus guiding them, the Snakes were to return to Fort Henry, as the new trading post was called, and take charge of the horses which the party would leave there, of which, after all the hunters were supplied, there remained seventy-seven. These matters being all arranged, Mr. Miller set out with his companions, under guidance of the two Snakes, on the 10th of October; and much did it grieve the friends of that gentleman to see him thus wantonly casting himself loose upon savage life. How he and his comrades fared in the wilderness, and how the Snakes acquitted themselves of their trust, respecting the horses, will hereafter appear in the course of these rambling anecdotes.

CHAPTER XIV.

WHILE the canoes were in preparation, the hunters
ranged about the neighbourhood, but with little success.
Tracts of buffaloes were to be seen in all directions, but
none of a fresh date. There were some elk, but extremely
wild; two only were killed. Antelopes were likewise
seen, but too shy and fleet to be approached. A few beavers were taken every night, and salmon trout of a small
size, so that the camp had principally to subsist upon
dried buffalo meat.

On the 14th, a poor, half-naked Snake Indian, one of
that forlorn caste called the Shuckers, or diggers, made
his appearance at the camp. He came from some lurking
place among the rocks and cliffs, and presented a picture
of that famishing wretchedness to which these lonely fugitives among the mountains are sometimes reduced. Having received wherewithal to allay his hunger, he disappeared, but in the course of a day or two returned to the
camp, bringing with him his son, a miserable boy, still
more naked and forlorn than himself. Food was given to
both; they skulked about the camp like hungry hounds,
seeking what they might devour, and having gathered up
the feet and entrails of some beavers that were lying
about, slunk off with them to their den among the rocks.

By the 18th of October, fifteen canoes were completed,
and on the following day the party embarked with their
effects; leaving their horses grazing about the banks, and
trusting to the honesty of the two Snakes, and some
special turn of good luck, for their future recovery.

The current bore them along at a rapid rate; the light
spirits of the Canadian voyageurs, which had occasionally
flagged upon land, rose to their accustomed buoyancy on
finding themselves again upon the water. They wielded

their paddles with their wonted dexterity, and for the first time made the mountains echo with their favourite boat songs.

In the course of the day the little squadron arrived at the confluence of Henry and Mad rivers, which, thus united, swelled into a beautiful stream of a light pea-green colour, navigable for boats of any size, and which, from the place of junction, took the name of Snake river, a stream doomed to be the scene of much disaster to the travellers. The banks were here and there fringed with willow thickets and small cotton-wood trees. The weather was cold, and it snowed all day, and great flocks of ducks and geese, sporting in the water or streaming through the air, gave token that winter was at hand; yet the hearts of the travellers were light, and, as they glided down the little river, they flattered themselves with the hope of soon reaching the Columbia. After making thirty miles in a southerly direction, they encamped for the night in a neighbourhood which required some little vigilance, as there were recent traces of grizzly bears among the thickets.

On the following day the river increased in width and beauty; flowing parallel to a range of mountains on the left, which at times were finely reflected in its light green waters. The three snowy summits of the Pilot Knobs, or Tetons, were still seen towering in the distance. After pursuing a swift but placid course for twenty miles, the current began to foam and brawl, and assume the wild and broken character common to the streams west of the Rocky mountains. In fact, the rivers which flow from those mountains to the Pacific, are essentially different from those which traverse the great prairies on their eastern declivities. The latter, though sometimes boisterous, are generally free from obstructions, and easily navigated; but the rivers to the west of the mountains descend more steeply and impetuously, and are continually liable to cascades and rapids. The latter abounded in the part of the river which the travellers were now descending. Two of the canoes filled among the breakers; the crews were saved, but much of the lading was lost or damaged, and one of the canoes drifted down the stream and was broken among the rocks.

On the following day, October 21st, they made but a short distance when they came to a dangerous strait, where the river was compressed for nearly half a mile between perpendicular rocks, reducing it to the width of twenty yards, and increasing its violence. Here they were obliged to pass the canoes down cautiously by a line from the impending banks. This consumed a great part of a day ; and after they had re-embarked they were soon again impeded by rapids, when they had to unload their canoes, and carry them and their cargoes for some distance by land. It is at these places, called " portages," that the Canadian voyageur exhibits his most valuable qualities ; carrying heavy burdens, and toiling to and fro, on land and in the water, over rocks and precipices, among brakes and brambles, not only without a murmur, but with the greatest cheerfulness and alacrity, joking and laughing, and singing scraps of old French ditties.

The spirits of the party, however, which had been elated on first varying their journey from land to water, had now lost some of their buoyancy. Every thing ahead was wrapped in uncertainty. They knew nothing of the river on which they were floating. It had never before been navigated by a white man, nor could they meet with an Indian to give them any information concerning it. It kept on its course through a vast wilderness of silent and apparently uninhabited mountains, without a savage wigwam upon its banks, or bark upon its waters. The difficulties and perils they had already passed, made them apprehend others before them, that might effectually bar their progress. As they glided onward, however, they regained heart and hope. The current continued to be strong ; but it was steady, and though they met with frequent rapids, none of them were bad. Mountains were constantly to be seen in different directions, but sometimes the swift river glided through prairies, and was bordered by small cotton-wood trees and willows. These prairies at certain seasons are ranged by migratory herds of the wide-wandering buffalo, the tracks of which, though not of recent date, were frequently to be seen. Here, too, were to be found the prickly pear or Indian fig, a plant which loves a more southern climate. On the land were large flights of magpies, and American robins; whole fleets of ducks and geese navigated the river, or flew off in long streaming files at the approach of the canoes; while the frequent establishments of the pains-taking and quiet-loving beaver, showed that the solitude of these waters was rarely disturbed, even by the all-per-vading savage.

They had now come near two hundred and eighty miles since leaving Fort Henry, yet without seeing a human being, or a human habitation; a wild and desert solitude extended on either side of the river, apparently almost destitute of animal life. At length, on the 24th of October, they were gladdened by the sight of some savage tents, and hastened to land, and visit them, for they were anxious to procure information to guide them on their route. On their approach, however, the savages fled in consternation. They proved to be a wandering band of Shoshonies. In their tents were great quantities of small fish about two inches long, together with roots and seeds, or grain, which they were drying for winter provisions. They appeared to be destitute of tools of any kind, yet there were bows and arrows very well made; the former were formed of pine, cedar, or bone, strength-ened by sinews, and the latter of the wood of rose bushes, and other crooked plants, but carefully straightened, and tipped with stone of a bottle-green colour.

There were also vessels of willow and grass, so closely wrought as to hold water, and a seine neatly made with meshes, in the ordinary manner, of the fibres of wild flax or nettle. The humble effects of the poor savages re-mained unmolested by their visiters, and a few small arti-cles, with a knife or two, were left in the camp, and were no doubt regarded as invaluable prizes.

Shortly after leaving this deserted camp, and re-em-barking in the canoes, the travellers met with three of the Snakes on a triangular raft made of flags or reeds; such was their rude mode of navigating the river. They were entirely naked excepting small mantles of hare skins over their shoulders. The canoes approached near enough to gain a full view of them, but they were not to be brought to a parley.

All further progress for the day was barred by a fall in the river of about thirty feet perpendicular; at the head of which the party encamped for the night.

The next day was one of excessive toil, and but little progress: the river winding through a wild rocky country, and being interrupted by frequent rapids, among which the canoes were in great peril. On the succeeding day they again visited a camp of wandering Snakes, but the inhabitants fled with terror at the sight of a fleet of canoes, filled with white men, coming down their solitary river.

As Mr. Hunt was extremely anxious to gain information concerning his route, he endeavoured by all kinds of friendly signs to entice back the fugitives. At length one, who was on horseback, ventured back with fear and trembling. He was better clad, and in better condition than most of his vagrant tribe that Mr. Hunt had yet seen. The chief object of his return appeared to be to intercede for a quantity of dried meat and salmon trout, which he had left behind; on which, probably, he depended for his winter's subsistence. The poor wretch approached with hesitation, the alternate dread of famine and of white men operating upon his mind. He made the most abject signs, imploring Mr. Hunt not to carry off his food. The latter tried in every way to reassure him, and offered him knives in exchange for his provisions: great as was the temptation, the poor Snake could only prevail upon himself to spare a part; keeping a feverish watch over the rest, lest it should be taken away. It was in vain Mr. Hunt made inquiries of him concerning his route, and the course of the river. The Indian was too much frightened and bewildered to comprehend him or to reply; he did nothing but alternately commend himself to the protection of the Good Spirit, and supplicate Mr. Hunt not to take away his fish and buffalo meat; and in this state they left him, trembling about his treasures.

In the course of that and the next day they made nearly

eighty miles; the river inclining to the south of west, and being clear and beautiful, nearly half a mile in width, with many populous communities of the beaver along its banks. The 28th of October, however, was a day of disaster. The river again became rough and impetuous, and was chafed and broken by numerous rapids. These grew more and more dangerous, and the utmost skill was required to steer among them. Mr. Crooks was seated in the second canoe of the squadron, and had an old experienced Canadian for steersman, named Antoine Clappine, one of the most valuable of the voyageurs. The leading canoe had glided safely among the turbulent and roaring surges, but in following it, Mr. Crooks perceived that his canoe was bearing towards a rock. He called out to the steersman, but his warning voice was either unheard or unheeded. In the next moment they struck upon the rock. The canoe was split and overturned. There were five persons on board. Mr. Crooks and one of his companions were thrown amidst roaring breakers and a whirling current, but succeeded, by strong swimming, to reach the shore. Clappine and two others clung to the shattered bark, and drifted with it to a rock. The wreck struck the rock with one end, and, swinging round, flung poor Clappine off into the raging stream, which swept him away, and he perished. His comrades succeeded in getting upon the rock, from whence they were afterwards taken off.

This disastrous event brought the whole squadron to a halt, and struck a chill into every bosom. Indeed, they had arrived at a terrific strait, that forbade all further progress in the canoes, and dismayed the most experienced voyageur. The whole body of the river was compressed into a space of less than thirty feet in width, between two ledges of rocks, upwards of two hundred feet high, and formed a whirling and tumultuous vortex, so frightfully agitated, as to receive the name of "The Caldron Linn." Beyond this fearful abyss, the river kept raging and roaring on, until lost to sight among impending precipices.

CHAPTER XV.

MR. HUNT and his companions encamped upon the borders of the Caldron Linn, and held gloomy council as to their future course. The recent wreck had dismayed even the voyageurs, and the fate of their popular comrade, Clappine, one of the most adroit and experienced of their fraternity, had struck sorrow to their hearts ; for, with all their levity, these thoughtless beings have great kindness towards each other.

The whole distance they had navigated since leaving Henry's fort, was computed to be about three hundred and forty miles ; strong apprehensions were now entertained that the tremendous impediments before them would oblige them to abandon their canoes. It was determined to send exploring parties on each side of the river, to ascertain whether it was possible to navigate it further. Accordingly, on the following morning, three men were despatched along the south bank, while Mr. Hunt and three others proceeded along the north. The two parties returned after a weary scramble among swamp, rocks, and precipices, and with very disheartening accounts. For nearly forty miles that they had explored, the river foamed and roared along through a deep and narrow channel, from twenty to thirty yards wide, which it had worn in the course of ages, through the heart of a barren rocky country. The precipices on each side were often two and three hundred feet high, sometimes perpendicular and sometimes overhanging, so that it was impossible, excepting in one or two places, to get down to the margin of the stream. This dreary strait was rendered the more dangerous by frequent rapids, and occasionally perpendicular falls from ten to forty feet in height ; so that it seemed almost hopeless to attempt to pass the

canoes down it.   The party, however, who had explored
the south side of the river had found a place, about six
miles from the camp, where they thought it possible the
canoes might be carried down the bank and launched
upon the stream, and from whence they might make their
way with the aid of occasional portages.   Four of the
best canoes were accordingly selected for the experiment,
and were transported to the place on the shoulders of
sixteen of the men.   At the same time, Mr. Reed, the
clerk, and three men, were detached to explore the river
still further down than the previous scouting parties had
been, and at the same time to look out for Indians, from
whom provisions might be obtained and a supply of horses,
should it be found necessary to proceed by land.

The party who had been sent with the canoes returned
on the following day, weary and dejected.   One of the
canoes had been swept away with all the weapons and
effects of four of the voyageurs, in attempting to pass it
down a rapid by means of a line.   The other three had
stuck fast among the rocks, so that it was impossible to
move them ; the men returned, therefore, in despair, and
declared the river unnavigable.

The situation of the unfortunate travellers was now
gloomy in the extreme.   They were in the heart of an
unknown wilderness, untraversed as yet by a white man.
They were at a loss what route to take, and how far they
were from the ultimate place of their destination, nor
could they meet, in these uninhabited wilds, with any
human being to give them information.   The repeated
accidents to their canoes had reduced their stock of provisions to five days' allowance, and there was now every
appearance of soon having famine added to their other
sufferings.

This last circumstance rendered it more perilous to keep
together than to separate.   Accordingly, after a little
anxious but bewildered council, it was determined that
several small detachments should start off in different directions, headed by the several partners.   Should any of
them succeed in falling in with friendly Indians, within a
reasonable distance, and obtaining a supply of provisions

and horses, they were to return to the aid of the main
body : otherwise, they were to shift for themselves, and
shape their course according to circumstances ; keeping
the mouth of Columbia river as the ultimate point of their
wayfaring.   Accordingly, three several small parties set
off from the camp at Caldron Linn, in opposite directions.   Mr. M‘Lellan, with three men, kept down along
the bank of the river.   Mr. Crooks, with five others,
turned their steps up it ; retracing by land the wary course
they had made by water, intending, should they not find
relief nearer at hand, to keep on until they should reach
Henry's fort, where they hoped to find the horses they had
left there, and to return with them to the main body.

The third party, composed of five men, was headed by
Mr. M‘Kenzie, who struck to the northward, across the
desert plains, in hopes of coming upon the main stream
of the Columbia.

Having seen these three adventurous bands depart
upon their forlorn expeditions, Mr. Hunt turned his
thoughts to provide for the subsistence of the main body
left to his charge, and to prepare for their future march.
There remained with him thirty-one men, besides the
squaw and two children of Pierre Dorion.   There was no
game to be met with in the neighbourhood ; but beavers
were occasionally trapped about the river banks, which
afforded a scanty supply of food ; in the mean time they
comforted themselves that some or other of the foraging
detachments would be successful, and return with relief.

Mr. Hunt now set to work with all diligence, to prepare *caches*, in which to deposit the baggage and merchandise, of which it would be necessary to disburden
themselves, preparatory to their weary march by land ;
and here we shall give a brief description of those con-
trivances so noted in the wilderness.

A cache is a term common among traders and hunters,
to designate a hiding place for provisions and effects.   It
is derived from the French word *cacher*, to conceal, and
originated among the early colonists of Canada and Louisiana ; but the secret depository which it designates was
in use among the aboriginals long before the intrusion of

the white men.   It is, in fact, the only mode that migratory hordes have of preserving their valuables from robbery, during their long absences from their villages or accustomed haunts, on hunting expeditions, or during the vicissitudes of war.   The utmost skill and caution are required to render these places of concealment invisible to the lynx eye of an Indian.   The first care is to seek out a proper situation, which is generally some dry low bank of clay, on the margin of a water course.   As soon as the precise spot is pitched upon, blankets, saddle cloths, and other coverings, are spread over the surrounding grass and bushes, to prevent foot tracks, or any other derangement; and as few hands as possible are employed.   A circle of about two feet in diameter is then nicely cut in the sod, which is carefully removed, with the loose soil immediately beneath it, and laid aside in a place where it will be safe from any thing that may change its appearance. The uncovered area is then digged perpendicularly to the depth of about three feet, and is then gradually widened so as to form a conical chamber six or seven feet deep. The whole of the earth displaced by this process, being of a different colour from that on the surface, is handed up in a vessel, and heaped into a skin or cloth, in which it is conveyed to the stream and thrown into the midst of the current, that it may be entirely carried off.   Should the cache not be formed in the vicinity of a stream, the earth thus thrown up is carried to a distance, and scattered in such a manner as not to leave the minutest trace. The cave being formed, is well lined with dry grass, bark, sticks and poles, and occasionally a dried hide.   The property intended to be hidden is then laid in, after having been well aired: a hide is spread over it, and dried grass, brush, and stones, thrown in, and trampled down until the pit is filled to the neck, the loose soil, which had been put aside, is then brought, and rammed down firmly, to prevent its caving in, and is frequently sprinkled with water, to destroy the scent, lest the wolves and bears should be attracted to the place, and root up the concealed treasure.   When the neck of the cache is nearly level with the surrounding surface, the sod is again fitted in with the utmost exactness, and any bushes, stocks, or stones, that may have originally been about the spot, are restored to their former places.   The blankets and other coverings are then removed from the surrounding herbage: all tracks are obliterated; the grass is gently raised by the hand to its natural position, and the minutest chip or straw is scrupulously gleaned up and thrown into the stream.   After all is done, the place is abandoned for the night, and, if all be right next morning, is not visited again, until there be a necessity for re-opening the cache. Four men are sufficient in this way to conceal the amount of three tons' weight of provisions or merchandize, in the course of two days.   Nine caches were required to contain the goods and baggage which Mr. Hunt found it necessary to leave at this place.

Three days had been thus employed since the departure of the several detachments, when that of Mr. Crooks unexpectedly made its appearance.   A momentary joy was diffused through the camp, for they supposed succour to be at hand.   It was soon dispelled.   Mr. Crooks and his companions had become completely disheartened by this retrograde march through a bleak and barren country: and had found, computing from their progress and the accumulating difficulties besetting every step, that it would be impossible to reach Henry's fort, and return to the main body in the course of the winter.   They had determined, therefore, to rejoin their comrades, and share their lot.

One avenue of hope was thus closed upon the anxious sojourners at the Caldron Linn; their main expectation of relief was now from the two parties under Reed and M'Lellan, which had proceeded down the river; for, as to Mr. M'Kenzie's detachment, which had struck across the plains, they thought it would have sufficient difficulty in struggling forward through the trackless wilderness. For five days they continued to support themselves by trapping and fishing.   Some fish of tolerable size were speared at night by the light of cedar torches; others, that were very small, were caught in nets with fine meshes. The product of their fishing, however, was very scanty.

Their trapping was also precarious; and the tails and bellies of the beavers were dried and put by for the journey.

At length, two of the companions of Mr. Reed returned, and were hailed with the most anxious eagerness. Their report served but to increase the general despondency. They had followed Mr. Reed for some distance below the point to which Mr. Hunt had explored, but had met with no Indians, from whom to obtain information and relief. The river still presented the same furious aspect, brawling and boiling along a narrow and rugged channel, between rocks that rose like walls.

A lingering hope, which had been indulged by some of the party, of proceeding by water, was now finally given up: the long and terrific strait of the river set all further progress at defiance, and in their disgust at the place, and their vexation at the disasters sustained there, they gave it the indignant, though not very decorous appellation of the Devil's Scuttle Hole.

CHAPTER XVI.

Determination of the party to proceed on foot—Dreary deserts between Snake river and the Columbia—Distribution of effects preparatory to a march—Division of the party—Rugged march along the river—Wild aud broken scenery—Shoshonies—Alarm of a Snake encampment—Intercourse with the Snakes—Horse-dealing—Value of a tin kettle—Sufferings from thirst—A horse reclaimed—Fortitude of an Indian woman—Scarcity of food—Dogs' flesh a dainty—News of Mr. Crooks and his party—Painful travelling among the mountains—Snow storms—A dreary mountain prospect—A bivouac during a wintry night—Return to the river bank.

THE resolution of Mr. Hunt and his companions was now taken to set out immediately on foot. As to the other detachments that had in a manner gone forth to seek their fortunes, there was little chance of their return; they would probably make their own way through the wilderness. At any rate, to linger in the vague hope of relief from them, would be to run the risk of perishing with hunger. Besides, the winter was rapidly advancing, and they had a long journey to make through an unknown country, where all kinds of perils might await them. They were yet, in fact, a thousand miles from Astoria, but the distance was unknown to them at the time: every thing before and around them was vague and conjectural, and wore an aspect calculated to inspire despondency.

In abandoning the river, they would have to launch forth upon vast trackless plains destitute of all means of subsistence, where they might perish of hunger and thirst. A dreary desert of sand and gravel extends from Snake river almost to the Columbia. Here and there is a thin and scanty herbage, insufficient for the pasturage of horse or buffalo. Indeed these treeless wastes between the Rocky mountains and the Pacific, are even more desolate and barren than the naked upper prairies on the Atlantic side: they present vast desert tracts that must ever defy cultivation, and interpose dreary and thirsty wilds between the habitations of man, in traversing which, the wanderer will often be in danger of perishing.

Seeing the hopeless character of these wastes, Mr. Hunt and his companions determined to keep along the course of the river, where they would always have water at hand, and would be able occasionally to procure fish and beaver, and might perchance meet with Indians, from whom they could obtain provisions.

They now made their final preparations for the march. All their remaining stock of provisions consisted of forty pounds of Indian corn, twenty pounds of grease, about five pounds of portable soup, and a sufficient quantity of dried meat to allow each man a pittance of five pounds and a quarter, to be reserved for emergencies. This being properly distributed, they deposited all their goods and superfluous articles in the caches, taking nothing with them but what was indispensable to the journey. With all their management, each man had to carry twenty pounds' weight, beside his own articles and equipments.

That they might have the better chance of procuring subsistence in the scanty regions they were to traverse, they divided their party into two bands; Mr. Hunt, with eighteen men, beside Pierre Dorion and his family, was to proceed down the north side of the river, while Mr. Crooks, with eighteen men, kept along the south side.

On the morning of the 9th of October, the two parties separated, and set forth on their several courses. Mr. Hunt and his companions followed along the right bank of the river, which made its way far below them, brawling at the foot of perpendicular precipices of solid rock, two and three hundred feet high. For twenty-eight miles that they travelled this day, they found it impossible to get down to the margin of the stream. At the end of this distance, they encamped for the night at a place which admitted a scrambling descent. It was with the greatest difficulty, however, that they succeeded in getting up a kettle of water from the river, for the use of the camp. As some rain had fallen in the afternoon, they passed the night under the shelter of the rocks.

The next day they continued thirty-two miles to the north-west, keeping along the river, which still ran in its deep-cut channel. Here and there a sandy beach, or a narrow strip of soil, fringed with dwarf willows, would extend for a little distance along the foot of the cliffs, and sometimes a reach of still water would intervene like a smooth mirror between the foaming rapids.

As through the preceding day, they journeyed on without finding, except in one instance, any place where they could get down to the river's edge, and they were fain to allay the thirst caused by hard travelling, with the water collected in the hollow of the rocks.

In the course of their march on the following morning, they fell into a beaten horse path, leading along the river, which showed that they were in the neighbourhood of some Indian village or encampment. They had not proceeded far along it, when they met with two Shoshonies, or Snakes. They approached with some appearance of uneasiness, and, accosting Mr. Hunt, held up a knife, which, by signs they let him know, they had received from some of the white men of the advance parties. It was with some difficulty that Mr. Hunt prevailed upon one of the savages to conduct him to the lodges of his people. Striking into a trail or path which led up from the river, he guided them for some distance in the prairie, until they came in sight of a number of lodges, made of straw, and shaped like haystacks. Their approach, as on former occasions, caused the wildest affright among the inhabitants. The women hid such of their children as were too large to be carried, and too small to take care of themselves, under straw, and, clasping their infants to their breasts, fled across the prairie. The men awaited the approach of the strangers, but evidently in great alarm.

Mr. Hunt entered the lodges, and, as he was looking about, observed where the children were concealed; their black eyes glistening like those of snakes from beneath the straw. He lifted up the covering to look at them; the poor little beings were horribly frightened, and their fathers stood trembling, as if a beast of prey were about to pounce upon the brood.

The friendly manner of Mr. Hunt soon dispelled these apprehensions; he succeeded in purchasing some excellent dried salmon, and a dog, an animal much esteemed as food, by the natives; and when he returned to the river, one of the Indians accompanied him. He now came to where lodges were frequent along the banks, and, after a day's journey of twenty-six miles to the north-west, encamped in a populous neighbourhood. Forty or fifty of the natives soon visited the camp, conducting themselves in a very amicable manner. They were well clad, and all had buffalo robes, which they procured from some of the hunting tribes, in exchange for salmon. Their habitations were very comfortable; each had its pile of wormwood at the door for fuel, and within was abundance of salmon, some fresh, but the greater part cured. When the white men visited the lodges, however, the women and children hid themselves through fear. Among the supplies obtained here were two dogs, on which our travellers breakfasted, and found them to be very excellent, well-flavoured, and hearty food.

In the course of the three following days, they made about sixty-three miles, generally in a north-west direction. They met with many of the natives in their straw-built cabins, who received them without alarm. About their dwellings were immense quantities of the heads and skins of salmon, the best parts of which had been cured, and hidden in the ground. The women were badly clad; the children worse; their garments were buffalo robes, or the skins of foxes, wolves, hares, and badgers, and sometimes the skins of ducks, sewed together, with the plumage on. Most of the skins must have been procured by traffic with other tribes, or in distant hunting excursions, for the naked prairies in the neighbourhood afforded few animals, excepting horses, which were abundant. There were signs of buffaloes having been there, but a long time before.

On the 15th of November, they made twenty-eight miles along the river, which was entirely free from rapids. The shores were lined with dead salmon, which tainted the whole atmosphere. The natives whom they met spoke of Mr. Reed's party having passed through that neighbourhood. In the course of the day, Mr. Hunt saw a few horses, but the owners of them took care to hurry them out of the way. All the provisions they were able to procure, were two dogs and a salmon. On the following day, they were still worse off, having to subsist on parched corn, and the remains of their dried meat. The river this day had resumed its turbulent character, forcing its way through a narrow channel between steep rocks, and down violent rapids. They made twenty miles over a rugged road, gradually approaching a mountain in the north-west, covered with snow, which had been in sight for three days past.

On the 17th, they met with several Indians, one of whom had a horse. Mr. Hunt was extremely desirous of obtaining it as a packhorse; for the men, worn down by fatigue and hunger, found the load of twenty pounds' weight, which they had to carry, daily growing heavier and more galling. The Indians, however, along this river, were never willing to part with their horses, having none to spare. The owner of the steed in question seemed proof against all temptation; article after article, of great value in Indian eyes, was offered, and refused. The charms of an old tin kettle, however, were irresistible, and a bargain was concluded.

A great part of the following morning was consumed in lightening the packages of the men and arranging the load for the horse. At this encampment there was no food for fuel, even the wormwood on which they had frequently depended, having disappeared. For the two last days they had made thirty miles to the north-west.

On the 19th of November, Mr. Hunt was lucky enough to purchase another horse for his own use, giving in exchange a tomahawk, a knife, a fire steel, and some beads and gartering. In an evil hour, however, he took the advice of the Indians to abandon the river, and follow a road or trail, leading into the prairies. He soon had cause to repent the change. The road led across a dreary waste, without verdure; and where there was neither fountain, nor pool, nor running stream. The men now began to experience the torments of thirst, aggravated by their usual diet of dried fish. The thirst of the Canadian voyageurs became so insupportable as to drive them to the most revolting means of allaying it. For twenty-five miles did they toil on across this dismal desert, and laid themselves down at night, parched and disconsolate beside their wormwood fires; looking forward to still greater sufferings on the following day. Fortunately it began to rain in the night, to their infinite relief ; the water soon collected in puddles, and afforded them delicious draughts.

Refreshed in this manner, they resumed their wayfaring as soon as the first streaks of dawn gave light enough for them to see their path. The rain continued all day, so that they no longer suffered from thirst, but hunger took its place ; for, after travelling thirty-three miles, they had nothing to sup on but a little parched corn.

The next day brought them to the banks of a beautiful little stream, running to the west, and fringed with groves of cotton-wood and willow. On its borders was an Indian camp, with a great many horses grazing around it. The inhabitants, too, appeared to be better clad than usual. The scene was altogether a cheering one to the poor half-famished wanderers. They hastened to the lodges, but on arriving at them, met with a check that at first dampened their cheerfulness.   An Indian immediately laid claim to the horse of Mr. Hunt, saying that it had been stolen from him.   There was no disproving a fact, supported by numerous bystanders, and which the horse-stealing habits of the Indians rendered but too probable; so Mr. Hunt relinquished his steed to the claimant, not being able to retain him by a second purchase.

At this place they encamped for the night, and made a sumptuous repast upon fish and a couple of dogs, procured from their Indian neighbours.   The next day they kept along the river, but came to a halt after ten miles march, on account of the rain.   Here they again got a supply of fish and dogs from the natives; and two of the men were fortunate enough each to get a horse in exchange for a buffalo robe.   One of these men was Pierre Dorion, the half-breed interpreter, to whose suffering family the horse was a most timely acquisition.   And here we cannot but notice the wonderful patience, perseverance, and hardihood of the Indian women, as exemplified in the conduct of the poor squaw of the interpreter.   She was now far advanced in her pregnancy, and had two children to take care of; one four, and the other two years of age.   The latter of course she had frequently to carry on her back, in addition to the burden usually imposed upon the squaw, yet she had borne all her hardships without a murmur, and throughout this weary and painful journey, had kept pace with the best of the pedestrians.   Indeed, on various occasions in the course of this enterprise, she displayed a force of character that won the respect and applause of the white men.

Mr. Hunt endeavoured to gather some information from these Indians concerning the country, and the course of the rivers.   His communications with them had to be by signs, and a few words which he had learnt, which of course were extremely vague.   All that he could learn from them was, that the great river, the Columbia, was still far distant, but he could ascertain nothing as to the route he ought to take to arrive at it.   For the two following days they continued westward upwards of forty miles along the little stream, until they crossed it just before its junction with Snake river, which they found still running to the north. Before them was a wintry-looking mountain, covered with snow on all sides.

In three days more they made about seventy miles; fording two small rivers, the waters of which were very cold. Provisions were extremely scarce; their chief sustenance was portable soup; a meager diet for weary pedestrians.

On the 27th of November the river led them into the mountains through a rocky defile where there was scarcely room to pass. They were frequently obliged to unload the horses to get them by the narrow places; and sometimes to wade through the water in getting round rocks and butting cliffs. All their food this day was a beaver which they had caught the night before; by evening, the cravings of hunger were so sharp, and the prospect of any supply among the mountains so faint, that they had to kill one of the horses. "The men," says Mr. Hunt, in his journal, "find the meat very good, and, indeed, so should I, were it not for the attachment I have to the animal."

Early in the following day, after proceeding ten miles to the north, they came to two lodges of Shoshonies; who seemed in nearly as great an extremity as themselves, having just killed two horses for food. They had no other provisions excepting the seed of a weed which they gather in great quantities, and pound fine. It resembles hemp seed. Mr. Hunt purchased a bag of it, and also some small pieces of horseflesh, which he began to relish, pronouncing them "fat and tender."

From these Indians he received information that several white men had gone down the river, some on one side, and a good many on the other; these last he concluded to be Mr. Crooks and his party. He was thus released from much anxiety about their safety, especially as the Indians spoke of Mr. Crooks having one of his dogs yet, which showed that he and his men had not been reduced to extremity of hunger.

As Mr. Hunt feared he might be several days in passing through this mountain defile, and run the risk of famine, he encamped in the neighbourhood of the Indians, for the purpose of bartering with them for a horse. The evening was expended in ineffectual trials. He offered a gun, a buffalo robe, and various other articles. The poor fellows had, probably, like himself, the fear of starvation before their eyes. At length the women, learning the object of his pressing solicitations and tempting offers, set up such a horrible hue and cry, that he was fairly howled and scolded from the ground.

The next morning early, the Indians seemed very desirous to get rid of their visiters, fearing probably for the safety of their horses. In reply to Mr. Hunt's inquiries about the mountains, they told him that he would have to sleep but three nights more among them; and that six days travelling would take him to the falls of the Columbia; information in which he put no faith, believing it was only given to induce him to set forward. These, he was told, were the last Snakes he would meet with, and that he would soon come to a nation called Sciatogas.

Forward then did he proceed on his tedious journey, which at every step grew more painful. The road continued for two days through narrow defiles, where they were repeatedly obliged to unload the horses. Sometimes the river passed through such rocky chasms and under such steep precipices, that they had to leave it, and make their way, with excessive labour, over immense hills, almost impassable for horses. On some of these hills were a few pine trees, and their summits were covered with snow. On the second day of this scramble one of the hunters killed a black-tailed deer, which afforded the half-starved travellers a sumptuous repast. Their progress these two days was twenty-eight miles, a little to the northward of east.

The month of December set in drearily, with rain in the valleys, and snow upon the hills. They had to climb a mountain with snow to the midleg, which increased their painful toil. A small beaver supplied them with a scanty meal, which they eked out with frozen blackberries, haws, and chokecherries, which they found in the course of their scamble. Their journey this day, though excessively fatiguing, was but thirteen miles; and all the next day they had to remain encamped, not being able to see half a mile ahead, on account of a snow storm. Having nothing else to eat, they were compelled to kill another of their horses. The next day they resumed their march in snow and rain, but with all their efforts could only get forward nine miles, having for a part of the distance to unload the horses and carry the packs themselves. On the succeeding morning they were obliged to leave the river, and scramble up the hills. From the summit of these, they got a wide view of the surrounding country, and it was a prospect almost sufficient to make them despair. In every direction they beheld snowy mountains, partially sprinkled with pines and other evergreens, and spreading a desert and toilsome world around them. The wind howled over the bleak and wintry landscape, and seemed to penetrate to the marrow of their bones, They waded on through the snow, which at every step was more than knee deep.

After toiling in this way all day, they had the mortification to find that they were but four miles distant from the encampment of the preceding night, such was the meandering of the river among these dismal hills. Pinched with famine, exhausted with fatigue, with evening approaching, and a wintry wild still lengthening as they advanced; they began to look forward with sad forebodings to the night's exposure upon this frightful waste. Fortunately they succeeded in reaching a cluster of pines about sunset. Their axes were immediately at work; they cut down trees, piled them up in great heaps, and soon had huge fires "to cheer their cold and hungry hearts."

About three o'clock in the morning it again began to snow, and at daybreak they found themselves, as it were, in a cloud; scarcely being able to distinguish objects at the distance of a hundred yards. Guiding themselves by the sound of running water, they set out for the river, and by slipping and sliding contrived to get down to its bank. One of the horses, missing his foot, rolled down several hundred yards with his load, but sustained no injury. The weather in the valley was less rigorous than on the hills. The snow lay but ankle deep, and there was a quiet rain now falling. After creeping along for six miles, they encamped on the border of the river. Being utterly destitute of provisions, they were again compelled to kill one of their horses to appease their famishing hunger.

CHAPTER XVII.

An unexpected meeting—Navigation in a skin canoe—Strange fears of suffering men—Hardships of Mr. Crooks and his comrades—Tidings of Mr. M'Lellan—A retrograde march—A willow raft—Extreme suffering of some of the party—Illness of Mr. Crooks—Impatience of some of the men—Necessity of leaving the laggards behind.

THE wanderers had now accomplished four hundred and seventy-two miles of their dreary journey since leaving the Caldron Linn : how much further they had yet to travel, and what hardships to encounter, no one knew.

On the morning of the 6th of December, they left their dismal encampment, but had scarcely begun their march, when, to their surprise, they beheld a party of white men coming up along the opposite bank of the river. As they drew nearer, they were recognised for Mr. Crooks and his companions. When they came opposite, and could make themselves heard across the murmuring of the river, their first cry was for food ; in fact, they were almost starved. Mr. Hunt immediately returned to the camp, and had a kind of canoe made out of the skin of the horse, killed on the preceding night. This was done after the Indian fashion, by drawing up the edges of the skin with thongs, and keeping them distended by sticks or thwarts pieces. In this frail bark, Sardepie, one of the Canadians, carried over a portion of the flesh of the horse to the famishing party on the opposite side of the river, and brought back with him Mr. Crooks, and the Canadian, Le Clerc. The forlorn and wasted looks, and starving condition of these two men, struck dismay into the hearts of Mr. Hunt's followers. They had been accustomed to each other's appearance, and to the gradual operation of hunger and hardship upon their frames, but the change in the looks of these men, since last they parted, was a type of the famine and desolation of the land; and they now began to indulge the horrible presentiment that they would all starve together, or be reduced to the direful alternative of casting lots!

When Mr. Crooks had appeased his hunger, he gave Mr. Hunt some account of his wayfaring. On the side of the river along which he had kept, he had met with but few Indians, and those were too miserably poor to yield much assistance. For the first eighteen days, after leaving the Caldron Linn, he and his men had been confined to half a meal in twenty-four hours; for three days following, they had subsisted on a single beaver, a few wild cherries, and the soles of old mocassins; and for the last six days, their only animal food had been the carcass of a dog. They had been three days' journey further down the river than Mr. Hunt, always keeping as near to its banks as possible, and frequently climbing over sharp and rocky ridges that projected into the stream. At length they had arrived to where the mountains increased in height, and came closer to the river, with perpendicular precipices, which rendered it impossible to keep along the streams. The river here rushed with incredible velocity through a defile not more than thirty yards wide, where cascades and rapids succeeded each other almost without intermission. Even had the opposite banks, therefore, been such as to permit a continuance of their journey, it would have been madness to attempt to pass the tumultuous current, either on rafts or otherwise. Still bent, however, on pushing forward, they attempted to climb the opposing mountains; and struggled on through the snow for half a day, until, coming to where they could command a prospect, they found that they were not half way to the summit, and that mountain upon mountain lay piled beyond them, in wintry desolation. Famished and emaciated as they were, to continue forward would be to perish; their only chance seemed to be to regain the river, and retrace their steps up its banks.

It was in this forlorn and retrograde march that they had met with Mr. Hunt and his party.

Mr. Crooks also gave information of some others of their fellow-adventurers. He had spoken several days previously with Mr. Reed and Mr. M‘Kenzie, who, with their men, were on the opposite side of the river, where it was impossible to get over to them. They informed him that Mr. M‘Lellan had struck across from the little river above the mountains, in the hope of falling in with some of the tribe of Flatheads, who inhabit the western skirts of the Rocky range. As the companions of Reed and M Kenzie were picked men, and had found provisions more abundant on their side of the river, they were in better condition, and more fitted to contend with the difficulties of the country than those of Mr. Crooks, and when he lost sight of them, were pushing onward, down the course of the river.

Mr. Hunt took a night to revolve over his critical situation, and to determine what was to be done. No time was to be lost; he had twenty men and more, in his own party, to provide for, and Mr. Crooks and his men to relieve. To linger would be to starve. The idea of retracing his steps was intolerable, and, notwithstanding all the discouraging accounts of the ruggedness of the mountains lower down the river, he would have been disposed to attempt them, but the depth of the snow with which they were covered, deterred him; having already experienced the impossibility of forcing his way against such an impediment.

The only alternative, therefore, appeared to be, to return and seek the Indian bands scattered along the small rivers and mountains. Perhaps, from some of these he might procure horses enough to support him until he could reach the Columbia; for he still cherished the hope of arriving at that river in the course of the winter, though he was apprehensive that few of Mr. Crook's party would be sufficiently strong to follow him. Even in adopting this course, he had to make up his mind to the certainty of several days of famine at the outset, for it would take that time to reach the last Indian lodges from which he had parted, and until they should arrive there, his people would have nothing to subsist upon but haws and wild berries, excepting one miserable horse, which was little better than skin and bone.

After a night of sleepless cogitation, Mr. Hunt announced to his men the dreary alternative he had adopted, and preparations were made to take Mr. Crooks and Le Clerc across the river, with the remainder of the meat, as the other party were to keep up along the opposite bank. The skin canoe had unfortunately been lost in the night; a raft was constructed, therefore, after the manner of the natives, of bundles of willows, but it could not be floated across the impetuous current. The men were directed, in consequence, to keep on along the river by themselves, while Mr. Crooks and Le Clerc would proceed with Mr. Hunt. They all, then, took up their retrograde march with drooping spirits.

In a little while, it was found that Mr. Crooks and Le Clerc were so feeble as to walk with difficulty, so that Mr. Hunt was obliged to retard his pace, that they might keep up with him. His men grew impatient at the delay. They murmured that they had a long and desolate region to traverse, before they could arrive at the point where they might expect to find horses; that it was impossible for Crooks and Le Clerc, in their feeble condition, to get over it; that to remain with them would only to be starve in their company. They importuned Mr. Hunt, therefore, to leave these unfortunate men to their fate, and think only of the safety of himself and his party. Finding him not to be moved, either by entreaties or their clamours, they began to proceed without him, singly and in parties. Among those who thus went off was Pierre Dorion, the interpreter. Pierre owned the only remaining horse, which was now a mere skeleton. Mr. Hunt had suggested, in their present extremity, that it should be killed for food; to which the half-breed flatly refused his assent, and cudgelling the miserable animal forward, pushed on sullenly, with the air of a man doggedly deter-

mined to quarrel for his right.   In this way Mr. Hunt
saw his men, one after another, break away, until but five
remained to bear him company.

On the following morning another raft was made, on
which Mr. Crooks and Le Clerc again attempted to ferry
themselves across the river, but after repeated trials, had
to give up in despair.   This caused additional delay;
after which they continued to crawl forward at a snail's
pace.   Some of the men who had remained with Mr.
Hunt now became impatient of these incumbrances, and
urged him, clamorously, to push forward, crying out that
they should all starve.   The night which succeeded was
intensely cold, so that one of the men was severely frost-
bitten.   In the course of the night, Mr. Crooks was taken
ill, and in the morning was still more incompetent to
travel.   Their situation was now desperate, for their stock
of provisions was reduced to three beaver skins.   Mr.
Hunt, therefore, resolved to push on, overtake his people,
and insist upon having the horse of Pierre Dorion sacrificed for the relief of all hands.   Accordingly, he left two
of his men to help Crooks and Le Clerc on their way,
giving them two of the beaver skins for their support; the
remaining skin he retained, as provision for himself and
the three other men who struck forward with him.

CHAPTER XVIII.

Mr. Hunt overtakes the advanced party—Pierre Dorion, and his skeleton
horse—A Shoshonie camp—A justifiable outrage—Feasting on horseflesh—
Mr. Crooks brought to the camp—Undertakes to relieve his men—The skin
ferry boat—Frenzy of Prevost—His melancholy fate—Enfeebled state of
John Day—Mr. Crooks again left behind—The party emerge from among
the mountains—Interview with Shoshonies—A guide procured to conduct
the party across a mountain—Ferriage across Snake river—Re-union with
Mr. Crooks's men—Final departure from the river.

ALL that day Mr. Hunt and his three comrades travelled without eating.   At night they made a tantalizing
supper on their beaver skin, and were nearly starved with
hunger and cold.   The next day, December 10th, they

overtook the advance party, who were all as much famished as themselves, some of them not having eaten since the morning of the 7th. Mr. Hunt now proposed the sacrifice of Pierre Dorion's skeleton horse. Here he again met with positive and vehement opposition from the half-breed, who was too sullen and vindictive a fellow to be easily dealt with. What was singular, the men, though suffering such pinching hunger, interfered in favour of the horse. They represented, that it was better to keep on as long as possible without resorting to this last resource. Possibly the Indians, of whom they were in quest, might have shifted their encampment, in which case it would be time enough to kill the horse to escape starvation. Mr. Hunt, therefore, was prevailed upon to grant Pierre Dorion's horse a reprieve.

Fortunately, they had not proceeded much further, when, towards evening, the came in sight of a lodge of Shoshonies, with a number of horses grazing around it. The sight was as unexpected as it was joyous. Having seen no Indians in this neighbourhood as they passed down the river, they must have subsequently come out from among the mountains. Mr. Hunt, who first descried them, checked the eagerness of his companions, knowing the unwillingness of these Indians to part with their horses, and their aptness to hurry them off and conceal them, in case of alarm. This was no time to risk such a disappointment. Approaching, therefore, stealthily and silently, they came upon the savages by surprise, who fled in terror. Five of their horses were eagerly seized, and one was despatched upon the spot. The carcass was immediately cut up, and a part of it hastily cooked and ravenously devoured. A man was now sent on horseback with a supply of the flesh to Mr. Crooks and his companions. He reached them in the night: they were so famished that the supply sent them seemed but to aggravate their hunger, and they were almost tempted to kill and eat the horse that had brought the messenger. Availing themselves of the assistance of the animal, they reached the camp early in the morning.

On arriving there, Mr. Crooks was shocked to find that,

while the people on this side of the river were amply supplied with provisions, none had been sent to his own forlorn and famishing men on the opposite bank. He immediately caused a skin canoe to be constructed, and called out to his men to fill their camp kettles with water, and hang them over the fire, that no time might be lost in cooking the meat the moment it should be received. The river was so narrow, though deep, that every thing could be distinctly heard and seen across it. The kettles were placed on the fire, and the water was boiling by the time the canoe was completed. When all was ready, however, no one would undertake to ferry the meat across. A vague, and almost superstitious, terror had infected the minds of Mr. Hunt's followers, enfeebled and rendered imaginative of horrors by the dismal scenes and sufferings through which they had passed. They regarded the haggard crew, hovering like spectres of famine on the opposite bank, with indefinite feelings of awe and apprehension, as if something desperate and dangerous was to be feared from them.

Mr. Crooks tried in vain to reason or shame them out of this singular state of mind. He then attempted to navigate the canoe himself, but found his strength incompetent to brave the impetuous current. The good feelings of Ben Jones, the Kentuckian, at length overcame his fears, and he ventured over. The supply he brought was received with trembling avidity. A poor Canadian, however, named Jean Baptiste Prevost, whom famine had rendered wild and desperate, ran franticly about the bank, after Jones had returned, crying out to Mr. Hunt to send the canoe for him, and take him from that horrible region of famine, declaring that otherwise he would never march another step, but would lie down there and die.

The canoe was shortly sent over again, under the management of Joseph Delaunay, with further supplies Prevost immediately pressed forward to embark. Delaunay refused to admit him, telling him that there was now a sufficient supply of meat on his side of the river. He replied that it was not cooked, and he should starve before it was ready; he implored, therefore, to be taken where he could get something to appease his hunger immediately. Finding the canoe putting off without him, he forced himself aboard. As he drew near the opposite shore, and beheld meat roasting before the fires, he jumped up, shouted, clapped his hands, and danced in a delirium of joy, until he upset the canoe. The poor wretch was swept away by the current, and drowned ; and it was with extreme difficulty that Delaunay reached the shore.

Mr. Hunt now sent all his men forward, excepting two or three. In the evening, he caused another horse to be killed, and a canoe to be made out of the skin, in which he sent over a further supply of meat to the opposite party. The canoe brought back John Day, the Kentucky hunter, who came to join his former employer and commander, Mr. Crooks. Poor Day once so active and vigorous, was now reduced to a condition even more feeble and emaciated than his companions. Mr. Crooks had such a value for the man, on account of his past services and faithful character, that he determined not to quit him ; he exhorted Mr. Hunt, however, to proceed forward, and join the party, as his presence was all important to the conduct of the expedition. One of the Canadians, Jean Baptiste Dubreuil, likewise remained with Mr. Crooks.

Mr. Hunt left two horses with them, and a part of the carcass of the last that had been killed. This, he hoped, would be sufficient to sustain them until they should reach the Indian encampment.

One of the chief dangers attending the enfeebled condition of Mr. Crooks and his companions, was their being overtaken by the Indians, whose horses had been seized : though Mr. Hunt hoped that he had guarded against any resentment on the part of the savages, by leaving various articles in their lodge, more than sufficient to compensate for the outrage he had been compelled to commit.

Resuming his onward course, Mr. Hunt came up with his people in the evening. The next day, December 13th, he beheld several Indians, with three horses, on the opposite side of the river, and, after a time, came to the two lodges which he had seen on going down. Here he endeavoured in vain to barter a rifle for a horse, but again succeeded in effecting the purchase with an old tin kettle, aided by a few beads.

The two succeeding days were cold and stormy; the snow was augmenting, and there was a good deal of ice running in the river. Their road, however, was becoming easier; they were getting out of the hills, and finally emerged into the open country, after twenty days of fatigue, famine, and hardship of every kind, in the ineffectual attempt to find a passage down the river.

They now encamped on a little willowed stream, running from the east, which they had crossed on the 26th of November. Here they found a dozen lodges of Shoshonies, recently arrived, who informed them that had they persevered along the river, they would have found their difficulties augment until they became absolutely insurmountable. This intelligence added to the anxiety of Mr. Hunt for the fate of Mr. M'Kenzie and his people, who had kept on.

Mr. Hunt now followed up the little river, and encamped at some lodges of Shoshonies, from whom he procured a couple of horses, a dog, a few dried fish, and some roots and dried cherries. Two or three days were exhausted in obtaining information about the route, and what time it would take to get to the Sciatogas, a hospitable tribe, on the west side of the mountains, represented as having many horses. The replies were various, but concurred in saying that the distance was great, and would occupy from seventeen to twenty-one nights. Mr. Hunt then tried to procure a guide; but though he sent to various lodges up and down the river, offering articles of great value in Indian estimation, no one would venture. The snow they said was waist deep in the mountains; and to all his offers they shook their heads, gave a shiver, and replied, " we shall freeze! we shall freeze!" at the same time they urged him to remain and pass the winter among them.

Mr. Hunt was in a dismal dilemma. To attempt the mountains without a guide, would be certain death to him and all his people; to remain there, after having already been so long on the journey, and at such great expense, was worse to him, he said, than "two deaths." He now changed his tone with the Indians, charged them with deceiving him in respect to the mountains, and talking with a "forked tongue," or, in other words, with lying. He upbraided them with their want of courage, and told them they were women to shrink from the perils of such a journey. At length one of them, piqued by his taunts, or tempted by his offers, agreed to be his guide; for which he was to receive a gun, a pistol, three knives, two horses, and a little of every article in the possession of the party; a reward sufficient to make him one of the wealthiest of his vagabond nation.

Once more then, on the 21st of December, they set out upon their wayfaring, with newly excited spirits. Two other Indians accompanied their guide, who led them immediately back to Snake river, which they followed down for a short distance, in search of some Indian rafts made of reeds, on which they might cross. Finding none, Mr. Hunt caused a horse to be killed, and a canoe to be made out of its skin. Here, on the opposite bank, they saw the thirteen men of Mr. Crooks's party, who had continued up along the river. They told Mr. Hunt, across the stream, that they had not seen Mr. Crooks, and the two men who had remained with him, since the day that he had separated from them.

The canoe proving too small, another horse was killed, and the skin of it joined to that of the first. Night came on before the little bark had made more than two voyages. Being badly made, it was taken apart and put together again, by the light of the fire. The night was cold; the men were weary and disheartened with such varied and incessant toil and hardship. They crouched, dull and drooping, around their fires; many of them began to express a wish to remain where they were for the winter. The very necessity of crossing the river dismayed some of them in their present enfeebled and dejected state. It was rapid and turbulent, and filled with float-ice, and they remembered that two of their comrades had already perished in its waters. Others looked forward with misgivings to the long and dismal journey through lonesome regions that awaited them, when they should have passed this dreary flood.

At an early hour of the morning, December 23d, they began to cross the river. Much ice had formed during the night, and they were obliged to break it for some distance on each shore. At length they all got over in safety to the west side; and their spirits rose on having achieved this perilous passage. Here they were rejoined by the people of Mr. Crooks, who had with them a horse and a dog, which they had recently procured. The poor fellows were in the most squalid and emaciated state. Three of them were so completely prostrated in strength and spirits, that they expressed a wish to remain among the Snakes. Mr. Hunt, therefore, gave them the canoe, that they might cross the river, and a few articles with which to procure necessaries, until they should meet with Mr. Crooks. There was another man, named Michael Carriere, who was almost equally reduced, but he determined to proceed with his comrades, who were now incorporated with the party of Mr. Hunt. After the day's exertions they encamped together on the banks of the river. This was the last night they were to spend upon its borders. More than eight hundred miles of hard travelling, and many weary days had it cost them; and the sufferings connected with it, rendered it hateful in their remembrance, so that the Canadian voyageurs always spoke of it as " La maudite rivière enragée"—the accursed mad river : thus coupling a malediction with its name.

CHAPTER XIX.

On the 24th of December, all things being arranged, Mr. Hunt turned his back upon the disastrous banks of Snake river, and struck his course westward for the mountains. His party, being augmented by the late followers of Mr. Crooks, amounted now to thirty-two white men, three Indians, and the squaw and two children of Pierre Dorion. Five jaded, half-starved horses were laden with their luggage, and, in case of need, were to furnish them with provisions. They travelled painfully about fourteen miles a day, over plains and among hills, rendered dreary by occasional falls of snow and rain. Their only sustenance was a scanty meal of horse flesh once in four and twenty hours.

On the third day the poor Canadian, Carriere, one of the famished party of Mr. Crooks, gave up in despair, and lying down upon the ground declared he could go no further. Efforts were made to cheer him up, but it was found that the poor fellow was absolutely exhausted and could not keep on his legs. He was mounted, therefore, upon one of the horses, though the forlorn animal was in little better plight than himself.

On the 28th, they came upon a small stream winding to the north, through a fine level valley; the mountains receding on each side. Here their Indian friends pointed out a chain of woody mountains to the left, running north and south, and covered with snow; over which they would have to pass. They kept along the valley for twenty-one miles on the 29th, suffering much from a continual fall of snow and rain, and being twice obliged to ford the icy stream. Early in the following morning the squaw of Pierre Dorion, who had hitherto kept on without murmuring or flinching, was suddenly taken in labour, and enriched her husband with another child. As the fortitude and good conduct of the poor woman had gained for her the good will of the party, her situation caused concern and perplexity. Pierre, however, treated the matter as an occurrence that could soon be arranged and need cause no delay. He remained by his wife in the camp, with his other children and his horse, and promised soon to rejoin the main body, who proceeded on their march.

Finding that the little river entered the mountains, they abandoned it and turned off for a few miles among hills. Here another Canadian, named La Bonté, gave out, and had to be helped on horseback. As the horse was too weak to bear both him and his pack, Mr. Hunt took the latter upon his own shoulders. Thus, with difficulties augmenting at every step, they urged their toilsome way among the hills half famished, and faint at heart, when they came to where a fair valley spread out before them of great extent, and several leagues in width, with a beautiful stream meandering through it. A genial climate seemed to prevail here, for though the snow lay upon all the mountains within sight, there was none to be seen in the valley. The travellers gazed with delight upon this serene sunny landscape, but their joy was complete on beholding six lodges of Shoshonies pitched upon the borders of the stream, with a number of horses and dogs about them. They all pressed forward with eagerness, and soon reached the camp. Here their first attention was to obtain provisions. A rifle, an old musket, a tomahawk, a tin kettle, and a small quantity of ammunition soon procured them four horses, three dogs, and some roots. Part of the live stock was immediately killed, cooked with all expedition, and as promptly devoured. A hearty meal restored every one to good spirits. In the course of the following morning the Dorion family made its appearance. Pierre came trudging in the advance, followed by his valued, though skeleton steed, on which was mounted his squaw with the new born infant in her arms, and her boy of two year's old, wrapped in a blanket and slung at her side. The mother looked as unconcerned as if nothing had happened to her; so easy is nature in her operations in the wilderness, when free from the enfeebling refinements of luxury, and the tamperings and appliances of art.

The next morning ushered in the new year (1812). Mr. Hunt was about to resume his march, when his men requested permission to celebrate the day. This was particularly urged by the Canadian voyageurs, with whom new year's day is a favourite festival; and who never willingly give up a holiday, under any circumstances. There was no resisting such an application; so the day was passed in repose and revelry; the poor Canadians

contrived to sing and dance in defiance of all their hardships; and there was a sumptuous new year's banquet of
dog's meat and horse flesh.

After two days of welcome rest, the travellers addressed
themselves once more to their painful journey. The Indians of the lodges pointed out a distant gap through
which they must pass in traversing the ridge of mountains.
They assured them that they would be but little incommoded by snow, and in three days would arrive among the
Sciatogas. Mr. Hunt, however, had been so frequently
deceived by Indian accounts of routes and distances, that
he gave but little faith to this information.

The travellers continued their course due west for five
days, crossing the valley and entering the mountains.
Here the travelling became excessively toilsome, across
rough stony ridges, and amidst fallen trees. They were
often knee deep in snow, and sometimes in the hollows
between the ridges sank up to their waists. The weather
was extremely cold; the sky covered with clouds, so that
for days they had not a glimpse of the sun. In traversing the highest ridge they had a wide but chilling prospect over a wilderness of snowy mountains.

On the 6th of January, however, they had crossed the
dividing summit of the chain, and were evidently under
the influence of a milder climate. The snow began to de-
crease; the sun once more emerged from the thick canopy
of clouds, and shone cheeringly upon them, and they
caught a sight of what appeared to be a plain, stretching
out in the west. They hailed it as the poor Israelites
hailed the first glimpse of the promised land, for they
flattered themselves that this might be the great plain of
the Columbia, and that their painful pilgrimage might be
drawing to a close.

It was now five days since they had left the lodges of
the Shoshonies, during which they had come about sixty
miles, and their guide assured them that in the course of
the next day they would see the Sciatogas.

On the following morning, therefore, they pushed forward with eagerness, and soon fell upon a small stream,
which led them through a deep, narrow defile, between

stupendous ridges. Here, among the rocks and precipices, they saw gangs of that mountain-loving animal, the black-tailed deer, and came to where great tracts of horses were to be seen in all directions, made by the Indian hunters.

The snow had entirely disappeared, and the hopes of soon coming upon some Indian encampment, induced Mr. Hunt to press on. Many of the men, however, were so enfeebled, that they could not keep up with the main body, but lagged, at intervals, behind ; and some of them did not arrive at the night encampment. In the course of this day's march, the recently born child of Pierre Dorion died.

The march was resumed early next morning, without waiting for the stragglers. The stream which they had followed throughout the preceding day, was now swollen by the influx of another river ; the declivities of the hills were green, and the valleys were clothed with grass. At length the joyful cry was given of " An Indian camp !" It was yet in the distance, in the bosom of the green valley, but they could perceive that it consisted of numerous lodges, and that hundreds of horses were grazing the grassy meadows around it. The prospect of abundance of horse flesh diffused universal joy, for by this time the whole stock of travelling provisions was reduced to the skeleton steed of Pierre Dorion, and another wretched animal, equally emaciated, that had been repeatedly reprieved during the journey.

A forced march soon brought the weary and hungry travellers to the camp. It proved to be a strong party of Sciatogas and Tus-che-pas. There were thirty-four lodges, comfortably constructed of mats : the Indians, too, were better clothed than any of the wandering bands they had hitherto met on this side of the Rocky mountains. Indeed they were as well clad as the generality of the wild hunter tribes. Each had a good buffalo or deer skin robe, and a deer skin hunting shirt and leggins. Upwards of two thousand horses were ranging the pastures around their encampment ; but what delighted Mr. Hunt was, on entering the lodges, to behold brass kettles, axes, copper tea kettles, and various other articles of civilized manufacture, which showed that these Indians had an indirect communication with the people of the sea-coast, who traded with the whites. He made eager inquiries of the Sciatogas, and gathered from them that the great river (the Columbia), was but two days' march distant, and that several white people had recently descended it; who he hoped might prove to be M'Lellan, M'Kenzie, and their companions.

It was with the utmost joy and the most profound gratitude to Heaven, that Mr. Hunt found himself and his band of weary and famishing wanderers, thus safely extricated from the most perilous part of their long journey, and within the prospect of a termination of their toils. All the stragglers who had lagged behind arrived, one after another, excepting the poor Canadian voyageur, Carriere. He had been late in the preceding afternoon, riding behind a Snake Indian, near some lodges of that nation, a few miles distant from the last night's encampment, and it was expected that he would soon make his appearance.

The first object of Mr. Hunt was to obtain provisions for his men. A little venison of an indifferent quality, and some roots, were all that could be procured that evening; but the next day he succeeded in purchasing a mare and colt, which were immediately killed, and the cravings of the half-starved people in some degree appeased.

For several days they remained in the neighbourhood of these Indians, reposing after all their hardships, and feasting upon horse flesh and roots, obtained in subsequent traffic. Many of the people ate to such excess, as to render themselves sick; others were lame from their past journey; but all gradually recruited in the repose and abundance of the valley. Horses were obtained here much more readily, and at a cheaper rate than among the Snakes. A blanket, a knife, or half a pound of blue beads, would purchase a steed, and at this rate many of the men bought horses for their individual use.

This tribe of Indians, who are represented as a proud spirited race, and uncommonly cleanly, never eat horses

nor dogs, nor would they permit the raw flesh of either to
be brought into their huts.   They had a small quantity of
venison in each lodge, but set so high a price upon it that
the white men, in their impoverished state, could not afford to purchase it.   They hunted the deer on horseback :
" ringing," or surrounding them, and running them down
in a circle.   They were admirable horsemen, and their
weapons were bows and arrows, which they managed with
great dexterity.   They were altogether primitive in their
habits, and seemed to cling to the usages of savage life,
even when possessed of the aids of civilization.   They had
axes among them, yet they generally made use of a stone
mallet wrought into the shape of a bottle, and wedges of
elk horn, in splitting their wood.   Though they might
have two or three brass kettles hanging in their lodges,
yet they would frequently use vessels made of willow, for
carrying water, and would even boil their meat in them,
by means of hot stones.   Their women wore caps of willow neatly worked and figured.

As Carriere, the Canadian straggler, did not make his
appearance for two or three days after the encampment in
the valley, two men were sent out on horseback in search
of him.   They returned, however, without success.   The
lodges of the Snake Indians near which he had been seen,
were removed, and they could find no trace of him.   Several days more elapsed, yet nothing was seen or heard of
him, or of the Snake horseman, behind whom he had been
last observed.   It was feared, therefore, that he had either
perished through hunger and fatigue, had been murdered
by the Indians, or, being left to himself, had mistaken
some hunting tracks for the trail of the party, and had
been led astray and lost.

The river on the banks of which they were encamped,
emptied into the Columbia, was called by the natives the
Eu-o-tal-la, or Umatalla, and abounded with beaver.   In
the course of their sojourn in the valley which it watered,
they twice shifted their camp, proceeding about thirty miles
down its course, which was to the west.   A heavy fall of
rain caused the river to overflow its banks, dislodged them

from their encampment, and drowned three of their horses, which were tethered in the low ground.

Further conversation with the Indians satisfied them that they were in the neighbourhood of the Columbia. The number of the white men who they said had passed down the river, agreed with that of M'Lellan, M'Kenzie, and their companions, and increased the hope of Mr. Hunt that they might have passed through the wilderness with safety.

These Indians had a vague story that white men were coming to trade among them; and they often spoke of two great men named Ke-Koosh and Jacquean, who gave them tobacco, and smoked with them. Jacquean, they said, had a house somewhere upon the great river. Some of the Canadians supposed they were speaking of one Jacquean Finlay, a clerk of the North-west Company, and inferred that the house must be some trading post on one of the tributary streams of the Columbia. The Indians were overjoyed when they found this band of white men intended to return and trade with them. They promised to use all diligence in collecting quantities of beaver skins, and no doubt proceeded to make deadly war upon that sagacious, but ill-fated animal, who, in general, lived in peaceful insignificance among his Indian neighbours, before the intrusion of the white trader. On the 20th of January, Mr. Hunt took leave of these friendly Indians, and of the river on which they were encamped, and continued westward.

At length, on the following day, the way-worn travellers lifted up their eyes, and beheld before them the long sought waters of the Columbia. The sight was hailed with as much transport as if they had already reached the end of their pilgrimage; nor can we wonder at their joy. Two hundred and forty miles had they marched, through wintry wastes and rugged mountains, since leaving Snake river; and six months of perilous wayfaring had they experienced since their departure from the Aricara village on the Missouri. Their whole route by land and water from that point had been, according to their computation, seventeen hundred and fifty-one miles in the course of which they had endured all kinds of hardships. In fact, the necessity of winding the dangerous country of the Blackfeet, had obliged them to make a bend to the south, and to traverse a great additional extent of unknown wilderness.

The place where they struck the Columbia was some distance below the junction of its two great branches, Lewis and Clarke rivers, and not far from the influx of the Wallah-Wallah. It was a beautiful stream, three quarters of a mile wide, totally free from trees; bordered in some places with steep rocks, in others with pebbled shores.

On the banks of the Columbia they found a miserable horde of Indians, called Akai-chies, with no clothing but a scanty mantle of the skins of animals, and sometimes a pair of sleeves of wolf's skin. Their lodges were shaped like a tent, and very light and warm, being covered with mats of rushes; beside which they had excavations on the ground, lined with mats, and occupied by the women, who were even more slightly clad than the men. These people subsisted chiefly by fishing; having canoes of a rude construction, being merely the trunks of pine trees split and hollowed out by fire. Their lodges were well stored witth dried salmon, and they had great quantities of fresh salmon trout, of an excellent flavour, taken at the mouth of the Umatalla, of which the travellers obtained a most acceptable supply.

Finding that the road was on the north side of the river, Mr. Hunt crossed, and continued five or six days travelling rather slowly down along its banks, being much delayed by the straying of the horses, and the attempts made by the Indians to steal them. They frequently passed lodges, where they obtained fish and dogs. At one place the natives had just returned from hunting, and had brought back a large quantity of elk and deer meat, but asked so high a price for it as to be beyond the funds of the travellers, so they had to content themselves with dog flesh. They had by this time, however, come to consider it very choice food, superior to horse flesh, and the minutes of the expedition speak rather exultingly now and then, of their having made a "famous repast," where this viand happened to be unusually plenty.

They again learnt tidings of some of the scattered members of the expedition, supposed to be M'Kenzie, M'Lellan, and their men, who had preceded them down the river, and had overturned one of their canoes, by which they lost many articles. All these floating pieces of intelligence of their fellow adventurers, who had separated from them in the heart of the wilderness, they received with eager interest.

The weather continued to be temperate, marking the superior softness of the climate on this side of the mountains. For a great part of the time, the days were delightfully mild and clear, like the serene days of October on the Atlantic borders. The country in general, in the neighbourhood of the river, was a continual plain, low near the water, but rising gradually : destitute of trees, and almost without shrubs or plants of any kind, excepting a few willow bushes. After travelling about sixty miles, they came to where the country became very hilly, and the river made its way between rocky banks, and down numerous rapids. The Indians in this vicinity were better clad and altogether in more prosperous condition than those above, and, as Mr. Hunt thought, showed their consciousness of ease by something like sauciness of manner. Thus prosperity is apt to produce arrogance in savage as well as in civilized life. In both conditions, man is an animal that will not bear pampering.

From these people Mr. Hunt for the first time received vague, but deeply interesting intelligence of that part of the enterprise which had proceeded by sea to the mouth of the Columbia. The Indians spoke of a number of white men who had built a large house at the mouth of the great river, and surrounded it with palisades. None of them had been down to Astoria themselves ; but rumours spread widely and rapidly from mouth to mouth among the Indian tribes, and are carried to the heart of the interior, by hunting parties and migratory hordes.

The establishment of a trading emporium at such a point, also, was calculated to cause a sensation to the most remote parts of the vast wilderness beyond the mountains. It, in a manner, struck the pulse of the great vital river, and vibrated up all its tributary streams.

It is surprising to notice how well this remote tribe of savages had learnt through intermediate gossips, the private feelings of the colonists at Astoria ; it shows that Indians are not the incurious and indifferent observers that they have been represented. They told Mr. Hunt that the white people at the large house had been looking anxiously for many of their friends, whom they had expected to descend the great river; and had been in much affliction, fearing that they were lost. Now, however, the arrival of him and his party would wipe away all their tears, and they would dance and sing for joy.

On the 31st of January, Mr. Hunt arrived at the falls of the Columbia, and encamped at the village of Wishram, situated at the head of that dangerous pass of the river called " the long narrows."

CHAPTER XX.

The village of Wish-ram—Roguery of the inhabitants—Their habitations—
Tidings of Astoria—Of the Tonquin massacre—Thieves about the camp—
A band of braggarts—Embarkation—Arrival at Astoria—A joyful reception
—Old comrades—Adventures of Reed, M'Lellan, and M'Kenzie, among
the Snake river mountains—Rejoicing at Astoria.

Of the village of Wish-ram, the aborigines' fishing mart of the Columbia, we have given some account in an early chapter of this work. The inhabitants held a taffic in the productions of the fisheries of the falls, and their village was the trading resort of the tribes from the coast and from the mountains. Mr. Hunt found the inhabitants shrewder and more intelligent than any Indians he had met with. Trade had sharpened their wits, though it had not improved their honesty; for they were a community of arrant rogues and freebooters. Their habitations comported with their circumstances, and were superior to any the travellers had yet seen west of the

Rocky mountains. In general the dwellings of the savages on the Pacific side of that great barrier, were mere tents and cabins of mats, or skins, or straw, the country being destitute of timber. In Wish-ram, on the contrary, the houses were built of wood, with long sloping roofs. The floor was sunk about six feet below the surface of the ground, with a low door at the gable end, extremely narrow, and partly sunk. Through this it was necessary to crawl, and then to descend a short ladder. This inconvenient entrance was probably for the purpose of defence ; there were loopholes also under the eaves, apparently for the discharge of arrows. The houses were larger, generally containing two or three families. Immediately within the doors were sleeping places, ranged along the walls, like berths in a ship; and furnished with pallets of matting. These extended along one-half of the building ; the remaining half was appropriated to the storing of dried fish.

The trading operations of the inhabitants of Wish-ram had given them a wider scope of information, and rendered their village a kind of head-quarters of intelligence. Mr. Hunt was able, therefore, to collect more distinct tidings concerning the settlement of Astoria and its affairs. One of the inhabitants had been at the trading post established by David Stuart on the Oakinagan, and had picked up a few words of English there. From him Mr. Hunt gleaned various particulars about that establishment, as well as about the general concerns of the enterprise. Others repeated the name of Mr. M'Kay, the partner who perished in the massacre on board of the Tonquin, and gave some account of that melancholy affair. They said Mr. M'Kay was a chief among the white men, and had built a great house at the mouth of the river, but had left it, and sailed away in a large ship to the northward, where he had been attacked by bad Indians in canoes. Mr. Hunt was startled by this intelligence, and made further inquiries. They informed him that the Indians had lashed their canoes to the ship, and fought until they had killed him and all his people. This is another instance of the clearness with which intelligence is transmitted from mouth to mouth among the Indian tribes. These tidings, though but partially credited by Mr. Hunt, filled his mind with anxious forebodings. He now endeavoured to procure canoes, in which to descend the Columbia, but none suitable for the purpose were to be obtained above the narrows ; he continued on, therefore, the distance of twelve miles, and encamped on the bank of the river. The camp was soon surrounded by loitering savages, who went prowling about, seeking what they might pilfer. Being baffled by the vigilance of the guard, they endeavoured to compass their ends by other means. Towards evening, a number of warriors entered the camp in ruffling style; painted and dressed out as if for battle, and armed with lances, bows and arrows, and scalping knives. They informed Mr. Hunt that a party of thirty or forty braves were coming up from a village below to attack the camp and carry off the horses, but that they were determined to stay with him, and defend him. Mr. Hunt received them with great coldness, and, when they had finished their story, gave them a pipe to smoke. He then called up all hands, stationed sentinels in different quarters, but told them to keep as vigilant an eye within the camp as without.

The warriors were evidently baffled by these precautions, and, having smoked their pipe, and vapoured off their valour, took their departure. The farce, however, did not end here. After a little while, the warriors returned, ushering in another savage, still more heroically arrayed. This they announced as the chief of the belligerent village, but as a great pacificator. His people had been furiously bent upon the attack, and would have doubtless carried it into effect, but this gallant chief had stood forth as the friend of white men, and had dispersed the throng by his own authority and prowess. Having vaunted this signal piece of service, there was a significant pause; all evidently expecting some adequate reward. Mr. Hunt again produced the pipe, smoked with the chieftain and his worthy compeers, but made no further demonstration of gratitude. They remained about the camp all night, but at daylight returned, baffled and crestfallen, to their homes, with nothing but smoke for their pains.

Mr. Hunt now endeavoured to procure canoes, of which he saw several about the neighbourhood, extremely well made, with elevated stems and sterns, some of them capable of carrying three thousand pounds weight. He found it extremely difficult, however, to deal with these slippery people, who seemed much more inclined to pilfer. Notwithstanding a strict guard maintained round the camp, various implements were stolen, and several horses carried off. Among the latter, we have to include the long-cherished steed of Pierre Dorion. From some wilful caprice, that worthy pitched his tent at some distance from the main body, and tethered his invaluable steed beside it, from whence it was abstracted in the night, to the infinite chagrin and mortification of the hybrid interpreter.

Having, after several days' negotiation, procured the requisite number of canoes, Mr. Hunt would gladly have left this thievish neighbourhood, but was detained until the 5th of February, by violent head winds, accompanied by snow and rain. Even after he was enabled to get under way, he had still to struggle against contrary winds and tempestuous weather. The current of the river, however, was in his favour; having made a portage at the grand rapid, the canoes met with no further obstruction, and, on the afternoon of the 15th of February, swept round an intervening cape, and came in sight of the infant settlement of Astoria. After eleven months' wandering in the wilderness, a great part of the time over trackless wastes, where the sight of a savage wigwam was a rarity, we may imagine the delight of the poor, weatherbeaten travellers, at beholding the embryo establishment, with its magazines, habitations, and picketed bulwarks, seated on a high point of land, dominating a beautiful little bay, in which was a trim-built shallop riding quietly at anchor. A shout of joy burst from each canoe at the long-wished-for sight. They urged their canoes across the bay, and pulled with eagerness for shore, where all hands poured down from the settlement to receive and welcome them. Among the first to greet them on their landing, were some of their old comrades and fellow-sufferers, who, under the conduct of Reed, M'Lellan, and M'Kenzie, had parted from them at the Caldron Linn. These had reached Astoria nearly a month previously, and, judging from their own narrow escape from starvation, had given up Mr. Hunt and his followers as lost. Their greeting was the more warm and cordial. As to the Canadian voyageurs, their mutual felicitations, as usual, were loud and vociferous, and it was almost ludicrous to behold these ancient " comrades" and " confrères" hugging and kissing each other on the river bank.

When the first greetings were over, the different bands interchanged accounts of their several wanderings, after separating at Snake river; we shall briefly notice a few of the leading particulars. It will be recollected by the reader, that a small exploring detachment had proceeded down the river, under the conduct of Mr. John Reed, a clerk of the company; that another had set off under M'Lellan, and a third in a different direction, under M'Kenzie. After wandering for several days without meeting with Indians, or obtaining any supplies, they came together fortuitously among the Snake river mountains, some distance below that disastrous pass or strait, which had received the appellation of the Devil's Scuttle Hole.

When thus united, their party consisted of M'Kenzie, M'Lellan, Reed, and eight men, chiefly Canadians. Being all in the same predicament, without horses, provisions, or information of any kind, they all agreed that it would be worse than useless to return to Mr. Hunt and encumber him with so many starving men, and that their only course was to extricate themselves as soon as possible from this land of famine and misery, and make the best of their way for the Columbia. They accordingly continued to follow the downward course of Snake river; clambering rocks and mountains, and defying all the difficulties and dangers of that rugged defile, which subsequently, when the snows had fallen, was found impassable by Messrs. Hunt and Crooks.

Though constantly near to the borders of the river, and

for a great part of the time within sight of its current, one of their greatest sufferings was thirst. The river had worn its way in a deep channel through rocky mountains, destitute of brooks or springs. Its banks were so high and precipitous, that there was rarely any place where the travellers could get down to drink of its waters. Frequently they suffered for miles the torments of Tantalus; water continually in sight, yet fevered with the most parching thirst. Here and there they met with rain water collected in the hollows of the rocks, but more than once they were reduced to the utmost extremity; and some of the men had recourse to the last expedient to avoid perishing.

Their sufferings from hunger were equally severe. They could meet with no game, and subsisted for a time on strips of beaver skin, broiled on the coals. These were doled out in scanty allowances, barely sufficient to keep up existence, and at length failed them altogether. Still they crept feebly on, scarce dragging one limb after another, until a severe snow storm brought them to a pause. To struggle against it, in their exhausted condition, was impossible; so, cowering under an impending rock at the foot of a steep mountain, they prepared themselves for that wretched fate which seemed inevitable.

At this critical juncture, when famine stared them in the face, M'Lellan casting up his eyes, beheld an ahsahta, or bighorn, sheltering itself under a shelving rock on the side of the hill above them. Being in more active plight than any of his comrades, and an excellent marksman, he set off to get within shot of the animal. His companions watched his movements with breathless anxiety, for their lives depended upon his success. He made a cautious circuit; scrambled up the hill with the utmost silence, and at length arrived, unperceived, within a proper distance. Here levelling his rifle he took so sure an aim, that the bighorn fell dead on the spot; a fortunate circumstance, for, to pursue it, if merely wounded, would have been impossible in his emaciated state. The declivity of the hill enabled him to roll the carcass down to his companions, who were too feeble to climb the rocks,

They fell to work to cut it up; yet exerted a remarkable self-denial for men in their starving condition, for they contented themselves for the present with a soup made from the bones, reserving the flesh for future repasts. This providential relief gave them strength to pursue their journey, but they were frequently reduced to almost equal straits, and it was only the smallness of the party, requiring a small supply of provisions, that enabled them to get through this desolate region with their lives.

At length, after twenty-one days of toil and suffering, they got through these mountains, and arrived at a tributary stream of that branch of the Columbia called Lewis river, of which Snake river forms the southern fork. In this neighbourhood they met with wild horses, the first they had seen west of the Rocky mountains. From hence they made their way to Lewis river, where they fell in with a friendly tribe of Indians, who freely administered to their necessities. On this river they procured two canoes, in which they dropped down the stream to its confluence with the Columbia, and then down that river to Astoria, where they arrived haggard and emaciated, and perfectly in rags.

Thus, all the leading persons of Mr. Hunt's expedition were once more gathered together, excepting Mr. Crooks, of whose safety they entertained but little hope, considering the feeble condition in which they had been compelled to leave him in the heart of the wilderness.

A day was now given up to jubilee, to celebrate the arrival of Mr. Hunt and his companions, and the joyful meeting of the various scattered bands of adventurers at Astoria. The colours were hoisted; the guns, great and small, were fired ; there was a feast of fish, of beaver, and venison, which relished well with men who had so long been glad to revel on horse flesh and dogs' meat; a genial allowance of grog was issued, to increase the general animation, and the festivities wound up, as usual, with a grand dance at night, by the Canadian voyageurs.*

* The distance from St. Louis to Astoria, by the route travelled by Hunt and M'Kenzie, was upwards of thirty-five hundred miles, though; in a direct line it does not exceed eighteen hundred.

CHAPTER XXI.

THE winter had passed away tranquilly at Astoria. The apprehensions of hostility from the natives had subsided; indeed, as the season advanced, the Indians for the most part had disappeared from the neighbourhood, and abandoned the sea coast, so that, for want of their aid, the colonists had at times suffered considerably for want of provisions. The hunters belonging to the establishment made frequent and wide excursions, but with very moderate success. There were some deer and a few bears to be found in the vicinity, and elk in great numbers; the country, however, was so rough, and the woods so close and entangled, that it was almost impossible to beat up the game. The prevalent rains of winter, also, rendered it difficult for the hunter to keep his arms in order. The quantity of game, therefore, brought in by the hunters was very scanty, and it was frequently necessary to put all hands on very moderate allowance. Towards spring, however, the fishing season commenced,—the season of plenty on the Columbia. About the beginning of February, a small kind of fish, about six inches long, called by the natives the uthlecan, and resembling the smelt, made its appearance at the mouth of the river. It is said to be of delicious flavour, and so fat as to burn like a candle, for which it is often used by the natives. It enters the rivers in immense shoals, like solid columns, often extending to the depth of five or more feet, and is scooped up by the natives with small nets at the end of poles. In this way they will soon fill a canoe, or form a great heap on the river banks. These fish constitute a principal article of their food; the women drying them and stringing them on cords.

As the uthlecan is only found in the lower part of the river, the arrival of it soon brought back the natives to coast; who again resorted to the factory to trade, and from that time furnished plentiful supplies of fish.

The sturgeon makes its appearance in the river shortly after the uthlecan, and is taken in different ways, by the natives; sometimes they spear it; but oftener they use the hook and line, and the net. Occasionally, they sink a cord in the river by a heavy weight, with a buoy at the upper end, to keep it floating. To this cord several hooks are attached by short lines, a few feet distant from each other, and baited with small fish. This apparatus is often set towards night, and by the next morning several sturgeon will be found hooked by it; for though a large and strong fish, it makes but little resistance when insnared.

The salmon, which are the prime fish of the Columbia, and as important to the piscatory tribes as are the buffaloes to the hunters of the prairies, do not enter the river until towards the latter part of May, from which time, until the middle of August, they abound, and are taken in vast quantities, either with the spear or seine, and mostly in shallow water. An inferior species succeeds, and continues from August to December. It is remarkable for having a double row of teeth, half an inch long and extremely sharp, from whence it has received the name of the dog-toothed salmon. It is generally killed with the spear in small rivulets, and smoked for winter provision. We have noticed in a former chapter the mode in which the salmon are taken and cured at the falls of the Columbia, and put up in parcels for exportation. From these different fisheries of the river tribes, the establishment at Astoria had to derive much of its precarious supplies of provisions.

A year's residence at the mouth of the Columbia, and various expeditions in the interior, had now given the Astorians some idea of the country. The whole coast is described as remarkably rugged and mountainous with dense forests of hemlock, spruce, white and red cedar, cotton-wood, white oak, white and ·swamp ash, willow, and a few walnut. There is likewise an undergrowth of aromatic shrubs, creepers, and clambering vines, that render the forest almost impenetrable ; together with berries of various kinds, such as gooseberries, strawberries, raspberries,, both red and yellow, very large and finely-flavoured whortleberries, cranberries, serviceberries, blackberries, currants, sloes, and wild and choke cherries.

Among the flowering vines is one deserving of particular notice. Each flower is composed of six leaves or petals, about three inches in length, of a beautiful crimson, the inside spotted with white. Its leaves, of a fine green, are oval, and disposed by threes. This plant climbs upon the trees without attaching itself to them ; when it has reached the topmost branches, it descends perpendicularly, and as it continues to grow extends from tree to tree, until its various stalks interlace the grove like the rigging of a ship. The stems or trunks of this vine are tougher and more flexible than willow, and are from fifty to one hundred fathoms in length. From the fibres, the Indians manufacture baskets of such close texture as to hold water.

The principal quadrupeds that had been seen by the colonists in their various expeditions, were the stag, fallow deer, hart, black and grizzly bear, antelope, ahsahta or bighorn, beaver, sea and river otter, muskrat, fox, wolf, and panther, the latter extremely rare. The only domestic animals among the natives were horses and dogs.

The country abounded with aquatic and land birds, such as swans, wild geese, brant, ducks of almost every description, pelicans, herons, gulls, snipes, curlews, eagles, vultures, crows, ravens, magpies, woodpeckers, pigeons, partridges, pheasants, grouse, and a great variety of singing birds.

There were few reptiles ; the only dangerous kinds were the rattlesnake, and one striped with black, yellow, and white, about four feet long. Among the lizard kind was one about nine or ten inches in length, exclusive of the tail, and three inches in circumference. The tail was round, and of the same length as the body. The head was triangular, covered with small square scales. The upper part of the body was likewise covered with small scales, green, yellow, black, and blue. Each foot had five toes, furnished with strong nails, probably to aid it in burrowing, as it usually lived under ground on the plains.

A remarkable fact, characteristeric of the country west of the Rocky mountains, is the mildness and equability of the climate. That great mountain barrier seems to divide the continent into different climates, even in the same degrees of latitude. The rigorous winters and sultry summers, and all the capricious inequalities of temperature prevalent on the Atlantic side of the mountains, are but little felt on their western declivities. The countries between them and the Pacific are blest with milder and steadier temperature, resembling the climates of parallel latitudes in Europe. In the plains and valleys, but little snow falls throughout the winter, and usually melts while falling. It rarely lies on the ground more than two days at a time, except on the summits of the mountains. The winters are rainy rather than cold. The The rains for five months, from the middle of October to the middle of March, are almost incessant, and often accompanied with tremendous thunder and lightning. The winds prevalent at this season are from the south and southeast, which usually bring rain. Those from the north to the southwest are the harbingers of fair weather and a clear sky. The residue of the year, from the middle of March to the middle of October, an interval of seven months, is serene and delightful. There is scarcely any rain throughout this time, yet the face of the country is kept fresh and verdant by nightly dews, and occasionally by humid fogs in the mornings. These are not considered prejudicial to health, since both the natives and the whites sleep in the open air with perfect impunity. While this equable and bland temperature prevails throughout the lower country, the peaks and ridges of the vast mountains by which it is dominated, are covered with perpetual snow. This renders them discernible at a great distance, shining at times like bright summer clouds, at other times assuming the most aerial tints, and always forming brilliant and striking features in the vast landscape. The mild temperature prevalent throughout the country is attributed by some to the succession of winds from the Pacific ocean, extending from latitude twenty degrees to at least fifty degrees north. These temper the heat of summer, so that in the shade no one is incommoded by perspiration : they also soften the rigours of winter, and produce such a moderation in the climate, that the inhabitants can wear the same dress throughout the year.

The soil in the neighbourhood of the sea-coast is of a brown colour, inclining to red, and generally poor ; being a mixture of clay and gravel. In the interior, and especially in the valleys of the Rocky mountains, the soil is generally blackish ; though sometimes yellow. It is frequently mixed with marl and with marine substances, in a state of decomposition. This kind of soil extends to a considerable depth, as may be perceived in the deep cuts made by ravines, and by the beds of rivers. The vegetation in these valleys is much more abundant than near the coast ; in fact, it is in these fertile intervals, locked up between rocky sierras, or scooped out from barren wastes, that population must extend itself, as it were, in veins and ramifications, if ever the regions beyond the mountains should become civilized.

CHAPTER XXII.

Natives in the neighbourhood of Astoria—Their persons and characteristics— Causes of deformity—Their dress—Their contempt of beards—Ornaments— Armour and weapons—Mode of flattening the head—Extent of the custom —Religious belief—The two great spirits of the air and of the fire—Priests or medicine men—The rival idols—Polygamy a cause of greatness—Petty warfare—Music, dancing, gamblng—Thieving a virtue—Keen traders— —Intrusive habits—Abhorrence of drunkenness—Anecdote of Comcomly.

A BRIEF mention has already been made of the tribes or hordes existing about the lower part of the Columbia at the time of the settlement ; a few more particulars concerning them may be acceptable. The four tribes nearest

to Astoria, and with whom the traders had most intercourse, were, as has heretofore been observed, the Chinooks,
the Clatsops, the Wahkiacums, and the Cathlamets.
The Chinooks resided chiefly along the banks of a river
of the same name, running parallel to the sea-coast,
through a low country studded with stagnant pools, and
emptying itself into Baker's bay, a few miles from Cape
Disappointment. This the tribe over which Comcomly,
the one-eyed chieftain, held sway; it boasted two hundred
and fourteen fighting men. Their chief subsistence was
on fish, with an occasional regale of the flesh of elk and
deer, and of wild fowl from the neighbouring ponds.

The Clatsops resided on both sides of Point Adams;
they were the mere reliques of a tribe which had been
nearly swept off by the smallpox, and did not number
more than one hundred and eighty fighting men.

The Wahkiacums, or Waak-i-cums, inhabited the north
side of the Columbia, and numbered sixty-six warriors.
They and the Chinooks were originally the same; but a
dispute arising about two generations previous to the time
of the settlement between the ruling chief and his brother
Wahkiacum; the latter seceded, and, with his adherents,
formed the present horde which continues to go by his
name. In this way new tribes or clans are formed, and
lurking causes of hostility engendered.

The Cathlamets lived opposite to the lower village of
the Wahkiacums, and numbered ninety-four warriors.

These four tribes, or rather clans, have every appearance
of springing from the same origin, resembling each other
in person, dress, language, and manners. They are rather
a diminutive race, generally below five feet five inches,
with crooked legs and thick ankles; a deformity caused
by their passing so much of their time sitting or squatting
upon the calves of their legs, and their heels, in the bottom
of their canoes; a favourite position, which they retain,
even when on shore. The women increase the deformity
by wearing tight bandages round the ankles, which prevent
the circulation of the blood, and cause a swelliug of the
muscles of the leg.

Neither sex can boast of personal beauty. Their faces

are round, with small, but animated eyes. Their noses are broad and flat at top, and fleshy at the end, with large nostrils. They have wide mouths, thick lips, and short, irregular, and dirty teeth. Indeed, good teeth are seldom to be seen among the tribes west of the Rocky mountains, who live chiefly on fish.

In the early stages of their intercourse with white men, these savages were but scantily clad. In summer time the men were entirely naked ; in the winter and in bad weather, the men wore a small robe, reaching to the middle of the thigh, made of the skins of animals, or of the wool of the mountain sheep. Occasionally, they wore a kind of mantle of matting, to keep off the rain ; but, having thus protected the back and shoulders, they left the rest of the body naked.

The women wore similar robes, though shorter, not reaching below the waist ; beside which, they had a kind of petticoat, or fringe, reaching from the waist to the knee, formed of the fibres of cedar bark, broken into strands, or a tissue of silk grass twisted and knotted at the ends. This was the usual dress of the women in summer; should the weather be inclement, they added a vest of skins, similar to the robe.

The men carefully eradicated every vestige of a beard considering it a great deformity. They looked with disgust at the whiskers and well-furnished chins of the white men, and in derision called them Longbeards. Both sexes, on the other hand, cherished the hair of the head, which with them is generally black and rather coarse. They allowed it to grow to a great length, and were very proud and careful of it, sometimes wearing it plaited, sometimes wound round the head in fanciful tresses. No greater affront could be offered to them than to cut off their treasured locks.

They had conical hats with narrow rims, neatly woven of bear grass or of the fibres of cedar bark, interwoven with designs of various shapes and colours ; sometimes merely squares and triangles, at other times rude representations of canoes, with men fishing and harpooning. These hats were nearly water-proof, and extremely durable.

The favourite ornaments of the men were collars of
bears' claws, the proud trophies of hunting-exploits; while
the women and children wore similar decorations of elks'
tusks.   An intercourse with the white traders, however,
soon effected a change in the toilets of both sexes.   They
became fond of arraying themselves in any article of civilized dress which they could procure, and often made a
most grotesque appearance.   They adapted many articles
of finery, also, to their own previous tastes.   Both sexes
were fond of adorning themselves with bracelets of iron,
brass, or copper.   They were delighted, also, with blue
and white beads, particularly the former, and wore broad
tight bands of them round the waist and ankles : large
rolls of them round the neck, and pendants of them in
the ears.   The men, especially, who in savage life carry
a passion for personal decoration further than the females,
did not think their gala equipments complete, unless they
had a jewel of haiqua, or wampum, dangling at the nose.
Thus arrayed, their hair besmeared with fish oil, and their
bodies bedaubed with red clay, they considered themselves irresistible.

When on warlike expeditions, they painted their faces
and bodies in the most hideous and grotesque manner,
according to the universal practice of American savages.
Their arms were bows and arrows, spears, and war-clubs.
Some wore a corslet, formed of pieces of hard wood,
laced together with bear-grass, so as to form a light coat
of mail, pliant to the body; and a kind of casque of cedar bark, leather, and bear-grass, sufficient to protect the
head from an arrow or a war-club.   A more complete
article of defensive armour was a buff jerkin or shirt of
great thickness, made of doublings of elk-skin, and reaching to the feet, holes being left for the head and arms.
This was perfectly arrow proof; add to which, it was often
endowed with charmed virtues, by the spells and mystic
ceremonials of the medicine man, or conjurer.

Of the peculiar custom, prevalent among these people,
of flattening the head, we have already spoken.   It is one
of those instances of human caprice, like the crippling of
the feet of females in China, which are quite incompre-

hensible. This custom prevails principally among the tribes on the sea-coast, and about the lower parts of the rivers. How far it extends along the coast we are not able to ascertain. Some of the tribes, both north and south of the Columbia, practise it; but they all speak the Chinook language, and probably originated from the same stock. As far as we can learn, the remoter tribes, which speak an entirely different language, do not flatten the head. This absurd custom declines, also, in receding from the shores of the Pacific; few traces of it are to be found among the tribes of the Rocky mountains, and after crossing the mountains it disappears altogether. Those Indians, therefore, about the head waters of the Columbia, and in the solitary mountain regions, who are often called Flatheads, must not be supposed to be characterized by this deformity. It is an appellation often given by the hunters east of the mountain chain, to all the western Indians, excepting the Snakes.

The religious belief of these people was extremely limited and confined; or rather, in all probability, their explanations were but little understood by their visiters. They had an idea of a benevolent and omnipotent spirit, the creator of all things. They represent him as assuming various shapes at pleasure, but generally that of an immense bird. He usually inhabits the sun, but occasionally wings his way through the aerial regions, and sees all that is doing upon earth. Should any thing displease him, he vents his wrath in terrific storms and tempests, the lightning being the flashes of his eyes, and the thunder the clapping of his wings. To propitiate his favour they offer to him annual sacrifices of salmon and venison, the first fruits of their fishing and hunting.

Besides this aerial spirit they believe in an inferior one, who inhabits the fire, and of whom they are in perpetual dread, as, though he possesses equally the power of good and evil, the evil is apt to predominate. They endeavour, therefore, to keep him in good humour by frequent offerings. He is supposed also to have great influence with the winged spirit, their sovereign protector and benefactor. They implore him, therefore, to act as their interpreter and procure them all describable things, such as success in fishing and hunting, abundance of game, fleet horses, obedient wives, and male children.

These Indians have likewise their priests, or conjurers, or medicine men, who pretend to be in the confidence of the deities, and the expounders and enforcers of their will. Each of these medicine men has his idols carved in wood, representing the spirits of the air and of the fire, under some rude and grotesque form of a horse, a bear, a beaver, or other quadruped, or that of a bird or fish. These idols are hung round with amulets and votive offerings, such as beavers' teeth, and bears' and eagles' claws.

When any chief personage is on his deathbed, or dangerously ill, the medicine men are sent for. Each brings with him his idols, with which he retires into a canoe to hold a consultation. As the doctors are prone to disagree, so these medicine men have now and then a violent altercation as to the malady of the patient, or the treatment of it. To settle this they beat their idols soundly against each other; whichever first loses a tooth or a claw is considered as confuted, and his votary retires from the field.

Polygamy is not only allowed, but considered honourable, and the greater number of wives a man can maintain, the more important is he in the eyes of the tribe. The first wife, however, takes rank of all the others, and is considered mistress of the house. Still the domestic establishment is liable to jealousies and cabals, and the lord and master has much difficulty in maintaining harmony in his jangling household.

In the manuscript from which we draw many of these particulars, it is stated, that he who exceeds his neighbours in the number of his wives, male children, and slaves, is elected chief of the village; a title to office which we do not recollect ever before to have met with.

Feuds are frequent among these tribes, but are not very deadly. They have occasionally pitched battles, fought on appointed days, and at specified places, which are generally the banks of a rivulet. The adverse parties post themselves on the opposite sides of the stream, and at such distances that the battles often last a long while before any blood is shed. The number of killed and wounded seldom exceed half a dozen. Should the damage be equal on each side, the war is considered as honourably concluded: should one party lose more than the other, it is entitled to a compensation in slaves or other property, otherwise hostilities are liable to be renewed at a future day. They are much given also to predatory inroads into the territories of their enemies, and sometimes of their friendly neighbours. Should they fall upon a band of inferior force, or upon a village, weakly defended, they act with the ferocity of true poltroons, slaying all the men and carrying off the women and children as slaves. As to the property it is packed upon horses which they bring with them for the purpose. They are mean and paltry as warriors, and altogether inferior in heroic qualities to the savages of the buffalo plains on the east side of the mountains.

A great portion of their time is passed in revelry, music, dancing, and gambling. Their music scarcely deserves the name; the instruments being of the rudest kind. Their singing is harsh and discordant, the songs are chiefly extempore, relating to passing circumstances, the persons present, or any trifling object that strikes the attention of the singer. They have several kinds of dances, some of them lively and pleasing. The women are rarely permitted to dance with the men, but form groups apart, dancing to the same instrument and song.

They have a great passion for play, and a variety of games. To such a pitch of excitement are they sometimes roused, that they gamble away every thing they possess, even to their wives and children. They are notorious thieves, also, and proud of their dexterity. He who is frequently successful, gains much applause and popularity; but the clumsy thief, who is detected in some bungling attempt, is scoffed at and despised, and sometimes severely punished.

Such are a few leading characteristics of the natives in the neighbourhood of Astoria. They appear to us inferior in many respects to the tribes east of the mountains, the bold rovers of the prairies; and to partake much of the Esquimaux character; elevated in some degree by a more genial climate, and more varied style of living.

The habits of traffic engendered at the cataracts of the Columbia, have had their influence along the coast. The Chinooks and other Indians at the mouth of the river, soon proved themselves keen traders, and in their early dealings with the Astorians, never hesitated to ask three times what they considered the real value of an article. They were inquisitive, also, in the extreme, and impertinently intrusive; and were prone to indulge in scoffing and ridicule, at the expense of the strangers.

In one thing, however, they showed superior judgment and self-command, to most of their race; this was, in their abstinence from ardent spirits, and the abhorrence and disgust with which they regarded a drunkard. On one occasion, a son of Comcomly had been induced to drink freely at the factory, and went home in a state of intoxication, playing all kinds of mad pranks, until he sank into a stupor, in which he remained for two days. The old chieftain repaired to his friend, M'Dougal, with indignation flaming in his countenance, and bitterly reproached him for having permitted his son to degrade himself into a beast, and to render himself an object of scorn and laughter to his slaves.

CHAPTER XXIII.

Spring arrangements at Astoria—Various expeditions set out—The Long Narrows—Pilfering Indians—Thievish tribe at Wish-ram—Portage at the falls—Portage by moonlight—An attack, a route, and a robbery—Indian cure for cowardice—A parley and compromise—The despatch party turn back—Meet Crooks and John Day—Their sufferings—Indian perfidy—Arrival at Astoria.

As the spring opened, the little settlement of Astoria was in agitation, and prepared to send forth various expeditions. Several important things were to be done. It was necessary to send a supply of goods to the trading post of Mr. David Stuart, established in the preceding autumn on the Oakinagan. The cache, or secret deposit, made by Mr. Hunt at the Caldron Linn, was likewise to be visited, and the merchandise and other effects left there to be brought to Astoria. A third object of moment was to send despatches overland to Mr. Astor at New York, informing him of the state of affairs at the settlement, and the fortunes of the several expeditions.

The task of carrying supplies to Oakinagan was assigned to Mr. Robert Stuart, a spirited and enterprising young man, nephew to the one who had established the post. The cache was to be sought out by two of the clerks, named Russell Farnham and Donald M'Gilles, conducted by a guide, and accompanied by eight men, to assist in bringing home the goods.

As to the despatches, they were confided to Mr. John Reed, the clerk, the same who had conducted one of the exploring detachments of Snake river. He was now to trace back his way across the mountains by the same route by which he had come, with no other companions or escort than Ben Jones, the Kentucky hunter, and two Canadians. As it was still hoped that Mr. Crooks might be in existence, and that Mr. Reed and his party might meet with him in the course of their route, they were charged with a small supply of goods and provisions, to aid that gentleman on his way to Astoria.

When the expedition of Reed was made known, Mr. M'Lellan announced his determination to accompany it. He had long been dissatisfied with the smallness of his share in the copartnership, and had requested an additional number of shares; his request not being complied with, he resolved to abandon the company. M'Lellan was a man of a singularly self-willed and decided character, with whom persuasion was useless; he was permitted, therefore, to take his own course without opposition.

As to Reed, he set about preparing for his hazardous journey with the zeal of a true Irishman. He had a tin case made in which the letters and papers addressed to Mr. Astor were carefully soldered up. This case he intended to strap upon his shoulders, so as to bear it about with him, sleeping and waking, in all changes and chances, by land or by water, and never to part with it but with his life!

As the route of these several parties would be the same for nearly four hundred miles up the Columbia, and within that distance would lie through the piratical pass of the rapids, and among the freebooting tribes of the river, it was thought advisable to start about the same time, and to keep together. Accordingly, on the 22d of March, they all set off, to the number of seventeen men, in two canoes;—and here we cannot but pause to notice the hardihood of these several expeditions, so insignificant in point of force, and severally destined to traverse immense wildernesses, where larger parties had experienced so much danger and distress. When recruits were sought in the preceding year among the experienced hunters and voyageurs at Montreal and St. Louis, it was considered dangerous to attempt to cross the Rocky mountains with less than sixty men; and yet, here we find Reed ready to push his way across those barriers with merely three companions. Such is the fearlessness, the insensibility to danger, which men acquire by the habitude of constant risk. The mind, like the body, becomes callous by exposure.

The little associated band proceeded up the river, under the command of Mr. Robert Stuart, and arrived early in the month of April at the Long Narrows, that notorious plundering place. Here it was necessary to unload the canoes, and to transport both them and their cargoes to the head of the Narrows by land. Their party was too few in number for the purpose. They were obliged, therefore, to seek the assistance of the Cathlasco Indians, who undertook to carry the goods on their horses. Forward then they set, the Indians with their horses well freighted, and the first load convoyed by Reed and five men well armed; the gallant Irishman striding along at the head, with his tin case of despatches glittering on his back. On passing, however, through a rocky and intri-

cate defile, some of the freebooting vagabonds turned
their horses up a narrow path and gallopped off, carrying
with them two bales of goods, and a number of smaller
articles. To follow them was useless; indeed, it was
with much ado that the convoy got into port with the
residue of the cargoes; for some of the guards were pillaged of their knives and pocket handkerchiefs, and the
lustrous tin case of Mr. John Reed was in imminent
jeopardy.

Mr. Stuart heard of these depredations, and hastened
forward to the relief of the convoy, but could not reach
them before dusk, by which time they had arrived at the
village of Wish-ram, already noted for its great fishery,
and the knavish propensities of its inhabitants. Here
they found themselves benighted in a strange place, and
surrounded by savages bent on pilfering, if not upon open
robbery. Not knowing what active course to take, they
remained under arms all night, without closing an eye,
and at the very first peep of dawn, when objects were yet
scarce visible, everything was hastily embarked, and,
without seeking to recover the stolen effects, they pushed
off from shore ; " glad to bid adieu," as they said, " to
this abominable nest of miscreants."

The worthies of Wish-ram, however, were not disposed
to part so easily with their visiters. Their cupidity had
been quickened by the plunder which they had already
taken, and their confidence increased by the impunity
with which their outrage had passed. They resolved,
therefore, to take further toll of the travellers, and, if
possible, to capture the tin case of despatches ; which
shining conspicuously afar off, and being guarded by
John Reed with such especial care, must, as they supposed,
be " a great medicine."

Accordingly, Mr. Stuart and his comrades had not proceeded far in the canoes, when they beheld the whole
rabble of Wish-ram stringing in groups along the bank,
whooping and yelling, and gibbering in their wild jargon ;
and when they landed below the falls, they were surrounded by upwards of four hundred of these river
ruffians, armed with bows and arrows, war-clubs, and

other savage weapons. These now pressed forward, with offers to carry the canoes and effects up the portage. Mr. Stuart declined forwarding the goods, alleging the lateness of the hour; but, to keep them in good humour, informed them that, if they conducted themselves well, their offered services might probably be accepted in the morning; in the mean while, he suggested that they might carry up the canoes. They accordingly set off with the two canoes on their shoulders, accompanied by a guard of eight men well armed.

When arrived at the head of the falls, the mischievous spirit of the savages broke out, and they were on the point of destroying the canoes, doubtless with a view to impede the white men from carrying forward their goods, and laying them open to further pilfering. They were with some difficulty prevented from committing this outrage by the interference of an old man, who appeared to have authority among them; and, in consequence of his harangue, the whole of the hostile band, with the exception of about fifty, crossed to the north side of the river, where they lay in wait, ready for further mischief.

In the mean time, Mr. Stuart, who had remained at the foot of the falls with the goods, and who knew that the proffered assistance of the savages was only for the purpose of having an opportunity to plunder, determined, if possible, to steal a march upon them, and defeat their machinations. In the dead of the night, therefore, about one o'clock, the moon shining brightly, he roused his party, and proposed that they should endeavour to transport the goods themselves, above the falls, before the sleeping savages could be aware of their operations. All hands sprang to the work with zeal, and hurried it on in the hope of getting all over before daylight. Mr. Stuart went forward with the first loads, and took his station at the head of the portage, while Mr. Reed and Mr. M'Lellan remained at the foot to forward the remainder.

The day dawned before the transportation was completed. Some of the fifty Indians who had remained on the south side of the river, perceived what was going on, and, feeling themselves too weak for an attack, gave the

alarm to those on the opposite side, upwards of a hundred of whom embarked in several large canoes. Two
loads of goods yet remained to be brought up.   Mr.
Stuart despatched some of the people for one of the loads,
with a request to Mr. Reed to retain with him as many
men as he thought necessary to guard the remaining load,
as he suspected hostile intentions on the part of the Indians.   Mr. Reed, however, refused to retain any of
them, saying that M'Lellan and himself were sufficient to
protect the small quantity that remained.   The men
accordingly departed with the load, while Reed and
M'Lellan continued to mount guard over the residue. By
this time a number of the canoes had arrived from the
opposite side. As they approached the shore, the unlucky tin box of John Reed, shining afar like the brilliant helmet of Euryalus, caught their eyes.   No sooner
did the canoes touch the shore, than they leaped forward
on the rocks, set up a war-whoop, and sprang forward to
secure the glittering prize. Mr. M'Lellan, who was at
the river bank, advanced to guard the goods, when one of
the savages attempted to hoodwink him with his buffalo
robe with one hand, and to stab him with the other.
M'Lellan sprang back just far enough to avoid the blow,
and raising his rifle, shot the ruffian through the heart.

In the mean time, Reed who, with the want of forethought of an Irishman, had neglected to remove the
leathern cover from the lock of his rifle, was fumbling at
the fastenings, when he received a blow on the head with
a war-club that laid him senseless on the ground.   In a
twinkling he was stripped of his rifle and pistols, and the
tin box, the cause of all this onslaught, was borne off in
triumph.

At this critical juncture, Mr. Stuart, who had heard the
war-whoop, hastened to the scene of action with Ben
Jones, and seven others of the men.   When he arrived,
Reed was weltering in his blood, and an Indian standing
over him and about to despatch him with a tomahawk.
Stuart gave the word, when Ben Jones levelled his rifle,
and shot the miscreant on the spot.   The men then gave
a cheer, and charged upon the main body of the savages,

who took to instant flight. Reed was now raised from the ground, and borne senseless and bleeding to the upper end of the portage. Preparations were made to launch the canoes and embark in all haste, when it was found that they were too leaky to be put in the water, and that the oars had been left at the foot of the falls. A scene of confusion now ensued. The Indians were whooping and yelling, and running about like fiends. A panic seized upon the men, at being thus suddenly checked, the hearts of some of the Canadians died within them, and two young men actually fainted away. The moment they recovered their senses, Mr. Stuart ordered that they should be deprived of their arms, their under garments taken off, and that a piece of cloth should be tied round their waist, in imitation of a squaw; an Indian punishment for cowardice. Thus equipped, they were stowed away among the goods in one of the canoes. This ludicrous affair excited the mirth of the bolder spirits, even in the midst of their perils, and roused the pride of the wavering. The Indians having crossed back again to the north side, order was restored, some of the hands were sent back for the oars, others set to work to calk and launch the canoes, and in a little while all were embarked and were continuing their voyage along the southern shore.

No sooner had they departed, than the Indians returned to the scene of action, bore off their two comrades, who had been shot, one of whom was still living, and returned to their village. Here they killed two horses, and drank the hot blood to give fierceness to their courage. They painted and arrayed themselves hideously for battle; performed the dead dance round the slain, and raised the war song of vengeance. Then mounting their horses, to the number of four hundred and fifty men, and brandishing their weapons, they set off along the northern bank of the river, to get ahead of the canoes, lie in wait for them, and take a terrible revenge on the white men.

They succeeded in getting some distance above the canoes without being discovered, and were crossing the river to post themselves on the side along which the white men were coasting, when they were fortunately descried.

Mr. Stuart and his companions were immediately on the alert. As they drew near to the place where the savages had crossed, they observed them posted among steep and overhanging rocks, close along which the canoes would have to pass. Finding that the enemy had the advantage of the ground, the whites stopped short when within five hundred yards of them, and discharged and reloaded their pieces. They then made a fire, and dressed the wounds of Mr. Reed, who had received five severe gashes in the head. This being done, they lashed the canoes together, fastened them to a rock at a small distance from the shore, and there awaited the menaced attack.

They had not been long posted in this manner, when they saw a canoe approaching. It contained the war-chief of the tribe, and three of his principal warriors. He drew near, and made a long harangue, in which he informed them that they had killed one and wounded another of his nation; that the relations of the slain cried out for vengeance, and he had been compelled to lead them to the fight. Still he wished to spare unnecessary bloodshed; he proposed, therefore, that Mr. Reed, who, he observed, was little better than a dead man, might be given up to be sacrificed to the manes of the deceased warrior. This would appease the fury of his friends; the hatchet would then be buried, and all thenceforward would be friends.

The answer was a stern refusal and a defiance, and the war-chief saw that the canoes were well prepared for a vigorous defence. He withdrew, therefore, and returning to his warriors among the rocks, held long deliberations. Blood for blood is a principle in Indian equity and Indian honour; but though the inhabitants of Wish-ram were men of war, they were likewise men of traffic, and it was suggested that honour for once might give way to profit. A negotiation was accordingly opened with the white men, and after some diplomacy, the matter was compromised for a blanket to cover the dead, and some tobacco to be smoked by the living. This being granted, the heroes of Wish-ram crossed the river once more, returned to their village to feast upon the horses whose blood they had so vaingloriously drunk, and the travellers pursued their voyage without further molestation.

The tin case, however, containing the important despatches for New York, was irretrievably lost; the very precaution taken by the worthy Hibernian to secure his missives, had, by rendering them conspicuous, produced their robbery. The object of his overland journey, therefore, being defeated, he gave up the expedition. The whole party repaired with Mr. Robert Stuart to the establishment of Mr. David Stuart, on the Oakinagan river. After remaining here two or three days, they all set out on their return to Astoria, accompanied by Mr. David Stuart. This gentleman had a large quantity of beaver-skins at his establishment, but did not think it prudent to take them with him, fearing the levy of " black mail" at the falls.

On their way down, when below the forks of the Columbia, they were hailed one day from the shore in English. Looking around, they descried two wretched men, entirely naked. They pulled to shore; the men came up and made themselves known. They proved to be Mr. Crooks and his faithful follower, John Day.

The reader will recollect, that Mr. Crooks, with Day and four Canadians, had been so reduced by famine and fatigue, that Mr. Hunt was obliged to leave them, in the month of December, on the banks of the Snake river. Their situation was the more critical, as they were in the neighbourhood of a band of Shoshonies, whose horses had been forcibly seized by Mr. Hunt's party for provisions. Mr. Crooks remained here twenty days, detained by the extremely reduced state of John Day, who was utterly unable to travel, and whom he would not abandon, as Day had been in his employ on the Missouri, and had always proved himself most faithful. Fortunately the Shoshonies did not offer to molest them. They had never before seen white men, and seemed to entertain some superstitions with regard to them; for, though they would encamp near them in the day time, they would move off with their tents in the night; and finally disappeared, without taking leave.

When Day was sufficiently recovered to travel they kept feebly on, sustaining themselves as well as they could, until in the month of February, when three of the Canadians, fearful of perishing with want, left Mr. Crooks on a small river, on the road by which Mr. Hunt had passed in quest of Indians. Mr. Crooks followed Mr. Hunt's track in the snow for several days, sleeping as usual in the open air, and suffering all kinds of hardships. At length, coming to a low prairie, he lost every appearance of the " trail," and wandered during the remainder of the winter in the mountains, snbsisting sometimes on horse meat, sometimes on beavers and their skins, and a part of the time on roots.

About the last of March, the other Canadian gave out, and was left with a lodge of Shoshonies; but Mr. Crooks and John Day still kept on, and finding the snow sufficiently diminished, undertook, from Indian information, to cross the last mountain ridge. They happily succeeded, and afterwards fell in with the Wallah-Wallahs, a tribe of Indians inhabiting the banks of the river of the same name, and reputed as being frank, hospitable, and sincere. They proved worthy of the character, for they received the poor wanderers kindly, killed a horse for them to eat, and directed them on their way to the Columbia. They struck the river about the middle of April, and advanced down it one hundred miles, until they came within about twenty miles of the falls.

Here they met with some of the " chivalry" of that noted pass, who received them in a friendly way, and set food before them ; but, while they were satisfying their hunger, perfidiously seized their rifles. They then stripped them naked and drove them off, refusing the entreaties of Mr. Crooks for a flint and steel of which they had robbed him ; and threatening his life if he did not instantly depart.

In this forlorn plight, still worse off than before, they renewed their wanderings. They now sought to find their way back to the hospitable Wallah-Wallahs, and had advanced eighty miles along the river, when fortunately, on the very morning that they were going to leave the

Columbia, and strike inland, the canoes of Mr. Stuart hove in sight.

It is needless to describe the joy of these poor men at once more finding themselves among countrymen and friends, or of the honest and hearty welcome with which they were received by their fellow-adventurers. The whole party now continued down the river, passed all the dangerous places without interruption, and arrived safely at Astoria on the 11th of May.

CHAPTER XXIV.

Comprehensive views—To supply the Russian fur establishment—An agent sent to Russia—Project of an annual ship—The Beaver fitted out—Her equipment and crew—Instructions to the captain—The Sandwich Islands—Rumours of the fate of the Tonquin—Precautions at reaching the mouth of the Columbia.

HAVING traced the fortunes of the two expeditions by sea and land to the mouth of the Columbia, and presented a view of affairs at Astoria, we will return for a moment to the master spirit of the enterprise, who regulated the springs of Astoria, at his residence in New York.

It will be remembered, that a part of the plan of Mr. Astor was to furnish the Russian fur establishment on the north-west coast with regular supplies, so as to render it independent of those casual vessels which cut up the trade and supplied the natives with arms. This plan had been countenanced by our own government, and likewise by Count Pahlen, the Russian minister at Washington. As its views, however, were important and extensive, and might eventually affect a wide course of commerce, Mr. Astor was desirous of establishing a complete arrangement on the subject with the Russian American Fur Company, under the sanction of the Russian government. For this purpose, in March, 1811, he despatched a confidential agent to St. Petersburg, fully empowered to enter into the requisite negotiations. A passage was given to this gentleman by the government of the United States, in the John Adams, one of its armed vessels, bound to a European port.

The next step of Mr. Astor was, to despatch the annual ship contemplated on his general plan. He had as yet heard nothing of the success of the previous expeditions, and had to proceed upon the presumption that every thing had been effected according to his instructions. He accordingly fitted out a fine ship of four hundred and ninety tons, called the Beaver, and freighted her with a valuable cargo destined for the factory at the mouth of the Columbia, the trade along the coast, and the supply of the Russian establishment. In this ship embarked a reinforcement, consisting of a partner, five clerks, fifteen American labourers, and six Canadian voyageurs. In choosing his agents for his first expedition, Mr. Astor had been obliged to have recourse to British subjects experienced in the Canadian fur trade ; henceforth it was his intention, as much as possible, to select Americans, so as to secure an ascendancy of American influence in the management of the company, and to make it decidedly national.

Accordingly, Mr. John Clarke, the partner who took the lead in the present expedition, was a native of the United States, though he had passed much of his life in the north-west, having been employed in the fur trade since the age of sixteen. Most of the clerks were young gentlemen of good connexions in the American cities, some of whom embarked in the hope of gain, others through the mere spirit of adventure incident to youth.

The instructions given by Mr. Astor to Captain Sowle, the commander of the Beaver, were, in some respects, hypothetical, in consequence of the uncertainty resting upon the previous steps of the enterprise.

He was to touch at the Sandwich islands, inquire about the fortunes of the Tonquin, and whether an establishment had been formed at the mouth of the Columbia. If so, he was to take as many Sandwich islanders as his ship would accommodate, and proceed thither. On arriving at the river, he was to observe great caution, for even if an establishment should have been formed, it might have fallen into hostile hands. He was, therefore, to put in as if by casualty or distress, to give himself out as a coasting trader, and to say nothing about his ship being owned by Mr. Astor, until he had ascertained that every thing was right. In that case, he was to land such part of his cargo as was intended for the establishment, and to proceed to New Archangel with the supplies intended for the Russian post at that place, where he could receive peltries in payment. With these he was to return to Astoria; take in the furs collected there, and, having completed his cargo by trading along the coast, was to proceed to Canton. The captain received the same injunction that had been given to Captain Thorn of the Tonquin, of great caution and circumspection in his intercourse with the natives, and that he should not permit more than one or two to be on board at a time.

The Beaver sailed from New York on the 10th of October, 1811, and reached the Sandwich Islands without any occurrence of moment. Here a rumour was heard of the disastrous fate of the Tonquin. Deep solicitude was felt by every one on board for the fate of both expeditions, by sea and land. Doubts were entertained whether any establishment had been formed at the mouth of the Columbia, or whether any of the company would be found there. After much deliberation, the captain took twelve Sandwich islanders on board for the service of the factory, should there be one in existence, and proceeded on his voyage.

On the 6th of May he arrived off the mouth of the Columbia, and running as near as possible, fired two signal guns. No answer was returned, nor was there any signal to be descried. Night coming on, the ship stood out to sea, and every heart drooped as the land faded away. On the following morning they again ran in within four miles of the shore, and fired other signal guns, but still without reply. A boat was then despatched to sound the channel and attempt an entrance; but returned without success, there being a tremendous swell, and breakers. Signal guns were fired again in the evening, but equally in vain, and once more the ship stood off to sea for the night. The captain now gave up all hope of finding any establishment at the place, and indulged in the most gloomy apprehensions. He feared his predecessors had been massacred before they had reached their place of destination ; or if they should have erected a factory, that it had been surprised and destroyed by the natives.

In this moment of doubt and uncertainty, Mr. Clarke announced his determination, in case of the worst, to found an establishment with the present party, and all hands bravely engaged to stand by him in the undertaking. The next morning the ship stood in for the third time, and fired three signal guns, but with little hope of reply. To the great joy of the crew, three distinct guns were heard in answer. The apprehensions of all but Captain Sowle were now at rest. That cautious commander recollected the instructions given him by Mr. Astor, and determined to proceed with great circumspection. He was well aware of Indian treachery and cunning. It was not impossible, he observed, that these cannon might have been fired by the savages themselves. They might have surprised the fort, massacred its inmates ; and these signal guns might only be decoys to allure him across the bar, that they might have a chance of cutting him off, and seizing his vessel.

At length a white flag was descried hoisted as a signal on Cape Disappointment. The passengers pointed to it in triumph, but the captain did not yet dismiss his doubts. A beacon-fire blazed through the night on the same place, but the captain observed that all these signals might be treacherous.

On the following morning, May 9th, the vessel came to anchor off Cape Disappointment, outside of the bar. Towards noon an Indian canoe was seen making for the ship, and all hands were ordered to be on the alert. A few moments afterwards, a barge was perceived following the canoe. The hopes and fears of those on board of the ship were in tumultuous agitation, as the boat drew nigh that was to let them know the fortunes of the enterprise, and the fate of their predecessors. The captain who was haunted with the idea of possible treachery, did not suffer his curiosity to get the better of his caution, but ordered a party of his men under arms to receive the visiters. The canoe came first alongside, in which were Comcomly and six Indians; in the barge were M'Dougal, M'Lellan, and eight Canadians. A little conversation with these gentlemen dispelled all the captain's fears, and the Beaver, crossing the bar under their pilotage, anchored safely in Baker's bay.

END OF THE SECOND VOLUME.

CHAPTER I.

Active operations at Astoria—Various expeditions fitted out—Robert Stuart and a party destined for New York—Singular conduct of John Day—His fate—Piratical pass and hazardous portage—Rattlesnakes—Their abhorrence of tobacco—Arrival among the Wallah-Wallahs—Purchase of horses—Departure of Stuart and his band for the mountains.

THE arrival of the Beaver with a reinforcement and supplies, gave new life and vigour to affairs at Astoria. These were means for extending the operations of the establishment, and founding interior trading posts. Two parties were immediately sent on foot to proceed severally under the command of Messrs. M'Kenzie and Clarke, and establish posts above the forks of the Columbia, at points where most rivalry and opposition were apprehended from the North-west Company.

A third party, headed by Mr. David Stuart, was to repair with supplies to the post of that gentleman on the Oakinagan. In addition to these expeditions, a fourth was necessary, to convey despatches to Mr. Astor, at New York, in place of those unfortunately lost by John Reed. The safe conveyance of these despatches were highly important, as by them Mr. Astor would receive an account of the state of the factory, and regulate his reinforcements and supplies accordingly. The mission was one of peril and hardship, and required a man of nerve and vigour. It was confided to Robert Stuart, who, though he had never been across the mountains, and a very young man, had given proofs of his competency to the task. Four trusty and well-tried men, who had come over-land in Mr. Hunt's expedition, were given as his guides and hunters. These were Ben Jones and John Day, the Kentuckians, and Andri Vallar and Francis Le Clerc, Canadians. Mr. M'Lellan again expressed his determination to take this opportunity of returning to the Atlantic states. In this he was joined by Mr. Crooks, who, notwithstanding all that he had suffered in the dismal journey of the preceding winter, was ready to retrace his steps, and brave every danger and hardship, rather than remain at Astoria. This little handful of adventurous men we propose to accompany in its long and perilous peregrinations.

The several parties we have mentioned all set off in company on the 29th of June, under a salute of cannon from the fort. They were to keep together, for mutual protection, through the piratical passes of the river, and to separate, on their different destinations, at the forks of the Columbia. Their number, collectively, was nearly sixty, consisting of partners and clerks, Canadian voyageurs, Sandwich islanders, and American hunters; and they embarked in two barges and ten canoes.

They had scarcely got under way, when John Day, the Kentucky hunter, became restless, and uneasy, and extremely wayward in his deportment. This caused surprise, for in general he was remarked for his cheerful, manly deportment. It was supposed that the recollection of past sufferings might harass his mind in undertaking to retrace the scenes where they had been experienced. As the expedition advanced, however, his agitation increased. He began to talk wildly and incoherently, and to show manifest symptoms of derangement.

Mr. Crooks now informed his companions that in his desolate wanderings through the Snake river country during the preceding winter, in which he had been accompanied by John Day, the poor fellow's wits had been partially unsettled by the sufferings and horrors through which they had passed, and he doubted whether they had ever been restored to perfect sanity. It was still hoped that this agitation of spirit might pass away as they proceeded; but, on the contrary, it grew more and more violent. His comrades endeavoured to divert his mind, and to draw him into rational conversation, but he only became the more exasperated, uttering wild and incoherent ravings. The sight of any of the natives put him in an absolute fury, and he would heap on them the most opprobrious epithets; recollecting, no doubt, what he had suffered from Indian robbers.

On the evening of the 2nd of July he became absolutely frantic, and attempted to destroy himself. Being disarmed, he sank into quietude, and professed the greatest remorse for the crime he had meditated. He then pretended to sleep, and having thus lulled suspicion, suddenly sprang up, just before daylight, seized a pair of loaded pistols, and endeavoured to blow out his brains. In his hurry he fired too high, and the balls passed over his head. He was instantly secured, and placed under a guard in one of the boats. How to dispose of him was now the question, as it was impossible to keep him with the expedition. Fortunately Mr. Stuart met with some Indians accustomed to trade with Astoria. These undertook to conduct John Day back to the factory, and deliver him there in safety. It was with the utmost concern that his comrades saw the poor fellow depart; for, independent of his invaluable services as a first-rate hunter, his frank loyal qualities had made him a universal favourite. It may be as well to add that the Indians executed their tasks faithfully, and landed John Day among his friends at Astoria; but his constitution was completely broken by the hardships he had undergone, and he died within a year.

On the evening of the 6th of July the party arrived at the piratical pass of the river, and encamped at the foot of the first rapid. The next day, before the commencement of the portage, the greatest precautions were taken to guard against lurking treachery, or open attack. The weapons of every man were put in order, and his cartridge-box replenished. Each one wore a kind of surcoat made of the skin of the elk, reaching from his neck to his knees, and answering the purpose of a shirt of mail, for it was arrow-proof, and could even resist a musket-ball at the distance of ninety yards. Thus armed and equipped, they posted their forces in military style. Five of the officers took their stations at each end of the portage, which was between three and four miles in length ; a number of men mounted guard at short distances along the heights immediately overlooking the river, while the residue, thus protected from surprise, employed themselves below in dragging up the barges and canoes, and carrying up the goods along the narrow margin of the rapids. With these precautions they all passed unmolested. The only accident that happened was the upsetting of one of the canoes, by which some of the goods sunk, and others floated down the stream. The alertness and rapacity of the hordes which infest these rapids, were immediately apparent. They pounced upon the floating merchandise with the keenness of regular wreckers. A bale of goods which landed upon one of the islands was immediately ripped open, one half of its contents divided among the captives, and the other half secreted in a lonely hut in a deep ravine. Mr. Robert Stuart, however, set out in a canoe with five men and an interpreter, ferreted out the wreckers in their retreat, and succeeded in wresting from them their booty.

Similar precautions to those already mentioned, and to a still greater extent, were observed in passing the long narrows, and the falls, where they would be exposed to the depredations of the chivalry of Wish-ram, and its free-booting neighbourhood. In fact, they had scarcely set their first watch one night, when the alarm of " Indians !" was given. " To arms !" was the cry, and every man was at his post in an instant. The alarm was explained ; a war party of the Shoshonies had surprised a canoe of the natives just below the encampment, had murdered four men and two women, and it was apprehended they would attack the camp ; the boats and canoes were immediately hauled up, a breastwork was made of them and the packages, forming three sides of a square, with the river n the rear, and thus the party remained fortified throughout the night.

The dawn, however, dispelled the alarm ; the portage was conducted in peace ; the vagabond warriors of the vicinity hovered about them while at work, but were kept at a wary distance. They regarded the loads of merchandise with wistful eyes, but seeing the " long beards" so formidable in number, and so well prepared for action, they made no attempt, either by open force or sly pilfering, to collect their usual toll, but maintained a peaceful demeanour, and were afterwards rewarded for their good conduct with presents of tobacco.

Fifteen days were consumed in ascending from the foot of the first rapid to the head of the falls, a distance of about eighty miles, but full of all kinds of obstructions. Having happily accomplished these difficult portages, the party, on the 19th of July, arrived at a smoother part of the river, and pursued their way up the stream with greater speed and facility.

They were now in the neighbourhood where Mr. Crooks and John Day had been so perfidiously robbed and stripped a few months previously, when confiding in the proffered hospitality of a ruffian band. On landing at night, therefore, a vigilant guard was maintained about the camp. On the following morning a number of Indians made their appearance, and came prowling round the party while at breakfast. To his great delight, Mr. Crooks recognised among them two of the miscreants by whom he had been robbed. They were instantly seized, bound hand and foot, and thrown into one of the canoes. Here they lay in doleful fright, expecting summary execution. Mr. Crooks, however, was not of a revengeful disposition, and agreed to release the culprits as soon as the pillaged property should be restored. Several savages immediately started off in different directions, and before night the rifles of Crooks and Day were produced; several of the smaller articles pilfered from them, however, could not be recovered.

The bands of the culprits were then removed, and they lost no time in taking their departure, still under the influence of abject terror, and scarcely crediting their senses that they had escaped the merited punishment of their offences.

The country on each side of the river now began to assume a different character. The hills, and cliffs, and forests disappeared; vast sandy plains, scantily clothed here and there with short tufts of grass, parched by the summer sun, stretched far away to the north and south.

The river was occasionally obstructed with rocks and rapids, but often there were smooth placid intervals, where the current was gentle, and the boatmen were enabled to lighten their labours with the assistance of the sail.

The natives in this part of the river resided entirely on the northern side. They were hunters, as well as fishermen, and had horses in plenty. Some of these were purchased by the party, as provisions, and killed on the spot, though they occasionally found a difficulty in procuring fuel wherewith to cook them. One of the greatest dangers that beset the travellers in this part of their expedition, was the vast number of rattlesnakes which infested the rocks and portages, and on which the men were in danger of treading. They were often found, too, in quantities about the encampments. In one place, a nest of them lay coiled together, basking in the sun. Several guns loaded with shot were discharged at them, and thirty-seven killed and wounded. To prevent any unwelcome visits from them in the night, tobacco was occasionally strewed around the tents, a weed for which they have a very proper abhorrence.

On the 28th of July, the travellers arrived at the mouth of the Wallah-Wallah, a bright, clear stream, about six feet deep, and fifty-five yards wide, which flows rapidly over a bed of sand and gravel, and throws itself into the Columbia, a few miles below Lewis river. Here the combined parties that had thus far voyaged together, were to separate, each for its particular destination.

On the banks of the Wallah-Wallah lived the hospitable tribe of the same name who had succoured Mr. Crooks and John Day in the time of their extremity. No sooner did they hear of the arrival of the party, than they hastened to greet them. They built a great bonfire on the bank of the river, before the camp, and men and women danced round it. The Wallah-Wallahs are an equestrian tribe. The equipments of their horses were rude and inconvenient. High saddles, roughly made of deer skin, stuffed with hair, which chafe the horse's back, and leave it raw; wooden stirrups, with a thong of raw hide wrapped round them; and for bridles they have cords of twisted horse hair, which they tie round the under jaw. They are, like most

Indians, bold, but hard riders, and when on horseback, gallop about the dangerous places, without fear for themselves, or pity for their steeds.

From these people Mr. Stuart purchased twenty horses for his party; some for the saddle, and others to transport the baggage. He was fortunate in procuring a noble animal for his own use, which was praised by the Indians for its great speed and bottom, and a high price set upon it. No people understand better the value of a horse, than these equestrian tribes; and nowhere is speed a greater requisite, as they frequently engage in the chase of the antelope, one of the fleetest of animals. Even after the Indian who sold this boasted horse to Mr. Stuart had concluded his bargain, he lingered about the animal, seeming loth to part from him, and to be sorry for what he had done.

A day or two were employed by Mr. Stuart in arranging packages and pack saddles, and making other preparations for his long and arduous journey. His party, by the loss of John Day, was now reduced to six, a small number for such an expedition. They were young men, however, full of courage, health, and good spirits, and stimulated, rather than appalled, by danger.

On the morning of the 31st of July, all preparation being concluded, Mr. Stuart and his little band mounted their steeds and took a farewell of their fellow travellers, who gave them three hearty cheers as they set out on their dangerous journey. The course they took was to the southeast, towards the fated region of the Snake river. At an immense distance rose a chain of craggy mountains, which they would have to traverse; they were the same among which the travellers had experienced such sufferings from cold during the preceding winter, and from their azure tints, when seen at a distance, had received the name of the Blue mountains.

CHAPTER II.

In retracing the route which had proved so disastrous
to Mr. Hunt's party during the preceding winter, Mr.
Stuart had trusted, in the present more favourable season,
to find easy travelling and abundant supplies. On these
great wastes and wilds, however, each season has its
peculiar hardships. The travellers had not proceeded far
before they found themselves among naked and arid hills,
with a soil composed of sand and clay, baked and brittle,
that to all appearance had never been visited by the dews
of heaven.

Not a spring, or pool, or running stream was to be seen;
the sunburnt country was seamed and cut up by dry
ravines, the beds of winter torrents, serving only to balk
the hopes of man and beast, with the sight of dusty
channels where water had once poured along in floods.

For a long summer day they continued onward without
halting; a burning sky above their heads, a parched desert
beneath their feet, with just wind enough to raise the light
sand from the knolls, and envelop them in stifling clouds.
The sufferings from thirst became intense; a fine young
dog, their only companion of the kind, gave out, and
expired. Evening drew on without any prospect of relief,
and they were almost reduced to despair, when they
descried something that looked like a fringe of forest,
along the horizon. All were inspired with new hope, for
they knew that on these arid wastes, in the neighbourhood
of trees, there is always water.

They now quickened their pace; the horses seemed to
understand their motives, and to partake of their anticipations, for, though before, almost ready to give out, they
now required neither whip nor spur. With all their
exertions, it was late in the night before they drew near to

the trees. As they approached, they heard, with transport, the rippling of a shallow stream. No sooner did the refreshing sound reach the ears of the horses, than the poor animals snuffed the air, rushed forward with ungovernable eagerness, and, plunging their muzzles into the water, drank until they seemed in danger of bursting. Their riders had but little more discretion, and required repeated draughts to quench their excessive thirst. Their weary march that day had been forty-five miles, over a tract that might rival the deserts of Africa for aridity. Indeed, the sufferings of the traveller on these American deserts, are frequently more severe than in the wastes of Africa and Asia, from being less habituated and prepared to cope with them.

On the banks of this blessed stream the travellers encamped for the night; and so great had been their fatigue, and so sound and sweet was their sleep, that it was a late hour the next morning before they awoke. They now recognised the little river to be the Umatalla, the same on the banks of which Mr. Hunt and his followers had arrived after their painful struggle through the Blue mountains, and experienced such a kind relief in the friendly camp of the Sciatogas.

That range of Blue mountains now extended in the distance before them; they were the same among which poor Michael Carriere had perished. They form the southeast boundary of the great plains along the Columbia, dividing the waters of its main stream from those of Lewis river. They are, in fact, a part of a long chain, which stretches over a great extent of country, and includes in its links the Snake river mountains.

The day was somewhat advanced before the travellers left the shady banks of the Umatalla. Their route gradually took them among the Blue mountains, which assumed the most rugged aspect, on a near approach. They were shagged with dense and gloomy forests, and cut up by deep and precipitous ravines, extremely toilsome to the horses. Sometimes the travellers had to follow the course of some brawling stream, with a broken, rocky bed, which the shouldering cliffs and promontories on either side, obliged them frequently to cross and recross. For some miles they struggled forward through these savage and darkly wooded defiles, when all at once the whole landscape changed, as if by magic. The rude mountains and rugged ravines softened into beautiful hills and intervening meadows, with rivulets winding through fresh herbage, and sparkling and murmuring over gravelly beds, the whole forming a verdant and pastoral scene, which derived additional charms from being locked up in the bosom of such a hardhearted region.

Emerging from the chain of Blue mountains, they descended upon a vast plain, almost a dead level, sixty miles in circumference, of excellent soil, with fine streams meandering through it in every direction, their courses marked out in the wide landscape by serpentine lines of cotton-wood trees and willows, which fringed their banks, and afforded sustenance to great numbers of beavers and otters.

In traversing this plain, they passed, close to the skirts of the hills, a great pool of water, three hundred yards in circumference, fed by a sulphur spring, about ten feet in diameter, boiling up in one corner. The vapour from this pool was extremely noisome, and tainted the air for a considerable distance. The place was much frequented by elk, which were found in considerable numbers in the adjacent mountains, and their horns, shed in the spring time, were strewed in every direction around the pond.

On the 20th of August, they reached the main body of Woodpile creek, the same stream which Mr. Hunt had ascended in the preceding year, shortly after his separation from Mr. Crooks.

On the banks of this stream they saw a herd of nineteen antelopes; a sight so unusual in that part of the country, that at first they doubted the evidence of their senses. They tried by every means to get within shot of them, but they were too shy and fleet, and after alternately bounding to a distance, and then stopping to gaze with capricious curiosity at the hunter, they at length scampered out of sight.

On the 12th of August, the travellers arrived on the

banks of Snake river, the scene of so many trials and mishaps to all of the present party excepting Mr. Stuart. They struck the river just above the place where it entered the mountains, through which Messrs. Stuart and Crooks had vainly endeavoured to find a passage. The river was here a rapid stream four hundred yards in width, with high sandy banks, and here and there a scanty growth of willow. Up the southern side of the river they now bent their course, intending to visit the caches made by Mr. Hunt at the Caldron Linn.

On the second evening, a solitary Snake Indian visited their camp, at a late hour, and informed them that there was a white man residing at one of the encampments of his tribe, about a day's journey higher up the river. It was immediately concluded, that he must be one of the poor fellows of Mr. Hunt's party, who had given out, exhausted by hunger and fatigue, in the wretched journey of the preceding winter. All present, who had borne a part in the sufferings of that journey, were eager now to press forward, and bring relief to a lost comrade. Early the next morning, therefore, they pushed forward with unusual alacrity. For two days, however, did they travel without being able to find any trace of such a straggler.

On the evening of the second day, they arrived at a place where a large river came in from the east, which was renowned among all the wandering hordes of the Snake nation for its salmon fishery, that fish being taken in incredible quantities in this neighbourhood. Here, therefore, during the fishing season, the Snake Indians resort from far and near, to lay in their stock of salmon, which, with esculent roots, forms the principal food of the inhabitants of these barren regions.

On the bank of a small stream emptying into Snake river at this place, Mr. Stuart found an encampment of Shoshonies. He made the usual inquiry of them concerning the white man of whom he had received intelligence. No such person was dwelling among them, but they said there were white men residing with some of their nation on the opposite side of the river. This was still more animating information. Mr. Crooks now hoped that these might be the men of his party, who, disheartened by perils and hardships, had preferred to remain among the Indians. Others thought they might be Mr. Miller and the hunters who had left the main body at Henry's fort, to trap among the mountain streams. Mr. Stuart halted, therefore, in the neighbourhood of the Shoshonie lodges, and sent an Indian across the river to seek out the white men in question, and bring them to his camp.

The travellers passed a restless, miserable night. The place swarmed with myriads of musquitoes, which, with their stings and their music, set all sleep at defiance. The morning dawn found them in a feverish, irritable mood, and their spleen was completely aroused by the return of the Indian, without any intelligence of the white men. They now considered themselves the dupes of Indian falsehoods, and resolved to put no more confidence in Snakes. They soon, however, forgot this resolution. In the course of the morning, an Indian came galloping after them; Mr. Stuart waited to receive him; no sooner had he come up, than, dismounting and throwing his arms round the neck of Mr. Stuart's horse, he began to kiss and caress the animal, who, on his part, seemed by no means surprised or displeased with the salutation. Mr. Stuart, who valued his horse highly, was somewhat annoyed by these transports; the cause of them was soon explained. The Snake said the horse had belonged to him, and been the best in his possession, and that it had been stolen by the Wallah-Wallahs. Mr. Stuart was by no means pleased with this recognition of his steed, nor disposed to admit any claim on the part of its ancient owner. In fact, it was a noble animal, admirably shaped, of free and generous spirit, graceful in every movement, and fleet as an antelope. It was his intention, if possible, to take the horse to New York, and present him to Mr. Astor.

In the meantime some of the party came up, and immediately recognized in the Snake an old friend and ally. He was, in fact, one of the two guides who had conducted Mr. Hunt's party, in the preceding autumn, across Mad river mountain, to fort Henry, and who subsequently departed with Mr. Miller and his fellow trappers, to conduct them to a good trapping ground. The reader may recollect that these two trusty Snakes were engaged by Mr. Hunt to return and take charge of the horses which the party intended to leave at fort Henry, when they should embark in canoes.

The party now crowded round the Snake, and began to question him with eagerness. His replies were somewhat vague, and but partially understood. He told a long story about the horses, from which it appeared that they had been stolen by various wandering bands, and scattered in different directions. The cache, too, had been plundered, and the saddles and other equipments carried off. His information concerning Mr. Miller and his comrades, was not more satisfactory. They had trapped for some time about the upper streams, but had fallen into the hands of a marauding party of Crows, who had robbed them of horses, weapons, and every thing.

Further questioning brought forth further intelligence, but all of a disastrous kind. About ten days previously, he had met with three other white men, in very miserable plight, having one horse each, and but one rifle among them. They also had been plundered and maltreated by the Crows, those universal freebooters. The Snake endeavoured to pronounce the names of these three men, and as far as his imperfect sounds could be understood, they were supposed to be three of the party of four hunters, viz. Carson, St. Michael, Detayé, and Delannay, who were detached from Mr. Hunt's party on the 28th of September, to trap beaver on the head waters of the Columbia.

In the course of conversation, the Indian informed them that the route by which Mr. Hunt had crossed the Rocky mountains, was very bad and circuitous, and that he knew one much shorter and easier. Mr. Stuart urged him to accompany them as guide, promising to reward him with a pistol with powder and ball, a knife, an awl, some blue beads, a blanket, and a looking-glass. Such a catalogue of riches was too tempting to be resisted; beside, the poor Snake languished after the prairies; he was tired, he said, of salmon, and longed for buffalo meat, and to have a grand buffalo hunt beyond the mountains. He departed, therefore, with all speed, to get his arms and equipments for the journey, promising to rejoin the party the next day. He

kept his word, and, as he no longer said anything to Mr.
Stuart on the subject of the pet horse, they journeyed very
harmoniously together; though now and then, the Snake
would regard his quondam steed with a wistful eye.

They had not travelled many miles, when they came to
a great bend of the river. Here the Snake informed them
that, by cutting across the hills, they would save many
miles of distance. The route across, however, would be a
good day's journey. He advised them, therefore, to encamp here for the night, and set off early in the morning.
They took his advice, though they had come but nine
miles that day.

On the following morning they rose, bright and early,
to ascend the hills. On mustering their little party, the
guide was missing. They supposed him to be somewhere
in the neighbourhood, and proceeded to collect the horses.
The vaunted steed of Mr. Stuart was not to be found. A
suspicion flashed upon his mind. Search for the horse of
the Snake!—He likewise was gone—the tracks of two
horses, one after the other, were found, making off from
the camp. They appeared as if one horse had been mounted, and the other led. They were traced for a few miles
above the camp, until they both crossed the river. It
was plain the Snake had taken an Indian mode of recovering his horse, having quietly decamped with him in the
night.

New vows were made never more to trust in
Snakes, or any other Indians. It was determined, also,
to maintain, hereafter, the strictest vigilance over their
horses, dividing the night into three watches, and one
person mounting guard at a time. They resolved, also, to
keep along the river, instead of taking the short cut recommended by the fugitive Snake, whom they now set down
for a thorough deceiver. The heat of the weather was
oppressive, and their horses were, at times, rendered almost
frantic by the stings of the prairie flies. The nights were
suffocating, and it was almost impossible to sleep, from the
swarms of musquitoes.

On the 20th of August they resumed their march, keeping along the prairie parallel to Snake river. The day

was sultry, and some of the party, being parched with thirst, left the line of march, and scrambled down the bank of the river to drink. The bank was overhung with willows, beneath which, to their surprise, they beheld a man fishing. No sooner did he see them, than he uttered an exclamation of joy. It proved to be John Hoback, one of their lost comrades. They had scarcely exchanged greetings, when three other men came out from among the willows. They were Joseph Miller, Jacob Rezner, and Robinson, the scalped Kentuckian, the veteran of the Bloody Ground.

The reader will perhaps recollect the abrupt and wilful manner in which Mr. Miller threw up his interest as a partner of the company, and departed from fort Henry, in company with these three trappers, and a fourth, named Cass. He may likewise recognise in Robinson, Rezner, and Hoback, the trio of Kentucky hunters, who had originally been in the service of Mr. Henry, and whom Mr. Hunt found floating down the Missouri, on their way homeward; and prevailed upon, once more, to cross the mountains. The haggard looks and naked condition of these men proved how much they had suffered. After leaving Mr. Hunt's party, they had made their way about two hundred miles to the southward, where they trapped beaver, on a river which, according to their account, discharged itself into the ocean to the south of the Columbia, but which we apprehend to be Bear river, a stream emptying itself into lake Bonneville, an immense body of salt water, west of the Rocky mountains.

Having collected a considerable quantity of beaver skins, they made them into packs, loaded their horses, and steered two hundred miles due east. Here they came upon an encampment of sixty lodges of Arapahays, an outlawed band of the Arapahoes, and notorious robbers. These fell upon the poor trappers; robbed them of their peltries, most of their clothing, and several of their horses. They were glad to escape with their lives, and without being entirely stripped, and, after proceeding about fifty miles further, made their halt for the winter.

Early in the spring they resumed their wayfaring, but

were unluckily overtaken by the same ruffian horde, who levied still further contributions, and carried off the remainder of their horses, excepting two. With these they continued on, suffering the greatest hardships. They still retained rifles and ammunition, but were in a desert country, where neither bird nor beast was to be found. Their only chance was to keep along the rivers and subsist by fishing; but at times, no fish were to be taken, and then their sufferings were horrible. One of their horses was stolen among the mountains by the Snake Indians; the other, they said, was carried off by Cass, who, according to their account, " villainously left them in their extremities." Certain dark doubts and surmises were afterwards circulated concerning the fate of that poor fellow, which, if true, showed to what a desperate state of famine his comrades had been reduced.

Being now completely unhorsed, Mr. Miller and his three companions wandered on foot for several hundred miles, enduring hunger, thirst, and fatigue, while traversing the barren wastes, which abound beyond the rocky mountains. At the time they were discovered by Mr. Stuart's party, they were almost famished, and were fishing for a precarious meal. Had Mr. Stuart made the short cut across the hills, avoiding this bend of the river, or had not some of his party accidentally gone down to the margin of the stream to drink, these poor wanderers might have remained undiscovered, and have perished in the wilderness. Nothing could exceed their joy on thus meeting with their old comrades, or the heartiness with which they were welcomed. All hands immediately encamped; and the slender stores of the party were ransacked to furnish out a suitable regale.

The next morning they all set out together; Mr. Miller and his comrades being resolved to give up the life of a trapper, and accompany Mr. Stuart back to St. Louis.

For several days they kept along the course of Snake river, occasionally making short cuts, across hills and promontories, where there were bends in the stream. In their way they passed several camps of Shoshonies, from some of whom they procured salmon, but in general they were too wretchedly poor to furnish any thing. It was the wish of Mr. Stuart to purchase horses for the recent recruits to his party; but the Indians could not be prevailed upon to part with any, alleging that they had not enough for their own use.

On the 25th of August they reached a great fishing place, to which they gave the name of the Salmon Falls. Here there is a perpendicular fall of twenty feet on the north side of the river, while on the south side there is a succession of rapids. The salmon are taken here in incredible quantities, as they attempt to shoot the falls. It was now a favourable season, and there were about one hundred lodges of Shoshonies busily engaged killing and drying fish. The salmon begin to leap shortly after sunrise. At this time the Indians swim to the centre of the falls, where some station themselves on rocks, and others stand to their waists in the water, all armed with spears, with which they assail the salmon as they attempt to leap, or fall back exhausted. It is an incessant slaughter, so great is the throng of the fish.

The construction of the spears thus used is peculiar. The head is a straight piece of elk horn, about seven inches long; on the point of which an artificial barb is made fast, with twine well gummed. The head is stuck on the end of the shaft, a very long pole of willow, to which it is likewise connected, by a strong cord a few inches in length. When the spearsman makes a sure blow, he often strikes the head of the spear through the body of the fish. It comes off easily, and leaves the salmon struggling with the string through its body, while the pole is still held by the spearsman. Were it not for the precaution of the string, the willow shaft would be snapped by the struggles and the weight of the fish. Mr. Miller, in the course of his wanderings, had been at these falls, and had seen several thousand salmon taken in the course of one afternoon. He declared that he had seen a salmon leap a distance of about thirty feet, from the commencement of the foam at the foot of the fall, completely to the top.

Having purchased a good supply of salmon from the fishermen, the party resumed their journey, and on the

29th arrived at the Caldron Linn ; the eventful scene of the preceding autumn. Here, the first thing that met their eyes, was a memento of the perplexities of that period : the wreck of a canoe, lodged between two ledges of rocks. They endeavoured to get down to it, but the river banks were too high and precipitous.

They now proceeded to that part of the neighbourhood where Mr. Hunt and his party had made the caches, intending to take from them such articles as belonged to Mr. Crooks, M'Lellan, and the Canadians. On reaching the spot, they found, to their astonishment, six of the caches open and rifled of their contents, excepting a few books which lay scattered about the vicinity. They had the appearance of having been plundered in the course of the summer. There were tracks of wolves in every direction, to and from the holes, from which Mr. Stuart concluded that these animals had first been attracted to the place by the smell of the skins contained in the caches, which they had probably torn up, and that their tracks had betrayed the secret to the Indians.

The three remaining caches had not been molested : they contained a few dry goods, some ammunition, and a number of beaver traps. From these Mr. Stuart took whatever was requisite for his party ; he then deposited within them all his superfluous baggage, and all the books and papers scattered around ; the holes were then carefully closed up, and all traces of them effaced. And here we have to record another instance of the indomitable spirit of the western trappers. No sooner did the trio of Kentucky hunters, Robinson, Rezner, and Hoback, find that they could once more be fitted out for a campaign of beaver trapping, than they forget all that they had suffered, and determined upon another trial of their fortunes ; preferring to take their chance in the wilderness, rather than return home ragged and penniless. As to Mr. Miller, he declared his curiosity, and his desire of travelling throughhthe Indian countries, fully satisfied : he adhered to his determination, therefore, to keep on with the party to St. Louis, and to return to the bosom of civilized society.

The three hunters, therefore, Robinson, Rezner, and

Hoback, were furnished, as far as the caches and the means
of Mr. Stuart's party afforded, with the requisite munitions
and equipments for a "two years' hunt;" but as their
fitting out was yet incomplete, they resolved to wait
in this neighbourhood until Mr. Reed should arrive;
whose arrival might soon be expected, as he was to set
out for the caches about twenty days after Mr. Stuart
parted with him at the Wallah-Wallah river.

Mr. Stuart gave in charge to Robinson a letter to Mr.
Reed, reporting his safe journey thus far, and the state in
which he had found the caches. A duplicate of this letter
he elevated on a pole, and set it up near the place of deposit.

All things being thus arranged, Mr. Stuart and his
little band, now seven in number, took leave of the three
hardy trappers, wishing them all possible success in
their lonely and perilous sojourn in the wilderness; and
we, in like manner, shall leave them to their fortunes,
promising to take them up again at some future page,
and to close the story of their persevering and ill-fated
enterprise.

CHAPTER III.

The Snake river deserts—Scanty fare—Bewildered travellers—Prowling Indians—
A giant Crow chief—A bully rebuked—Indian signals—Smoke on the mountains
—Mad river—An alarm—An Indian foray—A scamper—A rude Indian joke—
A sharp-shooter balked of his shot.

ON the 1st of September, Mr. Stuart and his companions
resumed their journey, bending their course eastward, along
the course of Snake river. As they advanced, the country
opened. The hills which had hemmed in the river receded
on either hand, and great sandy and dusty plains extended
before them. Occasionally, there were intervals of pasturage, and the banks of the river were fringed with willows
and cotton-wood, so that its course might be traced from
the hill-tops, winding under an umbrageous covert, through
a wide sunburnt landscape. The soil, however, was generally poor; there was, in some places, a miserable growth
of wormwood, and of a plant called saltweed, resembling
pennyroyal; but the summer heat had parched the plains,
and left but little pasturage. The game, too, had disap-

peared.   The hunter looked in vain over the lifeless landscape; now and then a few antelope might be seen, but
not within reach of the rifle.   We forbear to follow the travellers in a week's wandering over these barren wastes,
where they suffered much from hunger; having to depend
upon a few fish from the streams, and now and then a little
dried salmon, or a dog, procured from some forlorn lodge of
Shoshonies.

Tired of these cheerless wastes, they left the banks of
Snake river on the 7th of September, under guidance of
Mr. Miller, who, having acquired some knowledge of the
country during his trapping campaign, undertook to conduct them across the mountains by a better route than that
by Fort Henry, and one more out of the range of the
Blackfeet.   He proved, however, but an indifferent guide,
and they soon became bewildered among rugged hills and
unknown streams, and burnt and barren prairies.

At length they came to a river on which Mr. Miller had
trapped, and to which they gave his name; though, as before
observed, we presume it to be the same called Bear river,
which empties itself into lake Bonneville.   Up this river
and its branches they kept for two or three days, supporting
themselves precariously upon fish.   They soon found that
they were in a dangerous neighbourhood.   On the 12th of
September, having encamped early, they sallied forth with
their rods to angle for their supper.   On returning, they
beheld a number of Indians prowling about their camp,
whom, to their infinite disquiet, they soon perceived to be
Upsarokas, or Crows.   Their chief came forward with a
confident air.   He was a dark, herculean fellow, full six
feet four inches in height, with a mingled air of the ruffian
and the rogue.   He conducted himself peaceably, however,
and dispatched some of his people to their camp, which
was somewhere in the neighbourhood, from whence they
returned with a most acceptable supply of buffalo meat.
He now signified to Mr. Stuart that he was going to trade
with the Snakes, who reside on the west base of the mountains, below Henry's fort. Here they cultivate a delicate kind
of tobacco, much esteemed and sought after by the mountain
tribes.   There was something sinister, however, in the
look of this Indian, that inspired distrust.   By degrees,

the number of his people increased, until, by midnight, there were twenty-one of them about the camp, who began to be impudent and troublesome. The greatest uneasiness was now felt for the safety of the horses and effects, and every one kept vigilant watch throughout the night.

The morning dawned, however, without any unpleasant occurrence, and Mr. Stuart, having purchased all the buffalo meat that the Crows had to spare, prepared to depart. His Indian acquaintance, however, were disposed for further dealings; and, above all, anxious for a supply of gunpowder, for which they offered horses in exchange. Mr. Stuart declined to furnish them with the dangerous commodity. They became more importunate in their solicitations, until they met with a flat refusal.

The gigantic chief now stepped forward, assumed a swelling air, and, slapping himself upon the breast, gave Mr. Crooks to understand that he was a chief of great power and importance. He signified, further, that it was customary for great chiefs, when they met, to make each other presents. He requested, therefore, that Mr. Stuart would alight, and give him the horse upon which he was mounted. This was a noble animal, of one of the wild races of the prairies, on which Mr. Stuart set great value; he, of course, shook his head at the request of the Crow dignitary. Upon this the latter strode up to him, and taking hold of him, moved him backwards and forwards in his saddle, as if to make him feel he was a mere child within his grasp. Mr. Stuart preserved his calmness, and still shook his head. The chief then seized the bridle, and gave it a jerk that startled the horse, and nearly brought the rider to the ground. Mr. Stuart instantly drew forth a pistol, and presented it at the head of the bully-ruffian. In a twinkling, his swaggering was at an end, and he dodged behind his horse to escape the expected shot. As his subject Crows gazed on the affray from a little distance, Mr. Stuart ordered his men to level their rifles at them, but not to fire. The whole crew scampered among the bushes, and throwing themselves upon the ground, vanished from sight.

The chieftain, thus left alone, was confounded for an

instant ; but, recovering himself, with true Indian shrewdness, burst into a loud laugh, and affected to turn off the
whole matter, as a piece of pleasantry.　Mr. Stuart by no
means relished such equivocal joking, but it was not his policy
to get into a quarrel ; so he joined, with the best grace he
could assume, in the merriment of the jocular giant ; and,
to console the latter for the refusal of the horse, made him
a present of twenty charges of powder.　They parted, according to all outward profession, the best friends in the
world ; it was evident, however, that nothing but the
smallness of his own force, and the martial array and alertness of the white men, had prevented the Crow chief from
proceeding to open outrage.　As it was, his worthy followers, in the course of their brief interview, had contrived
to purloin a bag containing almost all the culinary utensils
of the party.

The travellers kept on their way due east, over a chain
of hills.　The recent rencontre showed them that they
were now in a land of danger, subject to the wide roamings
of a predacious tribe ; nor, in fact, had they gone many
miles, before they beheld sights calculated to inspire
anxiety and alarm.　From the summits of some of the
loftiest mountains, in different directions, columns of smoke
began to rise.　These they concluded to be signals made
by the runners of the Crow chieftain, to summon the
stragglers of his band, so as to pursue them with greater
force.　Signals of this kind, made by outrunners from one
central point, will rouse a wide circuit of the mountains in
a wonderfully short space of time ; and bring the straggling hunters and warriors to the standard of their chieftain.

To keep as much as possible out of the way of these
freebooters, Mr. Stuart altered his course to the north, and,
quitting the main stream of Miller's river, kept up a large
branch that came in from the mountains.　Here they encamped, after a fatiguing march of twenty-five miles.　As
the night drew on, the horses were hobbled, or fettered,
and tethered close to the camp ; a vigilant watch was
maintained until morning, and every one slept with his
rifle on his arm.

At sunrise, they were again on the march, still keeping

to the north. They soon began to ascend the mountains, and occasionally had wide prospects over the surrounding country. Not a sign of a Crow was to be seen ; but this did not assure them of their security, well knowing the perseverance of these savages in dogging any party they intend to rob, and the stealthy way in which they can conceal their movements, keeping along ravines and defiles. After a mountain scramble of twenty-one miles, they encamped on the margin of a stream running to the north.

In the evening there was an alarm of Indians, and every one was instantly on the alert. They proved to be three miserable Snakes, who were no sooner informed that a band of Crows was prowling in the neighbourhood, than they made off with great signs of consternation.

A couple more of weary days and watchful nights brought them to a strong and rapid stream, running due north, which they concluded to be one of the upper branches of Snake river. It was probably the same since called Salt river. They determined to bend their course down this river, as it would take them still further out of the dangerous neighbourhood of the Crows. They then would strike upon Mr. Hunt's track of the preceding autumn, and retrace it across the mountains. The attempt to find a better route under guidance of Mr. Miller had cost them a large bend to the south ; in resuming Mr. Hunt's track, they would at least be sure of their road. They accordingly turned down along the course of this stream, and at the end of three days' journey, came to where it was joined by a larger river, and assumed a more impetuous character, raging and roaring among rocks and precipices. It proved, in fact, to be Mad river, already noted in the expedition of Mr. Hunt. On the banks of this river, they encamped on the 18th of September, at an early hour.

Six days had now elapsed since their interview with the Crows, during that time they had come nearly a hundred and fifty miles to the north and west, without seeing any signs of those marauders. They considered themselves, therefore, beyond the reach of molestation, and began to relax in their vigilance, lingering occasionally for part of a day, where there was good pasturage. The poor horses needed repose. They had been urged on by forced marches, over rugged heights, among rocks and fallen timber, or over low swampy valleys, inundated by the labours of the beaver. These industrious animals abounded in all the mountain streams and water courses, wherever there were willows for their subsistence. Many of them they had so completely dammed up as to inundate the low grounds, making shallow pools or lakes, and extensive quagmires; by which the route of the travellers was often impeded.

On the 19th of September, they rose at early dawn; some began to prepare for breakfast, and others to arrange the packs preparatory to a march. The horses had been hobbled, but left at large to graze about the adjacent pastures. Mr. Stuart was on the bank of the river, at a short distance from the camp, when he heard the alarm cry—" Indians! Indians!—to arms! to arms!"

A mounted Crow galloped past the camp, bearing a red flag. He reined his steed on the summit of a neighbouring knoll, and waved his flaring banner. A diabolical yell now broke forth on the opposite side of the camp, beyond where the horses were grazing, and a small troop of savages came galloping up, whooping and making a terrific clamour. The horses took fright, and dashed across the camp in the direction of the standard bearer, attracted by his waving flag. He instantly put spurs to his steed, and scoured off, followed by the panic stricken herd, their fright being increased by the yells of the savages in their rear.

At the first alarm, Mr. Stuart and his comrades had seized their rifles, and attempted to cut off the Indians who were pursuing the horses. Their attention was instantly distracted by whoops and yells in an opposite direction. They now apprehended that a reserve party was about to carry off their baggage. They ran to secure it. The reserve party, however, galloped by, whooping and yelling in triumph and derision. The last of them proved to be their commander, the identical giant joker already mentioned. He was not cast in the stern poetical mould of fashionable Indian heroism, but on the contrary, was

grievously given to vulgar jocularity. As he passed Mr.
Stuart and his companions, he checked his horse, raised
himself in the saddle, and clapping his hands on the most
insulting part of his body, uttered some jeering words,
which, fortunately for their delicacy, they could not
understand. The rifle of Ben Jones was levelled in an
instant, and he was on the point of whizzing a bullet into
the target so tauntingly displayed. " Not for your life !
not for your life !" exclaimed Mr. Stuart, " you will bring
destruction on us all !"

It was hard to restrain honest Ben, when the mark was
so fair and the insult so foul. " Oh, Mr. Stuart," exclaimed he, " only let me have one crack at the infernal
rascal, and you may keep all the pay that is due to me."

" By heaven, if you fire," cried Mr. Stuart, " I'll blow
your brains out."

By this time the Indian was far out of reach, and
had rejoined his men, and the whole dare-devil band, with
the captured horses, scuttled off along the defiles, their red
flag flaunting over head, and the rocks echoing to their
whoops and yells, and demoniac laughter.

The unhorsed travellers gazed after them in silent mortification and despair; yet Mr. Stuart could not but
admire the style and spirit with which the whole exploit
had been managed, and pronounced it one of the most
daring and intrepid actions he had ever heard of among
Indians. The whole number of the Crows did not
exceed twenty. In this way, a small gang of lurkers
will hurry off the cavalry of a large war party; for when
once a drove of horses are seized with a panic, they
become frantic, and nothing short of broken necks can stop
them.

No one was more annoyed by this unfortunate occurrence than Ben Jones. He declared he would actually
have given his whole arrears of pay, amounting to upwards
of a year's wages, rather than be balked of such a capital
shot. Mr. Stuart, however, represented what might have
been the consequence of so rash an act. Life for life is the
Indian maxim. The whole tribe would have made
common cause in avenging the death of a warrior. The

party were but seven dismounted men, with a wide mountain region to traverse, infested by these people, and which might all be roused by signal fires. In fact the conduct of the band of marauders in question, showed the perseverance of savages when once they have fixed their minds upon a project. These fellows had evidently been silently and secretly dogging the party for a week past, and a distance of a hundred and fifty miles, keeping out of sight by day, lurking about the encampment at night, watching all their movements, and waiting for a favourable moment when they should be off their guard. The menace of Mr. Stuart, in their first interview, to shoot the giant chief with his pistol, and the fright caused among the warriors by presenting the rifles, had probably added the stimulus of pique to their usual horse stealing propensities, and in this mood of mind they would doubtless have followed the party throughout their whole course over the Rocky mountains, rather than be disappointed in their scheme.

CHAPTER IV.

Travellers unhorsed—Pedestrian preparations—Prying spies—Bonfire of baggage—
A march on foot—Rafting a river—The wounded elk—Indian trails—Wilful
conduct of Mr. M'Lellan—Grand prospect from a mountain—Distant craters of
volcanoes—Illness of Mr. Crooks.

Few reverses in this changeful world are more complete and disheartening than that of a traveller, suddenly unhorsed, in the midst of the wilderness. Our unfortunate travellers contemplated their situation for a time in perfect dismay. A long journey over rugged mountains and immeasurable plains, lay before them, which they must painfully perform on foot, and every thing necessary for subsistence or defence, must be carried on their shoulders. Their dismay, however, was but transient, and they immediately set to work, with that prompt expediency produced by the exigencies of the wilderness, to fit themselves for the change in their condition.

Their first attention was to select from their baggage such articles as were indispensable to their journey; to make them up into convenient packs, and to deposit the residue in caches. The whole day was consumed in these occupations; at night, they made a scanty meal of their remaining provisions, and lay down to sleep with heavy hearts. In the morning, they were up and about at an early hour, and began to prepare their knapsacks for a march, while Ben Jones repaired to an old beaver trap which he had set in the river bank at some little distance from the camp. He was rejoiced to find a middle sized beaver there, sufficient for a morning's meal to his hungry comrades. On his way back with his prize, he observed two heads peering over the edge of an impending cliff, several hundred feet high, which he supposed to be a couple of wolves. As he continued on, he now and then cast his eye up; the heads were still there, looking down with fixed and watchful gaze. A suspicion now flashed across his mind that they might be Indian scouts; and, had they not been far above the reach of his rifle, he would undoubtedly have regaled them with a shot.

On arriving at the camp, he directed the attention of his comrades to these aerial observers. The same idea was at first entertained, that they were wolves; but their immovable watchfulness, soon satisfied every one that they were Indians. It was concluded that they were watching the movements of the party, to discover their place of concealment of such articles as they would be compelled to leave behind. There was no likelihood that the caches would escape the search of such keen eyes, and experienced rummagers, and the idea was intolerable, that any more booty should fall into their hands. To disappoint them, therefore, the travellers stripped the caches of the articles deposited there, and collecting together every thing that they could not carry away with them, made a bonfire of all that would burn, and threw the rest into the river. There was a forlorn satisfaction in thus balking the Crows, by the destruction of their own property; and, having thus gratified their pique, they shouldered their packs, about ten o'clock in the morning, and set out in their pedestrian wayfaring.

The route they took was down along the banks of Mad river. This stream makes its way through the defiles of the mountains, into the plain below fort Henry, where it terminates in Snake river. Mr. Stuart was in hopes of meeting with Snake encampments in the plain, where he might procure a couple of horses to transport the baggage. In such case, he intended to resume his eastern course across the mountains, and endeavour to reach the Cheyenne river before winter. Should he fail, however, of obtaining horses, he would probably be compelled to winter on the Pacific side of the mountains, somewhere on the head waters of the Spanish or Colorado river.

With all the care that had been observed in taking nothing with them that was not absolutely necessary, the poor pedestrians were heavily laden, and their burdens added to the fatigues of their rugged road. They suffered much, too, from hunger. The trout they caught were too poor to yield much nourishment; their main dependance, therefore, was upon an old beaver trap, which they had providentially retained. Whenever they were fortunate enough to entrap a beaver, it was cut up immediately and distributed, that each man might carry his share.

After two days of toilsome travel, during which they made but eighteen miles, they stopped on the 21st, to build two rafts on which to cross to the north side of the river. On these they embarked, on the following morning, four on one raft, and three on the other, and pushed boldly from shore. Finding the rafts sufficiently firm and steady to withstand the rough and rapid water, they changed their minds, and instead of crossing, ventured to float down with the current. The river was, in general, very rapid, and from one to two hundred yards in width, winding in every direction through mountains of hard black rock, covered with pines and cedars. The mountains to the east of the river, were spurs of the rocky range, and of great magnitude; those on the west, were little better than hills, bleak and barren, or scantily clothed with stunted grass.

Mad river, though deserving its name from the impetuosity of its current, was free from rapids and cascades, and flowed on in a single channel between gravel banks, often fringed with cotton-wood and dwarf willows in abundance. These gave sustenance to immense quantities of beaver, so that the voyageurs found no difficulty in procuring food. Ben Jones, also killed a fallow deer, and a wolverine; and as they were enabled to carry the carcasses on their rafts, their larder was well supplied. Indeed, they might have occasionally shot beavers that were swimming in the river as they floated by, but they humanely spared their lives, being in no want of meat at the time. In this way they kept down the river for three days, drifting with the current and encamping on land at night, when they drew up their rafts on shore. Towards the evening of the third day, they came to a little island on which they descried a gang of elk. Ben Jones landed, and was fortunate enough to wound one, which immediately took to the water, but, being unable to stem the current, drifted above a mile, when it was over-taken and drawn to shore. As a storm was gathering, they now encamped on the margin of the river, where they remained all the next day, sheltering themselves as well as they could from rain, and hail, and snow, a sharp foretaste of the impending winter. During their encampment, they employed themselves in jerking a part of the elk for future supply. In cutting up the carcass, they found that the animal had been wounded by hunters, about a week pre-viously, an arrow head and a musket ball remaining in the wounds. In the wilderness, every trivial circumstance is a matter of anxious speculation. The Snake Indians have no guns; the elk, therefore, could not have been wounded by one of them. They were on the borders of the country infested by the Blackfeet, who carry fire-arms. It was con-cluded, therefore, that the elk had been hunted by some of that wandering and hostile tribe, who, of course, must be in the neighbourhood. The idea put an end to the transient solace they had enjoyed in the comparative repose and abundance of the river.

For three days longer they continued to navigate with their rafts. The recent storm had rendered the weather extremely cold. They had now floated down the river about ninety-one miles, when, finding the mountains on the right diminished to moderate-sized hills, they landed, and prepared to resume their journey on foot. Accordingly, having spent a day in preparations, making mocassins, and parcelling out their jerked meat in packs of twenty pounds to each man, they turned their backs upon the river on the 29th of September, and struck off to the north-east; keeping along the southern skirt of the mountain on which Henry's fort was situated.

Their march was slow and toilsome; part of the time through an alluvial bottom, thickly grown with cottonwood, hawthorn, and willows, and part of the time over rough hills. Three antelopes came within shot, but they dared not fire at them, lest the report of their rifles should betray them to the Blackfeet. In the course of the day they came upon a large horse track, apparently about three weeks old, and in the evening encamped on the banks of a small stream, on a spot which had been the camping place of this same band.

On the following morning they still observed the Indian track, but after a time they came to where it separated in every direction, and was lost. This showed that the band had dispersed in various hunting parties, and was, in all probability, still in the neighbourhood; it was necessary, therefore, to proceed with the utmost caution. They kept a vigilant eye as they marched, upon every height where a scout might be posted, and scanned the solitary landscape and the distant ravines, to observe any column of smoke; but nothing of the kind was to be seen; all was indescribably stern and lifeless.

Towards evening they came to where there were several hot springs, strongly impregnated with iron and sulphur, and sending up a volume of vapour that tainted the surrounding atmosphere, and might be seen at the distance of a couple of miles.

Near to these they encamped, in a deep gulley, which afforded some concealment. To their great concern, Mr. Crooks, who had been indisposed for the two preceding days, had a violent fever in the night.

Shortly after daybreak they resumed their march. On emerging from the glen, a consultation was held as to their course. Should they continue round the skirt of the mountain, they would be in danger of falling in with the scattered parties of Blackfeet, who were probably hunting in the plain. It was thought most advisable, therefore, to strike directly across the mountain, since the route, though rugged and difficult, would be most secure. This counsel was indignantly derided by M'Lellan as pusillanimous. Hot-headed and impatient at all times, he had been rendered irascible by the fatigues of the journey, and the condition of his feet, which were chafed and sore. He could not endure the idea of encountering the difficulties of the mountain, and swore he would rather face all the Blackfeet in the country. He was overruled, however, and the party began to ascend the mountain, striving, with the ardour and emulation of young men, who should be first up. M'Lellan, who was double the age of some of his companions, soon began to lose breath, and fall in the rear. In the distribution of burdens, it was his turn to carry the old beaver trap. Piqued and irritated, he suddenly came to a halt, swore he would carry it no further, and jirked it half way down the hill. He was offered in place of it a package of dried meat, but this he scornfully threw upon the ground. They might carry it, he said, who needed it, for his part, he could provide his daily food with his rifle. He concluded by flinging off from the party, and keeping along the skirts of the mountain, leaving those, he said, to climb rocks, who were afraid to face Indians. It was in vain that Mr. Stuart represented to him the rashness of his conduct, and the dangers to which he exposed himself: he rejected such counsel as craven. It was equally useless to represent the dangers to which he subjected his companions; as he could be discovered at a great distance on those naked plains, and the Indians, seeing him, would know that there must be other white men within reach. M'Lellan turned a deaf ear to every remonstrance, and kept on his wilful way.

It seems a strange instance of perverseness in this man thus to fling himself off alone, in a savage region, where solitude itself was dismal, but every encounter with his fellow man full of peril. Such, however, is the hardness of spirit, and the insensibility to danger, that grow upon men in the wilderness. M'Lellan, moreover, was a man of peculiar temperament, ungovernable in his will, of a courage that absolutely knew not fear, and somewhat of a braggart spirit, that took a pride in doing desperate and hairbrained things.

Mr. Stuart and his party found the passages of the mountain somewhat difficult, on account of the snow, which in many places was of considerable depth, though it was now but the 1st of October. They crossed the summit early in the afternoon, and beheld below them a plain about twenty miles wide, bounded on the opposite side by their old acquaintances, the Pilot Knobs, those towering mountains which had served Mr. Hunt as landmarks in part of his route of the preceding year. Through the intermediate plain wandered a river about fifty yards wide, sometimes gleaming in open day, but oftener running through willowed banks, which marked its serpentine course.

Those of the party who had been across these mountains, pointed out much of the bearings of the country to Mr. Stuart. They showed him in what direction must lie the deserted post called Henry's fort, where they had abandoned their horses and embarked in canoes, and they informed him that the stream which wandered through the plain below them, fell into Henry river, half way between the fort and the mouth of Mad or Snake river. The character of all this mountain region was decidedly volcanic; and to the northwest, between Henry's fort and the source of the Missouri, Mr. Stuart observed several very high peaks covered with snow, from two of which smoke ascended in considerable volumes, apparently from craters, in a state of eruption.

On their way down the mountain, when they had reached the skirts, they descried M'Lellan at a distance, in the advance, traversing the plain. Whether he saw them or not, he showed no disposition to rejoin them, but pursued his sullen and solitary way.

After descending into the plain, they kept on about six miles, until they reached the little river, which was here about knee deep, and richly fringed with willow. Here they encamped for the night. At this encampment the fever of Mr. Crooks increased to such a degree that it was impossible for him to travel. Some of the men were strenuous for Mr. Stuart to proceed without him, urging the imminent danger they were exposed to by delay in that unknown and barren region, infested by the most treacherous and inveterate of foes. They represented that the season was rapidly advancing ; the weather for some days had been extremely cold ; the mountains were already almost impassable from snow, and would soon present effectual barriers. Their provisions were exhausted ; there was no game to be seen ; and they did not dare to use their rifles, through fear of drawing upon them the Blackfeet.

The picture thus presented was too true to be contradicted, and made a deep impression on the mind of Mr. Stuart ; but the idea of abandoning a fellow being, and a comrade, in such a forlorn situation, was too repugnant to his feelings to be admitted for an instant.

He represented to the men that the malady of Mr. Crooks could not be of long duration, and that in all probability he would be able to travel in the course of a very few days. It was with great difficulty, however, that he prevailed upon them to abide the event.

CHAPTER V.

Ben Jones and a Grizzly Bear—Rocky heights—Mountain torrents—Traces of M'Lellan—Volcanic remains—Mineral earths—Peculiar clay for pottery—Dismal Plight of M'Lellan—Starvation—Shocking proposition of a desperate man—A broken down bull—A ravenous meal—Indian graves—Hospitable Snakes—A forlorn alliance.

As the travellers were now in a dangerous neighbourhood, where the report of a rifle might bring the savages upon them, they had to depend upon their old beaver-trap for subsistence. The little river on which they were encamped gave many " beaver signs," and Ben Jones set off at daybreak, along the willowed banks, to find a proper trapping place. As he was making his way among the thickets, with his trap on his shoulder, and his rifle in his hand, he heard a crashing sound, and turning, beheld a huge grizzly bear advancing upon him, with terrific growl. The sturdy Kentuckian was not to be intimidated by man or monster. Levelling his rifle, he pulled trigger. The bear was wounded, but not mortally ; instead, however, of rushing upon his assailant, as is generally the case with this kind of bear, he retreated into the bushes. Jones followed him for some distance, but with suitable caution, and Bruin effected his escape.

As there was every prospect of a detention of some days in this place, and as the supplies of the beaver trap were too precarious to be depended upon, it became absolutely necessary to run some risk of discovery by hunting in the neighbourhood. Ben Jones, therefore, obtained permission to range with his rifle some distance from the camp, and set off to beat up the river banks, in defiance of bear or Blackfeet.

He returned in great spirits in the course of a few hours, having come upon a gang of elk about six miles off, and killed five. This was joyful news, and the party immediately moved forward to the place where he had left the carcasses. They were obliged to support Mr. Crooks the whole distance, for he was unable to walk. Here they remained for two or three days, feasting heartily on elk meat, and drying as much as they would be able to carry away with them.

By the 5th of October, some simple prescriptions, together with an " Indian sweat," had so far benefited Mr. Crooks, that he was enabled to move about ; they, therefore, set forward slowly, dividing his pack and accoutrements among them, and made a creeping day's progress of eight miles south. Their route for the most part lay through swamps, caused by the industrious labours of the beaver ; for this little animal had dammed up numerous small streams, issuing from the Pilot Knob mountains, so that the low grounds on their borders were completely inundated. In the course of their march they killed a grizzly bear, with fat on its flanks upwards of three inches in thickness. This was an acceptable addition to their stock recruited in strength to be able to carry his rifle and pistols, and they made a march of seventeen miles along the borders of the plain.

Their journey daily became more toilsome, and their sufferings more severe, as they advanced. Keeping up the channel of a river, they traversed the rugged summit of the Pilot Knob mountain, covered with snow nine inches deep. For several days they continued, bending their course as much as possible to the east, over a succession of rocky heights, deep valleys, and rapid streams. Sometimes their dizzy path lay along the margin of perpendicular precipices several hundred feet in height, where a single false step might precipitate them into the rocky bed of a torrent which roared below. Not the least part of their weary task was the fording of the numerous windings and branchings of the mountain rivers, all boisterous in their currents, and icy cold.

Hunger was added to their other sufferings, and soon became the keenest. The small supply of bear and elk meat which they had been able to carry, in addition to their previous burdens, served but for a very short time. In their anxiety to struggle forward, they had but little time to hunt, and scarce any game came in their path. For three days they had nothing to eat but a small duck, and a few poor trout. They occasionally saw numbers of antelopes, and tried every art to get within shot; but the timid animals were more than commonly wild, and after tantallizing the hungry hunters for a time, bounded away beyond all chance of pursuit. At length they were fortunate enough to kill one: it was extremely meagre, and yielded but a scanty supply; but on this they subsisted for several days.

On the 11th, they encamped on a small stream, near the foot of the Spanish river mountain. Here they met with traces of that wayward and solitary being, M'Lellan, who was still keeping on ahead of them through these lonely mountains. He had encamped the night before on this stream; they found the embers of the fire by which he had slept, and the remains of a miserable wolf on which he had supped. It was evident he had suffered, like themselves, the pangs of hunger, though he had fared better at this encampment; for they had not a mouthful to eat.

The next day, they rose hungry and alert, and set out with the dawn to climb the mountain, which was steep and difficult. Traces of volcanic operations were to be seen in various directions. There was a species of clay also to be met with, out of which the Indians manufacture pots and jars and dishes. It is very fine and light, of an agreeable smell, and of a brown colour spotted with yellow, and dissolves readily in the mouth. Vessels manufactured of it, are said to impart a pleasant smell and flavour to any liquids. These mountains abound also with mineral earths, or chalks of various colours; especially two kinds of ochre, one a pale, the other a bright red, like vermilion; much used by the Indians, in painting their bodies.

About noon, the travellers reached the "drains" and brooks that formed the head waters of the river, and later in the day descended to where the main body, a shallow stream, about a hundred and sixty yards wide, poured through its mountain valley.

Here the poor famishing wanderers had expected to find buffalo in abundance, and had fed their hungry hopes during their scrambling toil, with the thoughts of roasted ribs, juicy humps, and broiled marrow bones. To their great disappointment, the river banks were deserted; a few old tracks, showed where a herd of bulls had some time before passed along, but not a horn nor hump was to be seen in the steril landscape. A few antelopes looked down upon them from the brow of a crag, but flitted away out of sight at the least approach of the hunter.

In the most starving mood they kept for several miles further, along the bank of the river, seeking for "beaver signs." Finding some, they encamped in the vicinity, and Ben Jones immediately proceeded to set the trap. They had scarce come to a halt, when they perceived a large smoke at some distance to the southwest. The sight was hailed with joy, for they trusted it might rise from some Indian camp, where they could procure something to eat, and the dread of starvation had now overcome even the terror of the Blackfeet. Le Clerc, one of the Canadians, was instantly despatched by Mr. Stuart, to reconnoitre; and the travellers sat up till a late hour, watching and listening for his return, hoping he might bring them food. Midnight arrived, but Le Clerc did not make his appearance, and they laid down once more supperless to sleep, comforting themselves with the hopes that their old beaver trap might furnish them with a breakfast.

At daybreak they hastened with famished eagerness to the trap—they found in it the fore paw of a beaver; the sight of which tantalized their hunger, and added to their dejection. They resumed their journey with flagging spirits, but had not gone far when they perceived Le Clerc approaching at a distance. They hastened to meet him, in hopes of tidings of good cheer. He had none such to give them! but news of that strange wanderer, M'Lellan. The smoke had risen from his encampment, which took fire while he was at a little distance from it fishing. Le Clerc found him in forlorn condition. His fishing had been unsuccessful. During twelve days that he had been wandering alone through these savage mountains, he had found scarce anything to eat. He had been ill, wayworn, sick at heart, still he had kept forward; but now his strength and his stubbornness were exhausted. He expressed his satisfaction at hearing that Mr. Stuart and his party were near, and said he would wait at his camp, for their arrival, in hopes they would give him something to eat, for without food he declared he should not be able to proceed much further.

When the party reached the place, they found the poor fellow lying on a parcel of withered grass, wasted to a perfect skeleton, and so feeble that he could scarce raise his head or speak. The presence of his old comrades seemed to revive him; but they had no food to give him, for they themselves were almost starving. They urged him to rise and accompany them, but he shook his head. It was all in vain, he said; there was no prospect of their getting speedy relief, and without it he should perish by the way; he might as well, therefore, stay and die where he was. At length, after much persuasion, they got him upon his legs; his rifle and other effects were shared among them, and he was cheered and aided forward. In this way they proceeded for seventeen miles, over a level plain of sand, until, seeing a few antelopes in the distance, they encamped on the margin of a small stream. All now that were capable of the exertion, turned out to hunt for a meal. Their efforts were fruitless, and after dark they returned to their camp, famished almost to desperation.

As they were preparing for the third time to lay down to sleep without a mouthful to eat, Le Clerc, one of the Canadians, gaunt and wild with hunger, approached Mr. Stuart, with his gun in his hand. " It was all in vain," he said, "to attempt to proceed any further without food. They had a barren plain before them, three or four days' journey in extent, on which nothing was to be procured. They must all perish before they could get to the end of it. It was better, therefore, that one should die to save the rest." He proposed, therefore, that they should cast lots; adding, as an inducement for Mr. Stuart to assent to the proposition, that he, as leader of the party, should be exempted.

Mr. Stuart shuddered at the horrible proposition, and endeavoured to reason with the man, but his words were unavailing. At length, snatching up his rifle, he threatened to shoot him on the spot if he persisted. The famished wretch dropped on his knees, begged pardon in the most abject terms, and promised never again to offend him with such a suggestion.

Quiet being restored to the forlorn encampment, each one sought repose. Mr. Stuart, however, was so exhausted by the agitation of the past scene, acting upon his emaciated frame, that he could scarce crawl to his miserable couch; where, notwithstanding his fatigues, he passed a sleepless night, revolving upon their dreary situation, and the desperate prospect before them.

Before daylight the next morning, they were up and on their way; they had nothing to detain them; no breakfast to prepare, and to linger was to perish. They proceeded, however, but slowly, for all were faint and weak. Here and there they passed the skulls and bones of buffaloes, which showed that those animals must have been hunted here during the past season; the sight of these bones served only to mock their misery. After travelling about nine miles along the plain, they ascended a range of hills, and had scarcely gone two miles further, when, to their great joy, they discovered " an old run-down buffalo bull;" the laggard probably of some herd that had been hunted and harassed through the mountains. They now all stretched themselves out to encompass and make sure of this solitary animal, for their lives depended upon their success. After considerable trouble and infinite anxiety, they at length succeeded in killing him. He was instantly flayed and cut up, and so ravenous was their hunger, that they devoured some of the flesh raw. The residue they carried to a brook near by, where they encamped, lit a fire, and began to cook.

Mr. Stuart was fearful that in their famished state they would eat to excess, and injure themselves. He caused a soup to be made of some of the meat, and that each should take a quantity of it as a prelude to his supper. This may have had a beneficial effect, for though they sat up the greater part of the night, cooking and cramming, no one suffered any inconvenience.

The next morning the feasting was resumed, and about mid-day, feeling somewhat recruited and refreshed, they set out on their journey with renovated spirits, shaping their course towards a mountain, the summit of which they saw towering in the east, and near to which they expected to find the head waters of the Missouri.

As they proceeded, they continued to see the skeletons of buffaloes scattered about the plain in every direction, which showed that there had been much hunting here by Indians in the recent season. Further on they crossed a large Indian trail, forming a deep path, about fifteen days old, which went in a north direction. They concluded it to have been made by some numerous band of Crows, who had hunted in this country for the greater part of the summer.

On the following day they forded a stream of considerable magnitude, with banks clothed with pine trees. Among these they found the traces of a large Indian camp, which had evidently been the head quarters of a hunting expedition, from the great quantities of buffalo bones strewed about the neighbourhood. The camp had apparently been abandoned about a month.

In the centre was a singular lodge, one hundred and fifty feet in circumference, supported by the trunks of twenty trees, about twelve inches in diameter, and forty-four feet long. Across these were laid branches of pine and willow trees, so as to yield a tolerable shade. At the west end, immediately opposite to the door, three bodies lay interred, with their feet towards the east. At the head of each grave was a branch of red cedar firmly planted in the ground. At the foot was a large buffalo's skull, painted black. Savage ornaments were suspended in various parts of the edifice, and a great number of children's mocassins. From the magnitude of this building, and the time and labour that must have been expended in erecting it, the bodies which it contained were probably those of noted warriors and hunters.

The next day, October 17th, they passed two large tributary streams of the Spanish river. They took their rise in the Wind river mountains, which ranged along to the east, stupendously high and rugged, composed of vast masses of black rock, almost destitute of wood, and covered in many places with snow. This day they saw a few buffalo bulls, and some antelopes, but could not kill any ; and their stock of provisions began to grow scanty as well as poor.

On the 18th, after crossing a mountain ridge, and traversing a plain, they waded one of the branches of Spanish river, and on ascending its bank, met with about a hundred and thirty Snake Indians. They were friendly in their demeanour, and conducted them to their encampment, which was about three miles distant. It consisted of about forty wigwams, constructed principally of pine branches. The Snakes, like most of their nation, were very poor ; the marauding Crows, in their late excursion through the country, had picked this unlucky band to the very bone, carrying off their horses, several of their squaws, and most of their effects. In spite of their poverty, they were hospitable in the extreme, and made the hungry strangers welcome to their cabins. A few trinkets procured from them a supply of buffalo meat, and of leather for mocassins, of which the party were greatly in need. The most valuable prize obtained from them, however, was a horse: it was a sorry old animal in truth, but it was the only one that remained to the poor fellows, after the fell swoop of the Crows; yet this they were prevailed upon to part with to their guests for a pistol, an axe, a knife, and a few other trifling articles.

They had doleful stories to tell of the Crows, who were encamped on a river at no great distance to the east, and were in such force that they dared not venture to seek any satisfaction for their outrages, or to get back a horse or a squaw. They endeavoured to excite the indignation of their visitors by accounts of robberies and murders committed on lonely white hunters and trappers by Crows and Black-feet. Some of these were exaggerations of the outrages already mentioned, sustained by some of the scattered members of Mr. Hunt's expedition; others were in all probability sheer fabrications, to which the Snakes seem to have been a little prone. Mr. Stuart assured them that the day was not far distant when the whites would make their power to be felt throughout that country, and take signal vengeance on the perpetrators of these misdeeds. The Snakes expressed great joy at the intelligence, and offered their services to aid the righteous cause, brightening at the thoughts of taking the field with such potent allies, and doubtless anticipating their turn at stealing horses and abducting squaws. Their offers of course were accepted; the calumet of peace was produced, and the two forlorn powers smoked eternal friendship between themselves and vengeance upon their common spoilers, the Crows.

CHAPTER VI.

By sunrise on the following morning (October 19th) the travellers had loaded their old horse with buffalo meat, sufficient for five days' provisions, and taking leave of their new allies, the poor, but hospitable Snakes, set forth in somewhat better spirits, though the increasing cold of the weather, and the sight of the snowy mountains, which they had yet to traverse, were enough to chill their very hearts. The country along this branch of the Spanish river, as far as they could see, was perfectly level, bounded by ranges of lofty mountains, both to the east and west. They proceeded about three miles to the south, where they came again upon the large trail of Crow Indians, which they had crossed four days previously, made, no doubt, by the same marauding band that had plundered the Snakes; and which, according to the account of the latter, was now encamped on a stream to the eastward. The trail kept on to the southeast, and was so well beaten by horse and foot, that they supposed at least a hundred lodges had passed along it. As it formed, therefore, a convenient highway, and ran in a proper direction, they turned into it, and determined to keep along it as far as safety would permit; as the Crow encampment must be some distance off, and it was not likely those savages would return upon their steps. They travelled forward, therefore, all that day, in the track of their dangerous predecessors, which led them across mountain streams, and along ridges, and through narrow valleys, all tending generally towards the southeast. The wind blew coldly from the north-east, with occasional flurries of snow, which made them encamp early, on the sheltered banks of a brook. The two Canadians, Vallée and Le Clerc, killed a young buffalo bull in the evening, which was in good condition, and afforded them a plentiful supply of fresh beef. They loaded their spits, therefore, and crammed their camp kettle with meat, and while the wind whistled, and the snow whirled around them, huddled round a rousing fire, basked in its warmth, and comforted both soul and body with a hearty and invigorating meal. No enjoyments have greater zest than these, snatched in the very midst of difficulty and danger ; and it is probable the poor wayworn and weatherbeaten travellers relished these creature comforts the more highly, from the surrounding desolation, and the dangerous proximity of the Crows.

The snow which had fallen in the night made it late in the morning before the party loaded their solitary pack-horse, and resumed their march. They had not gone far before the Crow trace which they were following, changed its direction, and bore to the north of east. They had already begun to feel themselves on dangerous ground, in keeping along it, as they might be descried by some scouts and spies of that race of marauders, whose predatory life required them to be constantly on the alert. On seeing the trace turn so much to the north, therefore, they abandoned it, and kept on their course to the southeast, for eighteen miles, through a beautifully undulating country, having the main chain of mountains on the left, and a considerably elevated ridge on the right. Here the mountain ridge which divides Wind river from the head waters of the Columbia and Spanish rivers, ends abruptly, and winding to the north of east, becomes the dividing barrier between a branch of the Bighorn and Cheyenne rivers, and those head waters which flow into the Missouri, below the Sioux country.

The ridge which lay on the right of the travellers having now become very low, they passed over it, and came into a level plain, about ten miles in circumference, and incrusted to the depth of a foot or eighteen inches with salt as white as snow. This is furnished by numerous salt springs of limpid water, which are continually welling up, overflowing their borders, and forming beautiful crystallizations. The Indian tribes of the interior are excessively fond of this salt, and repair to the valley to collect it ; but it is held in distaste by the tribes of the sea coast, who will eat nothing that has been cured or seasoned by it.

This evening they encamped on the banks of a small stream, in the open prairie. The north-east wind was keen and cutting; they had nothing wherewith to make a fire, but a scanty growth of sage, or wormwood, and were fain to wrap themselves up in their blankets, and huddle themselves in their "nests," at an early hour. In the course of the evening, Mr. M'Lellan, who had now regained his strength, killed a buffalo, but it was some distance from the camp, and they postponed supplying themselves from the carcass until the following morning.

The next day (October 21st), the cold continued, accompanied by snow. They set forward on their bleak and toilsome way, keeping to the east-northeast, towards the lofty summit of a mountain, which it was necessary for them to cross. Before they reached its base they passed another large trail, steering a little to the right of the point of the mountain. This they presumed to have been made by another band of Crows, who had probably been hunting lower down on the Spanish river.

The severity of the weather compelled them to encamp at the end of fifteen miles, on the skirts of the mountain, where they found sufficient dry aspen trees to supply them with fire, but they sought in vain about the neighbourhood for a spring or rill of water.

At daybreak they were up and on the march, scrambling up the mountain side for the distance of eight painful miles. From the casual hints given in the travelling memoranda of Mr. Stuart, this mountain would seem to offer a rich field of speculation for the geologist. Here was a plain three miles in diameter, strewed with pumice stones and other volcanic reliques, with a lake in the centre, occupying what had probably been the crater. Here were also, in some places, deposits of marine shells, indicating that this mountain crest had at some remote period been below the waves.

After pausing to repose, and to enjoy these grand but savage and awful scenes, they began to descend the eastern side of the mountain. The descent was rugged and romantic, along deep ravines and defiles, overhung with crags and cliffs, among which they beheld numbers of the ahsahta or bighorn, skipping fearlessly from rock to rock. Two of them they succeeded in bringing down with their rifles, as they peered fearlessly from the brow of their airy precipice.

Arrived at the foot of the mountain, the travellers found a rill of water oozing out of the earth, and resembling in look and taste, the water of the Missouri. Here they encamped for the night, and supped sumptuously upon their mountain mutton, which they found in good condition, and extremely well tasted.

The morning was bright and intensely cold. Early in the day they came upon a stream running to the east, between low hills of bluish earth, strongly impregnated with copperas. Mr. Stuart supposed this to be one of the head waters of the Missouri, and determined to follow its banks. After a march of twenty-six miles, however, he arrived at the summit of a hill, the prospect of which induced him to alter his intention. He beheld, in every direction south of east, a vast plain, bounded only by the horizon, through which wandered the stream in question, in a south-southeast direction. It could not, therefore, be a branch of the Missouri. He now gave up all idea of taking the stream for his guide, and shaped his course towards a range of mountains in the east, about sixty miles distant, near which he hoped to find another stream.

The weather was now so severe, and the hardships of travelling so great, that he resolved to halt for the winter, at the first eligible place. That night they had to encamp on the open prairie, near a scanty pool of water, and without any wood to make a fire. The north-east wind blew keenly across the naked waste, and they were fain to decamp from their inhospitable bivouac before the dawn.

For two days they kept on in an eastward direction, against wintry blasts and occasional snow storms. They suffered, also, from scarcity of water, having occasionally to use melted snow; this, with the want of pasturage, reduced their old packhorse sadly. They saw many tracks of buffalo, and some few bulls, which, however, got the wind of them, and scampered off.

On the 26th of October, they steered eastnortheast, for a wooded ravine, in a mountain at a small distance from the base of which, to their great joy, they discovered an abundant stream, running between willowed banks. Here they halted for the night, and Ben Jones having luckily trapped a beaver, and killed two buffalo bulls, they remained all the next day encamped, feasting and reposing, and allowing their jaded horse to rest from his labours.

The little stream on which they were encamped, was one of the head waters of the Platte river, which flows into the Missouri; it was, in fact, the northern fork, or branch of that river, though this the travellers did not discover until long afterwards. Pursuing the course of this stream for about twenty miles, they came to where it forced a passage through a range of high hills, covered with cedars, into an extensive low country, affording excellent pasture to numerous herds of buffalo. Here they killed three cows, which were the first they had been able to get, having hitherto had to content themselves with bull beef, which at this season of the year is very poor. The hump meat afforded them a repast fit for an epicure.

Late on the afternoon of the 30th, they came to where the stream, now increased to a considerable size, poured along in a ravine between precipices of red stone, two hundred feet in height. For some distance it dashed along, over huge masses of rock, with foaming violence, as if exasperated by being compressed into so narrow a channel, and at length leaped down a chasm that looked dark and frightful in the gathering twilight.

For a part of the next day, the wild river, in its capricious wanderings, led them through a variety of striking scenes. At one time they were upon high plains, like platforms among the mountains, with herds of buffaloes roaming about them; at another, among rude rocky defiles, broken into cliffs and precipices, where the black tailed deer bounded off among the crags, and the bighorn basked in the sunny brow of the precipice.

In the after part of the day, they came to another scene, surpassing in savage grandeur those already described. They had been travelling for some distance through a pass of the mountains, keeping parallel with the river, as it roared along, out of sight, through a deep ravine. Sometimes their devious path approached the margin of cliffs below which the river foamed, and boiled and whirled among the masses of rock that had fallen into its channel. As they kept cautiously on, leading their solitary pack-horse along these giddy heights, they all at once came to where the river thundered down a succession of precipices, throwing up clouds of spray, and making a prodigious din and uproar. The travellers remained, for a time, gazing with mingled awe and delight at this furious cataract, to which Mr. Stuart gave, from the colour of the impending rocks, the name of " the Fiery Narrows."

CHAPTER VII.

Wintry storms—A halt and council—Cantonment for the winter——Fine hunting country—Game of the mountains and plains—Sucessful hunting— Mr. Crooks and a grizzly bear — The wigwam — Bighorn and blacktails—Beef and Venison—Good quarters and good cheer—An alarm—An intrusion—Unwelcome guests—Desolation of the larder—Gormandizing exploits of hungry savages—Good quarters abandoned.

THE travellers encamped for the night on the banks of the river, below the cataract. The night was cold, with partial showers of rain and sleet. The morning dawned gloomily, the skies were sullen and overcast, and threatened further storms ; but the little band resumed their journey, in defiance of the weather. The increasing rigour of the season, however, which makes itself felt early in these mountainous regions, and on these naked and elevated plains, brought them to a pause, and a serious deliberation, after they had descended about thirty miles further along the course of the river.

All were convinced that it was vain to attempt to accomplish their journey on foot, at this inclement season. They had still many hundred miles to traverse before they should reach the main course of the Missouri, and their route would lay over immense prairies, naked and bleak, and destitute of fuel. The question then was, where to choose their wintering place, and whether or not to proceed further down the river. They had at first imagined it to be one of the head waters, or tributary streams, of the Missouri. Afterwards they had believed it to be Rapid, or Quicourt river, in which opinion they had not come nearer

to the truth ; they now, however, were persuaded, with
equal fallacy, by its inclining somewhat to the north of east,
that it was the Cheyenne.   If so, by continuing down it
much further they must arrive among the Indians, from
whom the river takes its name.   Among these they would
be sure to meet some of the Sioux tribe.   These would apprize their relatives, the piratical Sioux of the Missouri, of
the approach of a band of white traders ;   so that, in the
spring time they would be likely to be waylaid and robbed
on their way down the river, by some party in ambush
upon its banks.

Even should this prove to be the Quicourt or Rapid
river, it would not be prudent to winter much further down
upon its banks, as though they might be out of the range
of the Sioux, they would be in the neighbourhood of the
Poncas, a tribe nearly as dangerous.   It was resolved,
therefore, since they must winter somewhere on this
side of the Missouri, to descend no lower, but to keep
up in these solitary regions, where they would be in no
danger of molestation.

They were brought the more promptly and unanimously
to this decision, by coming upon an excellent wintering
place, that promised every thing requisite for their comfort.
It was on a fine bend of the river, just below where it issued
out from among a ridge of mountains, and bent towards
the northeast.   Here was a beautiful low point of land,
covered by cotton-wood, and surrounded by a thick growth
of willow, so as to yield both shelter and fuel, as well as
materials for building.   The river swept by in a strong
current, about a hundred and fifty yards wide.   To the
southeast were mountains of moderate height, the nearest
about two miles off, but the whole chain ranging to the
east, south, and southwest, as far as the eye could reach.
Their summits were crowned with extensive tracts of pitch
pine, chequered with small patches of the quivering aspen.
Lower down were thick forests of firs and red cedars, growing out in many places from among the very fissures of the
rocks.   The mountains were broken and precipitous, with
huge bluffs protruding from among the forests.   Their
rocky recesses, and beetling cliffs, afforded retreats to in-

n merable flocks of the bighorn, while their woody summits and ravines abounded with bears, and black-tailed deer. These, with the numerous herds of buffalo that ranged the lower grounds along the river, promised the travellers abundant cheer in their winter quarters.

On the 2nd of November, therefore, they pitched their camp for the winter; on the woody point, and their first thought was, to obtain a supply of provisions. Ben Jones and the two Canadians accordingly sallied forth, accompanied by two others of the party, leaving but one to watch the camp. Their hunting was uncommonly successful. In the course of two days, they killed thirty-two buffaloes, and collected their meat on the margin of a small brook, about a mile distant. Fortunately, a severe frost froze the river, so that the meat was easily transported to the encampment. On a succeeding day, a herd of buffalo came trampling through the woody bottom on the river banks, and fifteen more were killed.

It was soon discovered, however, that there was game of a more dangerous nature in the neighbourhood. On one occasion, Mr. Crooks had wandered about a mile from the camp, and had ascended a small hill commanding a view of the river. He was without his rifle, a rare circumstance; for in these wild regions, where one may put up a wild animal, or a wild Indian, at every turn, it is customary never to stir from the camp fire unarmed. The hill where he stood overlooked the place where the massacre of the buffalo had taken place. As he was looking round on the prospect, his eye was caught by an object below, moving directly towards him. To his dismay, he discovered it to be a grizzly bear, with two cubs. There was no tree at hand into which he could climb; to run would only be to provoke pursuit, and he should soon be overtaken. He threw himself on the ground, therefore, and lay motionless, watching the movements of the animal with intense anxiety. It continued to advance until at the foot of the hill, where it turned, and made into the woods, having probably gorged itself with buffalo flesh. Mr. Crooks made all haste back to the camp, rejoicing at his escape, and determining never to stir out again without his rifle. A few days after this circumstance, a grizzly bear was shot in the neighbour-hood, by Mr. Miller.

As the slaughter of so many buffaloes had provided the party with beef for the winter, in case they met with no further supply, they now set to work, heart and hand, to build a comfortable wigwam. In a little while the woody promontory rang with the unwonted sound of the axe. Some of its lofty trees were laid low, and by the second evening the cabin was complete. It was eight feet wide, and eighteen feet long. The walls were six feet high, and the whole was covered with buffalo skins. The fire-place was in the centre, and the smoke found its way out by a hole in the roof.

The hunters were next sent out, to procure deer-skins for garments, mocassins, and other purposes. They made the mountains echo with their rifles, and, in the course of two days' hunting, killed twenty-eight bighorns and black-tailed deer.

The party now revelled in abundance. After all that they had suffered from hunger, cold, fatigue, and watch-fulness; after all their perils from treacherous and savage men, they exulted in the snugness and security of their isolated cabin, hidden, as they thought, even from the prying eyes of Indian scouts, and stored with creature comforts; and they looked forward to a winter of peace and quietness; of roasting and boiling, and broiling, and feasting upon venison, and mountain mutton, and bear's meat, and marrow bones, and buffalo humps, and other hunter's dainties, and of dosing and reposing round their fire, and gossiping over past dangers and adven-tures, and telling long hunting stories, until spring should return; when they would make canoes of buffalo skins, and float themselves down the river.

From such halcyon dreams, they were startled one morning, at daybreak, by a savage yelp. They started up and seized their rifles. The yelp was repeated by two or three voices. Cautiously peeping out, they beheld, to their dismay, several Indian warriors among the trees, all armed and painted in warlike style; being evidently bent on some hostile purpose.

Miller changed countenance as he regarded them. "We are in trouble," said he, "these are some of the rascally Arapahays that robbed me last year." Not a word was uttered by the rest of the party, but they silently slung their powder horns and ball pouches, and prepared for battle. M'Lellan, who had taken his gun to pieces the evening before, put it together in all haste. He proposed that they should break out the clay from between the logs, so as to be able to fire upon the enemy.

"Not yet," replied Stuart; "it will not do to show fear or distrust; we must first hold a parley. Some one must go out and meet them as a friend."

Who was to undertake the task! it was full of peril, as the envoy might be shot down at the threshold.

"The leader of a party," said Miller, "always takes the advance."

"Good!" replied Stuart; "I am ready." He immediately went forth; one of the Canadians followed him; the rest of the party remained in garrison, to keep the savages in check.

Stuart advanced, holding his rifle in one hand, and extending the other to the savage that appeared to be the chief. The latter stepped forward and took it; his men followed his example, and all shook hands with Stuart, in token of friendship. They now explained their errand. They were a war party of Arapahay braves. Their village lay on a stream several days' journey to the eastward. It had been attacked and ravaged during their absence, by a band of Crows, who had carried off several of their women, and most of their horses. They were in quest of vengeance. For sixteen days they had been tracking the Crows about the mountains, but had not yet come upon them. In the mean time they had met with scarcely any game, and were half famished. About two days previously they had heard the report of fire-arms among the mountains, and on searching in the direction of the sound, had come to a place where deer had been killed. They had immediately put themselves upon the track of the hunters, and by following it up, had arrived at the cabin.

Mr. Stuart now invited the chief and another, who appeared to be his lieutenant, into the hut, but made signs that no one else was to enter. The rest halted at the door; others came straggling up, until the whole party, to the number of twenty-three, were gathered before the hut. They were armed with bows and arrows, tomahawks, and scalping knives, and some few with guns. All were painted and dressed for war, and had a wild and fierce appearance. Mr. Miller recognized among them some of the very fellows who had robbed him in the preceding year; and put his comrades upon their guard. Every man stood ready to resist the first act of hostility; the savages, however, conducted themselves peaceably, and showed none of that swaggering arrogance which a war party is apt to assume.

On entering the hut the chief and his lieutenant cast a wilful look at the rafters, laden with venison and buffalo meat. Mr. Stuart made a merit of necessity, and invited them to help themselves. They did not wait to be pressed. The rafters were soon cased of their burden; venison and beef were passed out to the crew before the door, and a scene of gormandizing commenced, of which few can have an idea, who have not witnessed the gastronomic powers of an Indian, after an interval of fasting. This was kept up throughout the day; they paused, now and then, it is true, for a brief interval, but only to return to the charge with renewed ardour. The chief and the lieutenant surpassed all the rest in the vigour and perseverance of their attacks; as if, from their station, they were bound to signalise themselves in all onslaughts. Mr. Stuart kept them well supplied with choice bits; for it was his policy to over-feed them, and keep them from leaving the hut, where they served as hostages for the good conduct of their followers. Once only, in the course of the day, did the chief sally forth. Mr. Stuart and one of the men accompanied him, armed with their rifles, but without betraying any distrust. The chieftain soon returned, and renewed his attack upon the larder. In a word, he and his worthy coadjutor, the lieutenant, ate until they were both stupified.

Towards evening the Indians made their preparations

for the night, according to the practice of war parties. Those outside of the hut threw up two breastworks, into which they retired at a tolerably early hour, and slept like over-fed hounds. As to the chief and his lieutenant, they passed the night in the hut, in the course of which, they, two or three times, got up to eat. The travellers took turns, one at a time, to mount guard until the morning.

Scarce had the day dawned, when the gormandizing was renewed by the whole band, and carried on with surprising vigour until ten o'clock, when all prepared to depart. They had six days' journey yet to make, they said, before they should come up with the Crows, who they understood were encamped on a river to the north-ward. Their way lay through a hungry country, where there was no game; they would, moreover, have but little time to hunt; they therefore craved a small quantity of provisions for the journey. Mr. Stuart again invited them to help themselves. They did so with keen forethought, loading themselves with the choicest parts of the meat, and leaving the larder far gone in a consumption. Their next request was for a supply of ammunition, having guns, but no powder and ball. They promised to pay mag-nificently out of the spoils of their foray. " We are poor now," said they, " and are obliged to go on foot, but we shall soon come back laden with booty, and all mounted on horseback, with scalps hanging at our bridles. We will then give each of you a horse, to keep you from being tired on your journey."

" Well," said Mr. Stuart, " when you bring the horses, you shall have the ammunition, but not before." The Indians saw, by his determined tone, that all further entreaty would be unavailing, so they desisted, with a goodhumoured laugh, and went off, exceedingly well freighted, both within and without, promising to be back again in the course of a fortnight.

No sooner were they out of hearing, than the luckless travellers held another council. The security of their cabin was at an end, and with it all their dreams of a quiet and cosey winter. They were between two fires. On one side were their old enemies, the Crows: on the other side, the Arapahays, no less dangerous freebooters. As to the moderation of this war party, they considered it assumed, to put them off their guard against some more favourable opportunity for a surprisal. It was determined, therefore, not to await their return, but to abandon, with all speed, this dangerous neighbourhood. From the accounts of their recent visitors, they were led to believe, though erroneously, that they were upon the Quicourt, or Rapid river. They proposed now to keep along it, to its confluence with the Missouri; but, should they be prevented by the rigours of the season, from proceeding so far, at least, to reach a part of the river where they might be able to construct canoes of greater strength and durability than those of buffalo skins.

Accordingly, on the 13th of December, they bade adieu, with many a regret, to their comfortable quarters, where, for five weeks, they had been indulging the sweets of repose, of plenty, and of fancied security. They were still accompanied by their veteran packhorse, which the Arapahays had omitted to steal, either because they intended to steal him on their return, or because they thought him not worth stealing.

CHAPTER VIII.

Rough wintry travelling—Hills and plains—Snow and ice—Disappearance of game—A vast dreary plain—A second halt for the winter—Another wigwam—New-year's feast—Buffalo humps, tongues, and marrow-bones—Return of spring—Launch of canoes—Bad navigation—Pedestrian march—Vast prairies—Deserted camps—Pawnee squaws—An Otto Indian—News of war—Voyage down the Platte and the Missouri—Reception at Fort Osage—Arrival at St. Louis.

THE interval of comfort and repose which the party had enjoyed in their wigwam, rendered the renewal of their fatigues intolerable for the first two or three days. The snow lay deep, and was slightly frozen on the surface, but not sufficiently to bear their weight. Their feet became sore by breaking through the crust, and their limbs weary by floundering on without firm foothold. So exhausted and dispirited were they, that they began to think it would be better to remain, and run the risk of being killed by the Indians, than to drag on thus painfully, with the probability of perishing by the way. Their miserable horse fared no better than themselves, having for the first day or two no other fodder than the ends of willow twigs, and the bark of the cotton-wood tree.

They all, however, appeared to gain patience and hardihood as they proceeded, and for fourteen days kept steadily on, making a distance of about three hundred and thirty miles. For some days the range of mountains which had been near to their wigwam, kept parallel to the river at no great distance, but at length subsided into hills. Sometimes they found the river bordered with alluvial bottoms, and groves with cotton-wood and willows; sometimes the adjacent country was naked and barren. In one place it ran for a considerable distance between rocky hills and promontories covered with cedar and pitch pines, and peopled with the bighorn and the mountain deer; at other places it wandered through prairies well stocked with buffaloes and antelopes. As they descended the course of the river, they began to perceive the ash and white oak here and there among the cotton-wood and willow, and at length caught a sight of some wild horses on the distant prairies.

The weather was various; at one time the snow lay deep; then they had a genial day or two, with the mildness and serenity of autumn; then again, the frost was so severe, that the river was sufficiently frozen to bear them upon the ice.

During the last three days of their fortnight's travel, however, the face of the country changed. The timber gradually diminished, until they could scarcely find fuel sufficient for culinary purposes. The game grew more and more scanty, and finally, none were to be seen but a few miserable broken-down buffalo bulls, not worth killing. The snow lay fifteen inches deep, and made the travelling grievously painful and toilsome. At length they came to an immense plain, where no vestige of timber was to be seen, nor a single quadruped to enliven the desolate landscape. Here, then, their hearts failed them, and they held another consultation. The width of the river, which was upwards of a mile, its extreme shallowness, the frequency of quicksands, and various other characteristics, had at length made them sensible of their errors with respect to it, and they now came to the correct conclusion that they were on the banks of the Platte or Shallow river. What were they to do? Pursue its course to the Missouri? To go on at this season of the year seemed dangerous in the extreme. There was no prospect of obtaining either food or firing. The country was destitute of trees, and though there might be drift wood along the river, it lay too deep beneath the snow for them to find it.

The weather was threatening a change, and a snow storm on these boundless wastes, might prove as fatal as a whirlwind of sand on an Arabian desert. After much dreary deliberation, it was at length determined to retrace their three last days' journey, of seventy-seven miles, to a place which they had remarked; where there was a sheltering growth of forest trees, and a country abundant in game. Here they would once more set up their winter quarters, and await the opening of the navigation to launch themselves in canoes.

Accordingly, on the 27th of December they faced about, retraced their steps, and on the 30th, regained the part of the river in question. Here the alluvial bottom was from one to two miles wide, and thickly covered with a forest of cotton-wood trees; while herds of buffalo were scattered about the neighbouring prairies, several of which soon fell beneath their rifles.

They encamped on the margin of the river, in a grove where there were trees large enough for canoes. Here they put up a shed for immediate shelter, and immediately proceeded to erect a hut. New-year's day dawned, when as yet but one wall of their cabin was completed; the genial and jovial day, however, was not permitted to pass uncelebrated, even by this weatherbeaten crew of wanderers. All work was suspended, except that of roasting and boiling. The choicest of the buffalo meat, with tongues and humps, and marrow bones, were devoured in quantities that would astonish any one that has not lived among hunters or Indians; and as an extra regale, having no tobacco left, they cut up an old tobacco pouch, still redolent with the potent herb, and smoked it in honour of the day. Thus for a time, in present revelry, however uncouth, they forgot all past troubles and all anxieties about the future, and their forlorn wigwam echoed to the sound of gaiety.

The next day they resumed their labours, and by the 6th of the month it was complete. They soon killed abundance of buffalo, and again laid in a stock of winter provisions.

The party were more fortunate in this their second cantonment. The winter passed away without any Indian visitors; and the game continued to be plenty in the neighbourhood. They felled two large trees, and shaped them into canoes; and, as the spring opened, and a thaw of several days' continuance melted the ice in the river, they made every preparation for embarking. On the 8th of March they launched forth in their canoes, but soon found that the river had not depth sufficient even for such slender barks. It expanded into a wide, but extremely shallow stream, with many sand bars, and occasionally various channels. They got one of their canoes a few miles down it, with extreme difficulty, sometimes wading and dragging it over the shoals; at length they had to abandon the attempt, and to resume their journey on foot, aided by their faithful old packhorse, who had recruited strength during the repose of the winter.

The weather delayed them for a few days, having suddenly become more rigorous than it had been at any time during the winter; but on the 20th of March they were again on their journey.

In two days they arrived at the vast naked prairie, the wintry aspect of which had caused them, in December, to pause and turn back. It was now clothed in the early verdure of spring, and plentifully stocked with game. Still, when obliged to bivouac on its bare surface, without any shelter, and by a scanty fire of dry buffalo dung, they found the night blasts piercing cold. On one occasion, a herd of buffalo, straying near their evening camp, they killed three of them merely for their hides, wherewith to make a shelter for the night.

They continued on for upwards of a hundred miles ; with vast prairies extending before them as they advanced ; sometimes diversified by undulating hills, but destitute of trees. In one place they saw a gang of sixty-five wild horses, but as for the buffaloes they seemed absolutely to cover the country. Wild geese abounded, and they passed extensive swamps that were alive with innumerable flocks of waterfowl, among which were a few swans, but an endless variety of ducks.

The river continued a winding course to the east-north-east, nearly a mile in width, but too shallow to float even an empty canoe. The country spread out into a vast level plain, bounded by the horizon alone, excepting to the north, where a line of hills seemed like a long promontory stretching into the bosom of the ocean. The dreary sameness of the prairie wastes began to grow extremely irksome. The travellers longed for the sight of a forest, or grove, or single tree, to break the level uniformity, and began to notice every object that gave reason to hope they were drawing towards the end of this weary wilderness. Thus the occurrence of a particular kind of grass was hailed as a proof that they could not be far from the bottoms of the Missouri ; and they were rejoiced at putting up several prairie hens, a kind of grouse seldom found far in the interior. In picking up drift wood for fuel, also, they found on some pieces the mark of an axe, which caused much speculation as to the time when and the persons by whom the trees had been felled. Thus they went on, like sailors at sea, who perceive in every floating weed and wandering bird, harbingers of the wished-for land.

By the close of the month the weather became very mild, and, heavily burdened as they were, they found the noontide temperature uncomfortably warm. On the 30th, they came to three deserted hunting camps, either of Pawnees or Ottoes, about which were buffalo skulls in all directions ; and the frames on which the hides had been stretched and cured. They had apparently been occupied the preceding autumn.

For several days they kept patiently on, watching every sign that might give them an idea as to where they were, and how near to the banks of the Missouri.

Though there were numerous traces of hunting parties and encampments, they were not of recent date. The country seemed deserted. The only human beings they met with were three Pawnee squaws, in a hut in the midst of a deserted camp. Their people had all gone to the south, in pursuit of the buffalo, and had left these poor women behind, being too sick and infirm to travel.

It is a common practice with the Pawnees, and probably with other roving tribes, when departing on a distant expedition, which will not admit of incumbrance or delay, to leave their aged and infirm with a supply of provisions sufficient for temporary subsistence. When this is exhausted they must perish, though sometimes their sufferings are abridged by hostile prowlers, who may visit the deserted camp.

The poor squaws in question expected some such fate at the hands of the white strangers ; and though the latter accosted them in the kindest manner, and made them presents of dried buffalo meat, it was impossible to soothe their alarm, or get any information from them.

The first landmark by which the travellers were enabled to conjecture their position with any degree of confidence, was an island about seventy miles in length, which they presumed to be Grand isle. If so, they were within one hundred and forty miles of the Missouri. They kept on, therefore, with renewed spirit, and at the end of three days met with an Otto Indian, by whom they were confirmed in their conjecture. They learnt at the same time another piece of information, of an uncomfortable nature. According to his account, there was war between the United States and England, and in fact it had existed for a whole year, during which time they had been beyond the reach of all knowledge of the affairs of the civilized world.

The Otto conducted the travellers to his village, situated a short distance from the Banks of the Platte. Here they were delighted to meet with two white men, Messrs. Dornin and Roi, Indian traders recently from St. Louis. Of these they had a thousand inquiries to make concerning all affairs, foreign and domestic, during their year of sepulture in the wilderness ; and especially about the events of the existing war.

They now prepared to abandon their weary travel by land, and to embark upon the water. A bargain was made with Mr. Dornin, who engaged to furnish them with a canoe and provisions for the voyage, in exchange for their venerable and well-tried fellow traveller, the old Snake horse.

Accordingly, in a couple of days, the Indians employed by that gentleman, constructed for them a canoe twenty feet long, four feet wide, and eighteen inches deep. The frame was of poles and willow twigs, on which were stretched five elk and buffalo hides, sewed together with sinews, and the seams payed with unctuous mud. In this they embarked at an early hour on the 16th of April, and drifted down ten miles with the stream, when the wind being high they encamped, and set to work to make oars, which they had not been able to procure at the Indian village.

Once more afloat, they went merrily down the stream, and after making thirty-five miles, immerged into the broad turbid current of the Missouri. Here they were borne along briskly by the rapid stream, though, by the time their fragile bark had floated a couple of hundred miles, its frame began to show the effects of the voyage. Luckily they came to the deserted wintering place of some hunting party, where they found two old wooden canoes. Taking possession of the largest, they again committed themselves to the current, and after dropping down fifty-five miles further, arrived safely at fort Osage.

Here they found Lieutenant Brownson still in command the officer who had given the expedition a hospitable reception on its way up the river, eighteen months previously. He received this remnant of the party with a cordial welcome, and endeavoured in every way to promote their comfort and enjoyment during their sojourn at the fort. The greatest luxury they met with on their return to the abode of civilized man, was bread, not having tasted any for nearly a year.

Their stay at fort Osage was but short. On re-embarking they were furnished with an ample supply of provisions by the kindness of Lieutenant Brownson, and performed the rest of their voyage without adverse circumstance. On the 30th of April they arrived in perfect health and fine spirits at St. Louis, having been ten months performing this perilous expedition from Astoria. Their return caused quite a sensation at the place, bringing the first intelligence of the fortune of Mr. Hunt and his party, in their adventurous route across the Rocky mountains, and of the new establishment on the shores of the Pacific.

CHAPTER IX.

Agreement between Mr. Astor and the Russian fur company—War between the United States and Great Britain—Instructions to Captain Sowle of the Beaver—Fitting out of the Lark—News of the arrival of Mr. Stuart.

It is now necessary, in linking together the parts of this excursive narrative, that we notice the proceedings of Mr. Astor, in support of his great undertaking. His project with respect to the Russian establishments along the northwest coast, had been diligently prosecuted. The agent sent by him to St. Petersburgh, to negotiate in his name as president of the American Fur Company, had, under sanction of the Russian government, made a provisional agreement with the Russian company.

By this agreement, which was ratified by Mr. Astor in 1813, the two companies bound themselves not to interfere with each other's trading and hunting grounds, nor to furnish arms and ammunition to the Indians. They were to act in concert, also, against all interlopers, and to succour each other in case of danger. The American company was to have the exclusive right of supplying the Russian posts with goods and necessaries, receiving peltries in payment at stated prices. They were, also, if so requested by the Russian governor, to convey the furs of the Russian company to Canton, sell them on commission, and bring back the proceeds, at such freight as might be agreed on at the time. This agreement was to continue in operation four years, and to be renewable for a similar term, unless some unforeseen contingency should render a modification necessary.

It was calculated to be of great service to the infant establishment at Astoria; dispelling the fears of hostile rivalry on the part of the foreign companies in its neighbourhood, and giving a formidable blow to the irregular trade along the coast. It was also the intention of Mr. Astor to have coasting vessels of his own, at Astoria, of small tonnage and draft of water, fitted for coasting service. These, having a place of shelter and deposit, could ply about the coast in short voyages, in favourable weather, and would have vast advantage over chance ships, which must make long voyages, maintain numerous crews, and could only approach the coast at certain seasons of the year. He hoped, therefore, gradually to make Astoria the great emporium of the American fur trade in the Pacific, and the nucleus of a powerful American state. Unfortunately for these sanguine anticipations, before Mr. Astor had ratified the agreement, as above stated, war broke out between the United States and Great Britain. He perceived, at once, the peril of the case. The harbour of New York would doubtless be blockaded, and the departure of the annual supply ship in the autumn prevented ; or, if she should succeed in getting out to sea, she might be captured on her voyage.

In this emergency, he wrote to Captain Sowle, commander of the Beaver. The letter, which was addressed to him at Canton, directed him to proceed to the factory at the mouth of the Columbia, with such articles as the establishment might need ; and to remain there, subject to the orders of Mr. Hunt, should that gentleman be in command there.

The war continued. No tidings had yet been received from Astoria ; the despatches having been delayed by the misadventure of Mr. Reed at the falls of the Columbia, and the unhorsing of Mr. Stuart, by the Crows among the mountains. A painful uncertainty, also, prevailed about Mr. Hunt and his party. Nothing had been heard of them since their departure from the Aricara village; Lisa, who parted from them there, had predicted their destruction; and some of the traders of the North-west Company, had actually spread a rumour of their having been cut off by the Indians.

It was a hard trial of the courage and means of an individual, to have to fit out another costly expedition, where so much had already been expended, so much uncertainty prevailed, and where the risk of loss was so greatly enhanced, that no insurance could be effected.

In spite of all these discouragements, Mr. Astor determined to send another ship to the relief of the settlement. He selected for this purpose a vessel called the Lark, remarkable for her fast sailing. The disordered state of the times, however, caused such delay, that February arrived, while the vessel was yet lingering in port.

At this juncture, Mr. Astor learnt that the North-west Company were preparing to send out an armed ship of twenty guns, called the Isaac Todd, to form an establishment at the mouth of the Columbia. These tidings gave him great uneasiness. A considerable proportion of the persons in his employ were Scotchmen and Canadians, and several of them had been in the service of the North-west Company. Should Mr. Hunt have failed to arrive at Astoria, the whole establishment would be under the controul of Mr. M'Dougal, of whose fidelity he had received very disparaging accounts from Captain Thorn. The British government, also, might deem it worth while to send a force against the establishment, having been urged to do so some time previously, by the North-west Company.

Under all these circumstances, Mr. Astor wrote to Mr. Monroe, then secretary of state, requesting protection from the government of the United States. He represented the importance of his settlement, in a commercial point of view, and the shelter it might afford to the American vessels in those seas. All he asked was, that the American government would throw forty or fifty men into the fort at his establishment, which would be sufficient for its defence, until he could send reinforcements over-land.

He waited in vain for a reply to this letter, the government, no doubt, being engrossed at the time by an over-whelming crowd of affairs. The month of March arrived, and the Lark was ordered by Mr. Astor to put to sea. The officer who was to command her, shrunk from his en-gagement, and in the exigency of the moment, she was given in charge to Mr. Northorpe, the mate. Mr. Nicholas G. Ogden, a gentleman on whose talents and integrity the highest reliance could be placed, sailed as supercargo. The Lark put to sea in the beginning of March 1813.

By this opportunity, Mr. Astor wrote to Mr. Hunt, as head of the establishment at the mouth of the Columbia, for he would not allow himself to doubt of his welfare. " I always think you are well," said he, " and that I shall see you again, which Heaven, I hope, will grant."

He warned him to be on his guard against any attempts to surprise the post ; suggesting the probability of armed hostility on the part of the North-west Company, and ex-pressing his indignation at the ungrateful returns made by that association for his frank and open conduct, and advan-tageous overtures. " Were I on the spot," said he, "and had the management of affairs, I would defy them all; but as it is, every thing depends upon you, and your friends about you. *Our enterprise is grand, and deserves success, and I hope in God it will meet it.* If my object was merely gain of money, I should say, think whether it is best to save what we can, and abandon the place; *but the very idea is like a dagger to my heart."* This extract is sufficient to show the spirit and the views which actuated Mr. Astor in this great undertaking.

Week after week, and month after month elapsed, with-out any thing to dispel the painful incertitude that hung over every part of this enterprise. Though a man of reso-lute spirit, and not easily cast down, the dangers impending over this darling scheme of his ambition, had a gradual effect upon the spirits of Mr. Astor. He was sitting one gloomy evening by his window, revolving over the loss of the Tonquin, and the fate of her unfortunate crew, and fearing that some equally tragical calamity might have be-fallen the adventurers across the mountains, when the even-ing newspaper was brought to him. The first paragraph that caught his eye, announced the arrival of Mr. Stuart and his party at St. Louis, with intelligence that Mr. Hunt and his companions had effected their perilous expedition to the mouth of the Columbia. This was a gleam of sunshine that for a time dispelled every cloud, and he now looked forward with sanguine hope to the accomplishment of all his plans.

CHAPTER X.

Banks of the Wallah-Wallah—Departure of David Stuart for the Oakinagan—Mr Clarke's route up Lewis River—Chipunnish, or Pierced-nosed Indians—Their character, appearance, and habits—Thievish habits—Laying-up of the boats—Post at Pointed Heart and Spokan rivers—M'Kenzie, his route up the Camoenum—Bands of travelling Indians—Expedition of Reed to the caches—Adventures of wandering voyageurs and trappers.

THE course of our narrative now takes us back to the regions beyond the mountains, to dispose of the parties that set out from Astoria, in company with Mr. Robert Stuart, and whom he left on the banks of the Wallah-Wallah. Those parties, likewise, separated from each other shortly after his departure, proceeding to their respective destinations, but agreeing to meet at the mouth of the Wallah-Wallah, about the beginning of June in the following year, with such peltries as they should have collected in the interior, so as to convoy each other through the dangerous passes of the Columbia.

Mr. David Stuart, one of the parties, proceeded with his men to the post already established by him at the mouth of the Oakinagan; having furnished this with goods and ammunition, he proceeded three hundred miles up that river, where he established another post in a good trading neighbourhood.

Mr. Clarke, another partner, conducted his little band up Lewis river to the mouth of a small stream coming in from the north, to which the Canadians gave the name of Pavion. Here he found a village or encampment of forty huts or tents, covered with mats, and inhabited by *Nez percés*, or Pierced-nosed Indians, as they are called by the traders; but Chipunnish, as they are called by themselves. They are a hardy, laborious, and somewhat knavish race, who lead a precarious life, fishing, and digging roots during the summer and autumn, hunting the deer on snow shoes during the winter, and traversing the rocky mountains in the spring, to trade for buffalo skins with the hunting tribes of the Missouri. In these migrations they are liable to be waylaid and attacked by the Blackfeet, and other warlike and predatory tribes, and driven back across the mountains with the loss of their horses, and of many of their comrades.

A life of this unsettled and precarious kind is apt to render men selfish, and such Mr. Clarke found the inhabitants of this village, who were deficient in the usual hospitality of Indians; parting with every thing with extreme reluctance, and showing no sensibility to any act of kindness. At the time of his arrival, they were all occupied in catching and curing salmon. The men were stout, robust, active, and good looking, and the women handsomer than those of the tribes nearer to the coast.

It was the plan of Mr. Clarke to lay up his boats here, and proceed by land to his place of destination, which was among the Spokan tribe of Indians, about a hundred and fifty miles distant. He accordingly endeavoured to purchase horses for the journey, but in this he had to contend with the sordid disposition of these people. They asked high prices for their horses, and were so difficult to deal with, that Mr. Clarke was detained seven days among them, before he could procure a sufficient number. During that time he was annoyed by repeated pilferings, for which he could get no redress. The chief promised to recover the stolen articles; but failed to do so, alleging that the thieves belonged to a distant tribe, and had made off with their booty. With this excuse Mr. Clarke was fain to content himself, though he laid up in his heart a bitter grudge against the whole pierced-nosed race, which it will be found he took occasion subsequently to gratify in a signal manner.

Having made arrangements for his departure, Mr. Clarke

laid up his barge and canoes in a sheltered place, on the
banks of a small bay, overgrown with shrubs and willows,
confiding them to the care of the Nezpercé chief, who on
being promised an ample compensation, engaged to have a
guardian eye upon them; then mounting his steed, and
putting himself at the head of his little caravan, he shook
the dust off his feet as he turned his back upon this village
of rogues and hard dealers. We shall not follow him
minutely in his journey; which lay at times over steep and
rocky hills, and among crags and precipices; at other
times over vast naked and sunburnt plains, abounding
with rattlesnakes, in traversing which, both men and
horses suffered intolerably from heat and thirst. The
place on which he fixed for a trading post was a fine point
of land at the junction of the Pointed Heart and Spokan
rivers. His establishment was intended to compete with
a trading-post of the North-west Company, situated at no
great distance, and to rival it in the trade with the Spokan
Indians; as well as with the Cootonais and Flatheads.
In this neighbourhood we shall leave him for the present.

Mr. M'Kenzie, who conducted the third party from the
Wallah-Wallah, navigated for several days up the south
branch of the Columbia, named the Camöenum by the
natives, but commonly called Lewis river, in honour of the
first explorer. Wandering bands of various tribes were
seen along this river, travelling in various directions; for
the Indians generally are restless roving beings, continually
intent on enterprises of war, traffic, and hunting. Some
of these people were driving large gangs of horses, as if to
a distant market. Having arrived at the mouth of the
Shahaptan, he ascended some distance up that river, and
established his trading post upon its banks. This appeared to be a great thoroughfare for the tribes from the
neighbourhood of the falls of the Columbia, in their expeditions to make war upon the tribes of the Rocky mountains; to hunt buffalo on the plains beyond, or to traffic
for roots and buffalo robes. It was the season of migration, and the Indians from various distant parts were
passing and repassing in great numbers.

Mr. M'Kenzie now detached a small band, under the

conduct of Mr. John Reed, to visit the caches made by Mr. Hunt at the Caldron Linn, and to bring the contents to his post; as he depended, in some measure, on them for his supplies of goods and ammunition. They had not been gone a week, when two Indians arrived of the Pallatapalla tribe, who live upon a river of the same name. These communicated the unwelcome intelligence that the caches had been robbed. They said that some of their tribe had, in the course of the preceding spring, been across the mountains, which separated them from Snake river, and had traded horses with the Snakes in exchange for blankets, robes, and goods of various descriptions. These articles the Snakes had procured from caches to which they were guided by some white men who resided among them, and who afterwards accompanied them across the Rocky mountains. This intelligence was extremely perplexing to Mr. M'Kenzie, but the truth of part of it was confirmed by the two Indians, who brought them an English saddle and bridle, which was recognized as having belonged to Mr. Crooks. The perfidy of the white men who revealed the secret of the caches, was, however, perfectly inexplicable. We shall presently account for it, in narrating the expedition of Mr. Reed.

That worthy Hibernian proceeded on his mission with his usual alacrity. His forlorn travels of the preceding winter had made him acquainted with the topography of the country, and he reached Snake river without any material difficulty. Here, in an encampment of the natives, he met with six white men, wanderers from the main expedition of Mr. Hunt, who, after having had their respective shares of adventures and mishaps, had fortunately come together at this place. Three of these men were Turcotte, La Chappelle, and Francis Landry; the three Canadian voyageurs who, it may be recollected, had left Mr. Crooks in February, in the neighbourhood of Snake river, being dismayed by the increasing hardships of the journey, and fearful of perishing of hunger. They had returned to a Snake encampment, where they passed the residue of the winter.

Early in the spring, being utterly destitute, and in great

extremity, and having worn out the hospitality of the Snakes, they determined to avail themselves of the buried treasures within their knowledge. They accordingly informed the Snake chieftains that they knew where a great quantity of goods had been left in caches, enough to enrich the whole tribe; and offered to conduct them to the place, on condition of being rewarded with horses and provisions. The chieftains pledged their faith and honour as great men and Snakes, and the three Canadians conducted them to the place of deposit at the Caldron Linn. This is the way that the savages got knowledge of the caches, and not by following the tracts of wolves, as Mr. Stuart had supposed. Never did money diggers turn up a miser's hoard with more eager delight, than did the savages lay open the treasures of the caches. Blankets and robes, brass trinkets and blue beads were drawn forth with chuckling exultation, and long strips of scarlet cloth, produced yells of ecstasy.

The rifling of the caches effected a change in the fortunes and deportment of the whole party. The Snakes were better clad and equipped than ever were Snakes before, and the three Canadians, suddenly finding themselves with horse to ride and weapon to wear, were, like beggars upon horseback, ready to ride on any wild scamper. An opportunity soon presented. The Snakes determined on a hunting match on the buffalo prairies, to lay in a supply of beef, that they might live on plenty, as became men of their improved condition. The three newly mounted cavaliers must fain accompany them. They all traversed the Rocky mountains in safety, descended to the head waters of the Missouri, and made great havoc among the buffaloes.

Their hunting camp was full of meat; they were gorging themselves like true Indians, with present plenty, and drying and jerking great quantities for a winter's supply. In the midst of their revelry and good cheer, the camp was surprised by the Blackfeet. Several of the Snakes were slain on the spot; the residue, with their three Canadian allies, fled to the mountains, stripped of horses, buffalo meat, every thing; and made their way back to the old encampment on Snake river, poorer than ever, but esteeming themselves fortunate in having escaped with their lives. They had not been long there when the Canadians were cheered by the sight of a companion in misfortune, Dubreuil, the poor voyageur who had left Mr. Crooks in March, being too much exhausted to keep on with him. Not long afterwards, three other straggling members of the main expedition made their appearance. These were Carson, St. Michael, and Pierre Delaunay, three of the trappers who, in company with Pierre Detayé, had been left among the mountains by Mr. Hunt, to trap beaver, in the preceding month of September. They had departed from the main body well armed and provided, with horses to ride, and horses to carry the peltries they were to collect. They came wandering into the Snake camp as ragged and destitute as their predecessors. It appears that they had finished their trapping, and were making their way in the spring to the Missouri, when they were met and attacked by a powerful band of the all-pervading Crows. They made a desperate resistance, and killed seven of the savages, but were overpowered by numbers. Pierre Detayé was slain, the rest were robbed of horses and effects, and obliged to turn back, when they fell in with their old companions, as already mentioned.

We should observe, that at the heels of Pierre Delaunay came draggling an Indian wife, whom he had picked up in his wanderings; having grown weary of celibacy among the savages.

The whole seven of this forlorn fraternity of adventurers, thus accidentally congregated on the banks of Snake river, were making arrangements once more to cross the mountains, when some Indian scouts brought word of the approach of the little band headed by John Reed.

The latter, having heard the several stories of these wanderers, took them all into his party, and set out for the Caldron Linn, to clear out two or three of the caches which had not been revealed to the Indians.

At that place he met with Robinson, the Kentucky veteran, who, with his two comrades, Rezner and Hoback, had remained there when Mr. Stuart went on. This adventurous trio had been trapping higher up the river, but Robinson had come down in a canoe, to await the expected arrival of the party, and obtain horses and equipments. He told Reed the story of the robbery of his party by the Arapahays, but it differed, in some particulars, from the account given by him to Mr. Stuart. In that, he had represented Cass as having shamefully deserted his companions in their extremity, carrying off with him a horse; in the one now given, he spoke of him as having been killed in the affray with the Arapahays. This discrepancy, of which, of course, Reed could have had no knowledge at the time, concurred, with other circumstances, to occasion afterwards some mysterious speculations and dark surmises as to the real fate of Cass; but as no substantial grounds were ever adduced for them, we forbear to throw any deeper shades into this story of sufferings in the wilderness.

Mr. Reed having gathered the remainder of the goods from the caches, put himself at the head of his party, now augmented by the seven men thus casually picked up, and the squaw of Pierre Delaunay, and made his way successfully to M'Kenzie's post, on the waters of the Shahaptan.

CHAPTER XI.

Departure of Mr. Hunt in the Beaver—Precautions at the factory—Detachment to the Wollamut—Gloomy apprehensions—Arrival of M'Kenzie—Affairs at the Shahaptan—News of war—Dismay of M'Dougal—Determination to abandon Astoria—Departure of M'Kenzie for the interior—Adventure of the rapids—Visits to the ruffians of wish-ram—A perilous situation—Meeting with M'Tavish and his party—Arrival at the Shahaptan—Plundered caches—Determination of the wintering partners not to leave the country—Arrival of Clarke among the Nez-percés—The affair of the silver goblet—Hanging of an Indian—Arrival of the wintering partners at Astoria.

AFTER the departure of the different detachments, or *brigades*, as they are called by the fur traders, the Beaver prepared for her voyage along the coast, and her visit to the Russian establishment, at New Archangel, where she was to carry supplies. It had been determined in the council of partners at Astoria, that Mr. Hunt should embark in this vessel, for the purpose of acquainting himself with the coasting trade, and of making arrangements with the commander of the Russian post, and that he should be relanded in October, at Astoria, by the Beaver, on her way to the Sandwich islands and Canton.

The Beaver put to sea in the month of August. Her departure, and that of the various brigades, left the little fortress of Astoria but slightly garrisoned. This was soon perceived by some of the Indian tribes, and the consequence was, increased insolence of deportment, and a disposition to hostility. It was now the fishing season, when the tribes from the northern coast drew into the neighbourhood of the Columbia. These were warlike and perfidious in their dispositions; and noted for their attempts to surprise trading ships. Among them were numbers ef the Neweetees, the ferocious tribe that massacred the crew of the Tonquin.

Great precautions, therefore, were taken at the factory to guard against surprise, while these dangerous intruders were in the vicinity. Galleries were constructed inside of the pallisades; the bastions were heightened, and sentinels were posted day and night. Fortunately, the Chinooks and other tribes resident in the vicinity manifested the most pacific disposition. Old Comcomly, who held sway over them, was a shrewd calculator. He was aware of the advantages of having the whites as neighbours and allies, and of the consequence derived to himself and his people from acting as intermediate traders between them and the distant tribes. He had, therefore, by this time, become a firm friend of the Astorians, and formed a kind of barrier between them and the hostile intruders from the north.

The summer of 1812 passed away without any of the hostilities that had been apprehended; the Neweetees, and other dangerous visitors to the neighbourhood, finished their fishing and returned home, and the inmates of the factory once more felt secure from attack.

It now became necessary to guard against other evils. The season of scarcity arrived, which commences in October and lasts until the end of January.   To provide for the support of the garrison, the shallop was employed to forage about the shores of the river.   A number of the men, also, under the command of some of the clerks, were sent to quarter themselves on the banks of the Wollamut (the Multnomah, of Lewis and Clarke), a fine river which disembogues into the Columbia, about sixty miles above Astoria.   The country bordering on the river is finely diversified with prairies and hills, and forests of oak, ash, maple, and cedar.   It abounded at that time with elk and deer, and the streams were well stocked with beaver.   Here the party, after supplying their own wants, were enabled to pack up quantities of dried meat, and send it by canoes, to Astoria.

The month of October elapsed without the return of the Beaver.   November, December, January, passed away, and still nothing was seen or heard of her.   Gloomy apprehensions now began to be entertained : she might have been wrecked in the course of her coasting voyage, or surprised, like the Tonquin, by some of the treacherous tribes of the north.

No one indulged more in these apprehensions than M'Dougal, who had now the charge of the establishment. He no longer evinced the bustling confidence and buoyancy, which once characterized him.   Command seemed to have lost its charms for him ; or rather, he gave way to the most abject despondency, descrying the whole enterprise, magnifying every untoward circumstance, and foreboding nothing but evil.

While in this moody state, he was surprised, on the 16th of January, by the sudden appearance of M'Kenzie, wayworn and weatherbeaten by a long wintry journey from his post on the Shahaptan, and with a face the very frontispiece for a volume of misfortune.   M'Kenzie had been heartily disgusted and disappointed at his post.   It was in the midst of the Tushepaws, a powerful and warlike nation, divided into many tribes, under different chiefs, who possessed innumerable horses, but not having turned their attention to beaver trapping, had no furs to offer.   According to M'Kenzie, they were but a " rascally tribe ;" from which we may infer that they were prone to consult their own interests, more than comported with the interests of a greedy Indian trader.

Game being scarce, he was obliged to rely for the most part on horseflesh for subsistence, and the Indians discovering his necessities, adopted a policy usual in civilized trade, and raised the price of horses to an exorbitant rate, knowing that he and his men must eat or die. In this way, the goods he had brought to trade for beaver skins, were likely to be bartered for horseflesh, and all the proceeds devoured upon the spot.

He had despatched trappers in various directions, but the country around did not offer more beaver than his own station. In this emergency he began to think of abandoning his unprofitable post, sending his goods to the posts of Clarke and David Stuart, who could make a better use of them, as they were in a good beaver country, and returning with his party to Astoria, to seek some better destination. With this view he repaired to the post of Mr. Clarke, to hold a consultation. While the two partners were in conference in Mr. Clarke's wigwam, an unexpected visitor came bustling upon them.

This was Mr. John George M'Tavish, a partner of the North-west Company, who had charge of the rival trading posts established in that neighbourhood. Mr. M'Tavish was the delighted messenger of bad news. He had been to lake Winnipeg, where he received an express from Canada, containing the declaration of war, and President Madison's proclamation, which he handed with the most officious complaisance to Messrs. Clarke and M'Kenzie. He moreover told them, that he had received a fresh supply of goods from the north-west posts on the other side of the Rocky mountains, and was prepared for vigorous opposition to the establishments of the American company. He capped the climax of this obliging, but belligerent intelligence, by informing them that the armed ship, Isaac Todd, was to be at the mouth of the Columbia about the beginning of March, to get possession of the trade of the river, and that he was ordered to join her there at that time.

The receipt of this news determined M'Kenzie. He immediately returned to the Shahaptan, broke up his establishment, deposited his goods in *cache*, and hastened, with all his people, to Astoria.

The intelligence thus brought, completed the dismay of M'Dougal, and seemed to produce a complete confusion of mind. He held council of war with M'Kenzie, at which some of the clerks were present, but of course had no votes. They gave up all hope of maintaining their post at Astoria. The Beaver had probably been lost; they could receive no aid from the United States, as all the ports would be blockaded. From England nothing could be expected but hostility. It was determined, therefore, to abandon the establishment in the course of the following spring, and return across the Rocky mountains.

In pursuance of the resolution, they suspended all trade with the natives, except for provisions, having already more peltries than they could carry away, and having need of all the goods for the clothing and subsistence of their people during the remainder of their sojourn, and on their journey across the mountains. This intention of abandoning Astoria was, however, kept secret from the men, lest they should at once give up all labour, and become restless and insubordinate.

In the mean time, M'Kenzie set off for his post at the Shahaptan, to get his goods from the caches, and buy horses and provisions with them for the caravan, across the mountains. He was charged with despatches from M'Dougal to Messrs. Stuart and Clarke, apprizing them of the intended migration, that they might make timely preparations.

M'Kenzie was accompanied by two of the clerks, Mr. John Reed, the Irishman, and Mr. Alfred Seton of New York. They embarked in two canoes, manned by seventeen men, and ascended the river without any incident of importance, until they arrived in the eventful neighbourhood of the rapids. They made the portage of the narrows and the falls early in the afternoon, and having partaken of a scanty meal, had now a long evening on their hands.

On the opposite side of the river lay the village of Wish-ram, of freebooting renown. Here lived the savages who had robbed and maltreated Reed, when bearing his tin box of despatches. It was known that the rifle of which he was despoiled, was retained as a trophy at the village. M'Kenzie offered to cross the river, and demand the rifle, if any one would accompany him. It was a hair-brained project, for these villages were noted for the ruffian character of their inhabitants; yet two volunteers promptly stepped forward; Alfred Seton, the clerk, and Joe de la Pierre, the cook. The trio soon reached the opposite side of the river. On landing, they freshly primed their rifles and pistols. A path winding for about a hundred yards among rocks and crags, led to the village. No notice seemed to be taken of their approach. Not a solitary being, man, woman, or child greeted them.' The very dogs, those noisy pests of an Indian town, kept silence. On entering the village, a boy made his appearance, and pointed to a house of larger dimensions than the rest. They had to stoop to enter it; as soon as they had passed the thresh-hold, the narrow passage behind them was filled up by a sudden rush of Indians, who had before kept out of sight.

M'Kenzie and his companions found themselves in a rude chamber of about twenty-five feet long, and twenty wide. A bright fire was blazing at one end, near which sat the chief, about sixty years old. A large number of Indians, wrapped in buffalo robes, were squatted in rows, three deep, forming a semicircle round three sides of the room. A single glance around sufficed to show them the grim and dangerous assemblage into which they had in-truded, and that all retreat was cut off by the mass which blocked up the entrance.

The chief pointed to the vacant side of the room oppo-site to the door, and motioned for them to take their seats. They complied. A dead pause ensued. The grim warriors around sat like statues; each muffled in his robe, with his fierce eyes bent on the intruders. The latter felt they were in a perilous predicament.

" Keep your eyes on the chief, while I am addressing him," said M'Kenzie to his companions. " Should he give any sign to his band, shoot him, and make for the door."

M'Kenzie advanced, and offered the pipe of peace to the chief, but it was refused. He then made a regular speech, explaining the object of their visit, and proposing to give in exchange for the rifle, two blankets, an axe, some beads, and tobacco.

When he had done, the chief rose, began to address him in a low voice, but soon became loud and violent, and ended by working himself up into a furious passion. He upbraided the white men for their sordid conduct in passing and repassing through their neighbourhood, without giving them a blanket or any other article of goods, merely because they had no furs to barter in exchange; and he alluded with menaces of vengeance, to the death of the Indian killed by the whites in the skirmish at the falls.

Matters were verging to a crisis. It was evident the surrounding savages were only waiting a signal from the chief to spring upon their prey. M'Kenzie and his companions had gradually risen on their feet during the speech, and had brought their rifles to a horizontal position, the barrels resting in their left hands ; the muzzle of M'Kenzie's piece was within three feet of the speaker's heart. They cocked their rifles ; the click of the locks for a moment suffused the dark cheek of the savage, and there was a pause. They coolly, but promptly advanced to the door; the Indians fell back in awe, and suffered them to pass. The sun was just setting as they emerged from this dangerous den. They took the precaution to keep along the tops of the rocks as much as possible on their way back to the canoe, and reached their camp in safety, congratulating themselves on their escape, and feeling no desire to make a second visit to the grim warriors of Wish-ram.

M'Kenzie and his party resumed their journey the next morning. At some distance above the falls of the Columbia, they observed two bark canoes, filled with white men, coming down the river, to the full chaunt of a set of Canadian voyageurs. A parley ensued. It was a detachment of northwesters, under the command of Mr. John George

M'Tavish, bound, full of song and spirit, to the mouth of the Columbia, to await the arrival of the Isaac Todd.

M'Kenzie and M'Tavish came to a halt, and, landing, encamped together for the night. The voyageurs of either party hailed each other as brothers, and old comrades, and they mingled together as if united by one common interest, instead of belonging to rival companies, and trading under hostile flags.

In the morning they proceeded on their different ways, in style corresponding to their different fortunes : the one toiling painfully against the stream, the other sweeping down gaily with the current.

M'Kenzie arrived safely at his deserted post on the Shahaptan, but found, to his chagrin, that his caches had been discovered and rifled by the Indians. Here was a dilemma, for, on the stolen goods he had depended to purchase horses of the Indians. He sent out men in all directions to endeavour to discover the thieves, and despatched Mr. Reed to the posts of Messrs. Clarke and David Stuart, with the letters of Mr. M'Dougal.

The resolution announced in these letters, to break up and depart from Astoria, was condemned by both Clarke and Stuart. These two gentlemen had been very successful at their posts, and considered it rash and pusillanimous to abandon, on the first difficulty, an enterprise of such great cost and ample promise. They made no arrangements, therefore, for leaving the country, but acted with a view to the maintenance of their new and prosperous establishments.

The regular time approached, when the partners of the interior posts were to rendezvous at the mouth of the Wallah-Wallah, on their way to Astoria, with the peltries they had collected. Mr. Clarke accordingly packed all his furs on twenty-eight horses, and, leaving a clerk and four men to take charge of the post, departed on the 25th of May with the residue of his force.

On the 30th, he arrived at the confluence of the Pavion and Lewis rivers, where he had left his barge and canoes, in the guardianship of the old Pierced-nose chieftain. That dignitary had acquitted himself more faithfully of his charge than Mr. Clarke had expected, and the canoes were found in very tolerable order. Some repairs were necessary, and, while they were making, the party encamped close by the village. Having had repeated and vexatious proofs of the pilfering propensities of this tribe during his former visit, Mr. Clarke ordered that a wary eye should be kept upon them.

He was a tall, good-looking man, and somewhat given to pomp and circumstance, which made him an object of note in the eyes of the wondering savages. He was stately, too, in his appointments, and had a silver goblet or drinking cup, out of which he would drink with a magnificent air, and then lock it up in a large *garde vin*, which accompanied him in his travels, and stood in his tent. This goblet had originally been sent as a present from Mr. Astor to Mr. M'Kay, the partner who had unfortunately been blown up in the Tonquin. As it reached Astoria after the departure of that gentleman, it had remained in the possession of Mr. Clarke.

A silver goblet was too glittering a prize not to catch the eye of a Pierced-nose. It was like the shining tin case of John Reed. Such a wonder had never been seen in the land before. The Indians talked about it to one another. They marked the care with which it was deposited in the *garde vin*, like a relic in its shrine, and concluded that it must be a " great medicine." That night Mr. Clarke neglected to lock up his treasure; in the morning the sacred casket was open—the precious relic gone!

Clarke was now outrageous. All the past vexations that he had suffered from this pilfering community rose to mind, and he threatened, that, unless the goblet were promptly returned, he would hang the thief should he eventually discover him. The day passed away, however, without the restoration of the cup. At night, sentinels were secretly posted about the camp. With all their vigilance, a Pierced-nose contrived to get into the camp unperceived, and to load himself with booty; and it was only on his retreat that he was discovered and taken.

At daybreak, the culprit was brought to trial, and promptly convicted. He stood responsible for all the spoliations of the camp, the precious goblet among the number, and Mr. Clarke passed sentence of death upon him.

A gibbet was accordingly constructed of oars; the chief of the village and his people were assembled, and the culprit was produced, with his legs and arms pinioned. Clarke then made an harangue. He reminded the tribe of the benefits he had bestowed upon them during his former visit, and the many thefts and other misdeeds which he had overlooked. The prisoner, especially, had always been peculiarly well treated by the white men, but had repeatedly been guilty of pilfering. He was to be punished for his own misdeeds, and as a warning to his tribe.

The Indians now gathered round Mr. Clarke, and interceded for the culprit. They were willing he should be punished severely, but implored that his life might be spared. The companions, too, of Mr. Clarke considered the sentence too severe, and advised him to mitigate it; but he was inexorable. He was not naturally a stern or cruel man; but from his boyhood he had lived in the Indian country among Indian traders, and held the life of a savage extremely cheap. He was, moreover, a firm believer in the doctrine of intimidation.

Farnham, a clerk, a tall " Green-mountain boy" from Vermont, who had been robbed of a pistol, acted as executioner. The signal was given, and the poor Pierced-nose, resisting, struggling, and screaming, in the most frightful manner, was launched into eternity. The Indians stood round gazing in silence and mute awe, but made no attempt to oppose the execution, nor testified any emotion when it was over. They locked up their feelings within their bosoms until an opportunity should arrive to gratify them with a bloody act of vengeance.

To say nothing of the needless severity of this act, its impolicy was glaringly obvious. Mr. M'Lean and three men were to return to the post with the horses, their loads having been transferred to the canoes. They would have to pass through a tract of country infested by this tribe, who were all horsemen and hard riders, and might pursue them to take vengeance for the death of their comrade. M'Lean, however, was a resolute fellow, and made light of all dangers. He and his three men were present at the execution, and set off as soon as life was extinct in the victim; but, to use the words of one of their comrades, " they did not let the grass grow under the heels of their horses, as they clattered out of the Pierced-nose country," and were glad to find themselves in safety at the post.

Mr. Clarke and his party embarked about the same time in their canoes, and early on the following day reached the mouth of the Wallah-Wallah, where they found Messrs. Stuart and M'Kenzie awaiting them; the latter having recovered part of the goods stolen from his cache. Clarke informed them of the signal punishment he had inflicted on the Pierced-nose, evidently expecting to excite their admiration by such a hardy act of justice, performed in the very midst of the Indian country, but was mortified at finding it strongly censured as inhuman, unnecessary, and likely to provoke hostilities.

The parties thus united, formed a squadron of two boats and six canoes, with which they performed their voyage in safety down the river, and arrived at Astoria on the 12th of June, bringing with them a valuable stock of peltries.

About ten days previously, the brigade which had been quartered on the banks of the Wollamut, had arrived with numerous packs of beaver, the result of a few months' sojourn on that river. These were the first fruits of the enterprise, gathered by men as yet mere strangers in the land; but they were such as to give substantial grounds for sanguine anticipations of profit, when the country should be more completely explored, and the trade established.

CHAPTER XII.

THE partners found Mr. M'Dougal in all the bustle of preparation ; having about nine days previously announced at the factory his intention of breaking up the establishment, and fixed upon the 1st of July for the time of departure. Messrs. Stuart and Clarke felt highly displeased at his taking so precipitate a step, without waiting for their concurrence, when he must have known that their arrival could not be far distant.

Indeed the whole conduct of Mr. M'Dougal was such as to awaken strong doubts of his loyal devotion to the cause. His old sympathies with the North-west Company seemed to have revived. He had received M'Tavish and his party with uncalled-for hospitality, as though they were friends and allies, instead of being a party of observation, come to reconnoitre the state of affairs at Astoria, and to await the arrival of a hostile ship. Had they been left to themselves, they would have been starved off for want of provisions, or driven away by the Chinooks, who only wanted a signal from the factory to treat them as intruders and enemies. M'Dougal, on the contrary, had supplied them from the stores of the garrison, and had gained them the favour of the Indians, by treating them as friends.

Having set his mind fixedly on the project of breaking up the establishment at Astoria, in the current year, M'Dougal was sorely disappointed at finding that Messrs. Stuart and Clarke had omitted to comply with his request to purchase horses and provisions for the caravan, across the mountains. It was now too late to make the necessary preparations in time for traversing the mountains, before winter, and the project had to be postponed.

In the mean time, the non-arrival of the annual ship, and the apprehensions entertained of the loss of the Beaver and of Mr. Hunt, had their effect upon the minds of Messrs. Stuart and Clarke. They began to listen to the desponding representations of M'Dougal, seconded by M'Kenzie, who inveighed against their situation as desperate and forlorn; left to shift for themselves, or perish upon a barbarous coast; neglected by those who sent them there, and threatened with dangers of every kind. In this way they were brought to consent to the plan of abandoning the country in the ensuing year.

About this time M'Tavish applied at the factory to purchase a small supply of goods wherewith to trade his way back to his post on the upper waters of the Columbia, having waited in vain for the arrival of the Isaac Todd. His request brought on a consultation among the partners. M'Dougal urged that it should be complied with. He furthermore proposed, that they should give up to M'Tavish, for a proper consideration, the post on the Spokan, and all its dependencies, as they had not sufficient goods on hand to supply that post themselves, and to keep up a competition with the North-west Company, in the trade with the neighbouring Indians. This last representation has since been proved incorrect. By inventories, it appears that their stock in hand for the supply of the interior posts, was superior to that of the North-west Company; so that they had nothing to fear from competition.

Through the influence of Messrs. M'Dougal and M'Kenzie, this proposition was adopted, and was promptly accepted by M'Tavish. The merchandise sold to him, amounted to eight hundred and fifty-eight dollars, to be paid for, in the following spring, in horses, or in any other manner most acceptable to the partners at that period.

This agreement being concluded, the partners formed their plans for the year that they would yet have to pass in the country. Their objects were, chiefly, present subsistence, and the purchase of horses for the contemplated journey, though they were likewise to collect as much peltries as their diminished means would command. Accordingly, it was arranged, that David Stuart should return to his former post on the Oakinagan, and Mr. Clarke should make his sojourn among the Flatheads. John Reed, the sturdy Hibernian, was to undertake the Snake river country, accompanied by Pierre Dorion and Pierre Delaunay, as hunters, and Francis Landry, Jeane Baptiste Turcotte, André la Chapelle, and Gilles le Clerc, Canadian voyageurs.

Astoria, however, was the post about which they felt the greatest solicitude, and on which they all more or less depended. The maintenance of this in safety throughout the coming year, was, therefore, their grand consideration. Mr. M'Dougal was to continue in command of it, with a party of forty men. They would have to depend chiefly upon the neighbouring savages for their subsistence. These, at present, were friendly, but it was to be feared that, when they should discover the exigencies of the post, and its real weakness, they might proceed to hostilities; or, at any rate, might cease to furnish their usual supplies. It was important, therefore, to render the place as independent as possible, of the surrounding tribes for its support; and it was accordingly resolved that M'Kenzie, with four hunters, and eight common men, should winter in the abundant country of the Wollamut, from whence they might be enabled to furnish a constant supply of provisions to Astoria.

As there was too great a proportion of clerks for the number of privates in the service, the engagements of three of them, Ross Cox, Ross, and M'Lellan, were surrendered to them, and they immediately enrolled themselves in the service of the North-west Company; glad, no doubt, to escape from what they considered a sinking ship.

Having made all these arrangements, the four partners, on the 1st of July, signed a formal manifesto, stating the alarming state of their affairs, from the non-arrival of the annual ship, and the absence and apprehended loss of the Beaver, their want of goods, their despair of receiving any further supply, their ignorance of the coast, and their disappointment as to the interior trade, which they pronounced unequal to the expenses incurred, and incompetent to stand against the powerful opposition of the North-west Company. And as by the 16th article of the company's agreement, they were authorized to abandon this undertaking, and dissolve the concern, if, before the period of five years, it should be found unprofitable; they now formally announced their intention to do so on the 1st day of June, of the ensuing year, unless in the interim they should receive the necessary support and supplies from Mr. Astor, or the stockholders, with orders to continue.

This instrument, accompanied by private letters of similar import, was delivered to Mr. M'Tavish, who departed on the 5th of July. He engaged to forward the despatches to Mr. Astor, by the usual winter express sent over-land by the North-west Company.

The manifesto was signed with great reluctance by Messrs. Clarke and D. Stuart, whose experience by no means justified the discouraging account given in it, of the internal trade, and who considered the main difficulties of exploring an unknown and savage country, and of ascertaining the best trading and trapping grounds, in a great measure overcome. They were overruled, however, by the urgent instances of M'Dougal and M'Kenzie, who having resolved upon abandoning the enterprise, were desirous of making as strong a case as possible to excuse their conduct to Mr. Astor and to the world.

CHAPTER XIII.

Anxieties of Mr. Astor—Memorial of the North-west company—Tidings of a British naval expedition against Astoria—Mr. Astor applies to government for protection —The frigate Adams ordered to be fitted out—Bright news from Astoria—Sunshine suddenly overclouded.

WHILE difficulties and disasters had been gathering about the infant settlement of Astoria, the mind of its projector at New York, was a prey to great anxiety. The ship Lark, despatched by him with supplies for the establishment, sailed on the 6th of March, 1813. Within a fortnight afterwards he received intelligence which justified all his apprehensions of hostility on the part of the British.

The North-west Company had made a second memorial to that government, representing Astoria as an American establishment, stating the vast scope of its contemplated operations, magnifying the strength of its fortifications, and expressing their fears that, unless crushed in the bud, it would effect the downfall of their trade.

Influenced by these representations, the British government ordered the frigate Phœbe to be detached as a convoy for the armed ship, Isaac Todd, which was ready to sail with men and munitions for forming a new establishment. They were to proceed together to the mouth of the Columbia, capture or destroy whatever American fortress they should find there, and plant the British flag on its ruins.

Informed of these movements, Mr. Astor lost no time in addressing a second letter to the secretary of state, communicating this intelligence, and requesting that it might be laid before the president; as no notice, however, had been taken of his previous letter, he contented himself with this simple communication, and made no further application for aid.

Awakened now to the danger that menaced the establishment at Astoria, and aware of the importance of protecting this foothold of American commerce and empire on the shores of the Pacific, the government determined to send the frigate Adams, Captain Crane, upon this service. On hearing of this determination, Mr. Astor immediately proceeded to fit out a ship called the Enterprise, to sail in company with the Adams, freighted with additional supplies and reinforcements for Astoria.

About the middle of June, while in the midst of these preparations, Mr. Astor received a letter from Mr. R. Stuart, dated St. Louis, May 1st, confirming the intelligence, already received through the public newspapers, of his safe return, and of the arrival of Mr. Hunt and his party at Astoria, and giving the most flattering accounts of the prosperity of the enterprise.

So deep had been the anxiety of Mr. Astor, for the success of this great object of his ambition, that this gleam of good news was almost overpowering. " I felt ready," said he, " to fall upon my knees in a transport of gratitude."

At the same time he heard that the Beaver had made good her voyage from New York to Columbia. This was additional ground of hope for the welfare of the little colony. The post being thus relieved and strengthened with an American at its head, and a ship of war about to sail for its protection, the prospect for the future seemed full of encouragement, and Mr. Astor proceeded with fresh vigour to fit out his merchant ship.

Unfortunately for Astoria, this bright gleam of sunshine was soon overclouded. Just as the Adams had received her complement of men, and the two vessels were ready for sea, news came from Commodore Chauncy, commanding on lake Ontario, that a reinforcement of seamen was wanted in that quarter. The demand was urgent, the crew of the Adams was immediately transferred to that service, and the ship was laid up.

This was a most ill-timed and discouraging blow, but Mr. Astor would not yet allow himself to pause in his undertaking. He determined to send the Enterprise to sea alone, and let her take the chance of making her unprotected way across the ocean. Just at this time, however, a British force made its appearance off the Hook, and the port of New York was effectually blockaded. To send a ship to sea under these circumstances, would be to expose her to almost certain capture. The Enterprise was, therefore, unloaded and dismantled, and Mr. Astor was obliged to content himself with the hope that the Lark might reach Astoria in safety, and that aided by her supplies, and by the good management of Mr. Hunt and his associates, the little colony might be able to maintain itself until the return of peace.

CHAPTER XIV.

Affairs of state at Astoria—M'Dougal proposes for the hand of an Indian princess—Matrimonial embassy to Comcomly—Matrimonial notions among the Chinooks—Settlements and pin money—The bringing home of the bride—A managing father-in-law—Arrival of Mr. Hunt at Astoria.

WE have hitherto had so much to relate of a gloomy and disastrous nature, that it is with a feeling of momentary relief we turn to something of a more pleasing complexion, and record the first, and indeed only nuptials in high life that took place in the infant settlement of Astoria.

M'Dougal, who appears to have been a man of a thousand projects, and of great, though somewhat irregular ambition, suddenly conceived the idea of seeking the hand of one of the native princesses, a daughter of the one-eyed potentate Comcomly, who held sway over the fishing tribe of the Chinooks, and had long supplied the factory with smelts and sturgeons.

Some accounts give rather a romantic origin to this affair, tracing it to the stormy night, when M'Dougal, in the course of an exploring expedition, was driven by stress of weather, to seek shelter in the royal abode of Comcomly. Then and there he was first struck with the charms of this piscatory princess, as she exerted herself to entertain her father's guest.

The " journal of Astoria," however, which was kept under his own eye, records this union as a high state alliance, and great stroke of policy. The factory had to depend, in a great measure, on the Chinooks for provisions. They were at present friendly, but it was to be feared they would prove otherwise, should they discover the weakness and the exigencies of the post, and the intention to leave the country. This alliance, therefore, would infallibly rivet Comcomly to the interests of the Astorians, and with him the powerful tribe of the Chinooks. Be this as it may, and it is hard to fathom the real policy of governors and princes, M'Dougal despatched two of the clerks as ambassadors extraordinary, to wait upon the one-eyed chieftain, and make overtures for the hand of his daughter.

The Chinooks, though not a very refined nation, have notions of matrimonial arrangements that would not disgrace the most refined sticklers for settlements and pin money. The suitor repairs not to the bower of his mistress, but to her father's lodge, and throws down a present at his feet. His wishes are then disclosed by some discreet friend employed by him for the purpose. If the suitor and his present find favour in the eyes of the father, he breaks the matter to his daughter, and inquires into the state of her inclinations. Should her answer be favourable, the suit is accepted, and the lover has to make further presents to the father, of horses, canoes, and other valuables, according to the beauty and merits of the bride; looking forward to a return in kind whenever they shall go to housekeeping.

We have more than once had occasion to speak of the shrewdness of Comcomly; but never was it exerted more adroitly than on this occasion. He was a great friend of M'Dougal, and pleased with the idea of having so distinguished a son-in-law; but so favourable an opportunity of benefiting his own fortune, was not likely to occur a second time, and he determined to make the most of it. Accordingly, the negotiation was protracted with true diplomatic skill. Conference after conference was held with the two ambassadors: Comcomly was extravagant in his terms; rating the charms of his daughter at the highest price, and indeed she is represented as having one of the flattest and most aristocratical heads in the tribe. At length the preliminaries were all happily adjusted. On the 20th of July, early in the afternoon, a squadron of canoes crossed from the village of the Chinooks, bearing the royal family of Comcomly, and all his court.

That worthy sachem landed in princely state, arrayed in a bright blue blanket and red breech clout, with an extra quantity of paint and feathers, attended by a train of half-naked warriors and nobles. A horse was in waiting to receive the princess, who was mounted behind one of the clerks, and thus conveyed, coy but compliant, to the fortress. Here she was received with devout, though decent joy, by her expecting bridegroom.

Her bridal adornments, it is true, at first caused some little dismay, having painted and anointed herself for the occasion according to the Chinook toilet; by dint, however, of copious ablutions, she was freed from all adventitious tint and fragrance, and entered into the nuptial state the cleanest princess that had ever been known, of the somewhat unctuous tribe of the Chinooks.

From that time forward, Comcomly was a daily visitor at the fort, and was admitted into the most intimate councils of his son-in-law. He took an interest in every thing that was going forward, but was particularly frequent in his visits to the blacksmith's shop; tasking the labours of the artificer in iron for every kind of weapon and implement suited to the savage state, insomuch that the necessary business of the factory was often postponed to attend to his requisitions.

The honeymoon had scarce passed away, and M'Dougal was seated with his bride in the fortress of Astoria, when about noon of the 20th of August, Gassacop, the son of Comcomly, hurried into his presence with great agitation, and announced a ship at the mouth of the river. The news produced a vast sensation. Was it a ship of peace or war? Was it American or British? Was it the Beaver or the Isaac Todd? M'Dougal hurried to the water side, threw himself into a boat, and ordered the hands to pull with all speed for the mouth of the harbour. Those in the fort remained watching the entrance of the river, anxious to know whether they were to prepare for greeting a friend or fighting an enemy. At length the ship was descried crossing the bar, and bending her course towards Astoria. Every gaze was fixed upon her in silent scrutiny, until the American flag was recognised. A general shout was the first expression of joy, and next a salutation was thundered from the cannon of the fort.

The vessel came to anchor on the opposite side of the river, and returned the salute. The boat of Mr. M'Dougal went on board, and was seen returning late in the afternoon. The Astorians watched her with straining eyes, to discover who were on board, but the sun went down, and the evening closed in before she was sufficiently near. At length she reached the land and Mr. Hunt stepped on shore. He was hailed as one risen from the dead, and his return was a signal for merriment almost equal to that which prevailed at the nuptials of M'Dougal.

We must now explain the cause of this gentleman's long absence, which had given rise to such gloomy and dispiriting surmises.

CHAPTER XV.

IT will be recollected, that the destination of the Beaver, when she sailed from Astoria on the 4th of August in 1812, was to proceed northwardly along the coast to Sheetka, or New Archangel, there to dispose of that part of her cargo intended for the supply of the Russian establishment at that place, and then to return to Astoria, where it was expected she would arrive in October.

New Archangel is situated in Norfolk Sound, lat. 57° 2 N., long. 135° 50 W. It was the head quarters of the different colonies of the Russian Fur Company, and the common rendezvous of the American vessels trading along the coast.

The Beaver met with nothing worthy of particular mention in her voyage, and arrived at New Archangel on the 19th of August. The place at that time was the residence of Count Baranhoff, the governor of the different colonies : a rough, rugged, hospitable, hard-drinking, old Russian ; somewhat of a soldier, somewhat of a trader ; above all, a boon companion of the old roystering school, with a strong cross of the bear.

Mr. Hunt found this hyperborean veteran ensconced in a fort which crested the whole of a high rocky promontory. It mounted one hundred guns, large and small, and was impregnable to Indian attack, unaided by artillery. Here the old governor lorded it over sixty Russians, who formed the corps of the trading establishment, beside an indefinite number of Indian hunters of the Kodiak tribe, who were continually coming and going, or lounging and loitering about the fort like so many hounds round a sportsman's hunting quarters. Though a loose liver among his guests, the governor was a strict disciplinarian among his men ; keeping them in perfect subjection, and having seven on guard night and day.

Besides those immediate serfs and dependants just mentioned, the old Russian potentate exerted a considerable sway over a numerous and irregular class of maritime traders, who looked to him for aid and munitions, and through whom he may be said to have, in some degree, extended his power along the whole north-west coast. These were American captains of vessels engaged in a particular department of trade. One of these captains would come, in a manner, empty handed to New Archangel. Here his ship would be furnished with about fifty canoes and a hundred Kodiak hunters, and fitted out with provisions, and every thing necessary for hunting the sea otter on the coast of California, where the Russians have another establishment. The ship would ply along the Californian coast from place to place, dropping parties of otter hunters in their canoes, furnishing them only with water, and leaving them to depend upon their own dexterity for a maintenance. When a sufficient cargo was collected, she would gather up her canoes and hunters, and return with them to Archangel; where the captain would render in the returns of his voyage, and receive one half of the skins for his share.

Over these coasting captains, as we have hinted, the veteran governor exerted some sort of sway, but it was of a peculiar and characteristic kind; it was the tyranny of the table. They were obliged to join him in his " prosnics" or carousals, and to drink " potations pottle deep." His carousals, too, were not of the most quiet kind, nor were his potations as mild as nectar. " He is continually," said Mr. Hunt, " giving entertainments by way of parade, and if you do not drink raw rum, and boiling punch as strong as sulphur, he will insult you as soon as he gets drunk, which is very shortly after sitting down to table."

As to any " temperance captain" who stood fast to his faith, and refused to give up his sobriety, he might go elsewhere for a market, for he stood no chance with the governor. Rarely, however, did any cold water caitiff of the kind darken the door of old Baranhoff; the coasting captains knew too well his humour and their own interests; they joined in his revels, they drank, and sang, and whooped ,and hiccupped, until they all got "half seas over," and then affairs went on swimmingly.

An awful warning to all "flinchers" occurred shortly before Mr. Hunt's arrival. A young naval officer had recently been sent out by the emperor to take command of one of the company's vessels. The governor, as usual, had him at his "prosnics," and plied him with fiery potations. The young man stood on the defensive until the old count's ire was completely kindled; he carried his point, and made the greenhorn tipsy, willy nilly. In proportion as they grew fuddled they grew noisy, they quarrelled in their cups; the youngster paid old Baranhoff in his own coin by rating him soundly; in reward for which, when sober, he was taken the rounds of four pickets, and received seventy-nine lashes, taled out with Russian punctuality of punishment.

Such was the old grizzled bear with whom Mr. Hunt had to do his business. How he managed to cope with his humour; whether he pledged him in raw rum and blazing punch, and "clinked the can" with him as they made their bargains, does not appear upon record; we must infer, however, from his general observations on the absolute sway of this hard-drinking potentate, that he had to conform to the customs of his court, and that their business transactions presented a maudlin mixture of punch and peltry.

The greatest annoyance to Mr. Hunt, however, was the delay to which he was subjected, in disposing of the cargo of the ship, and getting the requisite returns. With all the governor's devotions to the bottle, he never obfuscated his faculties sufficiently to lose sight of his interest, and is represented by Mr. Hunt as keen, not to say crafty, at a bargain, as the most arrant water-drinker. A long time was expended negotiating with him, and by the time the bargain was concluded, the month of October had arrived. To add to the delay he was to be paid for his cargo in seal skins. Now it so happened that there was none of this kind of peltry at the fort of old Baranhoff. It was necessary, therefore, for Mr. Hunt to proceed to a seal catching establishment, which the Russian company had at the island of St. Paul, in the sea of Kamschatka. He accordingly set sail on the 4th of October, after having spent forty-five days at New Archangel, boosing and bargaining with its roystering commander, and right glad was he to escape from the clutches of this " old man of the sea."

The Beaver arrived at St. Paul's on the 31st of October ; by which time, according to agreement, he ought to have been back at Astoria. The island of St. Paul's is in latitude 57° N., longitude 170° or 171 W. Its shores, in certain places, and at certain seasons, are covered with seals, while others are playing about in the water. Of these, the Russians take only the small ones, from seven to ten months old, and carefully select the males, giving the females their freedom, that the breed may not be diminished. The islanders, however, kill the large ones for provisions, and for skins wherewith to cover their canoes. They drive them from the shore over the rocks, until within a short distance of their habitations, where they kill them. By this means, they save themselves the trouble of carrying the skins, and have the flesh at hand. This is thrown in heaps, and when the season for skinning is over, they take out the entrails, and make one heap of the blubber. This, with drift wood, serves for fuel, for the island is entirely destitute of trees. They make another heap of the flesh, which with the eggs of sea-fowls, preserved in oil, an occasional sea lion, a few ducks in winter, and some wild roots, composes their food.

Mr. Hunt found seven Russians at the island, and one hundred hunters, natives of Oonalaska, with their families. They lived in cabins that looked like canoes ; being for the most part formed of the jaw bone of a whale, put up as rafters, across which were laid pieces of drift wood covered over with long grass, the skins of large sea animals, and earth ; so as to be quite comfortable, in spite of the rigours of the climate ; though we are told they had as ancient and fish-like an odour, " as had the quarters of Jonah, when lodged within the whale."

In one of those odoriferous mansions, Mr. Hunt occasionally took up his abode, that he might be at hand to hasten the loading of the ship. The operation, however, was somewhat slow, for it was necessary to overhaul and inspect every pack, to prevent imposition, and the peltries had then been to be conveyed in large boats, made of skins, to the ship, which was some little distance from the shore, standing off and on.

One night, while Mr. Hunt was on shore, with some others of the crew, there rose a terrible gale. When the day broke, the ship was not to be seen. He watched for her with anxious eyes until night, but in vain. Day after day of boisterous storms, and howling wintry weather, were passed in watchfulness and solitude. Nothing was to be seen but a dark and angry sea, and a scowling northern sky; and at night he retired within the jaws of the whale, and nestled disconsolately among seal skins.

At length, on the 13th of November, the Beaver made her appearance; much the worse for the stormy conflicts she had sustained in those hyperborean seas. She had been obliged to carry a press of sail in heavy gales, to be able to hold her ground, and had consequently sustained great damage in her canvass and rigging.

Mr. Hunt lost no time in hurrying the residue of the cargo on board of her; then bidding adieu to his seal fishing friends, and his whale-bone habitation, he put forth once more to sea.

He was now for making the best of his way to Astoria, and fortunate would it have been for the interests of that place, and the interests of Mr. Astor, had he done so; but unluckily, a perplexing question rose in his mind. The sails and rigging of the Beaver had been much rent and shattered in the late storm; would she be able to stand the hard gales to be expected in making the Columbia river at this season? Was it prudent, also, at this boisterous time of the year, to risk the valuable cargo which she now had on board, by crossing and recrossing the dangerous bar of that river? These doubts were probably suggested or enforced by Captain Sowle, who, it has already been seen, was an over-cautious, or rather a timid seaman, and they may have had some weight with Mr. Hunt? but there were other considerations, which more strongly swayed his mind. The lateness of the season, and the unforeseen delays the ship had encountered at New Archangel, and by being obliged to proceed to St. Paul's, had put her so much back in her calculated time, that there was a risk of her arriving so late at Canton, as to come to a bad market, both for the sale of her peltries, and the purchase of a return cargo. He considered it to be the interest of the company, therefore, that, he should proceed at once to the Sandwich Islands; there wait the arrival of the annual vessel from New York, take passage in her to Astoria, and suffer the Beaver to continue on to Canton.

On the other hand, he was urged to the other course by his engagements; by the plan of the voyage marked out for the Beaver, by Mr. Astor; by his inclination, and the possibility that the establishment might need his presence, and by the recollection that there must already be a large amount of peltries collected at Astoria, and waiting for the return of the Beaver, to convey them to market.

These conflicting questions perplexed and agitated his mind, and gave rise to much anxious reflection, for he was a conscientious man, that seems ever to have aimed at a faithful discharge of his duties, and to have had the interests of his employers earnestly at heart. His decision in the present instance was injudicious, and proved unfortunate. It was, to bear away for the Sandwich islands. He persuaded himself that it was matter of necessity, and that the distressed condition of the ship left him no other alternative; but we rather suspect he was so persuaded by the representations of the timid captain. They accordingly stood for the Sandwich islands, arrived at Woahoo, where the ship underwent the necessary repairs, and again put to sea on the 1st of January, 1813; leaving Mr. Hunt on the island.

We will follow the Beaver to Canton, as her fortunes, in some measure, exemplify the evil of commanders of ships acting contrary to orders; and as they form a part of the tissue of cross purposes that marred the great commercial enterprise, we have undertaken to record.

The Beaver arrived safe at Canton, where Captain Sowle found the letter of Mr. Astor, giving him information of the war, and directing him to convey the intelligence to Astoria. He wrote a reply, dictated either by timidity or obstinacy, in which he declined complying with the orders of Mr. Astor, but said he would wait for the return of peace, and then come home. The other proceedings of Captain Sowle were equally wrong-headed and unlucky. He was offered one hundred and fifty thousand dollars for the fur he had taken on board at St. Paul's. The goods for which it had been procured, cost but twenty-five thousand dollars in New York. Had he accepted this offer, and re-invested the amount in nankeens, which, at that time, in consequence of the interruption to commerce by the war, were at two-thirds of their usual price, the whole would have brought three hundred thousand dollars in New York. It is true, the war would have rendered it unsafe to attempt the homeward voyage, but he might have put the goods in store at Canton, until after the peace, and have sailed without risk of capture to Astoria; bringing to the partners at that place tidings of the great profits realized on the outward cargo, and the still greater to be expected from the returns. The news of such a brilliant commencement to their undertaking, would have counterbalanced the gloomy tidings of the war; it would have infused new spirit into them all, and given them courage and constancy to persevere in the enterprise. Captain Sowle, however, refused the offer of one hundred and fifty thousand dollars, and stood wavering and chaffering for higher terms. The furs began to fall in value; this only increased his irresolution; they sunk so much that he feared to sell at all; he borrowed money on Mr. Astor's account at eighteen per cent., and laid up his ship to await the return of peace.

In the meanwhile, Mr. Hunt soon saw reason to repent the resolution he had adopted in altering the destination of his ship. His stay at the Sandwich islands was prolonged far beyond all expectation. He looked in vain for the annual ship in the spring. Month after month passed by, and still she did not make her appearance. He, too, proved the danger of departing from orders.

Had he returned from St. Paul's to Astoria, all the anxiety and despondency about his fate, and about the whole course of the undertaking, would have been obviated. The Beaver would have received the furs collected at the factory, and taken them to Canton, and great gains, instead of great losses, would have been the result. The greatest blunder, however, was that committed by Captain Sowle.

At length, about the 20th of June, the ship Albatross, Captain Smith, arrived from China, and brought the first tidings of the war to the Sandwich islands. Mr. Hunt was no longer in doubt and perplexity as to the reason of the non-appearance of the annual ship. His first thoughts were for the welfare of Astoria, and concluding that the inhabitants would probably be in want of provisions, he chartered the Albatross for two thousand dollars, to land him, with some supplies, at the mouth of the Columbia, where he arrived, as we have seen, on the 20th of August, after a year's sea-faring that might have furnished a chapter in the wanderings of Sinbad.

CHAPTER XVI.

Arrangements among the partners—Mr. Hunt sails in the Albatross—Arrives at the Marquesas—News of the frigate Phœbe—Mr. Hunt proceeds to the Sandwich islands—Voyage of the Lark—Her shipwreck—Transactions with the natives of the Sandwich islands—Conduct of Tamaahmaah.

Mr. Hunt was overwhelmed with surprise when he learnt the resolution taken by the partners to abandon Astoria. He soon found, however, that matters had gone too far, and the minds of his colleagues had become too firmly bent upon the measure, to render any opposition of avail. He was beset, too, with the same disparaging accounts of the interior trade, and of the whole concerns and prospects of the company that had been rendered to Mr. Astor. His own experience had been full of perplexities and discouragements. He had a conscientious anxiety for the interests of Mr. Astor, and, not comprehending the extended views of that gentleman, and his habit of operating with great amounts, he had from the first been daunted by the enormous expenses required, and had become disheartened by the subsequent losses sustained, which appeared to him to be ruinous in their magnitude. By degrees, therefore, he was brought to acquiesce in the step taken by his colleagues, as perhaps advisable in the exigencies of the case; his only care was to wind up the business with as little further loss as possible to Mr. Astor.

A large stock of valuable furs was collected at the factory, which it was necessary to get to a market. There were twenty-five Sandwich islanders, also in the employ of the company, whom they were bound by express agreement to restore to their native country. For these purposes a ship was necessary.

The Albatross was bound to the Marquesas, and thence to the Sandwich islands. It was resolved that Mr. Hunt should sail in her in quest of a vessel, and should return, if possible, by the 1st of January, bringing with him a supply of provisions. Should anything occur, however, to prevent his return, an arrangement was to be proposed to Mr. M'Tavish, to transfer such of the men as were so disposed, from the service of the American Fur Company into that of the North-west, the latter becoming responsible for the wages due to them, on receiving an equivalent in goods from the storehouse of the factory. As a means of facilitating the dispatch of business, Mr. M'Dougal proposed, that in case Mr. Hunt should not return, the whole arrangement with Mr. M'Tavish should be left solely to him. This was assented to; the contingency being considered possible, but not probable.

It is proper to note, that, on the first announcement by Mr. M'Dougal of his intention to break up the establishment, three of the clerks, British subjects, had, with his consent, passed into the service of the North-west Company, and departed with Mr. M'Tavish for his post in the interior.

Having arranged all these matters during a sojourn of six days at Astoria, Mr. Hunt set sail in the Albatross, on the 26th of August, and arrived, without accident, at the Marquesas. He had not been there long, when Porter arrived in the frigate Essex, bringing in a number of stout London whalers as prizes, having made a sweeping cruise in the Pacific. From Commodore Porter he received the alarming intelligence that the British frigate Phœbe, with a storeship, mounted with battering pieces, calculated to attack forts, had arrived at Rio Janeiro, where she had been joined by the sloops of war Cherub and Racoon, and that they had all sailed in company on the 6th of July for the Pacific, bound, as it was supposed, to Columbia river.

Here, then, was the death-warrant of unfortunate Astoria! The anxious mind of Mr. Hunt was in greater perplexity than ever. He had been eager to extricate the property of Mr. Astor from a failing concern with as little loss as possible; there was now danger that the whole would be swallowed up. How was it to be snatched from the gulf? It was impossible to charter a ship for the purpose, now that a British squadron was on its way to the river. He applied to purchase one of the whale ships brought in by Commodore Porter. The commodore demanded twenty-five thousand dollars for her. The price appeared exorbitant, and no bargain could be made. Mr. Hunt then urged the commodore to fit out one of his prizes, and send her to Astoria, to bring off the property and part of the people, but he declined, "from want of authority." He assured Mr. Hunt, however, that he would endeavour to fall in with the enemy, or, should he hear of their having certainly gone to the Columbia, he would either follow or anticipate them, should his circumstances warrant such a step.

In this tantalizing state of suspense, Mr. Hunt was detained at the Marquesas until November 23rd, when he proceeded in the Albatross to the Sandwich islands. He still cherished a faint hope that, notwithstanding the war, and all other discouraging circumstances, the annual ship might have been sent by Mr. Astor, and might have touched at the islands, and proceeded to the Columbia. He knew the pride and interest taken by that gentleman in his great enterprise, and that he would not be deterred by dangers and difficulties from prosecuting it : much less would he leave the infant establishment without succour and support in the time of trouble. In this, we have seen, he did but justice to Mr. Astor; and we must now turn to notice the cause of the non-arrival of the vessel which he had despatched with reinforcements and supplies. Her voyage forms another chapter of accidents in this eventful story.

The Lark sailed from New York on the 6th of March, 1813, and proceeded prosperously on her voyage, until within a few degrees of the Sandwich islands. Here a gale sprang up that soon blew with tremendous violence. The Lark was a stanch and noble ship, and for a time buffeted bravely with the storm. Unluckily, however, she " broached to," and was struck by a heavy sea that hove her on her beam ends. The helm, too, was knocked to leeward, all command of the vessel was lost, and another mountain wave completely overset her. Orders were given to cut away the masts. In the hurry and confusion, the boats also were unfortunately cut adrift. The wreck then righted, but was a mere hulk, full of water, with a heavy sea washing over it, and all the hatches off. On mustering the crew, one man was missing, who was discovered below in the forecastle, drowned.

In cutting away the masts, it had been utterly impossible to observe the necessary precaution of commencing with the lee rigging, that being, from the position of the ship, completely under water. The masts and spars, therefore, being linked to the wreck, by the shrouds and rigging, remained alongside for four days. During all this time, the ship lay rolling in the trough of the sea, the heavy surges breaking over her, and the spars heaving and banging to and fro, bruising the half-drowned sailors that clung to the bowsprit and the stumps of the masts. The sufferings of these poor fellows were intolerable. They stood to their waists in water, in imminent peril of being washed off by every surge. In this position they dared not sleep, lest they should let go their hold and be swept away. The only dry place on the wreck was the bowsprit. Here they took turns to be tied on, for half an hour at a time, and in this way gained short snatches of sleep.

On the 14th, the first mate died at his post, and was swept off by the surges. On the 17th, two seamen, faint and exhausted, were washed overboard. The next wave threw their bodies back upon the deck, where they remained, swashing backward and forward, ghastly objects to the almost perishing survivors. Mr. Ogden, the supercargo, who was at the bowsprit, called to the men nearest to the bodies, to fasten them to the wreck ; as a last horrible resource in case of being driven to extremity by famine !

On the 17th, the gale gradually subsided, and the sea became calm. The sailors now crawled feebly about the wreck, and began to relieve it from the main encumbrances. The spars were cleared away, the anchors and guns heaved overboard ; the spritsail yard was rigged for a jurymast, and a mizen topsail set upon it. A sort of stage was made of a few broken spars, on which the crew were raised above the surface of the water, so as to be enabled to keep themselves dry, and to sleep comfortably. Still their sufferings from hunger and thirst were great ; but there was a Sandwich islander on board, an expert swimmer, who found his way into the cabin, and occasionally brought up a few bottles of wine and porter, and at length got into the run, and secured a quarter cask of wine. A little raw pork was likewise procured, and dealt out with a sparing hand. The horrors of their situation were increased by the sight of numerous sharks prowling about the wreck, as if waiting for their prey. On the 24th, the cook, a black man, died and was cast into the sea, when he was instantly seized on by these ravenous monsters.

They had been several days making slow headway under their scanty sail, when, on the 25th, they came in sight of land. It was about fifteen leagues distant, and they remained two or three days drifting along in sight of it. On the 28th, they descried, to their great transport, a canoe approaching, managed by natives. They came alongside, and brought a most welcome supply of potatoes. They informed them that the land they had made was one of the Sandwich islands. The second mate and one of the seamen went on shore in the canoe for water and provisions, and to procure aid from the islanders in towing the wreck into a harbour.

Neither of the men returned, nor was any assistance sent from shore. The next day, ten or twelve canoes came alongside, but roamed round the wreck like so many sharks, and would render no aid in towing her to land.

The sea continued to break over the vessel with such violence, that it was impossible to stand at the helm without the assistance of lashings. The crew were now so worn down by famine and thirst, that the captain saw it would be impossible for them to withstand the breaking of the sea, when the ship should ground; he deemed the only chance for their lives, therefore, was to get to land in the canoes, and to stand ready to receive and protect the wreck when she should drift to shore. Accordingly, they all got safe to land, but had scarcely touched the beach when they were surrounded by the natives, who stripped them almost naked. The name of this inhospitable island was Tahoorowa.

In the course of the night, the wreck came drifting to the strand, with the surf thundering around her, and shortly afterwards bilged. On the following morning, numerous casks of provisions floated on shore. The natives staved them for the sake of the iron hoops, but would not allow the crew to help themselves to the contents, or to go on board of the wreck.

As the crew were in want of every thing, and as it might be a long time before any opportunity occurred for them to get away from these islands, Mr. Ogden, as soon as he could get a chance, made his way to the island of Owyhee, and endeavoured to make some arrangement with the king for the relief of his companions in misfortune.

The illustrious Tamaahmaah, as we have shown on a former occasion, was a shrewd bargainer, and in the present instance proved himself an experienced wrecker. His negotiations with M'Dougal, and the other "Eris of the great American Fur Company," had but little effect on present circumstances, and he proceeded to avail himself of their misfortunes. He agreed to furnish the crew with provisions during their stay in his territories, and to return to them all their clothing that could be found, but he stipulated that the wreck should be abandoned to him as a waif cast by fortune on his shores. With these conditions Mr. Ogden was fain to comply. Upon this the great Tamaahmaah deputed his favourite, John Young, the tarpawling governor of Owyhee, to proceed with a number of the royal guards, and take possession of the wreck on behalf of the crown. This was done accordingly, and the property and crew were removed to Owyhee. The royal bounty appears to have been but scanty in its dispensations. The crew fared but meagerly; though, on reading the journal of the voyage, it is singular to find them, after all the hardships they had suffered, so sensitive about petty inconveniences, as to exclaim against the king as a " savage monster," for refusing them a " pot to cook in," and denying Mr. Ogden the use of a knife and fork which had been saved from the wreck.

Such was the unfortunate catastrophe of the Lark; had she reached her destination in safety, affairs at Astoria might have taken a different course. A strange fatality seems to have attended all the expeditions by sea, nor were those by land much less disastrous.

Captain Northrop was still at the Sandwich islands, on December 20th, when Mr. Hunt arrived. The latter immediately purchased, for ten thousand dollars, a brig called the Pedlar, and put Captain Northrop in command of her. They set sail for Astoria on the 22nd January, intending to remove the property from thence as speedily as possible to the Russian settlements on the north-west coast, to prevent it from falling into the hands of the British. Such were the orders of Mr. Astor, sent out by the Lark.

We will now leave Mr. Hunt on his voyage, and return to see what has taken place at Astoria during his absence.

CHAPTER XVII.

Arrival of M'Tavish at Astoria—Conduct of his followers—Negotiations of M'Dougal and M'Tavish—Bargain for the transfer of Astoria—Doubts entertained of the loyalty of M'Dougal.

On the 2nd of October, about five weeks after Mr. Hunt had sailed in the Albatross from Astoria, Mr. M'Kenzie set off with two canoes and twelve men, for the posts of Messrs. Stuart and Clarke, to apprize them of the new arrangements determined upon in the recent conference of the partners at the factory.

He had not ascended the river a hundred miles, when he met a squadron of ten canoes, sweeping merrily down under British colours, the Canadian oarsmen, as usual, in full song.

It was an armament fitted out by M'Tavish, who had with him Mr. J. Stuart, another partner of the North-west Company, together with some clerks, and sixty-eight men —seventy-five souls in all. They had heard of the frigate Phœbe and the Isaac Todd being on the high seas, and were on their way down to await their arrival. In one of the canoes Mr. Clarke came passenger, the alarming intelligence having brought him down from his post on the Spokan. Mr. M'Kenzie immediately determined to return with him to Astoria, and, veering about, the two parties encamped together for the night. The leaders, of course, observed a due decorum; but some of the subalterns could not restrain their chuckling exultation, boasting that they would soon plant the British standard on the walls of Astoria, and drive the Americans out of the country.

In the course of the evening, Mr. M'Kenzie had a secret conference with Mr. Clarke, in which they agreed to set off privately, before daylight, and get down in time to apprize M'Dougal of the approach of these North-westers. The latter, however, were completely on the alert; just as M'Kenzie's canoes were about to push off, they were joined by a couple from the north-west squadron, in which was M'Tavish, with two clerks, and eleven men. With these, he intended to push forward and make arrangements, leaving the rest of the convoy, in which was a large quantity of furs, to await his orders.

The two parties arrived at Astoria on the 7th of October. The North-westers encamped under the guns of the fort, and displayed the British colours. The young men in the fort, natives of the United States, were on the point of hoisting the American flag, but were forbidden by Mr. M'Dougal. They were astonished at such a prohibition, and were exceedingly galled by the tone and manner assumed by the clerks and retainers of the North-west Company, who ruffled about in that swelling and braggart style which grows up among these heroes of the wilderness; they, in fact, considered themselves lords of the ascendant, and regarded the hampered and harassed Astorians as a conquered people.

On the following day M'Dougal convened the clerks, and read to them an extract of a letter from his uncle, Mr. Angus Shaw, one of the principal partners of the Northwest Company, announcing the coming of the Phœbe and Isaac Todd, "to take and destroy every thing American on the north-west coast."

This intelligence was received without dismay by such of the clerks as were natives of the United States. They had felt indignant at seeing their national flag struck by a Canadian commander, and the British flag flowed, as it were, in their faces. They had been stung to the quick, also, by the vaunting airs assumed by the North-westers. In this mood of mind, they would willingly have nailed their colours to the staff, and defied the frigate. She could not come within many miles of the fort, they observed, and any boats she might send could be destroyed by their cannon.

There were cooler and more calculating spirits, however, who had the control of affairs, and felt nothing of the patriotic pride and indignation of these youths. The extract of the letter had, apparently, been read by M'Dougal, merely to prepare the way for a preconcerted stroke of management. On that same day Mr. M'Tavish proposed to purchase the whole stock of goods and furs belonging to the company, both at Astoria and in the interior, at cost and charges. Mr. M'Dougal undertook to comply; assuming the whole management of the negotiation in virtue of the power vested in him, in case of the non-arrival of Mr. Hunt. That power, however, was limited and specific, and did not extend to an operation of this nature and extent; no objection, however, was made to his assumption, and he and M'Tavish soon made a preliminary arrangement, perfectly satisfactory to the latter.

Mr. Stuart, and the reserve party of North-westers, arrived shortly afterwards, and encamped with M'Tavish. The former exclaimed loudly against the terms of the arrangement, and insisted upon a reduction of the prices. New negotiations had now to be entered into. The demands of the North-westers were made in a peremptory tone, and they seemed disposed to dictate like conquerors. The Americans looked on with indignation and impatience. They considered M'Dougal as acting, if not a perfidious, certainly a craven part. He was continually repairing to the camp to negotiate, instead of keeping within his walls and receiving overtures in his fortress. His case, they observed, was not so desperate as to excuse such crouching. He might, in fact, hold out for his own terms. The Northwest party had lost their ammunition; they had no goods to trade with the natives for provisions; and were so destitute that M'Dougal had absolutely to feed them, while he negotiated with them. He, on the contrary, was well lodged and victualled; had sixty men, with arms, ammunition, boats, and every thing requisite either for defence or retreat. The party beneath the guns of his fort were at his mercy; should an enemy appear in the offing, he could pack up the most valuable part of the property and retire to some place of concealment, or make off for the interior.

These considerations, however, had no weight with Mr. M'Dougal, or were overruled by other motives. The terms of sale were lowered by him to the standard fixed by Mr. Stuart, and an agreement executed on the 16th of October, by which the furs and merchandise of all kinds in the country, belonging to Mr. Astor, passed into the possession of the North-west Company at about a third of their real value.*   A safe passage through the north-west posts was guaranteed to such as did not choose to enter into the service of that company, and the amount of wages due to them was to be deducted from the price paid for Astoria.

The conduct and motives of Mr. M'Dougal, throughout the whole of this proceeding, have been strongly questioned by the other partners. He has been accused of availing himself of a wrong construction of powers vested in him at his own request, and of sacrificing the interests of Mr. Astor to the North-west Company, under the promise or hope of advantage to himself.

He always insisted, however, that he made the best bargain for Mr. Astor that circumstances would permit; the frigate being hourly expected, in which case the whole property of that gentleman would be liable to capture. That the return of Mr. Hunt was problematical; the frigate intending to cruise along the coast for two years, and clear it of all American vessels. He moreover averred, and M'Tavish corroborated his averment by certificate, that he proposed an arrangement to that gentleman, by which the furs were to be sent to Canton, and sold there at Mr. Astor's risk, and for his account; but this proposition was not acceded to.

Notwithstanding all his representations, several of the persons present at the transaction, and acquainted with

* Not quite 40,000 dollars were allowed for furs worth upwards of 100,000 dollars. Beaver was valued at two dollars per skin, though worth five dollars. Land otter at fifty cents, though worth five dollars. Sea otter at twelve dollars, worth from forty-five to sixty dollars; and for several kinds of furs nothing was allowed. Moreover, the goods and merchandise for the Indian trade ought to have brought three times the amount for which they were sold.

The following estimate has been made of the articles on hand, and the prices:—

		DOLLARS.		DOLLARS.
17,705 lbs. beaver parchment, valued at		200	worth	500
465, old coat beaver	,, ,,	166	,,	350
907 land otter	,, ,,	50	,,	500
68 sea otter	,, ,,	1200	,, 4 to	6000
30 ,, ,,	,, ,,	500	,,	2500

Nothing was allowed for

179 mink skins	worth each			40
22 raccoon	,, ,,			40
38 lynx	,, ,,			200
18 fox	,, ,,			100
106 ,,	,, ,,			150
71 black bear	,, ,,			400
16 grizzly bear	,, ,,			1000

the whole course of the affair, and among the number Mr. M'Kenzie himself, his occasional coadjutor, remained firm in the belief that he had acted a hollow part. Neither did he succeed in exculpating himself to Mr. Astor; that gentleman declaring, in a letter written some time afterwards, to Mr. Hunt, that he considered the property virtually given away. " Had our place and our property," he adds, " been fairly captured, I should have preferred it. I should not feel as if I were disgraced."

All these may be unmerited suspicions; but it certainly is a circumstance strongly corroborative of them, that Mr. M'Dougal, shortly after concluding this agreement, became a member of the North-west Company, and received a share productive of a handsome income.

CHAPTER XVIII.

Arrival of a strange sail—Agitation at Astoria—Warlike offer of Comcomly—Astoria taken possession of by the British—Indignation of Comcomly at the conduct of his son-in-law.

On the morning of the 30th of November, a sail was descried doubling Cape Disappointment. It came to anchor in Baker's bay, and proved to be a ship of war. Of what nation? was now the anxious inquiry. If English, why did it come alone? where was the merchant vessel that was to have accompanied it? If American, what was to become of the newly-acquired possession of the North-west Company?

In this dilemma, M'Tavish, in all haste, loaded two barges with all the packages of furs bearing the mark of the North-west Company, and made off for Tongue point, three miles up the river. There he was to await a preconcerted signal from M'Dougal, on ascertaining the character of the ship. If it should prove American, M'Tavish would have a fair start, and could bear off his rich cargo to the interior. It is singular that this prompt mode of conveying valuable, but easily transportable effects, beyond the reach of a hostile ship, should not have suggested itself while the property belonged to Mr. Astor.

In the mean time, M'Dougal, who still remained nominal chief at the fort, launched a canoe, manned by men recently in the employ of the American Fur Company, and steered for the ship. On the way, he instructed his men to pass themselves for Americans or Englishmen, according to the exigencies of the case.

The vessel proved to be the British sloop of war Racoon, of twenty-six guns, and one hundred and twenty men, commanded by Captain Black. According to the account of that officer, the frigate Phœbe, and the two sloops of war Cherub and Racoon; had sailed in convoy of the Isaac Todd from Rio Janeiro. On board of the Phœbe, Mr. John M'Donald, a partner of the North-west Company, embarked as passenger, to profit by the anticipated catastrophe at Astoria. The convoy was separated by stress of weather off Cape Horn. The three ships of war came together again at the island of Juan Fernandez, their appointed rendezvous, but waited in vain for the Isaac Todd.

In the mean time, intelligence was received of the mischief that Commodore Porter was doing among the British whale ships. Commodore Hillyer immediately set sail in quest of him, with the Phœbe and the Cherub, transferring Mr. M'Donald to the Racoon, and ordering that vessel to proceed to the Columbia.

The officers of the Racoon were in high spirits. The agents of the North-west Company, in instigating the expedition, had talked of immense booty to be made by the fortunate captors of Astoria. Mr. M'Donald had kept up the excitement during the voyage, so that not a midshipman but revelled in dreams of ample prize-money, nor a lieutenant that would have sold his chance for a thousand pounds. Their disappointment, therefore, may easily be conceived, when they learned that their warlike attack upon Astoria had been forestalled by a snug commercial arrangement; that their anticipated booty had become British property in the regular course of traffic, and that all this had been effected by the very company which had been instrumental in getting them sent on what they now stigmatized as a fool's errand.

They felt as if they had been duped and made tools of, by a set of shrewd men of traffic, who had employed them to crack the nut, while they carried off the kernel. In a word, M'Dougal found himself so ungraciously received by his countrymen on board of the ship, that he was glad to cut short his visit, and return to shore. He was busy at the fort, making preparations for the reception of the Captain of the Racoon, when his one-eyed Indian father-in-law made his appearance, with a train of Chinook warriors, all painted and equipped in warlike style.

Old Comcomly had beheld, with dismay, the arrival of a " big war canoe" displaying the British flag. The shrewd old savage had become something of a politician in the course of his daily visits at the fort. He knew of the war existing between the nations, but knew nothing of the arrangement between M'Dougal and M'Tavish. He trembled, therefore, for the power of his white son-in-law, and the new fledged grandeur of his daughter, and assembled his warriors in all haste. " King George," said he, " has sent his great canoe to destroy the fort, and make slaves of all the inhabitants. Shall we suffer it ? The Americans are the first white men that have fixed themselves in the land. They have treated us like brothers. Their great chief has taken my daughter to be his squaw : we are, therefore, as one people."

His warriors all determined to stand by the Americans to the last, and to this effect they came painted and armed for battle. Comcomly made a spirited war speech to his son-in-law. He offered to kill every one of King George's men that should attempt to land. It was an easy matter. The ship could not approach within six miles of the fort ; the crew could only land in boats. The woods reached to the water's edge ; in these, he and his warriors would conceal themselves, and shoot down the enemy as fast as they put foot on shore.

M'Dougal was, doubtless, properly sensible of this parental devotion on the part of his savage father-in-law, and, perhaps a little rebuked by the game spirit, so opposite to his own. He assured Comcomly, however, that his solicitude for the safety of himself and the princess was superfluous ; as, though the ship belonged to King

George, her crew would not injure the Americans, nor their Indian allies. He advised him and his warriors, therefore, to lay aside their weapons and war shirts, wash off the paint from their faces and bodies, and appear like clean and civil savages, to receive the strangers courteously.

Comcomly was sorely puzzled at this advice, which accorded so little with his Indian notions of receiving a hostile nation; and it was only after repeated and positive assurances of the amicable intentions of the strangers that he was induced to lower his fighting tone. He said something to his warriors explanatory of this singular posture of affairs, and in vindication, perhaps, of the pacific temper of his son-in-law. They all gave a shrug and an Indian grunt of acquiescence, and went off sulkily to their village, to lay aside their weapons for the present.

The proper arrangements being made for the reception of Captain Black, that officer caused his ship's boats to be manned, and landed with befitting state at Astoria. From the talk that had been made by the North-west Company, of the strength of the place, and the armament they had required to assist in its reduction, he expected to find a fortress of some importance. When he beheld nothing but stockades and bastions, calculated for defence against naked savages, he felt an emotion of indignant surprise, mingled with something of the ludicrous. "Is this the fort," cried he, "about which I have heard so much talking? D—n me, but I'd batter it down in two hours, with a four pounder!"

When he learned, however, the amount of rich furs that had been passed into the hands of the North-westers, he was outrageous, and insisted that an inventory should be taken of all the property purchased of the Americans, "with a view to ulterior measures in England, for the recovery of the value from the North-west Company."

As he grew cool, however, he gave over all idea of preferring such a claim, and reconciled himself, as well as he could, to the idea of having been forestalled by his bargaining co-adjutors.

On the 12th of December, the fate of Astoria was consummated by a regular ceremonial. Captain Black, attended by his officers, entered the fort, caused the British standard to be erected, broke a bottle of wine, and declared, in a loud voice, that he took possession of the establishment and of the country, in the name of his Britannic majesty, changing the name of Astoria to that of Fort George.

The Indian warriors, who had offered their services to repel the strangers, were present on the occasion. It was explained to them as being a friendly arrangement and transfer, but they shook their heads grimly, and considered it an act of subjugation of their ancient allies. They regretted that they had complied with M'Dougal's wishes, in laying aside their arms, and remarked, that, however the Americans might conceal the fact, they were undoubtedly all slaves; nor could they be persuaded of the contrary, until they beheld the Racoon depart without taking away any prisoners.

As to Comcomly, he no longer prided himself upon his white son-in-law, but, whenever he was asked about him, shook his head, and replied, that his daughter had made a mistake, and instead of getting a great warrior for a husband, had married herself to a squaw.

CHAPTER XIX.

Arrival of the brig Pedlar at Astoria—Breaking up of the establishment—Departure of several of the company—Tragical story told by the Squaw of Pierre Dorion—Fate of Reed and his companions—Attempts of Mr. Astor to renew his enterprise—Disappointment—Concluding observations and reflections.

HAVING given the catastrophe at the fort of Astoria, it remains now but to gather up a few loose ends of this widely excursive narrative, and conclude. On the 28th of February, the brig Pedlar anchored in Columbia river. It will be recollected that Mr. Hunt had purchased this vessel at the Sandwich islands, to take off the furs collected at the factory, and to restore the Sandwich islanders to their homes. When that gentleman learned, however, the precipitate and summary manner in which the property had been bargained away by Mr. M'Dougal, he expressed his indignation in the strongest terms, and determined to make an effort to get back the furs. As soon as his wishes were known in this respect, M'Dougal came to sound him on behalf of the North-west Company, intimating that he had no doubt the peltries might be repurchased at an advance of fifty per cent. This overture was not calculated to soothe the angry feelings of Mr. Hunt, and his indignation was complete, when he discovered that M'Dougal had become a partner of the North-west Company, and had actually been so since the 23rd of December. He had kept his partnership a secret, however; had retained the papers of the Pacific Fur Company in his possession; and had continued to act as Mr. Astor's agent, though two of the partners of the other company, Mr. M'Kenzie and Mr. Clarke, were present. He had, moreover, divulged to his new associates all that he knew as to Mr. Astor's plans and affairs, and had made copies of his business letters for their perusal.

Mr. Hunt now considered the whole conduct of M'Dougal hollow and collusive. His only thought was, therefore, to get all the papers of the concern out of his hands, and bring the business to a close; for the interests of Mr. Astor were yet completely at stake: the drafts of the North-west Company in his favour, for the purchase-money, not having yet been obtained. With some difficulty he succeeded in getting possession of the papers. The bills or drafts were delivered without hesitation. The latter he remitted to Mr. Astor by some of his associates, who were about to cross the continent to New York. This done, he embarked on board the Pedlar, on the 3rd of April, accompanied by two of the clerks, Mr. Seton and Mr. Halsey, and bade a final adieu to Astoria.

The next day, April 4th, Messrs. Clarke, M'Kenzie, David Stuart, and such of the Astorians as had not entered into the service of the North-west Company, set out to cross the Rocky mountains. It is not our intention to take the reader another journey across those rugged barriers; but we will step forward with the travellers to a distance on their way, merely to relate their interview with a character already noted in this work.

As the party were proceeding up the Columbia, near the mouth of the Wallah-Wallah river, several Indian canoes put off from the shore to overtake them, and a voice called upon them in French, and requested them to stop. They accordingly put to shore, and were joined by those in the canoes. To their surprise, they recognised in the person who had hailed them the Indian wife of Pierre Dorion, accompanied by her two children. She had a story to tell, involving the fate of several of our unfortunate adventurers.

Mr. John Reed, the Hibernian, it will be remembered, had been detached during the summer to the Snake river. His party consisted of four Canadians, Gilles Le Clerc, François Landry, Jean Baptiste Turcot, and André La Chapelle, together with two hunters, Pierre Dorion and Pierre Delaunay; Dorion, as usual, being accompanied by his wife and children. The objects of this expedition were twofold: to trap beaver, and to search for the three hunters Robinson, Hoback, and Rezner.

In the course of the autumn, Reed lost one man, Landry, by death; another one, Pierre Delaunay, who was of a sullen, perverse disposition, left him in a moody fit, and was never heard of afterwards. The number of his party was not, however, reduced by these losses, as the three hunters, Robinson, Hoback, and Rezner, had joined it.

Reed now built a house on the Snake river, for their winter quarters; which being completed, the party set about trapping. Rezner, Le Clerc, and Pierre Dorion, went about five days' journey from the wintering house, to a part of the country well stocked with beaver. Here they put up a hut, and proceeded to trap with great success. While the men were out hunting, Pierre Dorion's wife remained at home to dress the skins and prepare the meals. She was thus employed one evening about the beginning of January, cooking the supper of the hunters, when she heard footsteps, and Le Clerc staggered, pale and bleeding, into the hut. He informed her that a party of savages had surprised them, while at their traps, and had killed Rezner and her husband. He had barely strength left to give this information, when he sank upon the ground.

The poor woman saw that the only chance for life was instant flight, but in this exigency, showed that presence of mind and force of character for which she had frequently been noted. With great difficulty, she caught two of the horses belonging to the party. Then collecting her clothes, and a small quantity of beaver meat and dried salmon, she packed them upon one of the horses, and helped the wounded man to mount upon it. On the other horse she mounted with her two children, and hurried away from this dangerous neighbourhood, directing her flight for Mr. Reed's establishment. On the third day, she descried a number of Indians on horseback proceeding in an easterly direction. She immediately dismounted with her children, and helped Le Clerc likewise to dismount, and all concealed themselves. Fortunately they escaped the sharp eyes of the savages, but had to proceed with the utmost caution. That night, they slept without fire or water; she managed to keep her children warm in her arms; but before morning, poor Le Clerc died.

With the dawn of day, the resolute woman resumed her course, and, on the fourth day, reached the house of Mr. Reed. It was deserted, and all around were marks of blood and signs of a furious massacre. Not doubting that Mr. Reed and his party had all fallen victims, she turned in fresh horror from the spot. For two days she continued hurrying forward, ready to sink for want of food, but more solicitous about her children than herself. At length she reached a range of the Rocky mountains, near the upper part of the Wallah-Wallah river. Here she chose a wild lonely ravine, as her place of winter refuge.

She had fortunately a buffalo robe and three deer skins; of these, and of pine bark and cedar branches, she constructed a rude wigwam, which she pitched beside a mountain spring. Having no other food, she killed the two horses, and smoked their flesh. The skins aided to cover her hut. Here she dragged out the winter, with no other company than her two children. Towards the middle of March, her provisions were nearly exhausted. She therefore packed up the remainder, slung it on her back, and with her helpless little ones, set out again on her wander-

ings.   Crossing the ridge of mountains, she descended to
the banks of the Wallah-Wallah, and kept along them
until she arrived where that river throws itself into the
Columbia.   She was hospitably received and entertained
by the Wallah-Wallahs, and had been nearly two weeks
among them when the two canoes passed.

On being interrogated, she could assign no reason for this
murderous attack of the savages ; it appeared to be perfectly wanton and unprovoked.   Some of the Astorians
supposed it an act of butchery by a roving band of Blackfeet ; others, however, and with greater probability of
correctness, have ascribed it to the tribe of Pierced-nose
Indians, in revenge for the death of their comrade hanged
by order of Mr. Clarke.   If so, it shows that these sudden
and apparently wanton outbreakings of sanguinary violence
on the part of savages, have often some previous, though
perhaps remote, provocation.

The narrative of the Indian woman closes the checkered
adventures of some of the personages of this motley story ;
such as the honest Hibernian Reed, and Dorion the hybrid
interpreter.   Turcot and La Chapelle were two of the men
who fell off from Mr. Crooks in the course of his wintry
journey, and had subsequently such disastrous times among
the Indians.   We cannot but feel some sympathy with
that persevering trio of Kentuckians, Robinson, Rezner, and
Hoback ; who twice turned back when on their way homeward, and lingered in the wilderness to perish by the hands
of savages.

The return parties from Astoria, both by sea and land,
experienced on the way as many adventures, vicissitudes,
and mishaps, as the far-famed heroes of the Odyssey ; they
reached their destination at different times, bearing tidings
to Mr. Astor of the unfortunate termination of his enterprise.

That gentleman, however, was not disposed, even yet, to
give the matter up as lost.   On the contrary, his spirit was
roused by what he considered ungenerous and unmerited
conduct on the part of the North-west Company.   " After
their treatment of me," said he, in a letter to Mr. Hunt,
" I have no idea of remaining quiet and idle."   He deter-

mined, therefore, as soon as circumstances would permit, to resume his enterprise.

At the return of peace, Astoria, with the adjacent country, reverted to the United States by the treaty of Ghent, on the principle of *status ante bellum*, and Captain Biddle was despatched in the sloop of war Ontario, to take formal possession.

In the winter of 1815, a law was passed by congress, prohibiting all traffic of British traders within the territories of the United States.

The favourable moment seemed now to Mr. Astor to have arrived for the revival of his favourite enterprise, but new difficulties had grown up to impede it. The North-west Company were now in complete occupation of the Columbia river, and its chief tributary streams, holding the posts which he had established, and carrying on a trade throughout the neighbouring region, in defiance of the prohibitory law of congress, which, in effect, was a dead letter beyond the mountains.

To dispossess them, would be an undertaking of almost a belligerent nature : for their agents and retainers were well armed and skilled in the use of weapons, as is usual with Indian traders. The ferocious and bloody contests which had taken place between the rival trading parties of the North-west and Hudson's Bay Companies, had shown what might be expected from commercial feuds in the lawless depths of the wilderness. Mr. Astor did not think it advisable, therefore, to attempt the matter without the protection of the American flag ; under which his people might rally in case of need. He accordingly made an informal overture to the President of the United States, Mr. Madison, through Mr. Gallatin, offering to renew his enterprise, and to re-establish Astoria, provided it would be protected by the American flag, and made a military post; stating that the whole force required would not exceed a lieutenant's command.

The application, approved and recommended by Mr. Gallatin, one of the most enlightened statesmen of our country, was favourably received, but no step was taken in consequence ; the president not being disposed, in all probability, to commit himself by any direct countenance or overt act. Discouraged by this supineness on the part of the government, Mr. Astor did not think fit to renew his overtures in a more formal manner, and the favourable moment for the re-occupation of Astoria was suffered to pass unimproved.

The British trading establishments were thus enabled, without molestation, to strike deep their roots, and extend their ramifications in despite of the prohibition of congress, until they had spread themselves over the rich field of enterprise opened by Mr. Astor. The British government soon began to perceive the importance of this region, and to desire to include it within their territorial domains. A question has consequently risen as to the right to the soil, and has become one of the most perplexing now open between the United States and Great Britain. In the first treaty relative to it, under date of October 20th, 1818, the question was left unsettled, and it was agreed that the country on the north-west coast of America, westward of the Rocky mountains, claimed by either nation, should be open to the inhabitants of both for ten years, for the purposes of trade, with the equal right of navigating all its rivers. When these ten years had expired, a subsequent treaty in 1828, extended the arrangement to ten additional years. So the matter stands at present.

On casting back our eyes over the series of events we have recorded, we see no reason to attribute the failure of this great commercial undertaking to any fault in the scheme, or omission in the execution of it, on the part of the projector. It was a magnificent enterprise; well concerted and carried on, without regard to difficulties or expense. A succession of adverse circumstances and cross purposes, however, beset it almost from the outset; some of them, in fact, arising from neglect of the orders and instructions of Mr. Astor. The first crippling blow was the loss of the Tonquin, which clearly would not have happened, had Mr. Astor's earnest injunctions with regard to the natives been attended to. Had this ship performed her voyage prosperously, and revisited Astoria in due time, the trade of the establishment would have taken its preconcerted course, and the spirits of all concerned been kept up by a confident prospect of success. Her dismal catastrophe struck a chill into every heart, and prepared the way for subsequent despondency.

Another cause of embarrassment and loss was the departure from the plan of Mr. Astor, as to the voyage of the Beaver, subsequent to her visiting Astoria. The variation from this plan produced a series of cross purposes, disastrous to the establishment, and detained Mr. Hunt absent from his post, when his presence there was of vital importance to the enterprise; so essential is it for an agent, in any great and complicated undertaking, to execute faithfully, and to the letter, the part marked out for him by the master mind which has concerted the whole.

The breaking out of the war between the United States and Great Britain, multiplied the hazards and embarrassments of the enterprise. The disappaintment as to convoy, rendered it difficult to keep up reinforcements and supplies; and the loss of the Lark added to the tissue of misadventures.

That Mr. Astor battled resolutely against every difficulty, and pursued his course in defiance of every loss, has been sufficiently shown. Had he been seconded by suitable agents, and properly protected by government, the ultimate failure of his plan might yet have been averted. It was his great misfortune, that his agents were not imbued with his own spirit. Some had not capacity sufficient to comprehend the real nature and extent of his scheme; others were alien in feeling and interest, and had been brought up in the service of a rival company. Whatever sympathies they might originally have had with him, were impaired, if not destroyed by the war. They looked upon his cause as desperate, and only considered how they might make interest to regain a situation under their former employers. The absence of Mr. Hunt, the only real representative of Mr. Astor, at the time of the capitulation with the Northwest Company, completed the series of cross purposes. Had that gentleman been present, the transfer, in all probability, would not have taken place.

It is painful, at all times, to see a grand and beneficial

stroke of genius fail of its aim, but we regret the failure of this enterprise in a national point of view; for had it been crowned with success, it would have redounded greatly to the advantage and extension of our commerce. The profits drawn from the country in question by the British Fur Company, though of ample amount, form no criterion by which to judge of the advantages that would have arisen had it been entirely in the hands of citizens of the United States. That company, as has been shown, is limited in the nature and scope of its operations, and can make but little use of the maritime facilities held out by an emporium and a harbour on that coast. In our hands, beside the roving bands of trappers and traders, the country would have been explored and settled by industrious husbandmen; and the fertile valleys, bordering its rivers, and shut up among its mountains, would have been made to pour forth their agricultural treasure to contribute to the general wealth.

In respect to commerce we should have had a line of trading posts from the Mississippi and the Missouri across the Rocky mountains, forming a high road from the great regions of the west to the shores of the Pacific. We should have had a fortified post and port at the mouth of the Columbia, commanding the trade of that river and its tributaries, and of a wide extent of country and sea coast; carrying on an active and profitable commerce with the Sandwich islands, and a direct and frequent communication with China. In a word, Astoria might have realized the anticipations of Mr. Astor, so well understood and appreciated by Mr. Jefferson, in gradually becoming a commercial empire beyond the mountains, peopled by " free and independent Americans, and linked with us by ties of blood and interest."

We repeat, therefore, our sincere regret, that our government should have neglected the overture of Mr. Astor, and suffered the moment to pass by, when full possession of this region might have been taken quietly, as a matter of course, and a military post established, without dispute, at Astoria. Our statesmen have become sensible, when too late, of the importance of this measure. Bills have repeatedly been brought into congress for the purpose, but without success;

and our rightful possessions on that coast, as well as our trade on the Pacific, have no rallying point protected by the national flag, and by a military force.

In the mean time, the second period of ten years is fast elapsing. In 1838, the question of title will again come up, and most probably, in the present amicable state of our relations with Great Britain will be again postponed. Every year, however, the litigated claim is growing in importance. There is no pride so jealous and irritable as the pride of territory. As one wave of emigration after another rolls into the vast regions of the west, and our settlements stretch towards the Rocky mountains, the eager eyes of our pioneers will pry beyond, and they will become impatient of any barrier or impediment in the way of what they consider a grand outlet of our empire. Should any circumstance, therefore, unfortunately occur to disturb the present harmony of the two nations, this ill-adjusted question, which now lies dormant, may suddenly start up into one of belligerent import, and Astoria become the watchword in a contest for dominion on the shores of the Pacific.

APPENDIX.

To the Honourable the Senate and House of Representatives of
the United States, in Congress assembled,

The Petition of the American Fur Company respectfully sheweth :

That the trade with the several Indian tribes of North America,
has, for many years past, been almost exclusively carried on by the
merchants of Canada ; who, having formed powerful and extensive
associations for that purpose, being aided by British capital, and
being encouraged by the favour and protection of the British Government, could not be opposed, with any prospect of success, by
individuals of the United States.

That by means of the above trade, thus systematically pursued, not
only the inhabitants of the United States have been deprived of commercial profits and advantages, to which they appear to have just and
natural pretensions, but a great and dangerous influence has been
established over the Indian tribes, difficult to be counteracted, and
capable of being exerted at critical periods, to the great injury and
annoyance of our frontier settlements.

That in order to obtain at least a part of the above trade, and more
particularly that which is within the boundaries of the United States,
your petitioners, in the year 1808, obtained an act of incorporation
from the state of New York, whereby they are enabled, with a competent capital, to carry on the said trade with the Indians in such
manner as may be conformable to the laws and regulations of the
United States, in relation to such commerce.

That the capital mentioned in the said act, amounting to one million of dollars, having been duly formed, your petitioners entered
with zeal and alacrity into those large and important arrangements,
which were necessary for, or conducive to, the object of their incorporation ; and among other things, purchased a great part of the
stock in trade, and trading establishments, of the Michilimackinac
Company of Canada. Your petitioners also, with the expectation of great
public and private advantage from the use of the said establishments,
ordered, during the spring and summer of 1810, an assortment of goods
from England, suitable for the Indian trade ; which, in consequence
of the President's proclamation of November of that year, were
shipped to Canada instead of New York, and have been transported,
under a very heavy expense, into the interior of the country. But as
they could not legally be brought into the Indian country within

the boundaries of the United States, they have been stored on the island of St. Joseph, in lake Huron, where they now remain.

Your petitioners, with great deference and implicit submission to the wisdom of the national legislature, beg leave to suggest for consideration, whether they have not some claim to national attention and encouragement, from the nature and importance of their undertaking; which, though hazardous and uncertain as it concerns their private emolument, must, at any rate, redound to the public security and advantage. If their undertaking shall appear to be of the description given, they would further suggest to your honourable bodies, that unless they can procure a regular supply for the trade in which they are engaged, it may languish, and be finally abandoned by American citizens; when it will revert to its former channel, with additional, and perhaps with irresistible, power.

Under these circumstances, and upon all those considerations of public policy which will present themselves to your honourable bodies in connexion with those already mentioned, your petitioners respectfully pray that a law may be passed to enable the President, or any of the heads of departments acting under his authority, to grant permits for the introduction of goods necessary for the supply of the Indians, into the Indian country that is within the boundaries of the United States, under such regulations, and with such restrictions, as may secure the public revenue, and promote the public welfare.

And your petitioners will ever pray, &c.

In witness whereof, the common seal of the American Fur Company, is hereunto affixed, the   day of March, 1812.

By order of the Corporation.

AN ACT to enable the American Fur Company, and other citizens, to introduce goods necessary for the Indian trade into the territories within the boundaries of the United States.

WHEREAS, the public peace and welfare require that the native Indian tribes, residing within the boundaries of the United States, should receive their necessary supplies under the authority and from the citizens of the United States : Therefore, be it enacted by the Senate and House of Representatives of the United States in congress assembled, that it shall be lawful for the President of the United States, or any of the heads of departments, thereunto by him duly authorised, from time to time to grant permits to the American Fur Company, their agents or factors, or any other citizens of the United States engaged in the Indian trade, to introduce into the Indian country within the boundaries of the United States, such goods, wares, and merchandise, as may be necessary for the said trade, under such regulations and restrictions as the said President or heads of departments may judge proper ; any law or regulation to the contrary, in anywise notwithstanding.

LETTER FROM MR. GALLATIN TO MR. ASTOR, DATED

New York, August 5, 1835.

DEAR SIR,

In compliance with your request, I will state such facts as I recollect, touching the subjects mentioned in your letter of the 28th ult. I may be mistaken respecting dates and details, and will only relate general facts, which I well remember.

In conformity with the treaty of 1794 with Great Britain, the citizens and subjects of each country were permitted to trade with the Indians residing in the territories of the other party. The reciprocity was altogether nominal. Since the conquest of Canada, the British had inherited from the French the whole fur trade, through the great lakes and their communications, with all the western Indians, whether residing in the British dominions or the United States. They kept the important western posts on those lakes till about the year 1797. And the defensive Indian war, which the United States had to sustain from 1776 to 1795, had still more alienated the Indians, and secured to the British their exclusive trade, carried through the lakes, wherever the Indians in that quarter lived. No American could, without imminent danger of property and life, carry on that trade, even within the United States, by the way of either Michilimackinac or St. Mary's. And independent of the loss of commerce, Great Britain was enabled to preserve a most dangerous influence over our Indians.

It was under these circumstances that you communicated to our government the prospect you had to be able, and your intention to purchase one-half of the interest of the Canadian Fur Company, engaged in trade by way of Michilimackinac with our own Indians. You wished to know whether the plan met with the approbation of government, and how far you could rely on its protection and encouragement. This overture was received with great satisfaction by the administration, and Mr. Jefferson, then President, wrote you to that effect. I was also directed, as secretary of the treasury, to write to you an official letter to the same purpose. On investigating the subject, it was found that the executive had no authority to give you any direct aid; and I believe that you received nothing more than an entire approbation of your plan, and general assurances of the protection due to every citizen engaged in lawful and useful pursuits.

You did effect the contemplated purchase, but in what year I do not recollect. Immediately before the war, you represented that a large quantity of merchandise, intended for the Indian trade, and including arms and munitions of war, belonging to that concern of which you owned one-half, was deposited at a post on lake Huron, within the British dominions; that, in order to prevent their ultimately falling into the hands of Indians who might prove hostile, you were desirous to try to have them conveyed into the United States; but that you were prevented by the then existing law of non-intercourse with the British dominions.

The executive could not annul the provisions of that law. But I was directed to instruct the collectors on the lakes, in case you or your agents should voluntarily bring in and deliver to them any parts of the goods above mentioned, to receive and keep them in their guard, and not to commence prosecutions until further instructions : the intention being then to apply to congress for an act remitting the forfeiture and penalties. I wrote accordingly, to that effect, to the collectors of Detroit and Michilimackinac.

The attempt to obtain the goods did not, however, succeed ; and I cannot say how far the failure injured you. But the war proved fatal to another much more extensive and important enterprise.

Previous to that time, but I also forget the year, you had undertaken to carry on a trade on your own account, though I believe under the New York charter of the American Fur Company, with the Indians west of the Rocky mountains. This project was also communicated to government, and met, of course, with its full approbation, and best wishes for your success. You carried it on the most entensive scale, sending several ships to the mouth of the Columbia river, and a large party by land across the mountains, and finally founding the establishment of Astoria.

This unfortunately fell into the hands of the enemy, during the war, from circumstances with which I am but imperfectly acquainted— being then absent on a foreign mission. I returned, in September 1815, and sailed again on a mission to France in June 1816. During that period I visited Washington twice—in October or November 1815, and in March 1816. On one of those two occasions, and I believe on the last, you mentioned to me that you were disposed once more to renew the attempt, and to re-establish Astoria, provided you had the protection of the American flag; for which purpose a lieutenant's command would be sufficient to you. You requested me to mention this to the president, which I did. Mr. Madison said he would consider the subject, and although he did not commit himself, I thought that he received the proposal favourably. The message was verbal, and I do not know whether the application was ever renewed in a more formal manner. I sailed soon after for Europe, and was seven years absent. I never had the pleasure, since 1816, to see Mr. Madison, and never heard again anything concerning the subject in question.

I remain, dear sir, very respectfully,

Your obedient servant,

ALBERT GALLATIN.

JOHN JACOB ASTOR, Esq.
New York.

NOTICES OF THE PRESENT STATE OF THE FUR TRADE, CHIEFLY
EXTRACTED FROM AN ARTICLE PUBLISHED IN SILLIMAN'S JOUR-
NAL FOR JANUARY 1834.

The North-west Company did not long enjoy the sway they had
acquired over the trading regions of the Columbia. A competition,
ruinous in its expenses, which had long existed between them and
the Hudson's Bay Company, ended in their downfall, and the ruin of
most of the partners. The relics of the company became merged in
the rival association, and the whole business was conducted under
the name of the Hudson's Bay Company.

This coalition took place in 1811. They then abandoned Astoria,
and built a large establishment sixty miles up the river, on the right
bank, which they called Fort Vancouver. This was in a neighbourhood were provisions could be more readily procured, and where
there was less danger from molestation by any naval force. The
company are said to carry on an active and prosperous trade, and
to give encouragement to settlers. They are extremely jealous,
however, of any interference or participation in their trade, and
monopolize it from the coast of the Pacific to the mountains, and for
a considerable extent north and south. The American traders and
trappers who venture across the mountains, instead of enjoying the
participation in the trade of the river and its tributaries, that had
been stipulated by treaty, are obliged to keep to the south, out of the
track of the Hudson's Bay parties.

Mr. Astor has withdrawn entirely from the American Fur Company, as he has, in fact, from active business of every kind. That
company is now headed by Mr. Ramsay Crooks; its principal establishment is at Michilimackinac, and it receives its furs from the
post depending on that station, and from those on the Mississippi,
Missouri, and Yellowstone rivers, and the great range of country
extending thence to the Rocky mountains. This company has steam-
boats in its employ, with which it ascends the rivers, and penetrates
to a vast distance into the bosom of those regions formerly so painfully explored in keel-boats and barges, or by weary parties on
horseback and on foot. The first irruption of steamboats into the
heart of these vast wildernesses, is said to have caused the utmost
astonishment and affright among their savage inhabitants.

In addition to the main companies already mentioned, minor associations have been formed, which push their way in the most
intrepid manner to the remote parts of the far west, and beyond the
mountain barriers. One of the most noted of these is Ashley's company, from St. Louis, which trap for themselves, and drive an
extensive trade with the Indians. The spirit, enterprise, and
hardihood of Ashley, are themes of the highest eulogy in the far
west, and his adventures and exploits furnish abundance of frontier
stories.

Another company of one hundred and fifty persons from New
York, formed in 1831, and headed by Captain Bonneville, of the

United States army, has pushed its enterprises into tracks before but little known, and has brought considerable quantities of furs from the region between the Rocky mountains and the coasts of Monterey and Upper California, on the Buenaventura and Timpanogos rivers.

The fur countries, from the Pacific, east to the Rocky mountains, are now occupied (exclusive of private combinations and individual trappers and traders) by the Russians; on the north-west, from Bahring's Strait to Queen Charlotte's Island, in north latitude fifty-three degrees, and by the Hudson's Bay Company, thence south of the Columbia river; while Ashley's company, and that under Captain Bonneville, take the remainder of the region to California. Indeed, the whole compass from the Mississippi to the Pacific Ocean is traversed in every direction. The mountains and forests, from the Arctic Sea to the Gulf of Mexico, are threaded, through every maze, by the hunter. Every river and tributary stream from the Columbia to the mouth of the Rio del Norte, and from the M'Kenzie to the Colorado of the west, from their head springs to their junction, are searched and trapped for beaver. Almost all the American furs, which do not belong to the Hudson's Bay Company, find their way to New York, and are either distributed thence for home consumption, or sent to foreign markets.

The Hudson's Bay Company ship their furs from their factories of York fort and from Moose river, on Hudson's Bay; their collection from Grand river, &c., they ship from Canada; and the collection from Columbia goes to London. None of their furs come to the United States, except through the London Market.

The export trade of furs from the United States is chiefly to London. Some quantities have been sent to Canton, and some few to Hamburgh; and an increasing export trade in beaver, otter, nutria, and vicunia wool, prepared for the hatter's use, is carried on in Mexico. Some furs are exported from Baltimore, Philadelphia, and Boston, but the principal shipments from the United States, are from New York to London, from whence they are sent to Leipsic, a well-known mart for furs, where they are disposed of during the great fair in that city, and distributed to every part of the continent.

The United States import from South America, nutria, vicunia, chinchilla, and a few deer skins; also fur seals from the Lobos Islands, off the river Plate. A quantity of beaver, otter, &c., are brought annually from Santa Fé. Dressed furs for edgings, linings, caps, muffs, &c., such as squirrel, gennet, fitch skins, and blue rabbit, are received from the north of Europe; also coney and hare's fur; but the largest importations are from London, where is concentrated nearly the whole of the North American fur trade.

Such is the present state of the fur trade, by which it will appear that the extended sway of the Hudson's Bay Company and its monopoly of the region of which Astoria was the key, has operated to turn the main current of this opulent trade into the coffers of Great Britain, and to render London the emporium, instead of New York, as Mr. Astor had intended.

We will subjoin a few observations on the animals sought after in this traffic, extracted from the same intelligent source with the preceding remarks.

Of the fur-bearing animals, " the precious ermine," so called by way of pre-eminence, is found, of the best quality, only in the cold regions of Europe and Asia*. Its fur is of the most perfect whiteness, except the tip of its tail, which is of a brilliant shining black. With these black tips tacked on the skins, they are beautifully spotted, producing an effect often imitated, but never equalled, in other furs. The ermine is of the genus mustela (weasel), and resembles the common weasel in its form ; is from fourteen to sixteen inches from the tip of the nose to the end of the tail. The body is from ten to twelve inches long. It lives in hollow trees, river banks, and especially in beech forests ; preys on small birds, is very shy, sleeping during the day, and employing the night in search of food. The fur of the older animals is preferred to the younger. It is taken by snares and traps, and sometimes shot with blunt arrows. Attempts have been made to domesticate it ; but it is extremely wild, and has been found untameable.

The sable can scarcely be called second to the ermine. It is a native of northern Europe, and Siberia, and is also of the genus mustela. In Samoieda, Yakutsk, Kamschatka, and Russian Lapland, it is found of the richest quality, and darkest colour. In its habits, it resembles the ermine. It preys on small squirrels and birds, sleeps by day, and prowls for food during the night. It is so like the marten in every particular except its size, and the dark shade of its colour, that naturalists have not decided whether it is the richest and finest of the marten tribe, or a variety of that species†. It varies in dimensions from eighteen to twenty inches.

The rich dark shades of the sable, and the snowy whiteness of the ermine, the great depth, and the peculiar, almost flowing softness, of their skins and fur, have combined to gain them a preference in all countries and in all ages of the world. In this age, they maintain the same relative estimate in regard to other furs, as when they marked the rank of the proud crusader, and were emblazoned in heraldry; but in most European nations they are now worn promiscuously by the opulent.

The martens from Northern Asia and the mountains of Kamschatka are much superior to the American, though in every pack of American marten skins there are a certain number which are beautifully shaded, and of a dark brown olive colour, of great depth and richness.

---

* An animal called the stoat, a kind of ermine, is said to be found in North America, but very inferior to the European and Asiatic.

† The finest fur and the darkest colour are most esteemed ; and whether the difference arises form the age of the animal, or from some peculiarity of location, is not known. They do not vary more from the common marten, than the Arabian horse from the shaggy Canadian.

Next these in value, for ornament and utility, are the sea otter, the mink, and the fiery fox.

The fiery fox is the bright red of Asia; is more brilliantly coloured and of finer fur than any other of the genus. It is highly valued for the splendour of its red colour and the fineness of its fur. It is the standard of value on the north-eastern coast of Asia.

The sea otter, which was first introduced into commerce in 1725, from the Aleutian and Kurile Islands, is an exceedingly fine, soft, close fur, jet black in winter, with a silken gloss. The fur of the young animal is of a beautiful brown colour. It is met with in great abundance in Bhering's Island, Kamschatka, Aleutian and Fox Islands, and is also taken on the opposite coasts of North America. It is sometimes taken with nets, but more frequently with clubs and spears. Their food is principally lobster and other shell fish.

In 1780 furs had become so scarce in Siberia, that the supply was insufficient for the demand in the Asiatic countries. It was at this time that the sea otter was introduced into the markets for China. The skins brought such incredible prices, as to originate immediately several American and British expeditions to the northern islands of the Pacific, to Nootka sound, and the north-west coast of America; but the Russians already had possession of the tract which they now hold, and had arranged a trade for the sea otter with the Koudek tribes. They do not engross the trade, however; the American north-west trading ships procure them, all along the coast, from the Indians.

At one period, the fur seals formed no inconsiderable item in the trade. South Georgia, in south latitude fifty-five degrees, discovered in 1675, was explored by Captain Cook in 1771. The Americans immediately commenced carrying seal skins thence to China, where they obtained the most exorbitant prices. One million two hundred thousand skins have been taken from that Island alone, and nearly an equal number from the island of Desolation, since they were first resorted to for the purposes of commerce.

The discovery of the South Shetlands, sixty-three degrees south latitude, in 1818, added surprisingly to the trade in fur seals. The number taken from the South Shetlands in 1821 and 1822, amounted to three hundred and twenty thousand. This valuable animal is now almost extinct in all these islands, owing to the exterminating system adopted by the hunters. They are still taken on the Lobos Islands, where the provident government of Montevideo restrict the fishery, or hunting, within certain limits, which insures an annual return of the seals. At certain seasons these amphibia, for the purpose of renewing their coat, come up on the dark frowning rocks and precipices, where there is not a trace of vegetation. In the middle of January, the islands are partially cleared of snow, where a few patches of short straggling grass spring up in favourable situations; but the seals do not resort to it for food. They remain on the rocks not less than two months, without any sustenance, when they return, much emaciated, to the sea.

Bears of various species and colours, many varieties of the fox, the wolf, the beaver, the otter, the marten, the raccoon, the badger, the wolverine, the mink, the lynx, the muskrat, the woodchuck, the rabbit, the hare, and the squirrel, are natives of North America.

The beaver, otter, lynx, fisher, hare, and raccoon, are used principally for hats; while the bears of several varieties furnish an excellent material for sleigh linings, for cavalry caps, and other military equipments. The fur of the black fox is the most valuable of any of the American varieties, and next to that the red, which is exported to China and Smyrna. In China, the red is employed for trimmings, linings, and robes; the latter being variegated, by adding the black fur of the paws, in spots or waves. There are many other varieties of American fox, such as the gray, the white, the cross, the silver, and the dun coloured. The silver fox is a rare animal, a native of the woody country below the falls of the Columbia river. It has a long, thick, deep lead-coloured fur, intermingled with long hairs, invariably white at the top, forming a bright, lustrous silver gray, esteemed by some more beautiful than any other kind of fox.

The skins of the buffalo, of the Rocky mountain sheep, of various deer, and of the antelope, are included in the fur trade with the Indians and trappers of the north and west.

Fox and seal skins are sent from Greenland to Denmark. The white fur of the arctic fox and polar bear is sometimes found in the packs brought to the traders by the most northern tribes of Indians, but is not particularly valuable. The silver-tipped rabbit is peculiar to England, and is sent thence to Russia and China.

Other furs are employed and valued according to the caprices of fashion, as well in those countries where they are needed for defences against the severity of the seasons, as among the inhabitants of milder climates, who, being of Tartar or Sclavonian descent, are said to inherit an attachment to furred clothing. Such are the inhabitants of Poland, of Southern Russia, of China, of Persia, of Turkey, and all the nations of Gothic origin in the middle and western parts of Europe. Under the burning suns of Syria and Egypt, and the mild climes of Bucharia and Independent Tartary, there is also a constant demand, and a great consumption, where there exists no physical necessity. In our own temperate latitudes, besides their use in the arts, they are in request for ornament and warmth during the winter, and large quantities are annually consumed for both purposes in the United States.

From the foregoing statements, it appears that the fur trade must henceforward decline. The advanced state of geographical science shows that no new countries remain to be explored. In North America the animals are slowly decreasing, from the persevering efforts and the indiscriminate slaughter practised by the hunters, and by the appropriation to the uses of man of those forests and rivers which have afforded them food and protection. They recede with the aborigines, before the tide of civilization; but a diminished supply will remain in the mountains, and uncultivated tracts of this and other countries, if the avidity of the hunter can be restrained within proper limitations.

HEIGHT OF THE ROCKY MOUNTAINS.

Various estimates have been made of the height of the Rocky mountains, but it is doubtful whether any have, as yet, done justice to their real altitude, which promises to place them only second to the highest mountains of the known world. Their height has been diminished to the eye by the great elevation of the plains from which they rise. They consist, according to Long, of ridges, knobs, and peaks, variously disposed. The more elevated parts are covered with perpetual snows, which contribute to give them a luminous, and, at a great distance, even a brilliant appearance ; whence they derived, among some of the first discoverers, the name of the Shining mountains.

James's Peak has generally been cited as the highest of the chain ; and its elevation above the common level has been ascertained, by a trigonometrical measurement, to be about eight thousand five hundred feet. Mr. Long, however, judged, from the position of the snow near the summits of other peaks and ridges at no great distance from it, that they were much higher. Having heard Professor Renwick, of New York, express an opinion of the altitude of these mountains, far beyond what had usually been ascribed to them, we applied to him for the authority on which he grounded his observation, and here subjoin his reply :—

Columbia College, New York, February 23, 1836.

Dear Sir,

In compliance with your request, I have to communicate some facts in relation to the heights of the Rocky mountains, and the sources whence I obtained the information.

In conversation with Simon M'Gillivray, Esq., a partner of the North-west Company, he stated to me his impression, that the mountains in the vicinity of the route pursued by the traders of that company were nearly as high as the Himalayas. He had himself crossed by this route, seen the snowy summits of the peaks, and experienced a degree of cold which required a spirit thermometer to indicate it. His authority for the estimate of the heights was a gentleman who had been employed for several years as surveyor of that company. This conversation occurred about sixteen years since.

A year or two afterwards, I had the pleasure of dining at Major Delafield's, with Mr. Thompson, the gentleman referred to by Mr. M'Gillivray. I inquired of him in relation to the circumstances mentioned by Mr. M'Gillivray, and he stated, that, by the joint means of the barometer and trigonometric measurement, he had ascertained the height of one of the peaks to be about twenty-five thousand feet, and there were others of nearly the same height in the vicinity.

I am, dear Sir,

Your's truly,

JAMES RENWICK.

To W. Irving, Esq.

SUGGEsTIONS WITH RESPECT TO THE INDIAN TRIBES, AND THE
PROTECTION OF OUR TRADE.

In the course of this work, a few general remarks have been
hazarded respecting the Indian tribes of the prairies, and the dangers
to be apprehended from them in future times, to our trade beyond the
Rocky mountains and with the Spanish frontiers. Since writing
those remarks, we have met with some excellent observations and
suggestions, in manuscript, on the same subject, written by Captain
Bonneville, of the United States army, who has lately returned from a
long residence among the tribes of the Rocky mountains. Captain
B. approves highly of the plan recently adopted by the United States
government for the organization of a regiment of dragoons for the
protection of our western frontier, and the trade across the prairies.
" No other species of military force," he observes, " is at all competent to cope with these restless and wandering hordes, who require
to be opposed with swiftness quite as much as with strength ; and the
consciousness that a troop, uniting those qualifications, is always on
the alert to avenge their outrages upon the settlers and traders, will
go very far towards restraining them from the perpetration of those
thefts and murders which they have heretofore committed with
impunity, whenever stratagem or superiority of force has given them
the advantage. Their interest already has done something towards
their pacification with our countrymen. From the traders among
them they receive their supplies in the greatest abundance, and upon
very equitable terms; and when it is remembered that a very considerable amount of property is yearly distributed among them by the government, as presents, it will readily be perceived that they are greatly
dependant upon us for their most valued resources. If, superadded
to this inducement, a frequent display of military prowess be made in
their territories, there can be little doubt that the desired security
and peace will be speedily afforded to our own people. But the idea
of establishing a permanent amity and concord amongst the various
east and west tribes themselves, seems to me, if not wholly impracticable, at least infinitely more difficult than many excellent philan-
thropists have hoped and believed. Those nations which have so
lately emigrated from the midst of our settlements to live upon our
western borders, and have made some progress in agriculture and the
arts of civilization, have, in the property they have acquired, and the
protection and aid extended to them, too many advantages to be
induced readily to take up arms against us, particularly if they can be
brought to the full conviction that their new homes will be permanent
and undisturbed ; and there is every reason and motive, in policy as
well as humanity, for our ameliorating their condition by every means
in our power. But the case is far different with regard to the Osages,
the Kanzas, the Pawnees, and other roving hordes beyond the frontiers of the settlements. Wild and restless in their character and
habits, they are by no means so susceptible of control or civilization;
and they are urged by strong, and, to them, irresistible causes in their

situation and necessities, to the daily perpetration of violence and fraud. Their permanent subsistence, for example, is derived from the buffalo hunting grounds, which lie a great distance from their towns. Twice a year they are obliged to make long and dangerous expeditions, to procure the necessary provisions for themselves and their families. For this purpose, horses are absolutely requisite, for their own comfort and safety, as well as for the transportation of their food, and their little stock of valuables; and without them they would be reduced, during a great portion of the year, to a state of abject misery and privation. They have no brood mares, nor any trade sufficiently valuable to supply their yearly losses, and they endeavour to keep up their stock by stealing horses from the other tribes to the west and south-west. Our own people, and the tribes immediately upon our borders, may indeed be protected from their depredations; and the Kanzas, Osages, Pawnees, and others, may be induced to remain at peace among themselves, so long as they are permitted to pursue the old custom of levying upon the Camanches and other remote nations for their complement of steeds for the warriors, and pack-horses for their transportations to and from the hunting ground. But the instant they are forced to maintain a peaceful and inoffensive demeanour towards the tribes along the Mexican border, and find that every violation of their rights is followed by the avenging arm of our government, the result must be, that, reduced to a wretchedness and want which they can ill brook, and feeling the certainty of punishment for every attempt to ameliorate their condition in the only way they as yet comprehend, they will abandon their unfruitful territory, and remove to the neighbourhood of the Mexican lands, and there carry on a vigorous predatory warfare indiscriminately upon the Mexicans, and our own people trading or travelling in that quarter.

"The Indians of the prairies are almost innumerable. Their superior horsemanship, which, in my opinion, far exceeds that of any other people on the face of the earth, their daring bravery, their cunning and skill in the warfare of the wilderness, and the astonishing rapidity and secrecy with which they are accustomed to move in their martial expeditions, will always render them most dangerous and vexatious neighbours, when their necessities or their discontents may drive them to hostility with our frontiers. Their mode and principles of warfare will always protect them from final and irretrievable defeat, and secure their families from participating in any blow, however severe, which our retribution might deal out to them.

"The Camanches lay the Mexicans under contribution for horses and mules, which they are always engaged in stealing from them in incredible numbers; and from the Camanches, all the roving tribes of the far west, by a similar exertion of skill and daring, supply themselves in turn. It seems to me, therefore, under all these circumstances, that the apparent futility of any philanthropic schemes for the benefit of these nations, and a regard for our own protection, concur in recommending that we remain satisfied with maintaining peace upon our own immediate borders, and leave the Mexicans and the Camanches, and all the tribes hostile to these last, to settle their differences and difficulties in their own way.

" In order to give full security and protection to our trading parties circulating in all directions through the great prairies, I am under the impression that a few judicious measures on the part of the government, involving a very limited expense, would be sufficient. And, in attaining this end, which of itself has already become an object of public interest and import, another, of much greater consequence, might be brought about, viz., the securing to the states a most valuable and increasing trade, now carried on by caravans directly to Santa Fé.

" As to the first desideratum: the Indians can only be made to respect the lives and property of the American parties, by rendering them dependant upon us for their supplies; which can alone be done with complete effect by the establishment of a trading post, with resident traders, at some point which will unite a sufficient number of advantages to attract the several tribes to itself in preference to their present places of resort for that purpose; for it is a well-known fact, that the Indians will always protect their trader, and those in whom he is interested, so as long as they derive benefits from him. The alternative presented to those at the north, by the residence of the agents of the Hudson's Bay Company amongst them, renders the condition of our people in that quarter less secure; but I think it will appear, at once, upon the most cursory examination, that no such opposition further south could be maintained, so as to weaken the benefits of such an establishment as is here suggested.

" In considering this matter, the first question which presents itself is, where do these tribes now make their exchanges, and obtain their necessary supplies? They resort almost exclusively to the Mexicans, who, themselves, purchase from us whatever the Indians most seek for. In this point of view, therefore, *cæteris paribus*, it would be an easy matter for us to monopolise the whole traffic. All that is wanting is some location more convenient for the natives than that offered by the Mexicans, to give us the undisputed superiority; and the selection of such a point requires but a knowledge of the single fact, that these nations invariably winter upon the head waters of the Arkansas, and there prepare all their buffalo robes for trade. These robes are heavy, and, to the Indian, very difficult of transportation. Nothing but necessity induces them to travel any great distance with such inconvenient baggage. A post, therefore, established upon the head waters of the Arkansas, must infallibly secure an uncontested preference over that of the Mexicans, even at their prices and rates of barter. Then let the dragoons occasionally move about among these people in large parties, impressing them with the proper estimate of our power to protect and to punish, and at once we have complete and assured security for all citizens whose enterprise may lead them beyond the border, and an end to the outrages and depredations which now dog the footsteps of the traveller in the prairies, and arrest and repress the most advantageous commerce. Such a post need not be stronger than fifty men ; twenty-five to be employed as hunters, to supply the garrison, and the residue as a defence against any hostility. Situated here upon the good lands of the Arkansas, in the midst of abundance of timber, while it might be kept up at a most inconsiderable expense, such an establishment within ninety miles of Santa Fé or Tous, would be more than justified by the other and more important advantages before alluded to, leaving the protection of the traders with the Indian tribes entirely out of the question.

" This great trade, carried on by caravans to Santa Fé, annually loads one hundred waggons with merchandise, which is bartered in the Northern provinces of Mexico for cash and for beaver furs. The numerous articles excluded as contraband, and the exorbitant duties laid upon all those that are admitted by the Mexican government, present so many obstacles to commerce, that I am well persuaded, that if a post, such as is here suggested, should be established on the Arkansas, it would become the place of deposit, not only for the present trade, but for one infinitely more extended. Here the Mexicans might purchase their supplies, and might well afford to sell them at prices which would silence all competition from any other quarter.

" These two trades, with the Mexicans and the Indians, centring at this post, would give rise to a large village of traders and labourers, and would undoubtedly be hailed, by all that section of country, as a permanent and invaluable advantage. A few pack-horses would carry all the clothing and ammunition necessary for the post during the first year, and two light field-pieces would be all the artillery required for its defence. Afterwards, all the horses required for the use of the establishment might be purchased from the Mexicans at the low price of ten dollars each ; and, at the same time, whatever animals might be needed to supply the losses among the dragoons traversing the neighbourhood, could be readily procured. The upper Missouri Indians can furnish horses, at very cheap rates, to any number of the same troops who might be detailed for the defence of the northern frontier; and, in other respects, a very limited outlay of money would suffice to maintain a post in that section of the country.

" From these considerations, and my own personal observation, I am, therefore, disposed to believe, that two posts established by the government, one at the mouth of the Yellowstone river, and one on the Arkansas, would completely protect all our people in every section of the great wilderness of the west; while other advantages, at least with regard to one of them, confirm and urge the suggestion. A fort at the mouth of Yellowstone, garrisoned by fifty men, would be perfectly safe. The establishment might be constructed simply with a view to the stores, stables for the dragoons' horses, and quarters for the regular garrison ; the rest being provided with sheds or lodges, erected in the vicinity, for their residence during the winter months."

THE END.